ADO Examples and Best Practices

WILLIAM R. VAUGHN

ADO Examples and Best Practices
Copyright © 2000 by Beta V Corporation

Library of Congress Control Number: 00-133575

ISBN: 1-893115-16-X

Printed and bound in the United States of America
10 9 8 7 6 5 4 3 2 1

Technical Reviewer: Edward Jerzierski
Developmental Editor: Andy Carroll
Copy Editor: Freelance Editorial Services
Production: TSI Graphics
Cover Design: Derek Yee Design

Distributed to the book trade worldwide by Springer-Verlag New York, Inc. 175 Fifth Avenue, New York, NY 10010 USA
In the United States, phone 1-800-SPRINGER; orders@springer-ny.com
www.springer-ny.com

For information on translations, please contact Apress directly:
901 Grayson Street, Berkeley, CA 94710-2617
www.apress.com

To my daughters Victoria and Chrissy,
of whom I couldn't be prouder.

Brief Contents

v

Detailed Contents

Introduction

I CAN'T TELL YOU HOW many people have asked when the next edition of *Hitchhiker's Guide to Visual Basic and SQL Server* is going to be written. So much of the technology has evolved since it was written that I can certainly see the need to update this tome. Since Visual Basic 6.0 shipped, ADO has changed at least eight times, so many of the examples and explanations in the 6th edition of the Guide are somewhat dated. However, Visual Basic 7.0 is not nearly done, so it's really too early to update the *Guide*.

When given an opportunity to write a book for Apress, though, I realized this was a perfect opportunity to focus on what has changed most—ADO. I could bring my readers up to speed on the newest features and techniques, without worrying about how Visual Basic will look in the future. But there are a lot of books out there on ADO programming. What I needed was a focus that would most appeal to you, the front-line, in-the-trenches developer. Thus *ADO Examples and Best Practices* was born.

Some of you will be migrating from other programming interfaces, such as Data Access Objects (DAO) or Remote Data Objects (RDO). On occasion, I make a passing comment about how to make this transition easier, but I don't dwell on those issues. Some of you will be transitioning (whether you want to or not) from an earlier version of ADO, and this book's for you.

Obviously, *ADO Examples and Best Practices* focuses on ActiveX Data Objects (ADO) version 2.5, but in a way that reflects what countless developers, trainers, and support engineers have passed on to me over the years. Yes, it's these people that provide the pathway to what I write in these books. For the last 14 years, I have made a living by writing, training, and documenting code—not by writing or supporting applications, as I did the first 12 years of my career. Because of this, I have to constantly work with others who do. When I can, I help them solve problems encountered in the "real world," but just as often the developer community provides me with innovative and tried-and-true ways of using the tools. These examples and "best practices" are techniques discussed, refined, and used by hundreds or thousands of the most talented developers in the world. And yes, many of the ideas come from "international" developers outside the USA. While some of the ideas come from inside Microsoft, where I am bound to a certain level of secrecy, many come from off campus, where developers often have to make do with what the folks on campus produce and shove out the door. I also regularly communicate with the product managers, developers, and product support teams here at Microsoft, who try to get the tools and interfaces to work better—based on your requests (and mine).

ADO Examples and Best Practices goes where the *Guide* did not—into the realm of the Web. It has fairly extensive discussions of how to best use ADO in ActiveX Server Pages (ASPs), as well as browser pages written in Visual Basic Script. While the book covers most of the new ADO 2.5 features, it also discusses other technologies such as XML and MSXML where it makes sense. Although this book is not a "programmer's reference," it does detail many of the individual objects, properties, and methods as I did in the *Guide*. Despite the Web hype out there, this book fully discusses client/server and middle-tier, along with Web-based ADO architectures, and the code development, deployment, and performance analysis issues associated with each paradigm.

Performance is a regular thread in *ADO Examples and Best Practices*. But to me, "performance" means more than writing code that runs fast. It means writing code that helps developers work more efficiently—write more solutions in less time and at a lower cost, not necessarily more code. This is especially important for developers working in teams. All too often the programs we write today were originally designed and implemented by others—or at least parts of them. This means that you have to deal with other developer's designs, techniques, and documentation—assuming the latter exists. And others have to deal with what you write. We are constantly challenged to create code that can be passed on to others to integrate, support, or debug. There are a lot of techniques you can use to make this process easy—easy for you and for the people who have to deal with what you write.

But this process requires what many programming shops, even those at Microsoft, don't have: discipline. No, I'm not talking about having a person walking the halls in leather and studs, cracking a whip (or at least I hope not)! I'm talking about establishing standards within the organization and sticking to them. It means writing spec, and coding to spec. It means curbing your desire to code outside the spec because you know how to do something better than the toads who created the spec. That might be the case, but unless you get your coworkers and managers to help change the spec, what you're creating is counterproductive. If you don't code to spec, your innovative code is not likely to work with other developers' code—now or in the future. Discipline also means curbing your arrogance. Deciding that the consumer of your code can take it or lump it is hardly a productive attitude—but it is not an uncommon mindset in some shops. Of course, if you are paid by the line, you are free to ignore these suggestions. Just don't look for repeat business.

We'll also look at ways to reduce COM overhead, reduce your applications' load time, and to better utilize the LAN, WAN, and Web, as well as RAM, disk space, and other system resources. We'll look at how to write programs that other developers can understand and support—without you having to interrupt that Saturday afternoon barbecue. (That's a barbecued SQL Server.)

Acknowledgments

THIS BOOK, LIKE THE REST OF MY WORKS, would not be possible if not for the patience, generosity, and knowledge passed on by countless contributors, reviewers, and mentors. These include, but are not limited to, David Sceppa, Dave Jezak, and many others at Microsoft mentioned elsewhere in the book. Edward Jezierski, my technical editor, also helped us get through a number of tough sections. And for help in the XML section, I'd like to thank Andrew Brust and his team. There are also a good number of contributors on the Microsoft and VBData-L alias who provided real-world issues to discuss, along with pragmatic working examples. My wife, Marilyn, has also been great at keeping the business side of the process straight and my body healthy.

About the Author

WILLIAM VAUGHN (Bill) earned his Bachelor's degree in Computer Science Education from Mary Hardin-Baylor and a Master's degree in interdisciplinary studies at the University of Texas at Dallas. Before that, he volunteered to fly helicopters in Southeast Asia for the U.S. Army. Bill has been knocking around the personal computer industry since it was born in the North Dallas area in the late '70s. By that time, Bill had already worked for a couple of mainframe companies, including stints with EDS and the Texas Department of Public Safety. He switched to PCs full-time when Ross Perot found out he was building PCs in his garage.

Over the years, Bill soaked up technology like a sponge. His home lab and every available space is stuffed with hardware, software and spare parts. He picked up PC-integrated circuit experience at Mostek, systems software experience at Challenge Systems, and a little of everything else at Digital Research. He championed the Z80, CP/M, and Concurrent PCDOS before he came to Microsoft in 1986. For the last fourteen years, he has had numerous roles at Microsoft—working with the Windows 1.0 Developer Liaison team, Microsoft University, the Visual Basic User Education team, the Visual Studio marketing team, and finally at Microsoft Technical Education. He has taught OS/2, SQL Server from the earliest versions, Basic, Visual Basic and every data access technology invented by Microsoft. He has also helped to guide, mentor, and train developers from all over the world by writing and delivering courses, lectures and whitepapers on all of these areas. Bill is probably best known for his (initially self-published) Hitchhiker's Guide to Visual Basic and SQL Server, now in its sixth edition. Data access developers who want to access SQL Server still recognize it as the "bible" of Visual Basic.

Bill has also managed to eke out a life between compiles. He has two beautiful and talented daughters: Victoria (George) and Chrissy (Fred). Victoria, who has a degree in Chemical Engineering and a Master's degree in Civil Engineering, has just provided him with his first grandchild. Chrissy graduates from Whitman College this spring with a degree in English—she writes even better than her dad does. Marilyn, Bill's wife of thirty-two years, is also the Treasurer and Executive Secretary of Beta V Corporation—which handles the business aspects of Bill's writing and publishing activities.

Working with ADO

YOU'RE NOT READING THIS BOOK FOR the jokes—at least, I hope not. I hope you're reading it for suggestions on how to write efficient ADO data access applications and how to write them efficiently. This first chapter walks you through some of the fundamentals—the stuff you must have in place to use ADO at all. I'll assume you know what you're doing in most respects, so I'll leave out some of the basic step-by-step stuff you'll find in the "Idiots" books. If you don't know what ADO is, what its object model looks like, or how the objects relate to one another, see the "ADO Fundamentals" appendix at the back of the book.

Choosing the "Right" Version of ADO

One of the challenges we all face is determining which version of ADO is the "right" version. Because there are so many versions and because they can work very differently, we often struggle with which version we should use. In some cases we don't have a choice—we have to use what the customer has installed or insists on using. When we do have a choice, we also have to worry about future versions changing (breaking) the software we've deployed. To better understand the myriad of choices, let's take a brief trip through ADO's history.

Since Visual Basic 6.0 shipped in the summer of '98, ADO has transmogrified several times—and yes, into some bizarre forms. Visual Basic 6.0 shipped with an early version of ADO 2.0, and then ADO changed when SQL Server 7.0 shipped, when Internet Explorer 5.0 shipped, and when Office 2000 shipped, and it was updated at least twice thereafter. While some of these changes were minor, some were not, and Visual Basic (Visual Studio) has not kept up very well.

Before ADO 2.0, there was the Microsoft ActiveX *Recordset* Library (ADOR). Initially, ADOR was intended to serve as a "lightweight" version of ADO—not requiring the complete install, and thus supporting a smaller footprint, less RAM, and faster download times. It turned out to be more trouble than it was worth so with ADO 2.0, the two libraries became one. As a result, setting your reference to the ADOR library is pointless.

Microsoft distributes ADO in the Microsoft Data Access Components (MDAC) package, a 6.35MB executable (mdac_typ.exe) that includes ADO, ODBC, and OLE DB drivers and providers. Yes, Microsoft bundles them all together in a take-one-get-them-all (whether you want them all or not) package. Packaging and installing all of these individual pieces together makes sense for maintaining stability.

The various MDAC pieces, but not necessarily all of them, are installed by many, many applications—applications from both Microsoft and third parties. If you're lucky, these applications "install" MDAC instead of just copying the files over and hoping for the best, as some applications seem to do. I'll show you how to install MDAC a little later in this chapter.

While MDAC moved to its "golden" or "general release" (2.1.2.4202.3 (GA)) in the fall of '99, the Visual Basic SP3, the Visual Studio 6.0 Plus Pack, and the Windows 2000 Readiness Kit did not contain this release. The Visual Basic team tells me that Visual Basic 6.0 SP4, due out in the spring of 2000, should upgrade Visual Basic 6.0 to address issues raised by the interface and functionality changes in ADO 2.1.

I "lurk" on a number of public and internal list servers (such as **VBDATA-L@peach.ease.lsoft.com**) where I see a number of questions about ADO. One frequently asked question is, "When one installs Internet Explorer 5.0, does it install ADO 2.1?" The answer is "sort of." That is, Internet Explorer 5.0 installs and uses ADO 2.1, but it does not install the providers and drivers that are installed with the full MDAC setup. So really, installing Internet Explorer 5.0 won't really (completely) install ADO—you will have to distribute and install the MDAC setup with your ADO 2.x client program.

ADO 2.5 Arrives

Now that ADO 2.5 has arrived, it's an integral part of Windows 2000, although it can still be installed separately on older versions of Windows by downloading it from the Web at http://microsoft.com/data. (Incidentally, this site is the best place to find out about the most recent version of ADO and MDAC.) This incorporation of ADO in Windows is supposed to mean that ADO will no longer change with every phase of the moon—it'll be harder for everyone to change ADO, even when they have to. It looks like everyone will have to upgrade/patch ADO through OS upgrades. This also means that the big players at Microsoft (Microsoft Office, Internet Explorer, Visual Studio, and others) will not be able to change MDAC willy-nilly (that's a technical term)—and that's good news.

> **WARNING** *Do not try to use the Office 2000 Installer to remove ADO. This is a fatal mistake that will force you to reinstall Windows 2000.*

The real problem with all of these changes is fundamental. When developing a COM component, you as a developer agree to conform to a recognized standard implementation regimen. One of the requirements is that future versions of the component will support all past versions (at least going back a couple of versions). This means that while the code for implementing these published interfaces might change, the interface names, properties, methods, events, and all of the arguments passed to them do *not* change.

ADO 2.1 broke the rules. ADO 2.0 applications crashed or misbehaved after their customers installed Internet Explorer 5.0 or one of the Office 2000 applications that upgraded ADO from 2.0 to 2.1. What's worse is that ADO kept changing over the months that followed. Even if the interfaces didn't change, MDAC did. In some cases, ODBC driver "improvements" changed security restrictions—locking out users that were previously able to access their databases using default behaviors. Even though ADO 2.1 and 2.5 both include ADO 2.0 typelibs that permit older applications to see their old familiar interfaces, when some of the revised ("improved") event handlers passed back an ADO 2.1 (or 2.5) Recordset instead of the ADO 2.0 Recordset, the applications broke. Some of the most serious "breakages" were in Visual Basic itself. None of the Visual Database Tools would work correctly with ADO 2.1 or later. This meant the Data Environment Designer was crippled. In addition, the ActiveX Data Control, the Data Form Wizard, and the Data Object Wizard were all dented.

At this writing, it's not clear what Microsoft and the MDAC team expect to do about this. They certainly can't revert to the old version. I have tried to get the Visual Studio team to upgrade Visual Basic 6.0 to fully support ADO 2.5, but it remains to be seen whether this will come to pass. Perhaps Visual Studio 6.0 SP4 will address these issues. I'm told that this will all be finally addressed when Visual Basic 7.0 arrives. I'll be long since retired by then…

What's New in ADO 2.5

ADO 2.5 continues to flesh out the original intent of ADO—to be the universal information interface. While there's plenty of bug fixes in this release, ADO also supports at least two entirely new objects—the Stream and the Record. You'll discover the Record object as soon as you slip and choose it instead of the Recordset object during statement completion time. But you'll learn.

> **NOTE** *The examples in the book are all written using ADO 2.5 on either a Windows 2000 or Windows 98 system. I don't expect them to compile or run on systems using older versions of ADO.*

Records and Streams

ADO 2.5 introduces the "Record" object, which can represent and manage things such as directories and files in a file system, and documents, folders, and messages in an e-mail system. A Record can also represent a row in a Recordset, but the Record object should not be confused with the Recordset object, as both have different methods and properties—also, some of the shared properties and methods behave differently.

The new Stream object provides the means to read, write, and manage the binary stream of bytes or text that comprises a file or message stream. Think of a Stream as an in-memory file. How many times have you had to write a block of data to disk when all you really wanted to do was hold on to it for a second or simply pass it to another component or tier?

URLs instead of Connection String

ADO 2.5 introduces the use of Uniform Resource Locators (URLs) to name data store objects, as an alternative to using connection strings and command text. URLs can be used with the existing Connection and Recordset objects, as well as with the new Record and Stream objects.

ADO 2.5 also supports OLE DB providers that recognize their own URL schemes. For example, the OLE DB Provider for Internet Publishing, which accesses the Windows 2000 file system, recognizes the existing HTTP scheme.

Special Fields for Document Source Providers

ADO 2.5 introduces access to a special class of providers, called document source providers, that can be used to manage directory folders and documents. When a Record object represents a document, or a Recordset object represents a folder of documents, the document source provider populates those objects with a unique set of fields that describe the characteristics of the document. These fields constitute a resource Record or Recordset.

New Reference Topics

A number of new properties, methods, and events were added to ADO 2.5 to support the Record and Stream objects. We'll discuss the Stream object in Chapter 9. These new properties help ADO define documents and files. The methods permit you to programmatically copy, add, delete, and modify characters, files, documents, or other data from source to destination.

The ADO Component Checker

Okay, so you just installed Visual Basic 6.0 SP3. Since you got it just last week, you assume it has the latest version of ADO, right? But do you know for sure which version of MDAC (thus ADO) you have installed on your development system, on your server, or on your client's system? Want to find out? Well as Yoda would say, "You will... you will." (Incidentally, Visual Basic 6.0 SP3 installs an older version of ADO 2.1—not the final "GA" release of ADO 2.1.)

However, you're in luck—the (Microsoft) Component Checker tool is designed to help you find out everything you want to know about MDAC (and perhaps some things you would rather not know). Component Checker runs on these operating systems: Microsoft Windows 98, Windows NT 4.0, and Windows 2000. Only 32-bit and 64-bit platforms are supported.

Component Checker is a customizable tool that performs the following tasks:

- Identifies the current MDAC installation on a computer.

- Creates a series of reports about the files identified for the current MDAC installation.

- (Optionally) removes the current MDAC installation after listing .dll conflicts and identifying programs that reference a given .dll.

Performing this last task is not always possible. After an ADO version is installed, such as ADO 2.1, the applications that depend on it will not work correctly (if at all) with an older ADO version. My understanding is that after ADO 2.5 is installed, it cannot be uninstalled—it becomes an integral part of the OS.

> **NOTE** *I installed ADO 2.1 (GA) on my new Visual Basic 6.0 SP3 system and ran the Component Checker. It turned up about a dozen difugelties[1]— a couple of missing Registry entries and a whole slew of "wrong version" errors. I tried the same thing after installing ADO 2.5. Ditto. Scary. They're working on it—or so they say.*

Installing ADO

If you're using Visual Basic 6.0, Visual Studio 6.0, Office 2000, or Internet Explorer 5.0, ADO is already installed. However, your customer's system might

---

1. Difugelties: (ancient computer term). Bug, error, screw-up, FUBAR.

not have ADO installed, and if it is installed, then the chances are pretty slim that system is running the same version of ADO as yours are. If you don't control what version your customer installs on its system, your ADO application might not work very long. Unfortunately, if the customer visits the Microsoft Windows Update site and decides to download a patch, or a new application, or simply upgrades Internet Explorer, it might end up with a newer version of ADO. So you can't depend on keeping an older version (or even a current version) of ADO in place on the target system—even if you hide it in a locked closet.

So, is there hope for all us ADO and COM users? Well, Windows 2000 technology is supposed to come to the rescue. In the latest version of MSDN News (January/February 2000, http://msdn.microsoft.com/voices/news/), there is an informative article that makes me think the problem is at least being studied. The article, "The End of DLL Hell," suggests that the new Windows Installer technology and Windows File Protection will prevent accidental (or intentional) damage to DLLs. What it does not say is whether ADO is considered to be one of the specially protected system DLLs. At this point, there's evidence it's not—but this might have to change.

> **TIP** *Windows 9x Users: DCOM95 for Windows 95 must be installed before installing MDAC 2.0x or 2.1x. MDAC installs components that rely on DLLs installed by DCOM95 to register correctly. DCOM95 is not required on Windows NT 4.0. In some cases, DCOM may not be installed on a Windows 98 computer. DCOM95 for Windows 95 is available for download at* **http://www.microsoft.com/com/tech/dcom.asp***.*

Sometimes you will want to handle the installation of Mdac_typ.exe yourself. Here's a tip. To use the underdocumented feature that installs MDAC "hands-free" on a user's machine, try these option flags:

```
Mdac_typ.exe /q /C:"Setup QN1"
```

While this is not a "quiet" install, it does the job and shows users what's going on (as if they really cared).

Deploying ADO

Deploying ADO on the target system is one of the most complex and troublesome issues facing any ADO (or COM) developer today. While tasks such as analysis, design, and testing have become regular steps in most development efforts, application deployment is often an overlooked step in the development process.

Deploying a COM solution generally involves many installation tasks, including the following:

- Distributing files

- Creating Registry entries

- Creating desktop icons

- Updating software components on client machines

Microsoft's Visual Basic Package and Deployment Wizard, and many third party deployment tools, are capable of automating the deployment process. However, many of these tools don't take advantage of the latest technologies to accomplish a conceptually simple task—installing the software!

For example, these tools often require that the author create installation scripts to set predefined paths and installation options. Developing installation scripts becomes increasingly difficult as solutions become more complicated and interdependent. Writing an installation script that copies three files is simple, but writing a script for a solution that shares a file with other applications is more difficult. Add uninstall logic, and these scripts become unmanageable.

Installation programs face an additional problem: How do you create an installation procedure that accounts for all of the differences between client machines? From what applications are installed to what operating system features are active, accounting for all of the variations that an installation procedure might encounter is a difficult, seemingly insurmountable, task. When scripts are created for installation procedures, authors need to anticipate the environment before the installation occurs. In other words, you have to know what the target system looks like, what's installed, what's not installed, and how many resources are available. Increasing the amount of information shared between the installer and the operating system can reduce the difficulty of this task.

Creating installation scripts is a difficult task that is required by most installer tools. Visual Studio Installer eliminates this step and other inherent difficulties associated with creating robust, efficient installation programs. When used in conjunction with the Windows Installer technology, Visual Studio Installer seems to be the best choice for creating fast, manageable, robust installation applications for Visual Studio-based solutions.

The Visual Studio and Windows Installers

To help solve some of the problems associated with installation programs, Microsoft has introduced the Windows Installer as a means of deploying applications. Windows Installer technology is a part of Microsoft Windows 2000 and is also available for Microsoft Windows 95, Windows 98, and Windows NT 4.0 operating systems. You'll see it install automatically when you install Office 2000 or any application that uses the Visual Studio Installer.

The Microsoft Windows Installer is not script-based like most other installation program development tools. Instead, the Windows Installer serves as a host for data-driven installation packages. Windows Installer uses "bundles" of data, called packages, to contain information about what components are required by a solution. The Windows Installer utilizes the information in a package to determine:

- How components are installed on a machine

- Which Registry settings need to be created or modified

- The default location of files

- Whether or not desktop icons need to be created

- Other installation-time information

All this is accomplished without the developer writing a single line of installation code. The highly interactive data-driven model represents a great advance over the traditional script-based approach. Data-driven installations avoid many of the complexities associated with script-based installers and reduce the workload of developers and operational support workers.

I saw this technology demonstrated at VBits in the fall of '99, and it was impressive. After a Visual Basic application was installed with the Visual Studio Installer, the speaker deleted some of the MDAC files and restarted the application. The system (Windows 98 in this case) went out, reinstalled those files and repaired the damage. Cool.

You can get the Visual Studio Installer from the Web (**http://msdn.Microsoft.com/vstudio**) or from the Visual Studio Plus Pack or Windows 2000 Readiness Kit (which is in the Visual Studio Plus Pack).

Getting More Help with ADO

Okay, so maybe you need more help on with ADO and don't know where to go. Well, I could send you to MSDN online or to the MSDN CDs that keep appearing on your doorstep every three months or so. However, while the information is likely there somewhere, finding it is a royal PIA (that's another technical term).

Both my *Hitchhiker's Guide to Visual Basic and SQL Server* (6th edition, Microsoft Press, ISBN: 1-57231-848-1) and the *ADO 2.0 Programmer's Reference* (Wrox Press, ISBN: 0-861001-83-5) are good basic references to ADO. However, the latter draws a number of conclusions about cursors that seem bizarre, at best. Microsoft Press also has a good, new ADO 2.5-oriented text by David Sceppa called *Programming ADO* (ISBN: 0-7356-0764-8) that I reviewed (and wrote the foreword for). Richard Waymire and Rick Sawtell's book *Teach Yourself Microsoft SQL Server 7.0 in 21 Days* (Sams, ISBN: 0-672-31290-5) seems to be a solid reference for SQL Server 7.0. *Active Server Pages* (Wrox Press, ISBN:1-861000-72-3) helped quite a bit with the Web side of development.

You can also get help online—and even for free. Several thousand folks and I hang out on a list server: **VBDATA@peach.ease.lsoft.com**. Lots of questions are asked and answered there.

CHAPTER 2

Introduction to ADO

I STRUGGLED WITH THIS CHAPTER IN the sense that I didn't want to bore you with material that you already understood. But the trainer in me said to lay some solid foundations before digging right into the coding techniques. So, this chapter has a few theoretical sections that describe ADO and where it fits in the bigger scheme of things. If you want to skip down to the techie stuff, go ahead. We start talking about cool coding stuff in Chapter 3. However, if you need a few more words on ADO, stick around.

ADO and OLE DB

When we start talking about getting at data from ADO, you might want to know a little more about what's going on behind the scenes. Well, as you know (or should know) ADO is a Component Object Model (COM) interface to OLE DB providers, and OLE DB expects to be accessed by consumers such as ADO. So, formally, an OLE DB Consumer is any piece of system or application code that consumes an OLE DB interface. This includes OLE DB components themselves. Figure 2-1 illustrates how ADO interfaces with OLE DB.

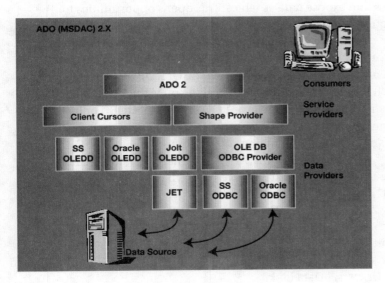

Figure 2-1: ADO connecting to OLE DB

A provider is any software component that exposes an OLE DB interface. *OLE DB providers* can be classified broadly into two classes: data providers and service components.

A *data provider* is any OLE DB provider that owns data and exposes its data in a tabular form as a rowset, which is defined later in this chapter. Examples of data providers include relational DBMSs, storage managers, spreadsheets, ISAMs, and e-mail data sources.

A *service component* is any OLE DB component that does not own its own data, but encapsulates some service by producing and consuming data through OLE DB interfaces. A service component is both a consumer and a provider. For example, a heterogeneous query processor is a service component—it has to draw data from one source, restructure it, and pass it up the food chain to the requesting component, the consumer. Suppose a consumer asks to join data from tables in two different data sources. In its role as a consumer, the query processor retrieves rows from rowsets created over each of the base tables. In its role as a provider, the query processor creates a rowset from these rows and returns it to the consumer.

A *database management system* (DBMS) is a type of data source whose job it is to return information in one form or another as an OLE DB data provider. In some implementations, a DBMS is segmented into functional pieces (components)—each handling a specific job. In theory, component DBMSs offer greater efficiency than traditional DBMSs because consumers generally require only a portion of the database management functionality offered, thereby reducing resource overhead. OLE DB enables simple tabular data providers to implement functionality native to their data store: at a minimum, they can use only the interfaces that expose data as tables. This opens opportunities for the development of query processor components, such as SQL or geographical query processors. These can consume tabular information from any provider that exposes its data through OLE DB. In addition, SQL DBMSs can expose their functionality in a more layered manner by using the OLE DB interfaces.

Okay, so much for the theory. What's really going on is this: ADO is a COM-based programming interface—like DAO or RDO. Instead of ODBC or Jet drivers that connect to the data sources, ADO uses OLE DB. It turns out that one of those OLE DB providers speaks ODBC, enabling you to connect to any ODBC data source (assuming you have the right ODBC driver). These drivers are called "data providers" in OLE DB speak. There are "native" OLE DB providers for Jet databases (called "Jolt" providers) that know how to access both Jet 3.x (Access 9x) and Jet 4.0 (Office 2000) databases. There are also native providers for SQL Server, Oracle, and other, more obscure data sources. See Figure 2-2 for the OLE DB dialog that lets you choose which provider to use. This dialog box is exposed whenever you use Visual Basic's Data View window, the ADO Data Control (ADC), or create an ADO Universal Data Link.

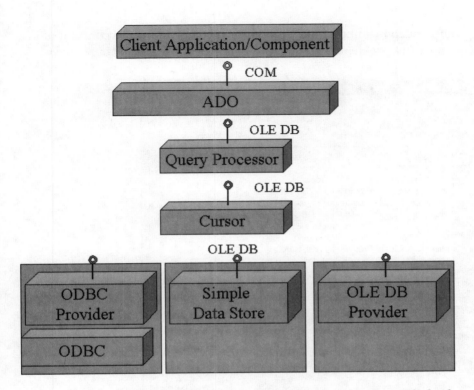

Figure 2-2: OLE DB Providers as exposed by the Data Link Properties dialog box

By default, ADO uses the OLE DB for ODBC provider—which might not be the best choice for your application. When you code your ADO program, you choose the provider either by taking the default or by naming a specific provider in the Connection object properties. Once connected, you can use other OLE DB providers to construct result sets, cursors, shapes (hierarchical representations of your data and its relationships to other datasets), or other data structures. You can also use ADO to help move data from tier to tier by persisting data to the new Stream object or to a file. As we progress through the book, more and more of this will become clear—I hope.

The ADO Object Model

Figure 2-3 illustrates the ADO 2.5 object model. It seems a lot simpler than the DAO or RDO models—at least on the surface. In the older DAO and RDO technologies, developers referenced object-based properties and methods to manipulate the underlying relational data sources. However, with ADO there are far fewer object-based properties, a lot fewer objects, and only four collections. Both DAO and RDO were choked (literally) with collections that consumed memory, and more importantly, CPU resources. They were also a constant source of memory leak problems, as objects were created and destroyed out of turn.

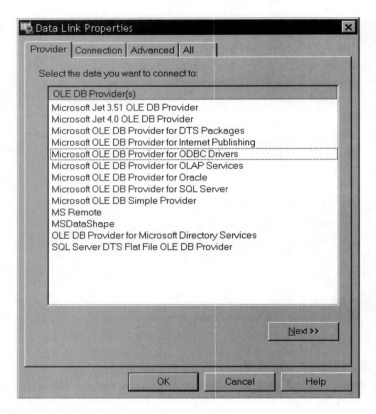

Figure 2-3: The ADO 2.5 Object Model

The ADO 2.5 object model has only five base objects—Connection, Command, Recordset, Record, and Stream. These can all be created independently. This means you don't have to create a Connection object or a Command object to create a Recordset—as a matter of fact, it often makes sense not to do so. Note that the Connection, Command, and Recordset objects are extended through the Properties collection associated with each object. These additional properties are generated (for the most part) by the provider.

When you connect to SQL Server, the Connection object's Properties collection is populated with properties specifically exposed by the selected "native" or ODBC SQL Server provider. These expose features and options specific to SQL Server. While other providers might also expose properties by the same name, they might not work in the same way—if they are implemented at all. I tell my ADO programming students to dump the Connection properties collection before connecting and again after connecting to their data provider. This illustrates how much the Properties collection is affected by the choice of provider and what's there regardless of the provider chosen.

> **TIP** *Visual Basic does not instantiate objects until they are referenced for the first time. If you touch the ADO Connection object in code (as when dumping the Connection.Properties collection), certain properties are set to their default values. To make sure your application behaves as expected, be sure to set the Connection.ConnectionString first, so that ADO knows which data provider will be used.*

These properties are actually documented—exactly *where* is the question. After some snooping around, I discovered that MSDN does not include OLEDB.CHM in its search path. This means that if you want to know what these properties do, you'll need to look there. I would set up a shortcut to that help file. On my system, OLEDB.CHM was loaded along with the other MSDN CHM files, but there's no telling where it will be on your system—go look for it. If you can't find it on your system, be sure to look back a couple of pages and download the latest version of ADO from **www.microsoft.com/data**. It's included there too.

Before you open an ADO Connection, but after having set the ConnectionString property, the Connection.Properties collection contains the following properties. Note that most of these properties don't need a lot of explanation once you understand the OLE DB jargon. For example, you might be used to seeing a Default Database property in DAO or RDO, but in OLE DB it's "Initial Catalog."

```
Password        =
Persist Security Info       =
User ID     =
Data Source     =
Window Handle           =
Location    =
Mode        =
Prompt      =   4
Connect Timeout         =       15
Extended Properties     =   DSN=LocalServer
Locale Identifier       =       1033
Initial Catalog =
OLE DB Services         =   -5
```

After you open the connection, a lot more properties are added to the list (there are about three pages of them, so I won't list them here). These properties are a little more obscure, but as I said before, they're documented in the OLE DB SDK. I'll show how to dump your property collections a little later.

Perusing the resulting properties after the Connection object is open can be very enlightening. Someone could write an entire book on these properties and how to make best use of them. The best source of information on the properties not discussed in this chapter or in later chapters is the OLE DB SDK.

Consider that the OLE DB provider developers have a lot of freedom when implementing these properties. That is, when an OLE DB developer builds a provider to access their data source, he or she is not *required* to implement many of the properties in any particular way. While most well-defined and understood properties are implemented uniformly, developers are granted quite a bit of slack when it comes to more obscure operations. They're also on their own when it comes to implementing features unique to their data provider.

Once your ADO Connection object is open, you can dump the Properties collection to see what additional lights, knobs, and switches are available to control your data provider as shown in the following code:

```
Dim cn As ADODB.Connection
Dim pr As Property


Private Sub Form_Load()
Set cn = New ADODB.Connection
cn.ConnectionString = "DSN=LocalServer"
For Each pr In cn.Properties
    Debug.Print pr.Name, " = ", pr.Value
Next pr
cn.Open "DSN=LocalServer", "SA", ""
For Each pr In cn.Properties
    Debug.Print pr.Name, " = ", pr.Value
Next pr
End Sub
```

CHAPTER 3

Creating ADO Objects

WHILE MANY OF YOU KNOW (or think you know) how to construct ADO or other COM objects, bear with me for a minute while I walk you through some basics. I've seen too many suspect examples in publications whose technical editors should know better, to skip over this. We'll talk about setting the references, or writing the code on an ASP to do so, and about a couple of mistakes that many developers are still making.

Instantiating ADO Objects

Okay, I want to get down to the technical coding stuff, but before you can use any of the ADO objects, you have to get Visual Basic to instantiate the objects—but you knew that. If you are working in the Visual Basic IDE, this process is drop-dead easy. All you have to do is reference the ADO library—and this might already be done for you if you start a "Data" project template, or reference the ADO Data control component.

If you're working in the Visual Basic IDE, you can select an appropriate ADO library by using the Project/References menu. Simply point to the "Microsoft ActiveX Data Objects 2.x Library" (where "x" is the version of ADO 2 that you want to use) in the dialog box shown in Figure 3-1. After the library is referenced, Visual Basic examines the typelibs and fills in your application's symbol table. This means that as you code, Visual Basic fills in the objects, properties, methods, and (especially) enumerated arguments. This single feature in Visual Basic dramatically improves your performance—your code-writing performance. It can verify that you have typed the object names correctly and that the objects will exist at runtime.

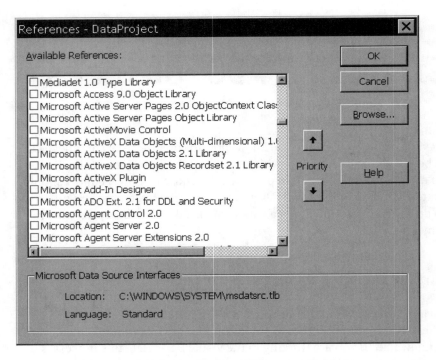

Figure 3-1: The Visual Basic IDE Project/References dialog box

TIP *What about the "Microsoft ActiveX Data Objects Recordset 2.1 Library"? Isn't this supposed to bring in a smaller, lighter, more limited version of ADO 2.1? Well, at one time it did—but no longer. It's now just a typelib that exposes a subset of the ADO 2.1 functionality, but it's really referencing the same MSADO15.DLL that's used by all versions of ADO.*

Okay, so how do you create these objects in code? All too many MSDN and documentation[1] examples show the very common syntax:

```
Dim cn as New ADODB.Connection          ' This is the wrong way...
```

However, when you use this syntax, you cause Visual Basic to add measurable overhead to each and every reference to the object. That is, each time Visual Basic touches the object "cn", the compiler adds:

```
If cn is Nothing then Set cn = New ADODB.Connection
```

---

1. Guilty: I also used the *Dim xx as New yy* syntax in early revisions of the HHG. When I discovered how this syntax impacted performance, I corrected them. Sorry 'bout that.

So, how do you declare and instantiate ADO (or any COM object) correctly? Simply break down the operation into two steps:

1. Declare the variable with Dim, Public, or Private as needed, but do not use the New operator.

2. Use a separate Set statement when (and only when) you need to reference the new object in code. In this case, use the New operator to construct a new instance of the desired object.

This correct syntax looks like this:

```
Dim cn as ADODB.Connection
...
Set cn = New ADODB.Connection
```

If you follow this best-practice coding convention, your applications will run a little faster, and you avoid crippling some of the features provided by ADO when working with multiple result set stored procedures. I explain that later.

> **TIP** *My students ask me if they need to use the ADODB qualifier when coding their Dim statements. I tell them that this is optional, but if there is even a remote chance that their code might invoke the Data Access Objects (DAO) library, that they had better include it to avoid name collisions. If you do include the ADODB prefix, changes that other bright minds make later won't break your golden code.*

Instantiating ADO Components in Visual Basic Script

Many of you will be using ADO from a Visual Basic Script running on IIS or the local browser (less likely). In this case, you won't be using the Visual Basic IDE to create your applications, which means that you'll have to code the ADO object instantiations yourself as in:

```
Dim cn          ' This will be our ADO connection object.
Set cn = Server.CreateObject("ADODB.Connection")
```

If you use Visual InterDev (VI) to develop your ASP or HTM pages, VI will try to help you populate objects it recognizes using statement completion—but it's not nearly as comprehensive and complete as the support in the Visual Basic IDE.

That's why you'll have to add an include file to your project to complete symbol table population for Web development, as shown in the following Visual Basic Script code. Without adovbs.inc., your ASP code will be unable to reference certain arguments and unenumerated options. Well, actually, that's not true. Your code can reference things such as adCmdText as an option on the Recordset Open method, but it won't compile or run.

```
<!-#include File="adovbs.inc"->
<%
Dim rs, cn
set cn = server.CreateObject ("ADODB.Connection")
Set rs = Server.CreateObject("ADODB.Recordset")
Set stm = Server.CreateObject("ADODB.Stream")
  cn.ConnectionString =  "dsn=WorkServer;uid=TestASP;pwd=Secret"
  cn.CursorLocation  = aduseclient
  cn.Open
  if err then
    BuildErrorRecord 0, err, err.Description
  Else
```

After your ASP ADO objects are created, they can be referenced in Visual Basic Script just as they are in "regular" Visual Basic. Neither Visual InterDev nor "Visual" Notepad (your Visual Basic Script editor automatically capitalizes the object names and properties as you code). Because of this, you don't (always) have a visual confirmation that the code you're pounding in is correct. Perhaps in Visual Basic 7.0...

ADO can be used in any tier—as long as it makes sense. For example, the ADO Command object might not be the best choice for every application. I've been having a running debate with others around here about the efficiency of creating Command objects in the middle tier as when working with MTS components or ASP pages. Just keep in mind that ADO objects (like all COM objects) take time to instantiate and additional time to tear down. Because these creation and destruction operations are carried out *each* time the object is referenced (no, MTS does not support pooled components yet), you'll find it pretty expensive to create *unnecessary* ADO objects. Yes, you can use the ODBC API to decrease the time it takes to get your components started and destroyed. If you're thinking about bypassing ADO and using OLE DB directly, forget it. You can't use OLE DB from Visual Basic—despite its performance benefits over ADO. I discuss this more fully in the chapters on middle-tier development.

CHAPTER 4

Getting Connected

WHEN YOU WANT ADO TO RETRIEVE data, you have to either create the data yourself or somehow connect to a data source and suck the data down. In some cases (as we'll discuss in the "Desperately Seeking Performance" and "Passing Data Between Tiers" sections), you can extract data from nontraditional data sources, such as an ActiveX Server Page (ASP) or an XML data Stream. But if you want to get data out of SQL Server, Access (Jet), Oracle, or any other "traditional" database, you have to use a connection—at least at first. This also holds true for any of the plethora of ODBC and OLE DB data sources available when you install MDAC 2.x (see Figure 4-1). However, you don't necessarily have to formally create your own ADO Connection object—in many cases ADO will create one for you.

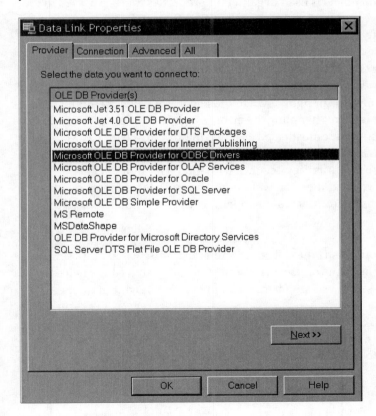

Figure 4-1: OLE DB Providers

This chapter discusses why, when, and how to use ADO Connection objects to get connected. While these objects won't help your social life, they will help you get in touch with your data. Frankly, based on the number of questions generated in my classes and the length of time the connection labs consume, getting connected (to databases) seems to be quite daunting for some people—and not just for those getting started with ADO. For example, there seems to be quite a bit of confusion regarding the ConnectionString and how to construct it correctly (and efficiently). I'll discuss a few tips and tricks in this regard as we go.

The ADO Connection Object

The ADO Connection object is your pipeline (almost literally) to client/server data sources. Although you might not realize it, ADO often creates one of these for you behind the scenes if you don't explicitly code one yourself. Of course, there are exceptions (aren't there always?), and I discuss them in this chapter, but suffice it to say that you usually need to build a Connection object at one point or another.

Your Connection object is used to gather up properties that are passed to the underlying data and service providers—such as ODBC, or OLE DB, or cursor providers. That's why the documentation for the providers (ODBC or OLE DB) provides vital low-level information about what should go into these parameters. Hopefully, you won't have to go there to get this information.

When working with Web pages, we often bypass the creation of the Connection object and sprint right down to the Recordset.Open method. That's cool and quick, but it makes handling the errors tough. Consider that VBScript's error handling is about as sophisticated as it was in MBASIC-80 for CP/M.[1] Because of this, you'll want to add a little more granularity to your Web-based code to help capture errors as they occur. See Chapter 9 for more details.

Never assume your connection will open. There are lots of reasons for a connection not opening (or not staying open). Let's take a quick look at the top 10 reasons:

1. The data source isn't there. The server name is misspelled or it's simply down. The filename or its path is wrong, or the system where it lives is down. The server was stolen in the night by animal rights activists.

2. The network is down. The hub, router, switch, or domain controller is down. One of those little boxes with the cool flashing lights was borrowed to enhance someone's holiday tree display.

---

1. CP/M is the 8-bit (8080/Z80) operating system I supported while working at Digital Research in the 80s. MBASIC-80 is one of the early versions of Microsoft Basic.

3. The net is up and the server is up, but it's full—you and everyone else have consumed all of the available connections. Your system administrator has been playing with the connections count again—his bonus did not come through.

4. You don't have enough licenses to upgrade the server to more users. Your boss said you paid too much for the software in the first place and you should have used one of those freeware systems anyway.

5. The connection was established, but you don't have permission to access the database specified as the initial catalog or default database. You made the SA mad yesterday when you accused him of playing with the connections count.

6. The server you're trying to connect to does not speak named pipes—only sockets. You forgot that the target server is MSDE.

7. The Data Source Name you specified in the ConnectionString does not exist. You forgot to install it on every single system in the universe where your application runs.

8. You chose the wrong provider for the database. You forgot that the right provider for an Access 2000 database is the Jolt 4.0 provider. You did not know that the SA converted all of your Jet 3.5 databases to 4.0 in the night—he's still mad about the connections crack.

9. You have been using the SA user-id for all of your applications—just like all of the examples in all of the books—and the *real* SA just changed the password. He won't even speak to you at this point—there are signs he has moved to Argentina.

10. The user pressed ctrl-alt-delete before your connection could time out because you set the ConnectionTimeout property to 0. They would have waited longer, but they had to leave for the airport—something about a trip south to join the SA.

Frankly, this list is far from complete. Each organization has its own situations that you have to deal with. While many of these errors are trappable, some simply require better organization, teamwork, and discipline on the part of your team, on the part of management, and, if at all possible, on the part of the SA. I know that's asking a lot, but if you expect to have a robust application, it's going to take a lot of work to keep your application connecting and running when things go "snap" somewhere.

A Connection object represents a unique session with a data source. In the case of a client/server database system, it may be equivalent to an actual network connection to the server. Depending on the functionality supported by the provider, some collections, methods, or properties of a Connection object might not be available. How can you tell which are available and which aren't? Again, check out the Properties collection after opening the Connection object.

Using the collections, methods, and properties of a Connection object, you can do the following:

- Configure the connection before opening it with the ConnectionString, ConnectionTimeout, and Mode properties. After the Connection object is open, examine the ConnectionString property to see what options were *actually* used to establish the connection.

- Set the CursorLocation property to invoke either the Client Cursor Provider, which supports batch updates, or server-side cursors, which support read-write cursors.

- Set the default database (initial catalog) for the connection with the DefaultDatabase property.

- Specify an OLE DB provider with the Provider property. Remember that the default provider is the OLE DB provider for ODBC. If you touch the Properties collection before setting the Provider property, it's set to MSDASQL (the provider name for the OLE DB Provider for ODBC).

- Manage transactions on the connection, including nested transactions if the provider supports them, with the IsolationLevel, BeginTrans, CommitTrans, and RollbackTrans methods and with the Attributes property.

- Establish—and later break—the physical connection to the data source with the Open and Close methods. Note that the Recordset object can open the Connection object on its own.

- Execute a command on the Connection object with the Execute method.

- Execute a named Command object against the Connection object— including managing parameters and returning a Recordset.

- Obtain schema information about your database with the OpenSchema method.

- Examine errors returned from the data source with the Errors collection.

- Read the version of the current ADO implementation with the Version property.

Using the Connection Object

As I indicated earlier, it's not always necessary to explicitly declare and open an ADO Connection object; sometimes ADO does this for you. However, the connection string you construct and use with the Recordset Open or the Command Execute method are all built using the same tenants as discussed here (so take notes!).

Connection Object Scope

Unless you knew better, you'd think that it might be cool to construct a Connection object in one process and hand it to another process to use as it saw fit. However, this is not an option—and it never has been. We've never been able to create DB-Library, ODBC, or OLE DB connections and pass the connection handles or objects to another process—even on the same system. While it's possible to marshal Recordset objects (even Command objects) across process boundaries, it's not an option for the Connection object.

There is, however, an alternative. You can remote a connection using the MS REMOTE provider—but with some limitations. The MS REMOTE provider enables the client to create a remote proxy on a remote server via HTTP, HTTPS, or DCOM. This remote proxy server makes the actual connection and performs the queries for you. It's like sending a trusted agent to an auction. The agent tells you what's up for bids and you communicate your instructions through the agent. If it works, you can end up with an antique worth owning; if not, you can end up with a stuffed moose head to hang in your hotel lobby. For security reasons, you should use the MSDFMAP.INI server-side security file whenever possible.

For example, you can code a remote connection like this:

```
Dim cn as adodb.connection
' I don't use MSDFMAP.INI here, and this is very insecure so don't do it.
Set cn = New Connection
cn.open "Provider=MS REMOTE;Remote Server=http://MyServer;" _
    "Remote Provider=SQLOLEDB;Data Source=SS_Hoo; " _
    & "Initial Catalog=Pubs;User Id=sa;Password=;"
cn.execute "create table MyDBTable(id int)"
```

Setting the Provider Property

Most of the time I ignore the Connection object's Provider property—at least I don't reference it except when debugging a connection string. The Provider property can be set in a number of ways, and usually automatically. It can be set by:

- *Not* mentioning a provider anywhere: not referencing the provider in the connection string, not referencing the Connection object's Properties collection in code, and (especially) not referencing the Provider property itself. In this case the Provider property defaults to "MSDASQL"—the OLE DB provider for ODBC.

- Mentioning a provider in the Connection string. In this case, the Provider property is set to the current *version* of the provider. For example, if the connection string has Provider= SQLOLEDB, the Provider property is set to SQLOLEDB.1.

- Setting the Provider property directly in code.

Switching the Provider property can be troublesome. I have seen situations where once the provider is set (as when referencing the Properties collection), trying to change it by using a different "Provider=" value confuses ADO.

Connecting to OLE DB "Native" and ODBC Data Providers

MDAC 2.5 ships with native providers for at least three "traditional" SQL relational data stores—SQL Server, Oracle, and Jet (.mdb).[2] The earliest versions of MDAC, required you to go through the OLE DB Provider for ODBC Data, which, in turn, used the appropriate ODBC driver to access these data stores. With MDAC 2.0, the developers think it's best to use *native* OLE DB providers. They are convinced that these access your data faster and impose a smaller disk and memory footprint. This is due (partially) to the fact that these native providers don't have to translate from ODBC-speak to the native tongue of the backend datasource. For example, the SQL Server provider is written to TDS, the Oracle provider to OCI, and the Jet provider to the Microsoft Jet Engine API interfaces.

---

2. The list of OLE DB providers included in my version of Visual Basic and ADO 2.5 has twelve providers in it, including the OLE DB Provider for ODBC. There are two versions of the Jet provider supplied—one for Jet 3.51 and one for Jet 4.0.

I'll divide the discussion into two parts—first, connecting through the default OLE DB provider for ODBC, and second, connecting through OLE DB native providers. There are native providers for SQL Server, Oracle, and both Jet 3.5 and Jet 4.0 (as well as many others).

Connecting with an ODBC Connection String

Let's start with the OLE DB provider for ODBC. It uses a connection string with which you might already be familiar. One challenge you face as an ADO programmer (even an experienced one), regardless of the provider you choose, is creating a connection string to pass to the ConnectionString property. These can be very simple:

```
cn.ConnectionString = "DSN=MyServer"          'Set the ConnectionString
cn.Open , "Admin", "pw"
```

In this case OLE DB takes most of the defaults. It uses the OLE DB provider for ODBC and opens the specified DSN by hitting the Windows Registry. The contents of that DSN Registry entry populate the "Extended Properties" Connection Property. The resulting ConnectionString ends up looking like this (behind the scenes):

```
Provider=MSDASQL.1;Password=pw;User ID=Admin;Connect Timeout=15;Extended
Properties="DSN=MyServer;Description=Local MSDE Server;
SERVER=(local);UID=Admin;PWD=pw;WSID=BETAV8;DATABASE=biblio";Locale
Identifier=1033
```

After the connection opens, the Connection.Properties("Extended Properties") contains:

```
DSN=MyServer;Description=Local MSDE
Server;SERVER=(local);UID=Admin;PWD=pw;WSID=BETAV8;DATABASE=biblio
```

Notice how ADO has inserted the UserID and password into the connection string. These were provided by the Connection.Open method—not stored with the DSN in the Registry. You can provide these values in the connection string and not have to specify them again in the Open method. And no, there is no way to encode these so that the source code maintains security of the password.

> **NOTE** *The password used in the Open is clearly available in these strings. Because of this, you might want to be careful about passing these objects and connections around.*

You'll also notice that the Connection string includes a Provider=MSDASQL.1 argument. This tells OLE DB to use the OLE DB provider for ODBC version 1. Removing the ".1" would simply tell OLE DB to use the most current provider by that name. At this point no such provider exists—but that's not to say one won't exist in the future. Note that ADO automatically sets the WSID (Workstation name), although you can override this with your own setting. I use this property in client/server applications to help identify specific clients. However, if your connection is running in the middle tier, changing the WSID argument is pointless—Microsoft Transaction Server sets it for you to keep the connection strings the same so they can be pooled.

Connecting Using OLE DB "Native" Providers

On the other hand, if you aren't planning to connect to SQL Server through an ODBC Data Source Name (DSN), you probably won't want to because of performance and security issues I discuss later. This means, you'll have to create a more complex connection string—at least, one that is a little more complicated, because each provider requires that its own arguments be passed to OLE DB from ADO. Yes, many of the arguments are the same, but there are unique differences.

Remember that if you "touch" the Connection object's Properties collection in code or the IDE, the "Provider Name" Connection property is set under the covers. Although this does *not* show up in the Properties collection, the value is set to ODBC (MSDASQL). So, if your first touch sets the ConnectionString, the Provider Name property is set based on what's specified in the ConnectionString. However, this means that once you touch the Properties collection—even using the Locals Windows in the Visual Basic IDE—you won't be able to change the Provider Name later. Thus, if you try to open a Jet or native Oracle provider, you'll get an *ODBC* error.

> **TIP** *You can use the string "(Local)" in the ODBC connect string to refer to the local server, but this won't work for the Data Source argument in an OLE DB Connection string.*

File-based Connections

When accessing file-based data sources, the Connection string can often simply point to the path and filename of the database file using the Data Source argument. However, you can also point to a file-based UDL or DSN using the File Name argument, as shown here:

```
cn.ConnectionString = "file name=c:\biblio.udl"
```

When working with Active Server Pages (ASP), you might want to make sure you fully qualify file path references so that your UDL file is stored outside of your Web site. Keeping with other unprotected files can expose your user ID and password to prying eyes (not good). In this case, place your UDL file outside of the /inetpub/ directory. Using Server.MapPath won't help, as it returns a directory relative to the virtual directory and you want to keep your common files outside of the virtual directory.

Connecting to Jet (Access) Databases

Let's take a brief look at the special issues involved in connecting to the native OLE DB provider for Jet databases. So you try to open a Jet database that has user accounts set up. You know that you have to provide a password and a UserID to the provider, but your application gets the following message: "-2147217843 Cannot start your application. The workgroup information file is missing or opened exclusively by another user." You're confused, so you check MSDN and find a description of the error message: "To ensure referential integrity in databases created by the Microsoft Jet database engine, your application must read the Microsoft Jet database's System.mdw file. Make sure the file is in the location specified in the SystemDB value of the \HKEY_LOCAL_MACHINE\SOFTWARE\ Microsoft\Office\8.0\Access\Jet\3.5\Engines\Jet key in the Windows Registry."

Oh, swell. Microsoft expects developers to dig into the Registry to make sure that the database can be opened with a password. And then you notice that the Registry entry in the message isn't right. You have Office 2000 installed—they never updated the error message. Sigh. So you dig into the Registry and find the right entry (HKEY_LOCAL_MACHINE\Software\Microsoft\Office\9.0\Access\Jet\4.0\Engines), but it's set to "c:\PROGRA~1\MICROS~1\OFFICE\SYSTEM.MDW". Double sigh—a DOS shortname.

What ADO is complaining about is the Jet workgroup information file (WIF). This is a file the Jet engine reads when the database is first opened. The WIF contains information about the users in a workgroup including users' account names, their passwords, and the groups of which they are members. You have to tell Jet where this file is located by setting an "Extended" property before trying to open the connection.

In Microsoft Access 95 and earlier, preference information for each user (specified in the Options dialog box) is stored in the workgroup information file. In Microsoft Access 97 and later, preference information is stored in the Windows Registry. In Microsoft Access version 2.0, the default name for the workgroup information file is System.mda. It is sometimes referred to just as a "workgroup" or the "system database." In Microsoft Access 95 and later, the default name for this file is System.mdw.

Okay, all of this is very interesting, but how do you open a secure .MDB? Well, thanks to a developer on the list service I subscribe to, I learned that you have to *manually* set the pathname of the Jet System.MDW file in code. For example, you can address the "Jet OLEDB:System Database" property in the connection string:

```
"data source=C:\Databases\Secure40.mdb;" _
    & "Jet OLEDB:System Database=C:\Windows\System\System.MDW;"
```

You also have to pass the correct UserID and password in the usual User-ID and Password properties to get connected.

> **TIP** *You have to set the Jet OLEDB:System Database property in the All tab of the Data View Properties dialog box to create a data link to a secure Jet database. When you do, the interface throws up a dialog box asking for the Admin password.*
>
> *Keep in mind that having a dialog box open up is not what you want to happen if you are connecting from MTS or an ASP page. You will not be able to see the dialog box, and the site will appear to be frozen—or it will crash and go down in flames right away.*

Post-Open Connection Strings

After the Connection object opens, ADO copies the provider-constructed connection string back to the Connection.ConnectionString property. This string includes all of the arguments you used in the original ConnectionString or in the Open method or both. It also includes all of the default arguments. This is the string that's cached and compared when using connection pooling in the middle tier.

Note that if ADO can't decide what to do with an argument, it might stick it into the "Extended Properties" section of the constructed ConnectionString. You'll notice that the constructed string contains both OLE DB *and* ODBC "extended" properties, as well as a host of default settings you never mentioned.

For example, this OLE DB ConnectionString:

```
Provider=SQLOLEDB.1;Data Source=betav8
```

returned the following post-open ConnectionString:

```
Provider=SQLOLEDB.1;Password=pw;User ID=Admin;Data Source=betav8;Locale
Identifier=1033;Connect Timeout=20;Use Procedure for Prepare=1;Auto
Translate=True;Packet Size=4096;Workstation ID=BETAV8
```

An ODBC Connection string starts out without an "Extended Properties" section:

```
Provider=MSDASQL;Driver={SQL Server};Server=Betav8;Database=pubs;uid=sa;pwd=;
```

but ends up with a fully populated Extended Properties section containing the OLE DB equivalents of the ODBC arguments:

```
Provider=MSDASQL.1;Password=pw;User ID=Admin;Connect Timeout=20;
Extended Properties="DRIVER=SQL Server;SERVER=Betav8 ;UID=Admin;PWD=pw;
WSID=BETAV8;DATABASE=pubs;Network=DBMSSOCN;
Address=betav8,1433";Locale Identifier=1033
```

Using Visual Database Tools to Create Connection Strings

Frankly, to connect to sources other than SQL Server using the OLE DB provider for ODBC, I steal (er, *leverage)* a connection string constructed by one of the Visual Database Tools or the ADO Data Control (ADODC). Because the error messages you get from ADO are, shall we say, sparse or simply confusing, you'll often be frustrated trying to figure out why a connection is not working. Let's walk through the process I show my students for getting the Visual Database Tools to create these connection strings for you.

The trick here is to use the IDE to construct the Connection and steal its connection. You have a couple of options here. I tend to use the ADODC for this exercise, because it is easier to extract the ConnectionString once it is constructed, so let's start there.

1. Start a new Visual Basic project using the Data Access template.

2. Draw an ADODC control from the toolbox on Form1 (or on any form).

3. Right-click the ADODC, check "Use Connection String", and click "Build" on the General tab.

4.   Choose the OLE DB provider from the providers list shown in the "Data Link Properties" dialog box (see Figure 4-1).

5.   Click Next. Based on the provider you choose, you'll be asked a series of questions that capture properties specific to that provider.

6.   After you have filled in the properties (such as filename or server name, UserID, and password), click Test Connection (see Figure 4-2). This verifies that the Connection string constructed for you will actually work (on your development system). Note that if the connection cannot be established, ADO won't be able to populate the Default Database list. If you get connected, the dialog box will populate the "Select the database on the server" dropdown list.

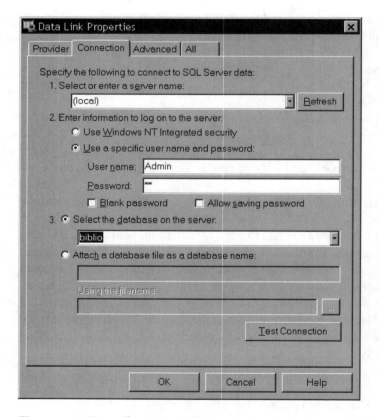

Figure 4-2: Using the Data Link Properties dialog box to build a Connection String

Let's pause here a second, because there are a few points to keep in mind. First, this Data Link Properties dialog box (Figure 4-2) actually *connects* to the target data provider, and to do that, you often need a valid UserID and password. This means the data source (network and server) must be available to you, and the account must have rights on the server or in the data source file so that the tools can connect. In addition, you might have to set the network library to reach the provider—as when you connect to MSDE (it *requires* TCP/IP). See the "Using the Client Network Utility" section later in this chapter.

Second, remember that the error handlers built in the Visual Database Tools are pretty crude. They don't seem to understand what to do when connections are exhausted; they can return some pretty silly error messages that won't mean much to you at the time. Because Visual Basic does not always release connections while you're experimenting, you might try shutting down Visual Basic and starting over. This releases any connections being held by Visual Basic itself. It's not enough to simply stop your application. No, it's not enough to simply stop your Visual Basic application and restart.

Third, the UserID and password collected in the Data Link Properties dialog box is not persisted in the Connection string unless you check the "Allow saving password" check box. Otherwise the Connection string is simply used to establish the connection, and capture the list of valid databases, after which it is discarded.

Finally, remember that just because you get connected here on your development system with this set of properties, it isn't a guarantee that your application, component, or Web page will be able to connect when you deploy.

Now, we're ready to proceed to the next step in the process of creating a Connection string using the Visual Database Tools.

1. Click OK if you are satisfied that the connection will open. This returns you to the populated ADODC control. It should look something similar to Figure 4-3.

2. Okay, now we have a working Connection String. Simply select the string in the Use Connection String text control and paste it in your code.

3. Delete the ADODC from your form.

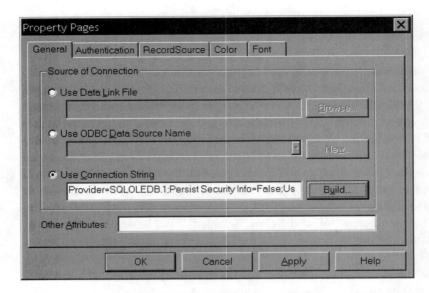

Figure 4-3: The ADODC Property Page after the ConnectionString is built

The connection string we just constructed looks like this:

```
Provider=SQLOLEDB.1;Persist Security Info=False;User ID=Admin;Initial
Catalog=biblio;Data Source=(local)
```

However, this is an easy one. If you use the same technique to create a connection string for a Jet data source, it would look like this when first extracted from the ADODC.

```
Provider=Microsoft.Jet.OLEDB.4.0;Data Source=C:\Program Files\Microsoft Visual
Studio\VB98\Nwind.mdb;Persist Security Info=False
```

Hmmmm, still looks pretty easy. So when does this get ugly? Well, if you did not use the ADODC to capture the connection string, but instead used the Data View window and the Data Environment Designer to do the same thing, you might want to extract the DataEnvironment1.Connection1 object's ConnectionSource property as exposed in the Visual Basic IDE property page. If you capture that string, after having pointed to the same Jet database, you get a dramatically different string:

```
Provider=Microsoft.Jet.OLEDB.4.0;Password="";User ID=Admin;Data Source=C:\Program
Files\Microsoft Visual Studio\VB98\Nwind.mdb;Mode=Share Deny None;Extended
Properties="";Locale Identifier=1033;Jet OLEDB:System database="";Jet
OLEDB:Registry Path="";Jet OLEDB:Database Password="";Jet OLEDB:Engine Type=4;Jet
OLEDB:Database Locking Mode=0;Jet OLEDB:Global Partial Bulk Ops=2;Jet
OLEDB:Global Bulk Transactions=1;Jet OLEDB:New Database Password="";Jet
OLEDB:Create System Database=False;Jet OLEDB:Encrypt Database=False;Jet
OLEDB:Don't Copy Locale on Compact=False;Jet OLEDB:Compact Without Replica
Repair=False;Jet OLEDB:SFP=False
```

Notice the plethora of pairs of double quotes. These are used to indicate empty arguments such as Password="". If you drop this into a Visual Basic string, you would certainly get errors. That's because Visual Basic interprets two double quotes as a single double quote. Clear? Well, anyway, if you want to use this connection string, you'll have to go through and remove *all* of the pairs of double quotes. But what if there are real quoted parameters passed? Well, that should not be a problem, because the Connection string constructor in the Data Environment Designer does not try to pass empty quoted strings for arguments with parameters. Bug? I suspect so.

You can see why I like the ADODC better. It's easier to steal (er, "leverage") its connection string.

Data Source Names and Microsoft Data Links

In the early days of ODBC, collecting and persisting connection string information was accomplished by using registered Data Source Names (DSNs). You can still reference these in ADO connection strings; I used one in an earlier example. The problem with this approach is that while you are fully capable of creating a DSN on your development system, getting one installed on the target system can be a royal PIA.[3] You have several alternatives to using registered DSNs:

- Use a file-based ODBC DSN that contains the same DSN information (in .INI file format) but that is stored in a file instead of in the Registry. Benefits: easy to deploy and install—just copy the file. Problems: slow to

---

3. PIA (a technical term).

access the first time, and easy for users to alter or destroy. It exposes internal UserIDs to prying eyes.

- Use a DSN-less ODBC connection. This approach means that you hard-code all of the required parameters in the connection string. You specify the specific server, driver, and all other required ODBC parameters. Benefits: fairly easy to code once you figure it out, and fast—very fast. Problems: you have hard-coded the server name in the application or component; but the server name does not change very often (or does it)?

  Basically, this is the approach we took when we passed an ADODC-generated connection string into our project.

  ```
  cn.ConnectionString = "Provider=SQLOLEDB.1;Persist Security Info=False;" _
      & "User ID=Admin;Initial Catalog=biblio;Data Source=(local)"
  cn.Open , , "pw"
  ```

> **TIP** *As a "best practice," don't break down strings using the concatenation operator as I have done in the example shown above. It causes Visual Basic to stop and reconstruct a string each time you do so. This approach is used to make the code more human readable for documentation, but it does not necessarily make it faster for Visual Basic to process.*

- Use an OLE DB Microsoft Data Link. In this case, you can create a file with a UDL extension that can be stored anywhere just like a file-based DSN. In this case, however, it simply contains a (Unicode) connection string (and nothing else). These are created in Windows 9x or Windows NT 4.0 or earlier through the file explorer (File | New | Microsoft Data Link). On Windows 2000, just create a text file and give it the UDL extension. Double-clicking this new file opens the Data Link Dialog box we just discussed. The connection string constructed is stored in the .UDL file. Referencing its path and name using the File Name argument in a connection string opens the UDL file and uses its contents (the ADO-generated ConnectionString) to open the ADO Connection.

  ```
  cn.ConnectionString = "File Name=c:\biblio.udl"
  cn.Open
  ```

ADO has improved quite a bit in version 2.5 in that it now caches all references to DSNs and UDLs—even if they come from files. This is why it takes longer to open file-based (and some Registry-based) data sources the *first* time.

> **TIP**   *The File | New | Microsoft Data Link shortcut is not built into Windows 2000. But you can create a .TXT file and give it the UDL extension manually. After this change, Windows and ADO treat it as a UDL file.*

Coding "Minimalist" Connection Strings

I tell my daughters (George and Fred) that ofttimes, less is more. With ADO connection strings this is still true. Connection strings can be very short:

```
Cn.Open "DSN=Fred"
```

This example assumes that your program can accept all of the default values. In this case, you assume the ODBC provider that the DSN is set to assume a "trusted" connection so that you don't even need the UserID and password, and that the SA has assigned the correct default database.

OLE DB connection strings can be short, too, but you have to specify the Provider first to prevent any confusion as the string is parsed:

```
Cn.Open "Provider=SQLOLEDB;Data Source=MyServer;"
```

Again, this assumes that you can accept the default settings. Here are some short sample connection strings for a wide variety of data sources:

- SQL Server Native OLE DB provider (sqloledb.dll):

  ```
  Provider=Sqloledb;Data Source=ServerXX;Initial Catalog=pubs;User
  Id=sa;Password=;
  ```

- Jet / Access 97 version 3.51 (msjtor35.dll):

  ```
  Provider=Microsoft.Jet.OLEDB.3.51;Data Source=c:\northwind.mdb
  ```

- Jet / Access 97 version 4.0 (msjetoledb40.dll):

  ```
  Provider=Microsoft.Jet.OLEDB.4.0;Data Source=c:\northwind.mdb
  ```

- Oracle (msdaora.dll):

```
Provider=Msdaora;Data Source=Serverxx.world; User ID=scott;Password=tiger"
```

- To use an old ODBC, driver use the following syntax:

```
"Provider=MSDASQL;Driver={SQL Server};
Server=MyServer;Database=pubs;uid=sa;pwd=;"
```

- Or for an ISAM, such as Excel, use this syntax:

```
"Provider=MSDASQL;Driver={Microsoft Excel Driver (*.xls)};
DBQ=D:\inetpub\wwwroot\testXL\pubs.xls;"
```

- MSDataShape (msadds.dll):

```
"Provider=MSDataShape;Data Provider=SQL Oledb;Data Source=ServerXX;Initial
Catalog=pubs;User Id=sa;".
```

- MS Remote (msdarem.dll)—you can execute three-tier parameterized hierarchies by combining MSDataShape and MS Remote:

```
"Provider=MSDataShape;Data Provider=MS Remote;Remote
Provider=sqloledb;Remote Server=http://your_IIS_server;Data
Source=ServerXX;Initial Catalog=pubs;User Id=sa;"
```

Creating a New Jet Database

In some cases, you might want to persist to a Microsoft Jet database. ADO knows how to do this, but you have to reference a different object library. Select Microsoft ADO Ext. 2.1 (or 2.5) for DDL and Security and use the following code:

```
Dim cat as ADOX.Catalog
Set Cat = New ADOX.Catalog
Cat.Create "Provider=Microsoft.Jet.OLEDB.4.0;Data Source=c:\MyNewDB.mdb"
```

Converting from ODBC to OLE DB Connection Strings

When the OLE DB engineers started to define the arguments to be recognized by the connection string parser, they did not want to make the process of converting *too* easy, so they redefined a number of the arguments. Table 4-1 lists some of these redefined arguments.

ODBC	OLE DB
UID=;PWD=;	User ID=, Password=
Database=	Initial Catalog=
Trusted_Connection=Yes	Integrated Security=SSPI;
Server	Data Source

Table 4-1: ODBC to OLE DB Provider Connection String Arguments

SQL Server Provider (SQLOLEDB) Connect String Arguments

While the Visual Studio documentation lists the initialization properties for the SQLOLEDB Provider, some of the property descriptions are incorrect. It's important to note that it is now possible to create a SQL Server 7.0 connection string that contains all of the parameters you can specify when creating a registered DSN. In earlier versions of ODBC, this was not an option; many of the arguments were reserved for the Registry-based DSN. Table 4-2 lists the SQL Server provider properties and describes their purpose.

PROPERTY	DESCRIPTION
"Data Source"	The SQL Server to connect to.
"Initial Catalog"	The "default" SQL Server database.
"Integrated Security"	A string containing the name of the authentication service. This can be set to "SSPI" or to "" for Windows NT Integrated security (Secured Support Provider Interface).
"Locale Identifier"	SQLOLEDB validates the locale ID and returns an error if the locale ID is not supported or is not installed on the client computer.
"Password"	The password assigned to a SQL Server login. This property is used when SQL Server Authentication Mode is selected for authorizing access to a SQL Server database.
"Persist Security Info"	SQLOLEDB persists authentication values, including an image of a password, if requested to do so. No encryption is provided.
"Prompt"	SQLOLEDB supports all prompting modes for data source initialization. SQLOLEDB uses 4 (no prompt) as its default setting for the property. The four possible values are these: (1): Always prompt the user for initialization information. (2): Prompt the user only if more information is needed. *(continued)*

39

	(3): Prompt the user only if more information is needed. Do not allow the user to enter optional information.
	(4): Do not prompt the user. Return a trappable error to the application if the UserID and password pair cannot be validated.
"User ID"	A SQL Server login. This property is used when SQL Server Authentication Mode is selected for authorizing access to a SQL Server database.
"Window Handle"	A window handle from the calling application. A valid window handle is required for the initialization dialog box displayed when prompting for initialization properties is allowed.
"Connect Timeout"	SQLOLEDB returns an error on initialization if a connection to the SQL Server cannot be established within the number of seconds specified. Approximately 10 seconds is the lower limit.

Table 4-2: SQL Server Provider (SQLOLEDB) Connect String Arguments

The properties in Table 4-3 are extended properties defined by the native OLE DB SQL Server (SQLOLEDB) provider. These are all exposed in the Connection Properties collection and they are all read/write.

EXTENDED PROPERTY	DESCRIPTION
"Application Name"	The client application name.
"Auto Translate"	If True, SQLOLEDB performs OEM/ANSI character conversion when multi-byte character strings are retrieved from, or sent to, the SQL Server. If False, no conversion is done.
"Current Languge" (Note the incorrect spelling.)	A SQL Server language name. Identifies the language used for system message selection and formatting. The language must be installed on the SQL Server or data source initialization will fail.
"Network Address"	The network address of the SQL Server specified by the property. These are used for IPX and NetBios protocols. See Q175472 on MSDN. It also appears that the Server Name followed by a port number is used for TCP/IP (BetaV9.1433).

"Network Library"	The name of the Net-Library (DLL) used to communicate with the SQL Server. The name should not include the path or the .dll filename extension. The default is provided by the SQL Server client configuration.
"Packet Size"	A network packet size in bytes. The packet size property value must be between 512 and 32767. The default is 4096.
"Use Procedure for Prepare"	Defines the use of SQL Server temporary stored procedures:
	0: A temporary stored procedure is not created when a command is prepared.
	1: Default. A temporary stored procedure is created when a command is prepared. The temporary stored procedures are dropped when the session is released.
	2: A temporary stored procedure is created when a command is prepared. The procedure is dropped when the command is unprepared, or when a new command is specified for the command object, or when all application references to the command are released.
"Workstation ID"	A string identifying the workstation.
"Initial File Name"	This property is for future use with SQL Server 7.0 database files.

Table 4-3: ODBC "Extended" property arguments for SQL Server 7.0.

Using the Client Network Utility

In cases where your server does not know how to open or create a named pipe, or you need to reference a server somewhere on the Web, you'll have to launch the Client Network Utility (shown in Figure 4.4) to advise ODBC that it should use an alternative network driver to access the specific server. This is a requirement for accessing Microsoft Database Engine (MSDE) versions of SQL Server 7.0 running on Windows 9x. In this case, the OS does not know how to work with named pipes (the default network interface). Frankly, the TCP/IP protocol is faster than named pipes, easier to install, and more reliable. However, you can't use domain-managed security unless you stick with named pipes.

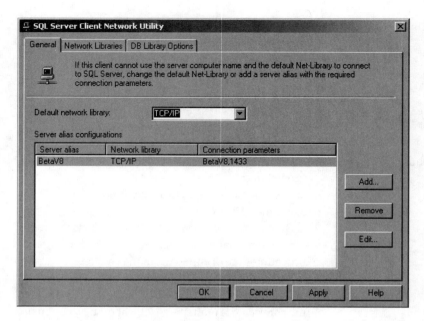

Figure 4-4: Use the SQL Server 7.0 Client Network Utility to select an alternative protocol.

To use the utility, simply launch it from Start | Programs | Microsoft SQL Server | Client Network Utility. Enter the name of the server in question and choose the appropriate network interface from the option button list on the left.

Actually, there is another option to force the use of TCP/IP (or other protocols) instead of the default (named pipes): add a "network=" argument to your connection string. For example, the following code forces the use of TCP/IP:

```
Network=dbmssocn;
```

Setting the CursorLocation Property

By default, ADO does *not* create a cursor to handle any rowsets[4] resulting from your queries, so the CursorLocation property does not really matter. ADO sets the default CursorLocation to server-side cursors (adUseServer). This means that if

---

4. A rowset is simply a set of rows containing the columns specified in the SELECT statement and meeting the membership requirements of the WHERE clause of a query.

you want to use the client-side cursor library's features, you have to switch to client-side cursors (adUseClient). When we get to the Recordset chapters, I discuss the impact of this choice. It turns out that you can switch back and forth between CursorLocation settings whenever you get the urge.

> **TIP** *If you are having problems with clumsy queries being sent to the server (as evidenced by the SQL Server Profiler or your data provider's trace routines), try switching CursorLocation. The data providers have distinctly different approaches to data access based on where the cursors are being created—even in cases where you are using cursorless result sets. For example, the Prepared property issues I discuss in the Command Object chapter 5 can be mitigated by switching the CursorLocation to adUseClient.*

Using Client-side or Server-side Cursors

I have been asked any number of times which are "better"—client-side or server-side cursors. I usually answer, "none-of-the-above." If you *must* use cursors, you need to consider how (and where) resources are to be used. Server-side cursors construct the rowset in a temporary location on the server, consuming server-side CPU and disk resources. You still have to move the rowset over the wire to the client, so in this regard there isn't much difference compared to client-side implementations. Client-side cursors instruct ADO to construct the keyset or static rowset in the client's RAM and disk space. Of course, in the middle tier, these resources might be the same as those shared by the local server.

Will you find significant differences in performance when using one type of cursor over another? I doubt it. An awful lot of work has gone into client-side cursor technology—the MDAC team is very proud of it. The (relatively) new shape provider is a testament to that. Many Microsoft developers are convinced that, to provide the most features and best performance, client-side cursors are the way to go. I'll let you decide for yourself. We'll look at a number of techniques that can only be implemented with server-side cursors and others only with client-side.

> **NOTE** *I've also seen some references to the use of the CREATE CURSOR TSQL syntax in a couple of books. However, this is not what server-side cursors are. That's because it's the ADO provider that generates the TSQL cursors—including server-side cursors when they are needed. While you can code and manage your own server-side cursors using this technique, it seems like a lot of trouble.*

Setting Timeout Properties

ADO exposes both ConnectionTimeout and CommandTimeout properties. This is great, but have you ever noticed how some of these timeout settings do not seem to work very well? Perhaps that is because they're not particularly well understood.

- **ConnectionTimeout** starts when a LAN connection is established to the database server and ends when the data source provider creates a connection. This means that the network component is *not* part of the timing. Because of this, if your network cable has been cut in two by your spouse's vacuum cleaner, your timeout will be a function of the system NetworkTimeout setting. Too bad there isn't one. Network interface card drivers handle timeouts on their own—there is no way to change how long these cards sit and wait for a network packet that will never come. The MDAC team wants to add an OLE DB-managed thread to timeout the operation based on the timeout settings.

- **CommandTimeout** starts when the database server has accepted the command and ends when the database server returns the first record. If the server or network is busy (or not answering at all), this setting won't help get control again.

Both property settings are dependent on network timeout—neither ADO timeout property setting accounts for the time ADO and the low-level providers require to connect to the LAN hardware. Because the low-level NIC driver makes a synchronous network API call, and because this call does not return until the network timeout expires, the ADO timeout code is blocked until the network answers—if it ever does.

In any case, if the network is working, most connections can be established in less than five seconds. Setting the ConnectionTimeout property to a value much larger than 15 seconds is silly—and it causes the client (the human) to timeout. That is, if your client application makes the user wait too long for some operation, the user might give up and Ctrl-Alt-Del your application.

> **NOTE** *Command and Recordset objects created against the Connection inherit the Connection object's CommandTimeout property. While this value can be reset in a Command object, it cannot be set in a Recordset— you have to take the Connection (or Command) setting.*

Prompting for UserID and Password

Humans don't initiate all ADO connections. No, I don't mean to imply that some of your users are rocks, animals, plants, or space aliens—even though some may behave as such. (Don't get me started on the lettuce-head I had to deal with last week.) What I mean is that some connections are launched by components that have no idea what "user" is requesting the operation. For example, a middle tier component simply connects to the data source and asks for data. It does not log on as "Fred" or any other specific UserID tied back to the user. Unless it uses "SA" (which is a very bad thing to do), the component uses a private UserID and password created specifically for this component and those like it.

However, some of you will feel the need to capture a UserID and password and pass these on to the ADO Connection to gain access to the DBMS. In my opinion, this approach is no longer needed and is usually not a particularly good idea as the following discussion explains. The problem you are trying to solve is user validation—should you permit the current human to access the database. There are several approaches to this problem—here are three suggestions:

- Use Windows network security to validate the user. This assumes that the user that logged in is the same user that's now using a program only available to the validated user. This permits you to use the Windows logon name as a UserID when opening a connection, but it assumes that the network protocol exposes this to the server—TCP/IP does not. This approach also assumes that the users are enrolled either in a group that the server recognizes or as individuals. The administration side of this approach can be fairly involved.

- Restrict access to the database so that end-users can neither see nor manipulate the DBMS base tables, views rules, triggers, queries, and so forth. In this case, only certain (perhaps secret) UserID/Passwords can access chosen stored procedures to perform queries and updates. This is my favorite approach, but it still requires a validation mechanism.

- Establish a secondary layer of security. This approach is often needed even in cases where users log on with specific roles. That is, after a user logs on to the application using an application-managed logon ID, either the application itself, or an underlying data access component, logs on with a secret UserID and password. This permits you to manage users with a much higher granularity of control. For example, you could restrict users' database access based on history, time of day, number of accesses, number of current users already logged on, job function, or number of legs.

Prompting Dialogs

Regardless of the type of user validation you choose, you do want to capture valid UserID and password strings yourself—you do *not* want the data provider to do it for you. That is, you *do not* want ODBC or OLE DB to throw up a dialog box (shown in Figure 4-5) requesting clarification of the UserID and Password (and database, data source, or server) that was supplied to the Connection Open method. If this dialog appears, the user is presented with an opportunity to guess another UserID/Password combination or to choose another database—and to keep guessing until they get it right. Not good.

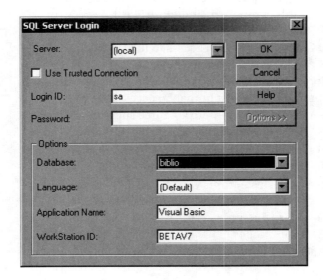

Figure 4-5: Be sure to set the prompting level to avoid exposing this dialog box.

ADO controls this behavior using the Connection object's Prompt property. Fortunately, the default behavior is "no prompt," which instructs ADO to raise a trappable error. However, the Visual Database Tools developers felt, for reasons I do not agree with, that the default behavior should be "prompt always." This means that if you use the Data Environment Designer to open connections, you'll have to disarm the Prompt property. This can be done via the Visual Basic property window when you select the DataEnvironment Connection object. Just be prepared to log on to the database about six times when you do so. Note that the Data Environment Designer supports both runtime and design-time Prompt behaviors.

"Trusted" Connections

Both the ODBC and OLE DB providers support domain-managed security. That is, they can capture the Windows login name and password and pass them to the data provider as a surrogate UserID and password. This assumes that the user's Windows logon name can be used because he or she is "trusted" to log on to the database using your application. This approach is not supported in TCP/IP-only configurations, such as MSDE, or where the "user" is really a component in the middle tier—these components aren't logged into the network.

In ODBC you can add "Trusted_Connection=Yes" to the connection string, indicating that this NT (domain-managed or integrated) authentication is to be used. All other UserID and Password entries in the ConnectionString, or that are passed from the Open statement are ignored. The default behavior with the ODBC provider is "Trusted_Connection=No." This enables mixed mode authentication, which means SQL server *or* NT authentication is used—whichever works.

Using integrated security (NT domain authentication) with ADO is typically more secure than using SQL server authentication. This is because with client-driven security (where humans are involved), developers often end up (unadvisedly) persisting server UserIDs and passwords to disk, either in their code or in a UDL or DSN file. Anyone perusing these files is able to compromise the password. Unfortunately, the way we have engineered our tools and services makes this an easy trap to fall into. For example, it is impossible to use integrated security when running ADO in process with IIS because IIS runs under the local system account and has no authorization to get to the network. If you run your application out of process, you can use integrated security, but the performance with today's IIS implementation will be inadequate for many scenarios. There are ways to deal with this problem by setting up runtime variables containing UserIDs and passwords, but I would bet that many developers do not follow these practices.

OLE DB also supports a similar security scheme, but it uses a different argument in the ConnectionString—"Integrated Security=SSPI" is equivalent to ODBC's "Trusted_Connection=Yes."

I wrote an application to test and log the error messages returned by ADO when performing various operations including management of UserIDs and passwords.[5] I started with simple connection permission issues and discovered a startling fact.

---

5. This application is available on the CD supplied with the book. Search for ConnErrTrap.exe.

Once the application connected using an ODBC DSN and a valid UserID and password (not necessarily SA), I no longer needed to provide a UserID and password again when connecting to the same DSN. If I provided a wrong UserID or password, ADO failed to connect, but just using the Open method with no UserID and Password would get me back in again. It turned out that my Windows logon name was being used in lieu of the missing UserID and password.

Using SA as Your UserID

Many of the security issues you'll face are masked when you choose to use SA as your UserID when accessing SQL Server. Because the SA account has rights to all resources on the server, it is permitted to do virtually anything—including dropping the entire database in a single stroke. It is a gross security violation to divulge the SA password. Without it, "ordinary" users are easily prevented from doing significant harm. Whether you're writing, speaking, training, or coding, make it a point to avoid using SA as your UserID.

Choosing the Default Database

When you connect to a DBMS such as SQL server that supports multiple, your UserID is associated with one of the databases on the system. If your SA is on the ball, the default database is changed to the working database you are most likely to use and that you have permission to access. If the default database (initial catalog) isn't preset, your default database could easily be "Master"—the system database where you (should) have no rights. Because you did not log on as "SA," you should not have to set the default database to be used by this connection. Remember that unless you specify otherwise in your query, your SELECT statements and action queries are executed against this default database.

> **TIP**   *If you get the dreaded ConnectionWrite("GetOverLappedResult") error, you might try changing network protocols. Anything except named pipes seems to work, but "multiprotocol" or TCP/IP seem to work best in this situation—especially if both client and server are configured to use TCP sockets. In most scenarios, TCP/IP is the best choice in terms of speed, stability, and ease of management.*

To select a new default database before the connection is opened, simply add an argument to the connection string. For example, to change your default database to "Fred", add "Database=Fred;" to an ODBC connection string or "Initial Catalog=Fred" to an OLE DB native connection string.

After the connection is open, it is possible to change the default database, but you have to be careful doing so. You cannot permit ADO to create another connection object for you in the process. Actually, ADO 2.5 seems to behave itself better than ADO 2.1 in this respect. If you were to try to change the default SQL Server database using the "Use <db>" TSQL command, and you used the Command object's Execute method to run the query, ADO *might* create another connection just to execute this query—especially if the current connection was busy working on another operation.

It's really safer to tell ADO that you're making the change—just set the "Current Catalog" property (ODBC or OLE DB connections) to the new database. ADO sends a "USE <db>" query for you on the current connection, but only if there are no results pending on the connection. After that, the queries executed will use the new default database. Of course, you could simply close and open the connection again, unless you were depending on other DB state settings. Because it's likely that the connection is pooled, this should not take a big performance hit.

The following code illustrates a typical Open method, and subsequently dumps the default database (current catalog) to show how the server changed it during the process of opening the connection. We then change it to another value using the Connection object Properties collection.

```
cn.Open "dsn=LocalServer;", "admin", "pw"    ' Logs on with SA-defined default DB
Debug.Print cn.Properties("Current Catalog")    ' See what the default DB is
cn.Properties("Current Catalog") = "adoclass"    ' Change it to whatever…
rs.Open "select ID from justinadoclass", cn
' Now you can reference objects in the new DB
```

> **TIP** *If you get a "Create File" error when connecting with the OLE DB for ODBC provider (the default), it might simply mean that ADO could not locate the specified server. You did specify one, didn't you? And it's running, isn't it?*

Managing Connection State

The default database is one of the database connection state properties maintained on the server and (to a limited extent) in the Connection object's Properties collection. These property settings are persisted for as long as the net connection to the server lives. If ADO creates another connection for you, it won't inherit any properties that you change after the connection is open. That's because it's created from the already constructed ConnectString property—even if you've changed one of the Command object properties, such as Current Catalog. However, if Microsoft Transaction Server pools the connection you create and close, other users will inherit the state maintained at the server (because the physical database connection is never closed).

This behavior could also occur on your ordinary client/server system because connection pooling is not restricted to Microsoft Transaction Server—it's implemented virtually *everywhere* unless you disable it. It's important that you realize the impact of changing state on the server in situations where it's possible that the connection could be reused by some pooling mechanism—even your own. The default database is not the only property that can wreak havoc with your system. Any time you use a SET statement in TSQL, the database state is changed. However ADO knows nothing about this change of state so it can't back out the change—even if it were designed to (it's not). For example, if you use SET NOCOUNT ON *outside of a stored procedure,* the change is persisted in the connection until it is closed. If you use a SET statement in a stored procedure, the state is reset when the stored procedure ends. When you create a temporary table or cursor, these are also maintained as part of the database state. Any application or component inheriting the connection gets all of these state changes, and it has no way of knowing what changes to the "virgin" state were made.

So, what happens when your development team starts tinkering with state? Well, this problem can be somewhat controlled because the connection won't be shared by other components or applications that don't share an identical connection string. However, if you plan to share connections across components (a desirable goal), you have to be far more careful. The symptom of corrupted state is components that work most of the time but fail at seemingly random times—perhaps after some other operation has just taken place—but not always. Ugly.

Using the Data View Window to Build Connections

The Data View window in the Visual Basic 6.0 IDE is designed to capture ADO provider connection strings and expose database schema to view and manipulate. Once you create a Data Link to one of the "enlightened" ADO providers, you'll see a list of tables (at least), and (perhaps) database diagrams, views, and stored procedures, as shown in Figure 4-6:

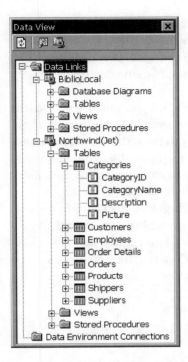

Figure 4-6: The Visual Basic 6.0 Data View window

Not all providers are smart enough to work with the Data View window—at least, not completely. If the provider is capable, you'll be able to use all of the Data View window features. Individual tables can be opened to examine and change data or schema—all using interactive graphical interfaces. When you make changes to the table, the Data View window submits the appropriate SQL query to the backend to make the changes. This means you can make changes to "live" databases, whether that makes sense or not. You'll also be given an option to simply save the SQL command script, which can then be submitted to your System Administrator (if you are still speaking, after having previously changed the database without her permission).

Want more information on the Data View window? My book *The Hitchhiker's Guide to Visual Basic and SQL Server* has a lengthy section on these tools.

IMHO   *Visual Basic tries to make getting at ADO data sources as easy as possible. Too bad the developers for this code didn't speak to each other any more than they did. As I see it, there are far too many "disconnects" between what was implemented and what could/should have been.*

Okay, now you have a data link set up. The next time you start Visual Basic 6.0, this data link will be exposed in the Data View window (shown in Figure 4-6) again for you to use. Did you expect the Microsoft Data Links to appear here? I did. They don't. The data links created here are persisted in the Registry—the Microsoft Data Links are not.

Using the data links to manage schema is cool, but you can also extract the Connection string from the data link to use in your own code. Unfortunately, it's not as easy as using the ADODC. You might try to go to the Properties page of a selected data link, but the dialog box there only *shows* the connection string; you can't copy it to the clipboard. I guess you could write out the salient parts in longhand, but that seems like a big oversight to me.

So how *do* you get at this pretested connect string? Well, you have to use the Data Environment Designer. The Data Links are not visible programmatically until you drag one of the elements (table, view, stored procedure, database diagram) to the Data Environment Designer's window. (Figure 4-7 shows a stored procedure dragged from the Data View Window.)

Figure 4-7: The Data Environment Designer exposing a stored procedure dragged from the Data View window.

Try this:

1. Start a new Visual Basic Datatemplate project. This adds the ADO 2.0 reference, a Data Environment Designer, and a Data Report Designer to your project. You can remove the Data Report Designer if you don't need it.

2. Establish a data link to your favorite data source (see Figure 4-8). In this case I'll connect to the Biblio test database on my local (MSDE)

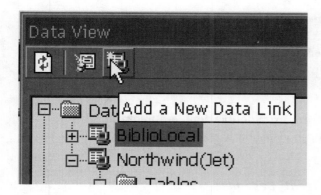

Figure 4-8: Using the Data View window to create a new Data Link

SQL Server. Simply click on Add a New Data Link and fill in the dialog boxes as we discussed when working with the ADC to create a ConnectionString. Yes, the Data View window uses the same OLE DB dialogs. (See Figure 4-8.)

3. When you are finished filling in the OLE DB provider properties, click OK and name your new data link. Use a name that reminds you of what it connects to; DataLink1 won't do.

4. Click the Tables icon under the new data link to expand the visible tables. If you can't see any tables, it could be that your provider is not smart enough to work with the Data View window, or that you don't have permission to view low-level tables. However, it's more likely that the tables will be visible despite the fact you don't have permission to access them. You won't find out about the permission violations until runtime. If you aren't the owner of the tables, you won't be able to change them using the Visual Database Tools.

5. Double-click the Data Environment Designer in the Project window to open a new Data Environment Designer window.

6. Select one of the tables and drag it to the Data Environment Designer window. At this point the Data Environment Designer and ADO construct a new Connection object (Connection2) based on your data link connection string and create an ADO Command object wrapped as a method of a DataEnvironment object.

7. To extract the data link connection string for Connection2, simply click the Connection2 icon in the Data Environment Designer window, press F4 to open the Visual Basic property page, and copy the ConnectionSource property to the clipboard—and into your application's code.

8. Remember to remove any extra double double-quote strings before trying to use the string in Visual Basic.

Using the Data Environment Designer

So, now that you have a Data Environment Designer set up in your Visual Basic project, how can you best use this in a Visual Basic program? Unfortunately there are a number of disconnects here that make it tough to use the Data Environment Designer efficiently. Sure, you can create applications using it, but I have had too many developers report mysterious problems and disappointed managers. Because of these poor reports, the Data Environment Designer no longer has a place of distinction on my "Best Practices" list. Don't get me wrong—there are some redeeming features of the Data Environment Designer, but there are also a number of issues that make it a challenge to use if you step over the yellow tape. See those ski-tips sticking out of the snow over there? That's Jim. He tried to use the Data Environment Designer on the other side of the DataEnvironment double-diamond area.

Understanding how the Data Environment Designer works can bring many of your expectations back to reality. First, remember that Data Environment Designer, like so many other tools, is simply a way of exposing ADO to the developer, but the Data Environment Designer does this by using another runtime engine. That is, a Visual Basic designer (unlike a Wizard) does not create any source code to tinker with. The DSR file contains binary instructions describing how the DataEnvironment runtime engine should construct the Connection, Command, and hierarchical Shape objects. This means that you won't be able to change the DataEnvironment object properties in code—at least not to any great extent. I've seen many people try to change the connection string or Command properties only to discover that their system is getting really confused.

Using Data Source Controls

Based on feedback I've received over the years, many developers migrate away from the use of Data Source controls, such as the ADO (ADODC), DAO (Data), and RDO (RDC) data controls. It's not that they don't have a place; it's just that when we start evolving our applications to handle more sophisticated situations, we find that these controls get in the way. Because the controls try to perform so many operations "for us" behind the scenes, we have too little control over what needs to be done. In the long run, we end up writing almost as much code anyway—and writing "around" the shortcomings and features of these "smart" controls.

Connection Query Execution Methods

Okay, now we're ready to try to run some queries against the Connection object. Nope, you don't need to construct a Command object, but if your query returns a rowset we'll have to build a Recordset—I discuss that in detail in the chapter "Working with Recordsets".

Suppose you opened the connection to run a query or run an action query. There are a few ways to do this after the connection is open.

- Use the Connection object's Execute method to execute a query string. This returns rows to a Recordset that you constructed ahead of time.

- Use the Connection object's Execute method to execute an action query that does not return rows.

- Execute a named ADO Command object against the Connection object. In this case, you pass in the Command arguments and a Recordset that was set up earlier.

- Execute any stored procedure by simply using it as a method of the Connection object. ADO accepts the stored procedure arguments as method arguments, accepting a named Recordset object as the last argument. (Cool!) We discuss the use (and implications) of this technique in the chapter "Working with Recordsets".

Because we haven't talked about the Command object yet, we'll postpone discussion of executing Command objects until we do, but let's take a look at the Connection object's ability to execute an SQL statement, run a maintenance query, or simply dump a table's rows back to a Recordset.

- The basic syntax for the Connection object's Execute method calls for:

- Command text—this argument can be a string containing an SQL statement, a table name, the name of a stored procedure, a URL, or text that makes sense to your data provider.

- Optionally, you can provide a Long variable to receive the number of rows affected by the query—assuming the provider sends back a result set.

- And optionally you can pass in a few parameters that help ADO decide how to execute the query. Basically, these describe the command text argument and tell ADO how to process the query. These are discussed in the Chapter 5.

For example, a typical Execute method invocation looks similar to this:

```
Set rs = cn.Execute("select City, State from publishers",,adCmdText)
```

And for "action" queries, it looks something like this:

```
cn.Execute"truncate table framis",, adExecuteNoRecords
```

Because ADO manufactures the Recordset object for you, it's always a read-only, forward-only, "cursorless" resultset.

> **TIP** *If you need a Recordset object with more functionality, create a Recordset object with the desired property settings and use the Recordset object's Open method to execute the query and return the desired cursor type. You can also use your own Recordset objects with the Command method. I discuss this in Chapter 5.*

Connection Pooling

ODBC implemented connection pooling quite some time ago, and OLE DB followed suit in the ADO 2.1 timeframe. This feature was developed to help increase throughput on Microsoft Transaction Server and IIS-managed servers. That is, instead of actually closing connections established by middle-tier components and Web pages, the connection pooling subsystem simply marks the connection as "reusable". If another application tries to open a connection with a connect string that matches an open connection (matches exactly—byte for byte), the connection handle is simply passed to the new "user". It seems that by default, connection pooling is enabled. If you don't want it, you can change the CPTimeout value in the Registry (HKEY_LOCAL_MACHINE\ Software\ODBC\ODBCINST.INI\SQL Server) to 0—or simply remove the entry.

By default, ADO uses OLE DB *session* pooling to maintain a pool of connections to the database. In some cases, you might want to use ODBC connection pooling instead of OLE DB session pooling.

To enable OLE DB session pooling in a desktop application, make sure that one reference to a connection object is retained at global scope in your Visual Basic application. In other words, Microsoft expects you to keep a connection open at all times for each application that wants a pool. Keeping a connection open maintains a reference to the IDataInitialize interface—the OLE DB Service Components where session pooling occurs. In MTS and ASP, however, you don't need to do this. These environments go hand-in-hand with ODBC Connection Pooling and OLE DB Session Pooling without making you jump through any hoops (at least most of the time). Microsoft recommends using session pooling unless there is some bug or other issue that prevents you from doing so. For more information on "free-session" pooling, consult the MSDN documentation and Web site—there are several articles on free-session pooling there.

Switching Connection Pooling in ODBC

To enable ODBC connection pooling from a Visual Basic/ADO application, Microsoft wants you to jump through a few hoops—with bricks tied to your ankles. There are two necessary steps:

I.   If you have ODBC Administrator 3.5 or later (and you should by now), open the ODBC Data Source Administrator from the control panel shown in Figure 4-9. Select the Connection Pooling tab. Find the driver that you are using in the list and double-click it. Check the option "Pool connections to this driver" and enter a timeout value in the dialog box.

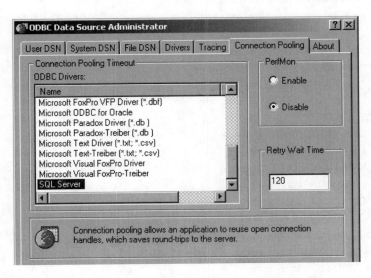

Figure 4-9: Using the ODBC Data Source Administrator to select connection pooling options.

2. Add an ODBC API function call to SQLSetEnvAttr in your application with the appropriate options to enable ODBC connection pooling for the process. Yes, I said an ODBC API function call. Sigh. This function should only be called once per process and must be called prior to executing any ADO code. If you aren't comfortable with the ODBC API, you can read all about them in the *Hitchhiker's Guide* and/or check out the following code example.

> **NOTE** *This code example was leveraged from a Microsoft Knowledge base article (Q237844). I dropped this into a class and put it out on the CD if you care to look there. Also note that this does not need to be called if you are opening your connections inside of MTS or ASP—they take care of this.*

This code creates the SQLSetEnvAttr value using the ODBC API. Good luck!

```
Dim rc As Integer
Const SQL_ATTR_CONNECTION_POOLING = 201
Const SQL_CP_ONE_PER_DRIVER = 1
Const SQL_IS_INTEGER = -6
Const SQL_CP_OFF = 0
Private Declare Function SQLSetEnvAttr Lib "odbc32.dll" ( _
                    ByVal EnvironmentHandle As Long, _
                    ByVal EnvAttribute As Long, _
                    ByVal ValuePtr As Long, _
                    ByVal StringLength As Long) As Integer
Public Function TurnOffPooling() As Integer
     TurnOffPooling = SQLSetEnvAttr(0&, _
             SQL_ATTR_CONNECTION_POOLING, _
             SQL_CP_OFF, _
             SQL_IS_INTEGER)
End Function
Public Function TurnOnPooling() As Integer
     TurnOnPooling = SQLSetEnvAttr(0&, _
             SQL_ATTR_CONNECTION_POOLING, _
             SQL_CP_ONE_PER_DRIVER, _
             SQL_IS_INTEGER)
     If rc <> 0 Then
         Debug.Print "SQLSetEnvAttr Error " & rc
     End If
End Function
```

If you're serious about using SQLSetEnvAttr, be sure to RTFM: page 943 of ODBC3.0 Programmer's Reference, Volume 2 (Microsoft Press) discusses the details of the API call and the ramifications of the call on your system and on everyone else's system. You've been officially warned.

Switching Connection Pooling Options in OLE DB

For OLE DB, you can "permanently" deactivate connection pooling—at least until some other program re-enables it. (I don't recommend dinking with the Registry because, like self-directed brain surgery in the mirror, it is fraught with danger. About the time you think you have it right, your daughter comes in and bumps your elbow while looking for her makeup.) However, in this case you have to locate the provider's GUID (search by name in the Registry). For example, the SQLOLEDB provider entry is located at: HKEY_LOCAL_MACHINE\Software\CLASSES\CLSID\{0C7FF16C-38E3-11d0-97AB-00C04FC2AD98}. Be sure to memorize this GUID—just so you can impress your geeky friends at the bar. After you find the GUID, you can (safely?) change its *OLEDB_SERVICES* key using the values in Table 4-4:

SERVICE	VALUE
All services (the default)	0xffffffff
All except Pooling and AutoEnlistment	0xfffffffc
All except Client Cursor	0xfffffffb
All except pooling, enlistment, and cursor	0xfffffff0
No services	0x00000000

Table 4-4: OLEDB_Services Options Registry Settings

I don't know how uncomfortable you are about changing the Registry, but I certainly don't like to. It not only affects your code, but everyone else's, too. That's why "best practices" dictate that you simply amend the connect string to set the "OLE DB Services" argument to one of the same options, as shown in Table 4-5:

SERVICE	VALUE
All services (the default)	"OLE DB Services = -1;"
All except Pooling and AutoEnlistment	"OLE DB Services = -4;"
All except Client Cursor	"OLE DB Services = -5;"
All except pooling, enlistment, and cursor	"OLE DB Services = -7;"
No services	"OLE DB Services = 0;"

Table 4-5: OLEDB_Services ConnectionString Arguments

For additional information on connection and session pooling, consult MSDN. The following Knowledge Base articles might also be of interest: Q189410, Q237844, and Q169470, and one of the best: Q176056 "INFO: ADO/ASP Scalability FAQ". See http://www.msdn.microsoft.com. No, not all of them are on the MSDN CD(s).

> **WARNING** *When ADO feels it's necessary, it might spawn a new Connection to carry out some request for you. When this happens, ADO creates a new transaction scope and database connection quietly behind the scenes and closes it when it's done.*

Tracing Orphaned Connections When Pooling Connections

There has been a lot of advice passed around about connection pooling and how to figure out whether the connections are being reused, abused, or unused and left to fend for themselves. I think this snippet pulled from my mail is probably one of the best lists so far:

1. Use the SQL Server 7.0 Profiler (shown in Figure 4-10) to determine if your connections are constantly getting created and never reused. You should be able to use the Connection ID and SPID columns to verify this:

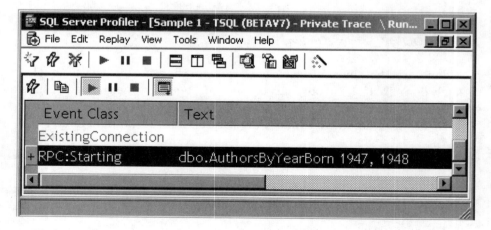

Figure 4-10: Using the SQL Server Profiler to trace TSQL queries

2. Check to see whether any of these connections time out after 60 seconds or whether they remain active but never appear to be reused. If connections are never reused and time out after 60 seconds, then session pooling is not correctly reusing connections.

3. Next, try to verify whether all connections are only used once, or whether only a few are left unused but they are accumulating. If some accumulate and never time-out, then an interface probably is not being released correctly, so the connections don't get put back in the pool.

4. If only a few are left unused but they are accumulating, see if they can be tied to any particular activity. Use "dbcc inputbuffer(spid)" in Query Analyzer to help see the last activity done on that particular connection.

5. Check whether any transactional work is being done. Try watching for some pages having an "@transaction=required" tag, while others do not.

6. Check whether the authentication of the ASP pages is Anonymous, Basic, or NTLM. Basic and NTLM can cause connections to be made on a per-user basis, thereby negating any benefit of session pooling. On a multiprocedure system, this can cause connections to accumulate very rapidly.

7. Add "Use Procedure for Prepare=0" to your connection strings and see if it helps. This prevents the provider from attempting to create temporary stored procedures in the process of executing the query.

8. And of course, there's always the last resort; try disabling session pooling.

Disabling session pooling can be accomplished in a number of ways. But this list of suggestions seems to make sense. Remember that with ADO 2.1, or later service packs of ADO 2.1, all ODBC drivers by default are enrolled in session pooling when using the OLE DB Provider for ODBC (MSDASQL). (Note that if you are using an ODBC driver from ADO you are using MSDASQL.) Within a user application, this means that if you have at least one connection open, subsequent connections opened are *automatically* pooled, even if the ODBC connection pooling for the driver is turned *off* in the ODBC Administrator. If connections are pooled, they remain open in the pool, even after you close them, for a hard-coded 60 seconds.

To attempt to disable pooling, here are a few things to try:

- Ensure that ODBC Connection pooling is turned off for the ODBC Driver. You can check this via the ODBC Administrator "Connection Pooling" tab (see Figure 4-10)—you should see <not pooled> next to the driver name. If not, double-click the appropriate driver (the one you're using) in the list box and turn it off.

- Add "OLE DB Services = -2;" to all connection strings to turn off session pooling for ADO. See "Pooling in the Microsoft Data Access Components" white paper in MSDN for more information on the OLE DB Services setting in ADO. A typical connection string would look something like this:

```
conn.open "DSN=MyDB2DataSource;UID=Me;PWD=My;OLE DB Services=-2;"
```

The rule requiring one persistent connection per set of unique user credentials applies *only* if your application is *not* running under either IIS (4.0) or MTS (2.0). IIS maintains the pool *as well* as MTS (at least until the connection times out or is no longer reused). That is, outside of these two environments, the (OLE DB Resource) pool goes away when the last connection in your application that has the unique set of user credentials used to create the pool is closed. MTS and IIS make the pool persistent.

Persistent connections can be a PIA—especially if you design your app not knowing that this is a requirement. However, remember that ODBC Connection Pooling jumbles connections together, regardless of authentication and underlying source driver/datastore. When your application requests a connection, it is blocked while this potentially huge pool of connection strings is searched for a match. In contrast, session pooling is optimized so that this doesn't happen. The only pool searched for an open connection is the pool (if it exists) that matches your user authentication. Session pooling has less locking contention on any given pool, which means that you should get your connection back much faster. OLE DB also manages "sets" of pools, depending on the number of processors in the computer, to further optimize finding a free connection as fast as possible.

Opening a Connection Asynchronously

In a traditional client/server application, I often (usually) open the Connection object asynchronously. Yes, this qualifies as another "best practice" because it makes better use of your user's time. In my applications, it gets the form painted faster, and no, I don't enable the controls on the form that require access to the connection to work—not until the connection is open.

The Visual Basic code for connecting asynchronously is simple—just add the adAsyncConnect option to the Open method:

```
cn.Open "dsn=localserver", "admin", "pw", adAsyncConnect
```

> **NOTE** *Not all of the providers support asynchronous operations, and there are no additional properties in the Connection object to inspect to determine whether you can connect or run queries asynchronously.*

Connecting asynchronously starts ADO working on the process of getting the connection established while my client thread finishes other work, such as completing Form_Load. While the connection operation is in progress, the Connection object's State property is set to adStateConnecting.

After ADO completes connecting, successfully or not, ADO fires the ConnectComplete event and turns off the adStateConnecting bit in the Connection object's State property. If the event handler returns an Error object set to nothing, the connection operation succeeded. If something went wrong, the Connection object's Errors collection has the details. Along with a pointer to the Error object, you get (at no extra charge) a Status object that also reports whether or not the operation worked. Checking Status for adStatusOK does the job.

So do you have to create an event handler to check whether the connection operation has completed? Nope, you can simply check the State property, waiting for the adStateOpen bit to turn on (and the adStateConnecting bit to turn off).

Testing for a Live Connection

Want to see if the connection is still open? Well, there aren't any properties on the Connection object that change when the connection is lost. And, you can't just check the State property, because ADO does not poll or check on its own. You might feel the need to poll yourself. Try sending a low-impact query, such as SELECT 1. This query takes about three packets and is fairly efficient. If it works, the connection is still open. Not that it'll be open when you need it, but it won't time out for another *n* seconds.

Managing Transactions

ADO can manage transactions for you—it does so at the Connection level, assuming that the data provider supports transactions. If your provider supports transactions, the Connection.Properties("Transaction DDL") is present. If the provider does not support transactions, you'll trip a trappable error if you try to reference this property. I guess that's a sure sign it's not supported.

So, let's assume your provider supports transactions. Now you can start a new transaction with the BeginTrans Connection object method, commit a transaction with CommitTrans, and roll back transactions with RollbackTrans. After you call the BeginTrans method, the provider will no longer instantaneously commit any changes you make until you call CommitTrans or RollbackTrans to end the transaction.

Just remember the scope of transactions. If you execute several queries on a Connection, all of the operations are under the same transaction umbrella. If you (or ADO) open an additional connection, its transaction scope is unaffected by other transactions on other connections.

For providers that support nested transactions, calling the BeginTrans method within an open transaction starts a new, nested transaction. The return value indicates the level of nesting: a return value of 1 indicates you have opened a top-level transaction (that is, the transaction is not nested within another transaction), 2 indicates that you have opened a second-level transaction (a transaction nested within a top-level transaction); and so forth. Calling CommitTrans or RollbackTrans affects only the most recently opened transaction; you must close or roll back the current transaction before you can resolve any higher-level transactions.

Depending on the Connection object's Attributes property, calling either the CommitTrans or RollbackTrans methods may automatically start a new transaction. If the Attributes property is set to *adXactCommitRetaining*, the provider automatically starts a new transaction after a CommitTrans call. If the Attributes property is set to *adXactAbortRetaining*, the provider automatically starts a new transaction after a RollbackTrans call.

Connection Object Events

ADO 2.0 implemented a comprehensive set of events. This moved ADO ahead in the race, when compared to RDO, which implemented the first (albeit limited) set of data access events. Unfortunately, these event handlers were redefined in ADO 2.1—that's the bad news if you were using the ADO 2.0 events. The good news is that they were not revised again in ADO 2.5. Basically, the new event handlers pass back an ADO 2.1 format Recordset (and the same format was used in ADO 2.5). This broke the event handlers in existing ADO 2.0 applications, which expected 2.0-format Recordsets. To deal with this problem, you have to recode your existing ADO 2.0 event handlers after having set your Project Reference to ADO 2.1 or 2.5. This should not involve more than a cut-and-paste operation.

> **TIP**   *When debugging event handlers, remember that Visual Basic has a tendency to "lose" events. That is, they might fire when your code is stopped at a breakpoint or dialog box (such as a MsgBox). However, if this happens, the events can be tossed. Bug? Bug.*

In some cases, however, just cutting and pasting the event handlers into the new prototype statements is not an option. Suppose your code uses the ADODC, the Data Form Wizard, or any of the Visual Database Tools, such as the Data Environment Designer, and you set your project reference to ADO 2.1 or 2.5. In this case, you have to take more drastic corrective action because all of these tools have been specifically written to support (just) ADO 2.0 Recordset objects. To fix this problem, edit your source code, and wherever your event handler (as generated by the Data Environment Designer, for example) plugs in its event handler prototype, modify the code to reference the ADO 2.0 Recordset—specifically. For example, notice how I replaced the ADODB.Recordset with ADODB.Recordset20 in the following event-handler prototype statement.

```
Private Sub Connection1_WillExecute(Source As String, _
    CursorType As ADODB.CursorTypeEnum, _
    LockType As ADODB.LockTypeEnum, Options As Long, _
    adStatus As ADODB.EventStatusEnum, _
    ByVal pCommand As ADODB.Command, ByVal pRecordset As ADODB.Recordset20, _
    ByVal pConnection As ADODB.Connection)
End Sub
```

The ADO 2.1 and 2.5 type libraries include definitions for both the older and newer Recordset objects. However, the newer Recordset 2.1 properties, methods, and options won't be available on the 2.0 version of the Recordset.

When you want to expose ADO object event handlers, you must declare the objects using the *WithEvents* operand. For example, the following code instructs Visual Basic to include any ADODB Connection events amongst the other objects and events in the code pane.

Let's walk through a code sample that illustrates the use of several of these events:

```
Option Explicit
Dim WithEvents cn As ADODB.Connection
Dim er As ADODB.Error
Dim strMsg As String
```

This first section sets up the cn (Connection) object using the WithEvents syntax to expose the event handlers.

```
Private Sub Form_Load()
    Set cn = New Connection
    cn.Open "dsn=localserver", "admin", "pw", adAsyncConnect
End Sub
```

The Form_Load event sets up the Connection object and tells ADO to begin opening it. We drop through to the end of the sub so that the initial form is painted. The Command button is still disabled. This means that if we don't enable it later, we won't be able to execute the query.

```
Private Sub cn_ConnectComplete(ByVal pError As ADODB.Error, _
    adStatus As ADODB.EventStatusEnum, ByVal pConnection As ADODB.Connection)
    If adStatus = adStatusOK Then
        cmdTestPrint.Enabled = True
        MsgBox strMsg, vbInformation, "Connect Complete"
    Else
        MsgBox "Could not connect." & pError.Description
    End If
    strMsg = ""
End Sub
```

The connection operation finishes and fires the ConnectComplete event. The code tests to determine whether the connection succeeded. If it did (adStatus = adStatusOK), the Command button control is enabled;. otherwise, a MsgBox dialog is displayed and nothing is done.

```
Private Sub cmdTestPrint_Click()
    cn.Execute "Execute TestPrint 'This is a test message'" , , adCmdText
End Sub
```

We're ready to test the stored procedure. In this case, it executes a couple of TSQL Print statements. These will end up in the Connection object's Errors collection. We could have executed this statement asynchronously, but there was no need to do so.

```
Private Sub cn_ExecuteComplete(ByVal RecordsAffected As Long, ByVal pError As
ADODB.Error, adStatus As ADODB.EventStatusEnum, ByVal pCommand As ADODB.Command,
ByVal pRecordset As ADODB.Recordset, ByVal pConnection As ADODB.Connection)
    DumpErrors
```

```
    MsgBox strMsg, vbInformation, "Execute Complete"
    strMsg = ""
End Sub
```

When the query finishes, the ExecuteComplete event fires, as it does for *all* operations on this Connection (pConnection). Note that a Command object is exposed here even though we didn't create one explicitly. There's a pointer to a Recordset here too, whose State property shows the query "adStateExecuting".

```
Private Sub cn_InfoMessage(ByVal pError As ADODB.Error, _
    adStatus As ADODB.EventStatusEnum, ByVal pConnection As ADODB.Connection)
    strMsg = "Info message: " & pError.Description
    DumpErrors
End Sub
```

During the course of opening the Connection object, the InfoMessage event fired to tell us that we switched the default database to "Biblio"—but it did so twice. Why? BHOM.[6] At that point it would/should not be opening another connection.

The following code simply dumps the errors collection into a single string we can use to debug the operation—not a string we can show users.

```
Sub DumpErrors()
    For Each er In cn.Errors
        strMsg = strMsg & "Errors:" & er.Description & vbCrLf
    Next er
End Sub
```

Do Events Make Much Sense in the Middle Tier?

Some developers have asked about the wisdom and practicality of implementing asynchronous operations in the middle tier. Sure, you can. The middle-tier component event handler can notify your application via DCOM if you have a mind to, but this approach implies maintaining state in the middle tier—something that's not a "best practice". So, you can do it, but try not to. It will make your application more complicated than it really needs to be, and it opens the door to random crashes.

---

6. BHOM: an old army term. "Beats the hell out of me" or "dunno."

The InfoMessage Event

Some providers, such as SQL Server, return "informational" messages when certain operations occur on the server. For example, when the current database changes, SQL Server reports back that this operation succeeded by sending the provider a message. The provider discards the message unless there is an InfoMessage event handler to deal with it. In most cases these messages are unimportant.

Error Handling

Trying to figure out what went wrong when opening a connection can be a challenge. Most of the errors seem to be grouped under three error numbers, with varying descriptions. Yes, that means that you'll have to parse the strings for the salient information and respond accordingly. Best practices dictates that you do not simply pass on these messages to end-users. They are the least likely people to be able to solve the problem.

- Error.Number –2147467259 (0x80004005) is fired for connection-related issues. This includes wrong protocol, missing (or misspelled) server, network permissions issues—basically anything that prevents ADO from creating a link to the remote server. The description often (but not always) has useful information for the developer about what went wrong.

- Error.Number –2147217843 (0x80040E4D) is fired for logon issues. However, you might have the "right" UserID but the wrong server and receive these errors if the server you specify is a working server.

- Error.Number –2147221020 (0x800401E4) is fired when the syntax of the ConnectionString is incorrect. This is fairly rare and should not occur after the application is debugged. If it occurs with a compiled application, it probably means that the DSN or UDL is contaminated.

> **TIP** *Don't make the user debug your program. Trap the errors and figure out what went wrong yourself.*

The Error.Description returned is prefixed with the source "stack" of the error. Apparently, each layer that handles the error adds an additional bracketed expression to the Description string, so that when you get your error message, it looks something like this:

```
[Microsoft][ODBC SQL Server Driver][SQL Server]Login failed for user 'Fred'.
```

TIP   *If you get ConnectionWrite(GetOverlappedResult) errors, switch to TCP/IP (away from named pipes).*

CHAPTER 5

ADO Command Strategies

WHEN WE GET TO CHAPTERS 6 and 7, which are all about Recordsets, you'll learn lots of different ways to execute queries—many of which don't require use of the Command object. The one important case where the Command object is required is when you have to capture parameters *returned* from stored procedures. ADO is very smart when it comes to handling stored procedures, so if you aren't returning OUTPUT parameters, and if you don't care about the stored procedure return status, you don't have to construct a Command object.

However, there are advantages to using Command objects. In this chapter, you'll learn that the Command object leverages new SQL Server and MDAC technology to execute all kinds of queries more efficiently. This means that when you execute rowset-returning or action queries, setting up the Command object can make the process of managing the query and its parameters far more sane. After a Command object is created, you no longer have to worry about putting single quotes around strings or figuring out how to deal with embedded apostrophes. This means you won't have to remove all of the Irish surnames from your database—such as O'Malley or O'Brien. This chapter also discusses how you can tell what your query is doing. We'll spend a significant amount of time pouring over SQL Profiler logs to see exactly what unnatural acts SQL Server is being asked to perform.

When it comes time to execute your SQL query, the best object to use is often the ADO Command. However, as you'll learn, it's not *always* the best choice. Fortunately, due to ADO's flexibility, there are other alternatives to draw on, as I discuss when we get to the Recordset object in Chapter 6. One thing you might not know—because it's underdocumented—is that all ADO Command objects appear as methods on their associated Connection objects. This innovative technique (well, it was stolen from RDO) enables you to code the Command by name, followed by its parameters, followed by the Recordset to contain the rowset. Cool. I discuss how to set this up later in this chapter.

Inner Workings of the Command Object

The Command object's biggest benefit is performance. Not only does it make your queries run efficiently, but it also makes *you* work more efficiently. That is, using the Command object can reduce the length of time it takes to code, debug, test, and deploy complex parameter-based queries—including queries executing stored procedures. For example, when accessing SQL Server 7.0, the ODBC and OLE DB providers have been tuned to access the new sp_executesql system stored procedure. There's quite a write-up on this in SQL Server Books Online,[1] and I have summarized it here.

Basically, the Command object is driven from the CommandType argument that instructs ADO how to transmit your query to the data provider. Suppose you have a parameter-based ad hoc query[2] that you wish to execute.

```
Select author, au_id, year_born from authors where year_born = ?
```

You placed a parameter marker (?) where you want ADO to insert the parameter, so you're ready to have ADO execute this query. For this query, ADO manufactures an SQL statement that looks like this:

```
sp_executesql N'Select author, au_id, year_born from authors where year_born =
@P1', N'@P1 int', 1947[3]
```

The sp_executesql system stored procedure was introduced in Microsoft SQL Server version 7.0. The MDAC developers want us to use it instead of the EXECUTE statement to execute a query string. The support for parameter substitution makes sp_executesql more versatile than EXECUTE; it also makes sp_executesql more efficient because it generates execution plans that are more likely to be reused by SQL Server.

ADO and the SQL Server data provider have also implemented another (proprietary) interface to handle server-side cursors. These are implemented as system-level sp_cursor stored procedures that open, fetch, close, and perform various other operations on your data. When using the default server-side CursorLocation setting, you'll find that many queries are executed using these stored procedures.

---

1. Books Online is the copious set of help topics and examples that ships with SQL Server in lieu of printed documentation. Most (if not all) of it is also available through MSDN via subscription or online.

2. An ad hoc query is simply a hard-coded SQL query or action. Using these queries is not a good idea for performance, maintainability and security reasons. If you can, use a stored procedure instead, but many developers depend on them, at least initially.

3. Note the "N" prefix on the generated code (N'Select au...). This uppercase N indicates that the following quoted string is in *Unicode* format. Unicode data is stored using 2 bytes per character, as opposed to 1 byte per character for character data. For more information, see "Constants" in Books Online.

> **TIP** *When working with SQL Server, it's essential that you turn on and leave on the Profiler (or SQL Server 6.5 Trace) while you are tuning your code. Leaving it on shows you exactly what's being sent to SQL Server in as much detail as you can handle (and sometimes more). Turn it off when you're happy with your code's performance.*

Substituting Parameter Values

The sp_executesql procedure and the sp_cursor stored procedures support the substitution of parameter values for any parameters specified in the Transact-SQL string—unlike the (obsolete) TSQL EXECUTE statement. Transact-SQL strings generated by sp_executesql are more similar to the original SQL query than those generated by the EXECUTE statement, which gives the SQL Server query optimizer a better chance to match the Transact-SQL statements from sp_executesql with execution plans from the previously executed statements. This dramatically reduces the need to compile a new execution plan with each execution of your parameter query. That's good.

With the TSQL EXECUTE statement, all parameter values must be converted to character or Unicode and made part of the Transact-SQL string, as shown in this code example:

```
DECLARE @IntVariable INT
DECLARE @SQLString NVARCHAR(500)
/* Build and execute a string with one parameter value. */
SET @IntVariable = 35
SET @SQLString = N'SELECT * FROM pubs.dbo.employee WHERE job_lvl = ' +
CAST(@IntVariable AS NVARCHAR(10))
EXEC(@SQLString)
/* Build and execute a string with a second parameter value. */
SET @IntVariable = 201
SET @SQLString = N'SELECT * FROM pubs.dbo.employee WHERE job_lvl = ' +
CAST(@IntVariable AS NVARCHAR(10))
EXEC(@SQLString)
```

If the statement is executed repeatedly, a completely new Transact-SQL string must be built for each execution, even when the only differences are in the values supplied for the parameters. This generates extra overhead in several ways:

- The ability of the SQL Server query optimizer to match the new Transact-SQL string with an existing execution plan is hampered by the constantly changing parameter values in the text of the string, especially in complex Transact-SQL statements.

- The entire string must be rebuilt for each execution.

- Parameter values (other than character or Unicode values) must be cast to a character or Unicode format for each execution.

In contrast, sp_executesql supports the setting of parameter values separately from the Transact-SQL string.

```
DECLARE @IntVariable INT
DECLARE @SQLString NVARCHAR(500)
DECLARE @ParmDefinition NVARCHAR(500)
/* Build the SQL string once. */
SET @SQLString =N'SELECT * FROM pubs.dbo.employee WHERE job_lvl = @level'
/* Specify the parameter format once. */
SET @ParmDefinition = N'@level tinyint'
/* Execute the string with the first parameter value. */
SET @IntVariable = 35
EXECUTE sp_executesql @SQLString, @ParmDefinition,@level = @IntVariable
/* Execute the same string with the second parameter value. */
SET @IntVariable = 32
EXECUTE sp_executesql @SQLString, @ParmDefinition,@level = @IntVariable
```

This sp_executesql example accomplishes the same task as the TSQL EXECUTE example shown earlier, but with these additional benefits:

- Because the actual text of the Transact-SQL statement does not change between executions, the query optimizer should match the Transact-SQL statement in the second execution with the execution plan generated for the first execution. Therefore, SQL Server does not have to compile the second statement.

- The Transact-SQL string is built only once.

- The integer parameter is specified in its native format. Conversion to Unicode is not required.

> **NOTE** *For SQL Server to reuse the execution plan, object names in the statement string must be fully qualified.*

Reusing Execution Plans

In earlier versions of SQL Server, the only way to reuse execution plans was to define the Transact-SQL statements as a stored procedure and have an application execute the stored procedure. The sp_executesql procedure can be used instead of stored procedures when executing a Transact-SQL statement a number of times—especially when the only variation is in the parameter values supplied to the Transact-SQL statement. Because the Transact-SQL statements themselves remain constant and only the parameter values change, the SQL Server query optimizer is likely to reuse the execution plan it generates for the first execution. Existing ODBC applications ported to SQL Server 7.0 automatically acquire the performance gains without having to be rewritten. For more information, see "Using Statement Parameters" in Books Online.

The Microsoft OLE DB Provider for SQL Server also uses sp_executesql to implement the direct execution of statements with bound parameters. Applications using OLE DB or ADO gain the advantages provided by sp_executesql without having to be rewritten.

The ADO Command object does not use sp_executesql to execute ad hoc queries that don't have parameters or that simply reference parameter-less stored procedures.

Building Command Objects

Building a Command object takes a little time—both CPU and development time. But consider the alternatives. In the olden days, setting up a query was a lot tougher than what ADO provides for us today. Okay, no "I used to code with keypunch machines with no ribbons…" stories here, but the code you write to create the Command object is a lot easier to create, understand, and support than the ODBC API or even Remote Data Objects ever hoped to be. There are even wizards that will do it for you, so how much easier can it get?[4]

---

4. I worked with the "Developer Days" people to tune up a wizard they handed out at the conference. It generates "correct" source code for building Command objects and the Properties collection without you lifting a finger—well, almost. It's on the CD.

> **TIP** *When you create a Command object, it should be created **once**. That is, create as many objects as necessary—don't create one and change its properties (other than its parameters) to suit the immediate requirement. At one time there was evidence that ADO was making many round trips to the server to "figure out" how to execute the query. My tests show that this no longer happens in ADO 2.5—at least not always. The entire setup phase seems to be done entirely on the client. But this is still overhead that you don't have to tolerate more than once.*

So, how do you build a Command object? It's easy:

1. Declare your Command objects in a scope where they can be seen by all of the routines that need to access them. This means when creating client/server applications, create your Command objects at the Module or Form level. However, if you must create a Command object in the middle-tier (Microsoft Transaction Server/COM+), do so in the method procedure. That's because Command objects can't be shared across apartments, and using global or class-scope variables in Microsoft Transaction Server simply does not work very well—to be kind.

2. Name your Command object so that it can be executed as a method on the Connection object. Although this is an optional step, it really helps later in the process. Be sure to use a string to name your Command object.

3. Set the CommandText property to the SQL statement in the query, or to the name of a stored procedure, table, or view. ADO is terrible at guessing what goes here.

4. Set the CommandType property to reflect the way you want the CommandText string to be treated. By default, ADO sets this to adCmdUnknown, so don't make ADO guess what's best to do.

5. Set the ActiveConnection property to point to the appropriate ADO Connection object. You can't execute the Parameters.Refresh method or run the query until you do. Once set, the named Command becomes a method on the Connection specified.

6. If the query expects one or more parameters, decide whether to use the Refresh method to get ADO to construct the Parameters collection for you, or build it yourself using the Parameters.Append or Command.CreateParameter technique.

Setting ADO Command Properties

Setting ADO properties is really a matter of knowing what ADO expects. If you're supposed to provide a number, make sure it's in the correct range. Avoid using literals—use the typelib-defined constants instead. It makes for code that is more readable and it's easier to maintain later. If you are setting a property from a TextBox or other control, be sure to reference the correct property explicitly. Don't depend on the default property to work—sometimes it does, more often it doesn't. For example, when setting a Command Parameter, use:

```
Cmd(eParm.NameWanted) = txtNameWanted.Text
```

This code depends on the definition of an Enum and a TextBox control. Leaving off the .Text property qualifier can have, well, unexpected consequences. Just don't tell me I didn't warn you. For example, in some cases, ADO (and COM) think you're trying to pass the TextBox *object* instead of its default Text property.

The Name Property

If you want to use the (cool) "Command as Connection method" technique to execute your Command object, you *must* name it. It's not a bad idea to do so in any case. If you're executing a stored procedure, the name *must* match the name of the stored procedure. Otherwise, you're free to name the command after jungle plants if you are so inclined. Just remember to set your name early—before you set the ActiveConnection property. And don't forget to use a String constant or variable to name your Command.

> **TIP** *If you pass in an unquoted value instead of a String constant or declared variable, Visual Basic assumes it's the name of a Variant variable that'll have some value later at runtime, unless you have Option Explicit turned on (which you should). In this case, you'll get a healthy Variable Not Defined warning at compile time.*

The CommandText Property

This property tells ADO and the data provider what to do. It's the question you want to ask, or it can simply be the name of a table, stored procedure, or even a URL, where the data should be found.

Usually the CommandText is a SQL statement, such as a SELECT statement, but it can also be any other type of command statement recognized by the provider, such as a stored procedure call. Remember to code the SQL in the SQL dialect understood by the data provider. So, if you're connecting to Oracle, you can (and should) use Oracle SQL extensions, just as you can use TSQL extensions when querying SQL Server.

Depending on the CommandType property setting, ADO may alter the CommandText property. You can read the CommandText property at any time to see the actual command text that ADO will use during execution.

You can also use the CommandText property to set or return a relative URL that specifies a resource, such as a file or directory. The resource is relative to a location specified explicitly by an absolute URL, or implicitly by an open Connection object.

CommandText and Scalability

But wait. Because a lot of the problems associated with scalability are caused by the CommandText property, it is a good idea to spend some additional time here. Remember that the query you specify in the CommandText property is simply a request for services from the data provider. It's the provider's responsibility to perform the physical input/output (I/O) operations to execute this request, no matter how wrong they might seem to a person.

Suppose you called down to the Pizza Hut in the university district in Walla Walla, Washington, and asked for a thousand meat-lover's and two veggie pizzas (you wanted to feed the Whitman Women's Soccer team and its supporters). The manager would probably call you back and check your credit rating, veracity, and sanity before starting to process the order. An ADO data provider doesn't call you back and say, "You're kidding, right?" when you ask for 1,000 or 10,000 or 10 million rows from a database. It just starts fetching the data and sending it back up the pipe to you. As it arrives, ADO dutifully starts caching this data into RAM and then spools to your hard disk until both are full to overflowing—on the floor behind the computer. No, ADO does not have a "bear with me, I'm kinda new at this" property—it assumes that you know what you're doing.

Intelligent Query Authoring or Authoring Intelligent Queries

After you are connected, it's time to submit your question to the database engine. That is, you need to submit a query—usually a SELECT statement to return rows, or an action query of some kind to change the data. Improperly designed queries have a greater impact on overall performance than does all other performance factors combined. In other words, if you ask the database engine to do something that takes 5, 50, or 50,000 seconds, no amount of brilliance on the client-side of the query can make the rows start appearing a second earlier. In addition, improperly designed concurrency constraints can indefinitely block your application from fetching even a single row.

There is a wealth of information available about writing efficient queries, and most of that advice boils down to these guidelines:

- Fetch *just* the *columns*[5] (fields) you need, and no more. Thus, never use SELECT * even when you want all of the (currently defined) columns. SELECT * might needlessly fetch columns that are expensive to fetch or irrelevant to the task at hand. In addition, SELECT * does *not* guarantee the order in which columns are returned. That is, if some ambitious systems administrator chooses to alphabetize the table's columns or to simply insert a new column in the table, SELECT * applications can croak (that's a technical term).

    One aspect of performance is *developer* performance. That is, how efficient are the coders working on the application, how many mistakes do they make, and how many times do they miscommunicate their intentions to other developers? SELECT * might seem to address this problem by telling the server to simply return all columns of a result set. However, if the application does not add the code to automatically morph to changes in the underlying schema, you aren't making developers more productive. Quite the contrary—you are adding work to those who have to figure out what's wrong when the schema changes.

- Fetch *just* the rows (records) you need and no more. Scalable applications fetch enough rows to solve the immediate requirement and no more. It's up to your design to determine what "immediate" means, because there is also a cost if you need to return to the server for more data. Your code needs to balance round-trips with the expense of returning rows that are not, or might never be, needed. Fetching too many rows also increases the amount of locking done by the database. This may hurt the scalability of your application, and it increases the chances for deadlocks. Don't confuse interactive human-based applications with reporting applications that often have to work with far more rows.

- Incorporate cursors in your application only when absolutely necessary. As you build scalable applications using increasingly complex queries and stored procedures, you'll discover that ADO can't build sophisticated cursors against the generated rowsets. We have found that *cursorless* result sets (ADO's default behavior) are faster to create and retrieve anyway.

---

5. Okay, I was raised to use the terms *rows* and *columns* for relational databases. The ISAM world uses *records* and *fields*. The Microsoft people who wrote ADO apparently like the ISAM terms, so here we are with records and fields. Sigh.

Consider that when working with sophisticated table relationships, it is rarely sufficient to simply add a row to a base table. In many cases, you first have to successfully add rows to foreign-key tables. This implies that simple cursor updates just won't work and you'll have to rely on stored procedures or more client-intensive transaction-governed operations.

- Consider using Return Status, OUTPUT, or INPUT-OUTPUT parameters instead of Recordsets (cursors) to retrieve data values. These are considerably (dramatically) faster than having ADO construct a Recordset to return your single row of data.

- If you simply *must* create a cursor, build a scrollable cursor *only* when absolutely necessary. Scrollability dramatically impacts performance, as ADO has to run additional code to construct cursor keysets or static rowsets in memory. While this overhead forces your application to incur a considerable one-time expense on Recordset creation, using Dynamic cursors exacerbates the situation by forcing ADO to requery the database repeatedly as you scroll from page to page.

- If you choose pessimistic locking, be careful about the size of the fetched rowset, as all rows in that rowset (and perhaps the pages where they reside) will remain locked as long as the cursor is open—not just when you are editing a row. Don't use pessimistic locking until you have thoroughly investigated the locking side effects—and have a note from your high-school principal.

- When you initially fetch rows from the server, don't let the *user* govern when (or if) the rowset is completely fetched. That is, avoid the practice of fetching and displaying the first row and permitting the user to push a button to fetch the next set of rows. Consider strategies that fetch all of the rows at once. For example, consider disconnecting the Recordset or using the GetRows or GetString methods. However, GetRows might not be such a good idea after all. It seems that it generates quite a bit of overhead as it constructs the Variant array output structure. There are cases where transforming the Recordset to a Variant array makes sense—just don't send the arrays from tier to tier. Delaying population delays release of share locks on the rows fetched. While this won't affect *your* application's performance, you will be holding back other applications competing for the same data pages. As a general rule, to achieve higher scalability, avoid holding locks on data that will be displayed to the user.

- Don't run a hard-coded query when you can run a stored procedure. By precompiling your query code into a stored procedure, you can eliminate the need to wait while the server validates, compiles, and builds a query plan before executing your query.

- When running ad-hoc queries (which you do any time you set the Command object's CommandText property to a string that does not contain the name of a stored procedure), don't set the Prepared property to True. That's because, as far as I'm concerned, it's broken.

- Consider what your application does to the server and other users—not just what your query does to make *your* client application or component faster. Sometimes you can perform operations from your client that can make the local application run very quickly, while at the same time locking out other users or otherwise making scalability impossible. Scalability and performance don't always go hand in hand, especially when you have a handful of users.

- Be sure to monitor the impact your application has on the server. Use the SQL Profiler to view the low-level operations your code asks the server to perform—remember our discussions in Chapter 4 (see Figure 4.11). Try to balance round-trips with the volume of useful data being returned. The Profiler and the other diagnostic tools we discuss later can clearly show what impact your programs are having on the system and each other—if you learn how to interpret the dumps.

Some of these strategies have to do with making your client respond faster, and others make your overall system faster. That is, some suggestions help create applications that use system resources more efficiently—resources that all clients contend for. This makes all of your applications run faster, be more responsive, and be less likely to lock up while waiting for resources.

Performance: Opening Command Objects

As I said earlier, if the query is to be executed more than once, it saves execution and coding time if you build a Command object to manage the query—especially if the query requires parameters. However, in the middle tier and on Web pages, it's not unusual to execute singleton queries and exit—thus, negating the need to create Command objects for better performance. As a matter of fact, you might see a performance advantage if you *don't* create the Command object in code—especially if you are coding in Visual Basic Script on ASPs where each line of Visual Basic is interpreted. If you're executing against SQL Server, queries that can reuse a previously cached query plan are not recompiled.

Then, again, consider the way Command objects help you manage parameters. Sometimes it's necessary to capture return status or OUTPUT parameters and you don't really have any other choice. And because most queries are parameter driven, using Command objects to simply manage the parameters can also reduce the total number of lines of executed Visual Basic code.

CommandType Property

If you don't tell ADO *how* to interpret and process your command, its own logic takes over and it makes an educated guess as to how to proceed. It's better (far better) to set the CommandType property to give ADO a suggestion as to how the query should be interpreted. This saves (considerable) internal processing time. Another boost in processing performance can be achieved by using the *adExecuteNoRecords* option with adCmdText or adCmdStoredProc. This tells ADO that the query won't be sending back a rowset, so don't bother constructing a cursor.

The documentation says that if the CommandType property value equals adCmdUnknown (the default value), you may experience diminished performance because ADO must make calls to the provider to determine whether the CommandText property is an SQL statement, a stored procedure, or a table name. The SQL Profiler did not show any evidence of these DDL requests, but some providers might require them. If the CommandType property does not match the type of command in the CommandText property, an error occurs when you call the Execute method. Table 5-1 lists the valid CommandType property settings.

COMMANDTYPE	DESCRIPTION
adCmdUnspecified	Command does not specify the type of query.
adCmdText	Evaluates the CommandText as a SQL command or an SQL "call" statement.[6]
adCmdTable	Evaluates CommandText as a table name. ADO simply executes "SELECT * FROM <table>" when you use this option. You had better know what you're doing to scalability when you do this.
adCmdStoredProc	Evaluates CommandText as a stored procedure name.
adCmdUnknown	Default. Indicates that the type of command in the CommandText property is not known, which makes ADO guess, or after it guessed, it still didn't know.
adCmdFile	Evaluates CommandText as the file name of a file-based Recordset.
adCmdTableDirect	Evaluates CommandText as a table name whose columns are all returned. This is only available when working with Jet 4.0 databases and providers.

Table 5-1: Valid CommandType property settings

---

6. It's no longer necessary to call stored procedures using the Call syntax that we used in RDO.

Trying to Preset Execution Options

When you construct your Command object, it might make sense to preset one or more of the options that affect how ADO executes the query. For example, you might want to request asynchronous execution by using adAsyncExecute, or an option indicating that the Command does not return rows such as adExecuteNoRecords. Unfortunately, ADO does not let you set these options when you set the CommandType. The documentation says you can, but if you try, you'll get a 3001 runtime error. You have to pass these options to the Execute method until this is fixed.

The `ActiveConnection` Property

If you expect to execute your Command object against a specific data provider (and most of you do), you have to set the ActiveConnection property to a Connection object pointing at that data source. Attempting to execute a Command or even use the Parameters.Refresh method without a valid ActiveConnection property setting results in—you guessed it—a trappable error.

> **TIP** *Once you set the ActiveConnection property, the Command object's Name property is frozen. If you want to reference the Command by name, set the Name before setting the ActiveConnection.*

Before the Connection is opened, the ActiveConnection property contains a "definition" of the connection, and this definition is simply a connect string. This means that you can set the ActiveConnection property using the same string that you use for the Connection object's ConnectionString property. After the Connection is open, ActiveConnection contains a live Connection object reference. If you wish to execute a Command on a series of Connections, set the ActiveConnection property to Nothing followed by setting it to alternative Connection objects.

You need to set the ActiveConnection property before you try to use the Parameters.Refresh method. If you do use the Parameters.Refresh method to construct the Parameters collection, and you set the ActiveConnection property to Nothing, ADO clears the Parameters collection (for some reason). However, changing the ActiveConnection property has no effect on the Parameters collection if you construct in code. Closing the Connection object sets the ActiveConnection property to Nothing for each Command object associated with the Connection (how rude). Setting the ActiveConnection property to a closed Connection object generates an error (duhh).

The (So-called) Prepared Property

In *theory*, the Prepared property was designed to reduce work on the server by precompiling ad hoc queries so that subsequent executions would use a temporary stored procedure instead of repeating the compile phase each time the query is executed. However, this is *not* the case with ADO's implementation—keep reading.

Since ODBC was invented some years ago, SQL Server has gotten a lot smarter—it now knows how to leverage existing (in cache) compiled query plans. That is, once you execute a query from ADO (or by any means), SQL Server constructs a query plan, saves it in the procedure cache, and executes it. When the query is done, SQL Server marks the query plan as "discardable" but leaves it in memory as long as it can. When another identical (or close-enough) query comes in, which is very likely in systems running multiple clients, SQL Server simply reuses the cached plan. This saves a significant amount of time and greatly improves scalability. It makes SQL Server actually *faster* as more users are added—assuming they are doing about the same things with the same set of queries.

ADO and its ODBC and OLE DB data providers know about this strategy, and in most cases they leverage it by executing sp_executesql, which takes advantage of this feature. However, doing so puts the Prepared property in a quandary. It insists on creating temporary stored procedures, but the data providers insist on using sp_executesql. The result? Chaos. I describe what happens a little later in the chapter in my discussion of executing Command objects.

My recommendation for the Prepared property is this: forget it—at least for SQL Server. For other providers, set up a trace that shows exactly what's going on—what the server is being asked to do.

The CommandTimeout Property

The CommandTimeout property indicates how long to wait (in seconds) while executing a command before terminating the attempt and generating an error. Remember that CommandTimeout starts when the database server has accepted the command and ends when the database server returns the first record. If the server or network is busy (or not answering at all), this setting won't help you regain control.

It's important to set this value based on reality. That is, if, based on repeated full-load testing, you know that the query takes a long time to run, then set the CommandTimeout accordingly—and add a fudge factor. Remember that the server or network can delay things as load changes or when the database has to allocate more disk space or other resources. The default of 30 seconds might not be enough. However, don't be tempted to set this to 0, which disables the timeout. You don't want your application to freeze, waiting for a query that'll never end.

Twice this week I've helped users with timeout errors. Both discovered that increasing the timeout did not solve their problem. Timeouts are caused by the inability of the data provider to complete the requested operation in the specified number of seconds. While the causes that prevent completion are numerous, one of the most common is locking. That is, when one application is holding a lock on a page, row, or table, other applications (or even different parts of the same application) are unable to access that data. Any attempt to access the data has to wait until the locks are released. In a well-tuned system, this usually takes a couple of seconds or so. If the offending application does not release the locks (perhaps it's waiting for other locks to be freed) the other applications attempting to access the data are blocked indefinitely. Before looking far and wide seeking out the guilty party, I think you'll find that all too often your own application is holding the lock. For example, if you open an updatable Recordset and try to update the database using an UPDATE action query, you'll discover exactly what I'm talking about.

In RDO (and in the ODBC API), there was an option that was lost on conversion to ADO—retry on timeout. That is, if you wanted to keep waiting after a Command timeout, you could simply pass a flag back to the event handler and keep waiting. This is not implemented in ADO. Why? BHOM (another "technical" term I learned in the Army that means "beats the hell out of me").

NOTE *ADO timeout settings are independent of network timeout. Because the low-level network driver makes a synchronous network API call, and because this call does not return until the network timeout expires, the ADO timeout code is blocked.*

Handling Parameter-based Queries

Most queries that you execute require one or more parameters to govern the rowset created. These parameters are usually applied to the WHERE clause of a query, but they can be used in a variety of other ways. When you construct any parameter-based query, you have to describe the query parameters one way or another and supply the runtime values, but you don't *have* to use the Command object—not unless you expect to have to deal with a stored procedure return status or with output parameters. You can use other techniques to pass input parameters, and I discuss these other techniques next. Basically, there are several approaches that you can take when constructing parameter queries:

- Construct a Command object in code, which exposes an empty ADO Parameters collection. This approach can generate the Parameters collection using the Refresh method or by constructing the Parameters one-by-one.

- Construct an SQL statement that includes the parameters in the query string. This approach can construct a sp_executesql query instead of having ADO construct one for you.

- The Visual Database Tools, including the Data Environment Designer, can also construct parameter-based SQL statements and expose these as Data Environment Designer-based Command objects. These are discussed more completely in the *Hitchhiker's Guide to Visual Basic and SQL Server*. In this book, I stay focused on ADO coding.

- Use the Visual Basic Addin supplied with this book[7] that generates the code to construct Command objects.

How ADO Command Objects Manage Your Parameters

When you use the ADO Parameters collection to manage your parameters, it's ADO's responsibility to get these parameters crammed into the query in the right places and in the right format. ADO is also responsible for dealing with "framing" quotes. That is, if the parameter has embedded single-quotes to delineate strings (most do), ADO will automatically double these up (replacing a single quote with two single quotes). This way your query won't die the first time you work with an Irish surname, such as O'Malley or O'Brien.

When working with Command objects, it's your responsibility to describe the parameters correctly, unless you use the Refresh method. This means constructing the Parameters collection one parameter at a time, in the order the data provider expects them. No, ADO and its data providers do not support "named" parameters (not until version 2.6), so until then, you *have* to specify them in the right order. Knowing how to describe the Parameter datatype, size, precision, scale, and shoe size is your responsibility. If you get it wrong, you'll get an error. If you get them out of order, who knows what will happen....

---

7. This Visual Basic Addin is also provided to MSDN subscribers—or should be by the time this book is available.

There are a number of techniques that that will make your parameter-based queries more efficient and easier to construct. One of these is the Visual Basic AddIn supplied on the CD that constructs the Visual Basic code required to open a connection, build the Command object, construct the Parameters collection and execute Eventually, all of your production applications will evolve to depend on parameter queries to both improve performance (both system and developer performance) and to simplify the development of component-based designs.

> **TIP** *No, you don't necessarily need to construct a Command object to execute a parameter-based query. However, if you don't take advantage of sp_executesql where it makes sense, I suspect your query performance might be disappointing.*

Constructing the Parameters Collection

The ADO Command object's Parameters collection manages all flavors of parameters: gazintas (input), gazouta (output), and gazinta-gazouta (input-output–bidirectional) parameters. Remember that input parameters can be applied to ad hoc queries as well as to stored procedures. The trick is learning how and when to construct the Command object's Parameters collection in code. As I said before, there are two approaches:

- Use the Command.Parameters.Refresh method to get ADO and the associated provider to construct the Parameters collection for you based on the CommandText you provide.

- Construct the Command.Parameters collection yourself—parameter-by-parameter—based on your understanding of how the parameters are defined.

Each technique has its advantages and disadvantages in terms of developer and application performance.

IMHO (another technical term that means "in my humble opinion"), neither technique should be used from the middle tier if you can help it. Why? Well, consider that the time taken to execute the extra code to build the Command object and the appropriate Parameter objects (one at a time) is wasted. It has to be re-executed each time the ASP is referenced or the MTS component is executed. Yes, the Command objects make the process far simpler to code. If you are looking for a simple solution with somewhat limited scalability, then keep reading.

Using the Refresh Method

The Command.Parameters.Refresh method technique seems to do all of the work for you—it constructs the Command object's Parameters collection for you in a single line of code. That's good and bad. It's good in the sense that you don't have to worry about how ADO creates the Parameter objects (for the most part, that is—it usually gets them right). It's bad in that ADO and the provider take a round-trip to the server to figure out how to do so, which can be costly (as we have already discussed). However, because this can be a one-time performance hit early in the life of the application, it might not make that much difference.

Remember to set the ActiveConnection property *before* attempting to use the Refresh method—ADO needs a valid connection to hit the database to generate the parameters.

> **TIP** *Actually, you don't even have to use the Refresh method if you don't want to, and using it might even cause ADO to execute **an extra** round-trip. When you try to read a property of an uninitialized Command.Parameters collection for the first time, ADO constructs the Parameters collection for you—just as if you had executed the Refresh method.*

After executing the Parameters.Refresh method, you still might need to revisit some of the Parameter objects. For example, if your stored procedure expects OUTPUT parameters, the providers have a tendency to tell ADO to set the Parameter.Direction property to adParamInputOutput instead of adParamOutput. This is not disastrous, because you can simply provide empty, null, or default values when calling the stored procedure.

An advantage (sort of) to the Parameters.Refresh method technique is that if someone changes the number, position, or datatype of the parameters, your application can automatically morph to the new parameter requirements. Of course, if these changes are significant, your code might very easily pass in wrong values to these parameters. Your code references Parameter objects by position—*not* by name. Suppose the datatype of parameter four changes from SmallInteger to Integer—no big deal. But if it changes from VarChar to VarBinary…that's another matter.

Constructing the Parameters Collection in Code

The second technique also has its good and bad points. Constructing the Parameters collection in code assumes that you understand how ADO and the called procedure expect the Parameter objects to be created. This also assumes you understand ADO well enough to know how to code the Parameter objects yourself *and* that the definitions for the parameters are *not* subject to change.

Just choosing the right datatype for each object can be tricky—and there is often more to constructing Parameter objects that makes the task even more complex. That's why I often defer to the Data Environment Designer or the Parameters.Refresh method to do this for me. Although the Data Environment Designer makes the same mistakes that ADO makes when building parameter collections, using it can save quite a bit of guessing on my part. To leverage the prefabricated Parameters collection, I use the Data Environment Designer to construct a DataEnvironment object and copy out the generated settings for each Parameter property into my code—especially the individual parameter object data types.

The Other Side of the Refresh Method Story

Let's see what ADO does when you use the Refresh method—especially in conjunction with the so-called Prepared property. There are a couple of important points not covered in the documentation. For example, in the following code, I used the Refresh method to build the Parameters collection.

```
With cmd
    .Name = "GetTitles"
    .Prepared = False
    .CommandType = adCmdText
    .ActiveConnection = cn
    .CommandText = "Select title from titles " _
        & "where title like ? " _
        & "and year_published between ? and ?"
    .Parameters.Refresh        ' let ADO create the Parameters collection
```

According to the SQL Server 7.0 Profiler, when the Refresh method executes, the provider (SQL Server in this case) is asked to execute these two queries (two round-trips):

```
SET FMTONLY ON select  title, year_published, year_published from  titles SET
FMTONLY OFF
declare @P1 int
set @P1=NULL
sp_prepare @P1 output, N'@P1 varchar(255),@P2 smallint,@P3 smallint', N'Select
title from titles where title like @P1 and year_published between @P2 and @P3', 1
select @P1
```

However, when the application executes:

```
cmd(eParms.TitleWanted) = "Hitch%"
cmd(eParms.YearHigh) = 1950
cmd(eParms.YearLow) = 1999
Set rs = New Recordset
rs.Open cmd
```

The profiler tells us that the SQL Server data provider destroys (sp_unprepare) the temporary stored procedure (1). ADO and the SQL Server provider then proceed to use sp_executesql to run the query:

```
sp_unprepare
sp_executesql N'Select title from titles where title like @P1 and year_published
between @P2 and @P3', N'@P1 varchar(255),@P2 smallint,@P3 smallint', 'Hitch%',
1999, 1950
```

Each subsequent execution of the Command object, regardless of syntax, simply generates a call to sp_executesql with the new parameters.

```
sp_executesql N'Select title from titles where title like @P1 and year_published
between @P2 and @P3', N'@P1 varchar(255),@P2 smallint,@P3 smallint', 'Any%', 1999,
1950
```

Okay, that's not so terrible (only one unnecessary tear down and reconstruction), but what if we change Prepare to True? In this case, ADO and the SQL Server data provider seem to get confused. Just as before (when Prepare was left as False), the DDL queries are used to construct (sp_prepare) the temporary stored procedure when you use the Refresh method. Nothing has really changed. However, if you use the Command as Connection method technique, ADO uses the existing temporary stored procedure, but *each subsequent* execution tears down the temporary stored procedure and reconstructs it.

Constructing the Parameter Collection in Code

But what happens if you construct the parameters yourself—in code—instead of using the Refresh method? Well, if you set Prepared=True, then ADO follows about the same path as before, but instead of creating the temporary stored procedure with sp_prepare when the Refresh method is executed, it's now executed when the Command is executed for the first time, as expected. And ADO also reuses this temporary stored procedure until you use the Command as Connection method technique, when it reverts back to its old bad habits.

However, if you construct the Parameter collection in code and *don't* set the Prepared property to True (it defaults to False), ADO knows just what to do—it simply constructs sp_executesql statements to run your query. That much it knows how to do. No extra round-trips to set up the temporary stored procedures just to tear them down again. It just runs the queries.

```
sp_executesql N'Select title from titles where title like @P1 and year_published
between @P2 and @P3', N'@P1 varchar(20),@P2 int,@P3 int', 'Hitch%', 1999, 1950
sp_executesql N'Select title from titles where title like @P1 and year_published
between @P2 and @P3', N'@P1 varchar(20),@P2 int,@P3 int', 'Any%', 1999, 1950
sp_executesql N'Select title from titles where title like @P1 and year_published
between @P2 and @P3', N'@P1 varchar(20),@P2 int,@P3 int', 'Hitch%', 1940, 1999
```

The SQL Server team knows about this Prepared property bug, and while SQL Server 7.0 SP2 has not (so far) completely addressed this problem, it has gone a long way toward doing so. After SP2 is applied, this aberrant behavior is only triggered when you use the Command as Connection method technique. While I like the simplicity and flexibility of this technique, I use it cautiously until this bug is fully resolved.

This silliness prevents the use of the Refresh method as a best practice, especially when coupled with the Prepared property setting of True. If you build your Parameters collection in code, ADO does not make these mistakes.

So, in summary, how can you prevent these problems—at least until Microsoft fixes the bug?

- Don't set the Prepared property to True. It only makes matters worse.

- Construct the Parameters collection for ad hoc queries in code.

- Don't use the Refresh method for adCmdtext commands. Without it, ADO uses the sp_execute strategy for your queries. Because SQL Server seems to be optimized for the sp_execute strategy, this should help, not hurt, performance.

- Be careful if you use the Command as Connection method.

- Keep an eye on the Profiler to see whether your queries are generating extra sp_unprepare and sp_prepare operations.

- Consider using the stored procedure as Connection method technique discussed in the Recordset chapter or other strategies that don't use the Command object at all.

The Parameter.Direction Property

The Parameter object's Direction property tells ADO how and when to expect data for this parameter. The default is adParamInput, but as shown in Figure 5-1, there are several intuitive alternatives:

- **adParamReturnValue**: If declared, the return value parameter is the first in the Parameters collection. It's used to receive the stored procedure's return status integer.

- **adParamInput** (the default): The parameter is passed to the query at runtime.

- **adParamInputOutput**: The parameter is passed to the query at runtime, and the same parameter is used to receive a value from the stored procedure.

- **adParamOutput**: The parameter is used to receive a value from the stored procedure.

- **adParamUnknown**: If ADO cannot figure out how to deal with a parameter (or you can't), it gets set to this "unknown" value.

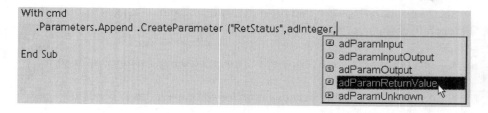

Figure 5-1: Direction property enumerated constants

The first Parameter object in the Parameters collection is special. It can hold either the return status from a stored procedure or the first parameter. Only the first Parameter object in the Properties collection can be set to adParamReturnValue. This position is reserved for stored procedures that return an integer status value (yes, it's always an integer). If you are executing an ordinary parameter query, not a stored procedure, you can define the first argument as adParamInput. For stored procedures, you can ignore the return status by setting the first (ordinal 0) Parameter object's Direction property to any other direction enumeration constant.

> **WARNING** *The Visual Basic Locals Window enumerates the Parameters collection using one-based referencing. That is, cmd.Parameters(0) is listed as Parameters(1). Swell.*

The Parameter.Type Property

When working in the Visual Basic integrated design environment (VB IDE), the statement completion feature can prompt you with a list of valid datatypes. The trick is to choose the right datatype. For instance, the other trainers, support staff, and I get quite a few questions on the Parameter object's Type property, which describes its datatype. Figure 5-2 shows how the VB IDE tries to prompt you, but there are many data types to choose from. By far the easiest way to determine the correct datatype to use is to ask ADO—at least initially. That is, use the Refresh method to populate the Parameters collection and examine the Type property settings for each parameter. While you're at it, also check the Size, Precision, and NumericScale property settings. Actually, there's an even easier way and it does not require any code. Use the Data View window to call up a table that has a field whose datatype you want ADO to access. Right-click the field in question, and the correct ADO-enumerated datatype constant will appear like magic.

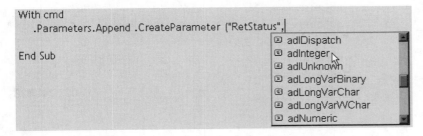

Figure 5-2: The VB IDE prompting with a list of ADO datatypes

Table 5-2 lists all of the SQL Server datatypes and some to watch out for. Checkout the datetime datatype—yep, you have to pass it as adDBTimeStamp.[8] The code for generating this table is on the CD, so you can run it against your own data provider.

SQL SERVER DATATYPE	ADO PARAMETER TYPE PROPERTY	PRECISION	SIZE
(RETURN_VALUE)	adInteger	10	0
Varchar	adVarChar		(You decide)
Char	adVarChar		(You decide)
Int	adInteger	10	0
Smallint	adSmallInt	5	0
Tinyint	adUnsignedTinyInt	3	0
Datetime	adDBTimeStamp		0
Smalldatetime	adDBTimeStamp		0
Bit	adBoolean		0
Text	adVarChar		2,147,483,647
Image	adVarBinary		2,147,483,647
Binary	adVarBinary		1
Varbinary	adVarBinary		1
Decimal	adNumeric	18	0
Smallmoney	adCurrency	10	0
Money	adCurrency	19	0
Numeric	adNumeric	18	0
Real	adSingle	7	0
Float	adDouble	15	0
Nchar	adVarWChar		1
Ntext	adVarWChar		1,073,741,823
Nvarchar	adVarWChar		1

Table 5-2: SQL Server data type and the correct ADO-enumerated datatype constants

The Parameter.Size Property

Use the Size property to determine the maximum size for values written to or read from the Value property of a Parameter object. If the size of the parameter exceeds this upper limit, you'll trip a trappable error.

---

8. The reason (rationale) for the use of the TimeStamp datatype instead of something more reasonable (adDateTime, or some such) is so thin it's not worth mentioning.

Yes, some datatypes don't require that you set the Size property. You *do* have to set it for Char and VarChar fields—where the size can vary. ADO and the data provider returned the default size properties shown in Table 5-2 (except for the Char and VarChar). Note that the (maximum) size for the NText (Unicode Text) is half the size of its equivalent ANSI Text datatype.

The Parameter.Precision and Parameter.NumericScale Properties

The Precision and NumericScale properties are used to describe numbers that have decimal points or varying degrees of accuracy. For numbers capable of storing a fractional value, use the NumericScale property to determine how many digits to the right of the decimal point are used to represent values. The Precision property is used to determine the maximum number of digits to be stored for any number—integer or floating point. These properties have to be set in code because they aren't supported by the CreateParameter method.

Constructing Parameter Objects with CreateParameter

You can create individual Parameter objects and add them to the Parameters collection using the Append method.

```
Dim Pr as Parameter
Set Pr = New Parameter
With Pr
    .Name = "P1"
    .Type = adVarChar
    .Direction = adParmInput
    .Size = 30
    .Value = "Fred graduates in 2000"
End With
Cmd.Append Pr
```

If you charge by the line, this is the best approach—but it's a lot easier to do all of this with a single line of code.

```
.Parameters.Append .CreateParameter("P1", adVarChar, adParamInput, 30, _
    "Fred graduates in 2000")
```

The CreateParameter method constructs the entire Parameter object in a single step. It does *not* include the NumericScale or Precision properties, but it does include the other essential properties—including Value. Because this method reminds you of all of the essential properties, prompting you for each one as you type in the Visual Basic IDE, its use qualifies as a best practice.

Rolling Your Own Parameter Queries

No, you don't have to use the Parameters collection to execute a parameter query, or queries without parameters for that matter. For instance, you can construct a query in a string and pass it to the Source property of a Recordset or the CommandText property of a Command object. You can also execute any stored procedure as a method of the Connection object. The stored procedure parameters are simply passed as method arguments.[9] If the query has parameters, you can concatenate parameters into the WHERE clause. If the stored procedure returns a Recordset, you pass that as the last argument, as shown below:

```
Set Rs = New Recordset
Cn.MySP "My parm1", 2, "O'Malley", RS
```

Here's an example that executes a parameter query without (apparent) use of the Command object at all—it simply sets the Recordset object's Source property to a constructed SELECT statement. Actually, behind the scenes ADO constructs a Command object to manage the query.

```
Set rs = New Recordset
With rs
    SQL = "Select title, Year_Published from titles " _
        & "where title like '" & txtParm1 & "'" _
        & "and year_published between " & txtParm2 & " and " & txtParm3
    .ActiveConnection = cn
    .Source = SQL
    .CursorType = adOpenStatic
    .LockType = adLockOptimistic
    .Open Options:=adCmdText
End With
```

The data provider is managed very differently depending on where the cursors are created. If a client-side cursor is selected prior to opening the Connection, then only these two SQL statements are sent to the server:

```
SET NO_BROWSETABLE ON
Select title, Year_Published from titles where title like 'Hitch%'and
year_published between 1900 and 1999
```

---

9. This "stored procedure as Connection method" technique is discussed in Chapter 6.

When rows are needed from the client-side cursor, ADO simply fetches them from locally cached data loaded from the single SELECT statement.

However, if server-side cursors are used, the ADO instructs the data provider to construct a server-managed cursor. When rows are needed, the provider runs another query to fetch rows from the cursor.

```
sp_cursoropen @P1 output, N'Select title, Year_Published from titles where title
like ''Hitch%''and year_published between 1900 and 1999', @P3 output, @P4 output,
@P5 output select @P1, @P3, @P4, @P5
sp_cursorfetch 531488860, 16, 1, 2048
sp_cursorfetch 531488860, 16, 1, 1
sp_cursorclose 531488860
```

Notice that the provider submits queries that execute stored procedures you might not see documented in Books Online—that's because they aren't documented. These sp_cursor... stored procedures are installed by the routines that set up the ODBC and OLE DB data access providers. Their source is encrypted so that you can't see what magic the provider is doing under the covers to implement your cursor. When I get permission, I'll document these new system stored procedures and publish the results.

What's Tough to Parameterize

While inserting constants into an SQL query's WHERE clause is easy, parameterizing other parts of the query is not so easy. Unless you use the concatenation technique I just discussed, changing table, field, or join syntax requires construction of a special type of query that's compiled each time it's run. That's a TSQL subject for another book.

Setting Parameter Values

At one point or another, you're going to want to pass a constant or variable to the query in one or more Parameters. The Value property serves to pass data to and from the procedure—depending on the Direction property setting. That is, before the Command object is executed, you must set the Value property for any input parameter that does *not* have a default value defined in the stored procedure, which means you have to provide a runtime parameter value for all ad hoc query parameters.

> **TIP**   *We'll discuss how to use and set default values in properties. See the "Using the Execute Method on a Command Object" section later in this chapter.*

Note that when you first set up your Command object, you can provide an initial Value property setting. However, this value is not read-only when the Command object is created, so it's not a *true* default value. When this value is set, though, ADO applies this value if a specific value is not provided before execution of the Command.

You can also provide default value settings when you write stored procedures. The following example illustrates coding a SQL Server stored procedure whose first argument has a default setting. That is, if a parameter is not passed to the stored procedure, the default value is used.

```
Create Procedure DefaultValues
    (@InputParm VarChar(20) = 'Fred', @InputParm2 integer)
As
    SELECT @InputParm Stuff
    return @InputParm2
```

The Command object's Value property can be referenced by name. ADO will name the Parameter objects for you as Param1, Param2, and so on, but remember that referencing any collection item by name is slower than referencing it by ordinal, as shown next. You can also name the Parameter objects if you use the (suggested) roll-your-own Parameters collection technique.

```
Set cmd = New Command
With cmd
    .ActiveConnection = cn
    .CommandText = "DefaultValues"
    .CommandType = adCmdStoredProc
    .Parameters.Refresh
    Set rs = .Execute
    Debug.Print .Parameters(0)  'return status
    Debug.Print .Parameters(1)  'Input param (default value?)
End With
```

What Happens When the Value Is Wrong

ADO has a fairly rude way of handling Field-constraint violations. Okay, so I'm a little sensitive, but when you assign a string containing 22 bytes to a Field or

Parameter you have described as VarChar(20), ADO trips a trappable error. I expected ADO to simply truncate the string, but I guess this is a better approach—you'll know about any violations of this field constraint. It also means you'll have to tighten up your parameter validation routines. The same thing happens when you pass an invalid date—February 30, 2000 for example, or an invalid integer (one that is too large, or too small, or that contains a decimal component).

No, you don't have to provide values for stored procedure parameters that have default values defined. This means that you might not have to supply any parameters. If you don't care about capturing return status or output parameters, you don't even have to code a Command object at all—just execute the stored procedure off of the Connection object.

```
Cn.spAllDefaultValues
```

The Parameters.Item(n).Value property is the default property for the Command object. So, to reference individual parameter values you can code:

```
MyCommand(3) = "George has a baby"        ' Notes Parameter
```

instead of:

```
MyCommand.Parameters.Item(3).Value = "George has a baby"    ' Notes Parameter
```

I discuss efficient COM object referencing later, but suffice it to say that while string referenced parameters are easier to read, they are almost twice as slow as ordinal references. This means that *neither* of the following alternatives is a good idea if runtime performance is the goal:

```
MyCommand("Notes") = "George has a baby"        ' Notes Parameter
MyCommand!Notes = "George has a baby"       ' Notes Parameter
```

So how do you add back in the human readability? One approach is to use enumerations for your parameters. So, if you had the following Enum defined:

```
Enum eParms
    ReturnStatus
    PName
    PGrade
    Notes
End Enum
```

you could refer to individual Value properties of selected Parameter objects as shown next:

```
MyCommand(eParms.Notes) = "It's a girl, and her name is Mary Anne!"
' And yes, ADO deals with the extra apostrophe
```

Referencing Field and Parameter objects by Enum or ordinal (with comments) is another best practice, as this improves human readability as well as performance.

If you don't provide the required Parameter values, ADO informs you with a trappable error. For example, I provided one of the three required parameters for an ad hoc query and got the following error (Err.Description):

```
[Microsoft][ODBC SQL Server Driver][SQL Server]Prepared statement '(@P1
varchar(255),@P2 smallint,@P3 smallint)Select title from ti' expects parameter
@P2, which was not supplied.
```

Considering that my query looks like this:

```
"Select title from titles where title like ? and year_published between ? and ?"
```

you might see where some developers would be as confused as ADO appeared to be. Well, because I asked that the query be "prepared" (Prepared = True), this Prepared statement syntax was not entirely unexpected. To add to the confusion, the error handler (in the data provider) truncated the query slightly (cutting it off shortly after the From clause). To prepare the query, ADO constructed a temporary stored procedure to execute the query—you can see the SQL for that query echoed in the error message. Make sense? I hope so.

Fetching Parameter Values

The return status from a stored procedure and the parameters that you marked as output (adParamOutput) or input/output (adParamInputOutput) are available, but only *after* the data provider sends them. This means that you won't see them until your Recordset reaches (EOF), unless the low-level protocol returns them earlier (not usually the case). Remember, the return status is always in the first (0th) Parameter in the Parameters collection—if you asked for it.

```
MyRetStatus = cmd(0)            ' Return Status parameter
```

Handling OUTPUT Parameters

ADO does not seem to know how to construct OUTPUT parameter queries very well. Because it can't really guess how you are going to use the parameters in code,[10] ADO assumes that simple OUTPUT parameters are really INPUT-OUTPUT parameters. Because of this, you usually have to change the Direction property to adParamOutput for each of your OUTPUT parameters. Because you're constructing your parameter collection using code, this should not be a problem. Of course, you could rewrite the stored procedure to pass SELECT rowsets instead of OUTPUT parameters....

It's really easy to make a mistake because the documentation for the process of setting up the Parameters collection leaves something to be desired. Also consider what happens when your database administrator changes the procedure in question to accommodate some other developer. If you have hard-coded the datatype for a particular procedure argument and it changes in the database, you have to recode, recompile, and redeploy—perhaps just before you resign.[11] Just remember to let the air out of the SA's tires before you leave the parking lot.

Parameter-based Ad Hoc Queries

You don't have to construct stored procedures or even ADO Command objects to execute parameter-based queries. Instead, you can construct an SQL query containing question marks (?) as parameter markers that ADO can handle for you—if you describe the parameters correctly in code. This saves you coding time.

Even though ADO can construct a prototype Parameters collection for you, you still have to add code to complete the process. For example, if you manage the parameters yourself in code, you still have to make sure that any string-based parameters do not contain single quotes (the SQL "framing" quote). You also need to set the ActiveConnection property before ADO will be able to construct the Parameters collection for you; yes, you guessed it, ADO has to query the database to construct the prototype Parameters collection. After you set the ActiveConnection property, you must visit each Parameter object in the Parameters collection and set any needed Type (the datatype), Direction (the default is adParamUnknown), Precision, NumericScale, and Attributes.

---

10. Unless you have the new "Read programmer's mind" add-in—available at a slight extra charge.

11. If your database is redefined regularly, then using the Parameters.Refresh method has more appeal.

Generating Parameters Collection Code Automatically

You can use a new Visual Basic Addin to make the process of generating correct code for parameter-based stored procedures easier. This code started circulating in the developer community after Developer Days 1999. While this addin will not automatically morph your code to changing procedure parameters, it does virtually eliminate the need to guess how to construct the Parameters collection in code. By simply providing enough information to get connected to your database and identifying which stored procedure to reference, you can have the addin write the needed code to construct the Command object's Parameters collection. Yes, you still need to go into the code and make sure that OUTPUT parameters are correctly coded, but the rest is automatic. This addin is provided on the CD.

> **TIP**   *When working with active server pages (and Visual Basic Script), you might weigh the extra cost of compiling the source code required to construct the Parameters collection against the cost of using the Refresh method. It might turn out that the round-trip costs less than compiling and executing 40 lines of code used to construct a large Parameters collection.*

Coding Command Objects for Oracle Stored Procedures

I don't think there's anything I missed in regard to using Command objects to run SQL Server stored procedures. We've discussed input, output, and input/output, as well as return-status parameters. When we get to the Recordset section of the book (in Chapters 6 and 7), I discuss the result sets generated by stored procedures. In other words, there are no other words to add—at least not here!

However, there are a number of issues that arise when calling Oracle stored procedures. There are a number of Knowledge Base articles on connecting to Oracle databases, and the following paragraphs are an update of one of the most helpful of those articles.

To begin, you really need to get the latest Oracle ODBC or OLE DB drivers. A lot of work was done in this area, so be sure to leverage these improvements and bug fixes by loading the most recent versions. Without these drivers, you'll find it impossible to retrieve Recordsets from Oracle stored procedures.

Oracle developers know that you can't just use Visual Basic or Visual Studio right out of the box with Oracle systems because you still need their proprietary drivers. These are installed on the client separately, and not being an Oracle expert, I won't try to explain that installation here.

With the release of the Microsoft ODBC Driver for Oracle version 2.0 and higher, you can now retrieve result sets from Oracle stored procedures. By creating Oracle stored procedures that return parameters of type TABLE, you can return row and column data that can then be manipulated and displayed as a result set. Knowledge Base article Q174679 uses the example in the Help file for the Microsoft ODBC Driver for Oracle v2.0 and shows how to use that example in Visual Basic.

> **NOTE** *The result sets created by the Microsoft ODBC Driver for Oracle version 2.0 and 2.5 using Oracle stored procedures are READ ONLY and STATIC. An Oracle Package must be created to retrieve a result set.*

Managing Command Objects

Remember that there are four phases to the creation and execution of Command objects:

1. Create the Command object and construct the Parameters collection.

2. Set the Parameter Value property for each input parameter.

3. Execute the query.

4. Process the results.

Phase 1 should be executed *once*. The remaining phases can be done on an "as required" basis, later in your application. If you review a client/server application that reruns the first phase repeatedly, revisit the source, and code the initialization process to a one-time-only event procedure. This is another best practice. Unfortunately, in the middle tier (and ASP) code, you have to construct the Command objects each time. But remember that Command objects are *not* required unless you're executing queries that return OUTPUT or Return Status values from the query.

Executing and Reexecuting Command Objects

After the Command object is constructed, the expensive part of constructing the Command object on the client is completed. We discussed some of the ways to execute queries in Chapter 4, so what follows won't be all that new. The Command's query can be executed in several ways:

- Using the Execute method on the constructed Command object.

- Using the Command object as a method on the Connection object.

- Referencing the Command with the Execute method on the Connection object.

- Referencing the Command with the Open method on the Recordset object. This technique is discussed in Chapter 6 where we focus on creating Recordsets.

Let's take a look at these techniques one at a time. Some of the primary differences you want to watch out for are how the Recordset is constructed (do you get to build it ahead of time or do you have to take the standard default) and how the parameters are passed to the Command object (do you have to provide them parameter-by-parameter or can you pass them as method arguments one way or another).

Using the Execute Method on a Command Object

One of the simplest and least flexible techniques is to simply "execute" the Command. This approach tells ADO to take the Command as it's currently populated and run it, and (optionally) construct a new Recordset object to receive the rowset. The Command object's Execute method is basically the same as when used against a Connection object (as we discussed in Chapter 4).

The following code example illustrates the use of the Execute method. (I use this Command object for the rest of the Command execution examples.) The principal difference here is that when you use the Execute method, ADO constructs a virgin Recordset set to ReadOnly/ForwardOnly to handle the rowset. If you use the Command as Connection method technique, you get to construct your own Recordset beforehand. Although the default Recordset constructed by the Execute method retrieves rows efficiently, if you expect updatability, you won't get it this way.

```
Set cmd = New Command
With cmd
    .Name = "GetTitles"
    .ActiveConnection = cn
```

```
      .CommandText = "Select title from titles " _
         & "where title like ? " _
         & "and year_published between ? and ?"
      .Parameters.Append CreateParameter("TitleWanted", adVarChar, adParamInput, 20)
      .Parameters.Append CreateParameter("YearLow", adInteger, adParamInput,, 1940)
      .Parameters.Append CreateParameter("YearHigh", adInteger, adParamInput)
      .Prepared = False
End With
```

Handling Parameter Default Values

Note that in the preceding example, the second parameter is set up in the Parameters collection with a value (1940). This tells ADO to reset the parameter to this value after each use of the Command object. After a Command object is executed, ADO resets each Parameter.Value back to the initial setting. In the case of the first and third Parameters, the Value is set back to empty.

Now that the Command is set up, we're ready to execute it. The following line might do the trick:

```
cmd.Execute
```

This code simply ignores the "rows affected" value—it won't return anything for this query anyway—and accepts the existing parameter value settings. Oops, because they weren't set, we get a trappable error. We should have set the parameter values first.

```
cmd(0) = "Hitch%"
cmd(1) = 1940
cmd(2) = 1990
cmd.Execute
```

Now the Execute method works fine. After the Command is executed, the Parameters are reset to their initial state—empty, 1940, and empty.

Passing Arguments with Variant Arrays

Another way to pass in input parameters is to use a Variant array. This approach is kinda cool. And better yet, if you don't provide one of the elements, ADO does not submit the parameter—it assumes the provider will insert the default value. If there is no default value set, either in the called stored procedure or in the initial

Parameter collection, ADO returns a trappable error: "-2147217900 Incorrect syntax near the keyword 'DEFAULT'."

```
vParms = Array("Hitch%", 1940, 1990)
cmd.Execute lRA, vParms
```

Let's try another variation:

```
cmd.Execute lRA, Array("Hitch%", 1940, 1990)
```

This technique bypasses the creation of a separate Variant array and simply uses the new Visual Basic Array function. In this case, we let the existing setting of the second parameter (cmd(1)) be used, because it has a default value. This variation, however, prevents you from reading the OUTPUT parameters off the array.

If you're executing an action query, it's nice to know how many rows are affected. If the provider can tell you, the value is returned in the Long variable passed as the first argument, RecordsAffected. It does not return the number of records in your rowset. It's passed to our routines above in the lRA variable.

Setting Additional Execution-time Options

When we defined the Command object, we specified the CommandType property, so we shouldn't have to provide it again when it comes time to execute a Command, but you can. There are also other more interesting options that do make sense when using the Execute method, including options that tell ADO you aren't expecting rows, that it should execute asynchronously, and several others, as shown in Table 5-3:

CONSTANT	DESCRIPTION
adAsyncExecute	Indicates that the command should execute asynchronously. This returns control to your application or component immediately (just after the first CacheSize rows are fetched), freeing up your thread for other tasks. It does not make a lot of sense to use this option for the middle tier, but it can really help "perceived" performance with client/server rigs.
adAsyncFetch	Tells ADO to asynchronously fetch the remaining rows after the initial quantity specified in the CacheSize are fetched. If this option is specified, ADO keeps fetching rows so that rowset population occurs more quickly. This is important for the overall

	system, as well as for your application, as rows past the initial cache are available more quickly. I discuss asynchronous fetching in Chapter 6.
adAsyncFetchNonBlocking	Prevents the main thread from blocking while retrieving. If the requested row has not been retrieved, the current row automatically moves to the end of the result set (EOF).
adExecuteNoRecords	Indicates that the command text is a command or stored procedure that does *not* return rows (for example, a command that only inserts data). If any rows are retrieved, they are discarded and not returned. This option is always combined with CommandType options of adCmdText or adCmdStoredProc. This option prevents ADO from constructing a Recordset object in cases where it's not needed.

Table 5-3: CommandType options

By using the right set of options you help ADO do less work to run your query and fetch rows more efficiently. You might have to "add" several of these together, as shown in the following code:

```
cn.Execute("MyUpdateSP", , adCmdStoredProcedure + adExecuteNoRecords)
```

When the Command object completes (successfully or not) an ExecuteComplete event fires.

Executing a Command Object as a Connection Method

Because we are also discussing *developer* performance, it makes sense to mention the Command as Connection method technique. This technique uses a named Command object as a method against the ADO Connection associated with it. That is, once you name a Command object (by setting its Name property) and set the ActiveConnection to a Connection object, you can use the following syntax to execute it:

```
Private Sub cmdRunQuery_Click()
    cnMyConnection.GetAuthors txtYearWanted.Text, rs
        ' parameter,  Recordset
    ProcessResults(rs)
End Sub
```

In this case, I'm executing a Command object called GetAuthors. The input parameters are passed as arguments to the method. The last argument passed is a reference to an instantiated Recordset object, which will contain the rowset when ADO completes executing the query.

> **TIP** *For reasons that have to do with how COM works behind the scenes,[12] you **must** fully qualify all object-sourced parameters when using this technique. This means that you can't just pass in txtYearWanted, which should refer to the default Text property of the TextBox control referenced. Instead, you must pass in txtYearWanted.Text. This prevents a number of strange behaviors, including confused parameters being passed to the data provider.*

This Command as Connection method technique is also very easy to code and yields excellent performance. In this case, you work with a preconstructed Recordset object configured with the correct CursorType, LockType, and other properties that make sense. Unlike the Command object's Execute method (discussed next), you get to describe how the Recordset object is to be constructed.

> **WARNING** *There is an outstanding bug posted against this technique. For more information, see "The Other Side of the Refresh Method Story" section, earlier in this chapter.*

Using the Command Object's Execute Method

The Command object's Execute method is far less flexible than other techniques. It also has a number of, well, interesting side effects that you might not be aware of. There are two flavors of the Execute method:

- Against a Connection object: In this case, you provide a Source argument, but you can't specify a Command object here as you can with the Recordset object's Open method (which I discuss in Chapter 6). You have to pass the SQL query as an SQL statement, a table name, a URL, or the name of a stored procedure. You also need to pass an appropriate CommandType in the Options argument—or let ADO guess the type of command to

---

12. All parameters are stored in a DISPARAMS structure of pure variants, but control references are valid variants, so Visual Basic just passes those—and ADO chokes.

execute—but you should always provide the CommandType to prevent ADO from "guessing" what's in the query you're submitting.

- Against a Command object: In this case, the Source argument is contained in the Command object, as are all of the other arguments needed to run the query, including the CommandType. But, again, ADO constructs the Recordset for you, so you have to settle for the "default" Recordset properties—read-only, forward-only.

In either case, if you want to return a rowset, you must capture the Recordset passed back from the Execute method. The Execute method always constructs the Recordset to the default specifications (read-only, forward-only) for you. For example:

```
Set rs = cmd.Execute
```

If you don't need a Recordset, use the alternative syntax:

```
cmd.Execute
```

However, there is an interesting side effect. In some cases, and especially when you create a Recordset using the Execute method against a Connection object, ADO opens *an additional* connection to run the query, and closes it afterwards. This is especially true if you use the Execute method again before fully populating the original Recordset.

Actually, the sequence of operations triggers this behavior. For example, if you set cmd.ActiveConnection to cn, and use the cmd.Execute method followed by cn.Execute, ADO does not open a new connection. However, if you use the cn.Execute method followed by the cmd.Execute method, ADO does create another connection to run the Command.

Tracing the Server and Data Provider

When you use ADO to execute your query, the server dutifully executes what ADO and the data provider sends it. However, how efficiently these statements are executed and how they affect scalability is an important consideration. The CursorLocation (client-side or server-side cursors), CursorType, LockType, and even the syntax you use can affect what type of query is sent to the backend. Because only SQL Server exposes enough trace information for you to be able to see what's actually getting transmitted to the server, I'm going to walk you through a number of configurations so that you can choose the query style that makes the most sense for your application or component. At least you'll understand which factors affect the resulting commands sent to SQL Server.

> **NOTE** *Yes, you can also dump the ODBC logs to get an idea of what the upper layer of ODBC is telling the driver to do. But this does not really show how the data driver implements this ODBC call. That's what the SQL Server Profiler (or SQLTrace) shows. And this does not show how OLE DB providers work behind the scenes.*

I'm going to step through these configurations one group at a time. First, server-side cursors with the default Recordset settings of read-only, forward-only are listed in Table 5-4. Table 5-5 lists server-side cursors with keyset/optimistic cursors. Notice the considerable difference in the number of round-trips and the complexity of the queries that the server has to process to execute basically the same Command but using different syntax to support the selected cursor types.

COMMAND SYNTAX	GENERATED QUERY
Cn.GetTitlesByYear	GetTitlesByYear 'Hitch%', 1900, 1999
rs.Open cmd	sp_executesql N'Select Top 50 title, ISBN, Year_Published from titles where title like @P1 and year_published between @P2 and @P3', N'@P1 varchar(20),@P2 int,@P3 int', 'Hitch%', 1900, 1999
rs.Open strSQL	Select Top 50 title, ISBN, Year_Published from titles where title like 'Hitch%' and year_published between 1900 and 1999
Cn.GetTitles	Sp_executesql N'Select Top 50 title, ISBN,...
Set rs = cmd.Execute...[13]	Sp_executesql N'Select Top 50 title, ISBN, ...

Table 5-4: Server-side Read-only/Forward-only Cursors

COMMAND SYNTAX	GENERATED QUERY
Cn.GetTitlesByYear	declare @P1 int declare @P3 int declare @P4 int declare @P5 int set @P1=NULL set @P3=102401 set @P4=311300 set @P5=NULL exec sp_cursoropen @P1 output, N'Select Top 50 title, ISBN, Year_Published from titles where title like @P1 and year_published between @P2 and @P3', @P3 output, @P4 output, @P5 output, N'@P1 varchar(20),@P2 int,@P3 int', 'Hitch%', 1900, 1999 select @P1, @P3, @P4, @P5

13. Using the Command.Execute method only makes sense with forward-only/read-only, because ADO manufactures the Recordset on each invocation.

rs.Open cmd	Sp_cursoropen ...
	sp_cursorfetch ... (several times)
rs.Open strSQL	Sp_cursoropen...
	sp_cursorfetch (several times)
Cn.GetTitles[14]	sp_cursoropen ... (several times)
	sp_cursorfetch ... (several times)

Table 5-5: Server-side Keyset/Optimistic Cursors

Client-side cursors are far less flexible than server-side cursors. In this case, only the Static CursorType is supported, and updatability is only provided if you choose adLockBatchOptimistic as the LockType. No, I don't expect you to study these tables that closely. I do expect you to try these tests on your own. The source code to set up all of these tests is on the book's CD. Dig into the ..\sample application\command objects\ directory for the code. Table 5-6 lists client-side static/optimistic cursors, and Table 5-7 lists client-side static/batch optimistic cursors.

COMMAND SYNTAX	GENERATED QUERY
rs.Open cmd	sp_executesql...
cmd.Execute	sp_executesql ...
Cn.GetTitlesByYear	GetTitlesByYear 'Hitch%', 1900, 1999
Cn.GetTitles	sp_executesql...
rs.Open strSQL	Select Top 50 title, ISBN, Year_Published from ...

Table 5-6: Client-side Static/Optimistic Cursors

COMMAND SYNTAX	GENERATED QUERY
rs.Open cmd	sp_executesql...
cmd.Execute	sp_executesql ...
Cn.GetTitlesByYear	GetTitlesByYear 'Hitch%', 1900, 1999
Cn.GetTitles	sp_executesql...
rs.Open strSQL	Select Top 50 title, ISBN, Year_Published from ...

Table 5-7: Client-side Static/Batch Optimistic Cursors

As you can see, there are a variety of approaches that the SQL Server data provider takes when executing queries on ADO's behalf. However, ADO seems to be fairly predictable, regardless of the cursor location setting. If you use client-side cursors and execute an ad hoc query using the Recordset Open method, or execute a

---

14. There seems to be some controversy about this technique. The ADO people are still working on it.

stored procedure, ADO simply takes the SQL and "passes it through," not attempting to leverage any of the system-level sp_cursor functions or even use the sp_executesql function. This is not necessarily wrong. SQL Server knows how to persist query plans for ad hoc queries, and the query plans for SQL Server are already compiled.

Calling stored procedures seems to be far more efficient than using ad hoc queries or Command objects. When you stick with forward-only/read-only concurrency, ADO just passes the stored procedure invocation on through to the server, even managing the parameters. If you ask for an updatable cursor, ADO prefixes the stored procedure call with a sp_cursoropen to handle scrolling and updating.

Detecting Command State

The Command object's State property is only really interesting when you execute a query asynchronously. That is, if you start executing a Command using any one of the techniques discussed in this chapter, the State property can indicate whether or not the query has completed. As long as ADO is busy managing the execution of your Command object, the Executing (adStateExecuting) bit of the State property (4) is on and the Open (adStateOpen) bit is off. Yes, you can poll the adStateExecuting bit as a way of waiting until an asynchronous operation is done, but I would rather use the ExecuteComplete event to do the job. Using the event consumes far less CPU resources when compared to polling—especially when compared to loop polling. It's like having your daughter sitting in the back seat on the way to grandma's house asking (every two minutes), "Are we there yet, daddy?"

The Cancel Method

So, you started the execution of your Command object with the adAsyncExecute option, and this returned control of your thread so that you could entertain the user with a progress bar or launch "Age of Empires II" while the user waits. If your user decides to quit waiting, you can use the Cancel method to stop processing the query—or at least you can try. Sometimes it's like trying to stop a train 40 feet from the rail crossing.

> **NOTE** *The Cancel method can also be applied to the Connection object to cancel an asynchronous open operation, but that's not as likely to be necessary—most connections complete before the user can blink, and if they are delayed longer than that, it's usually a network delay that can't be interrupted anyway.*

You get a trappable error if the operation is not stoppable, such as if you try to cancel an operation that wasn't started asynchronously.

Consider that it might not be safe to cancel an operation midstream—especially operations making changes to the database. SQL Server and other providers won't (necessarily) back out changes already made unless there was a transaction started beforehand.

ADO Command Object's "Fallback" Plan

The ADO named command fallback plan seems to be stored procedures. That is, if you don't create a Command object and you reference a named object off of the Connection object (like this):

```
cnOLEDB.TestQuery txtParm, rs
```

ADO will assume that TestQuery is a stored procedure. If it's not, you'll trip an error complaining that the stored procedure TestQuery could not be located. The same will happen if you use adCmdText as the Command.CommandType property and submit a single object name.

This means you can execute any stored procedure (parameters and all) using the following syntax (assuming GetTitles is a stored procedure):

```
Cn.GetTitles "1980", rsMyRecordset
```

The problem with the stored procedure as Connection method technique is that it cannot handle OUTPUT parameters. This means that if the stored procedure has OUTPUT parameters, this technique will not return them to you—no Command object is created to handle them. While you can execute the stored procedure, you have to pass placeholders for each of the OUTPUT parameters because ADO defaults OUTPUT Parameter.Direction to INPUT/OUTPUT (adParamInputOutput). But when the query is executed, there is no Command object created to fetch the returning parameters.

Command Object Tips and Warnings

As I was working with the Command object to develop the example and test code, I came across several miscellaneous tips. A summary of those tips and techniques appears below. I've also included a few suggestions that I picked up from my students and the folks I communicate with via e-mail:

- If you try to execute a stored procedure, and the parameters you describe don't match what SQL Server expects, almost anything can happen, including the error: "–2147418113 Unexpected failure."

- If you set the CommandType property to adCmdStoredProc and you reference a table instead of a stored procedure, you'll trip this trappable error: "–2147217900 — The request for procedure 'Publishers' failed because 'Publishers' is a table object." It's clear that ADO is watching out for you. The Profiler showed no signs of running round-trips to the server to figure this out, even though one actually takes place. However, this information might have been cached.

- If the argument passed to the Command object's parameter does not meet the datatype requirements (string, number, integer, date, currency, and so forth) your code will trigger a 3421 error: "The application is using a value of the wrong type for the current operation." Who writes these error messages anyway?

- If the CommandType is left at adCmdUnknown and the query contains a SELECT statement, ADO figures it out on its own and resets the CommandType to adCmdText.

- If the CommandType is adCmdTable, anything other than a table name in the CommandText trips the following syntax error when you attempt to execute the query: "–2147217900 Incorrect syntax near the keyword 'select'." However, the ODBC provider does not trap incorrect table names. I set up a Command object using adCmdTable with Fred as the CommandText, and when ADO submitted SELECT * FROM FRED, ADO did not complain. On the other hand, the OLE DB provider returned: "–2147217865 Invalid object name 'fred'." Interesting.

> **NOTE** *Error messages returned from the OLE DB provider arrive without any prefix indicating which layer caused the error. The ODBC messages come back looking like this:*
>
> ```
> [Microsoft][ODBC SQL Server Driver][SQL Server]Invalid object name 'fred'.
> ```

Handling Connection Object Events

This is easy because there aren't any events exposed on the Command object. You have to depend on the Connection or Recordset object to handle events associated with the Command. If you run a Command object asynchronously, you can trap the WillExecute or ExecuteComplete event on the associated Connection to determine when it's done, or poll the Command object's State property.

Performance Considerations: Using Command Objects Wisely

A common performance problem with Command objects is instantiating (creating), executing, and destroying them in a single Command_Click event, a middle-tier component, or on a Web page. This is a problem, because in these cases, the object setup expense is paid each time the Command is executed instead of once. Because you can't expect to scale an application or component that leaves Command objects lying around waiting for potential clients, we have to construct them "just in time." While there are certainly cases in which you must construct a Command object, you don't want to expend the resources to instantiate and prepare the object unless it is necessary. Of course, in the middle tier (Microsoft Transaction Server or ASP), you may have no choice. In this case, you really want to think out your query strategy to determine whether it's really necessary to create/use/destroy a Command object each time the method or ASP page is referenced—especially when other cheaper strategies are available. While Command objects make it easier to manage procedure parameters, the extra overhead of creating them might not pay off in better performance.

I used to think that the fundamental purpose of the Command object was to help ADO create a temporary stored procedure to run your query more quickly. However, I have seen ADO change its approach to the creation and execution of temporary stored procedures to leverage SQL Server and other providers' capabilities to deal more efficiently with repeated ad hoc query invocations.

The Command object's Execute method also constructs the Recordset object for you. That is, you can't specify the LockType, CursorType, CacheSize, MaxRecords, or other interesting (but performance robbing) Recordset properties ahead of time—you have to take the defaults. The default Recordset is a read-only, forward-only, CacheSize=1 "firehose" (or cursorless) result set that is very efficient, so this behavior works for a high-performance application. However, if you code the Options argument to the Execute, you can tell ADO that the query does not return rows at all (as shown next), which helps improve performance.

```
Set rs = cmd.Execute(Options:=adExecuteNoRecords)
```

Any information that you can give ADO to help it know how to process the "stuff" in the CommandText property helps performance. As with the Recordset object's Open method options, which I discuss in Chapter 6, you really must tell ADO whether or not this is the name of a stored procedure, a table, the name of a file, or just random SQL. No, adCmdTableDirect is not a valid choice for most providers. The CommandType default is adCmdUnknown, which means ADO will have to guess, which takes time.

In many cases, you can improve performance by avoiding client-to-server round-trips. For example, if you combine a number of related operations together in a single query, you can save quite a bit of system and backend overhead. However, not all providers support multiple operations—SQL Server does, but Jet/Access does not. I use this technique to perform bulk inserts or to execute a series of commands bound in a transaction. You have to understand how to deal with the more complex result sets that ADO generates using this technique. But that's not hard.

Recordset Strategies

FOLKS, I APOLOGIZE FOR TAKING SO long to get to this point—but we're now ready to talk about data and result sets. We've covered a lot of ground up to this point, and we still have a long way to go. So, let's get started.

The Recordset object is the interface that ADO uses to expose rowsets. Not all result sets include rowsets, so your query might not include a rowset at all. Recordset objects are expensive to create, so if you have a choice, don't ask ADO to create one. However, when you do need to manage the rowset component of your query, the ADO Recordset is the most powerful object ADO has to bring to bear on your data access problem.

The Recordset discussion is spread over three chapters. This chapter discusses the how, when, and why of constructing a Recordset by walking you through the creation of the ADO Recordset object and providing a number of tips on how to make efficient use of the data source. I also discuss populating, navigating, and updating Recordsets, and try to clear up some of the confusion about locking—both page and row-level locking. In Chapter 7, I discuss how to manipulate the Recordset. There I focus on binding, sorting, filtering, and finding the rowset. In Chapter 8, I discuss marshaling Recordsets. No, not how to help them line up in neat rows, but how to move them from tier to tier.

The technique that you use to construct the Recordset object can have a significant impact on the performance and scalability of your application or component, whether it runs on a Windows desktop or on an IIS server down in the data center. As we saw in the chapter on ADO Command Objects, the syntax used to execute the query can also dramatically affect what gets executed on the server and what gets returned.

Introducing Recordsets

When ADO runs your query, it returns the qualifying rows using a Recordset object.[1] However, you don't necessarily need to create a Recordset to retrieve information. You can run a query to return a set of results in the form of output parameters or simply as an integer passed back as the return status of a stored procedure. Output parameter information is all passed back in the Command object—not the Recordset.

---

1. Qualifying rows means rows returned from your database table(s) that meet the qualifications described in the SELECT statement and its WHERE clause.

What you need to understand is that ADO (and RDO, DAO, and the ODBC API) all return result sets that contains the answer to your SQL query—your question posed to the data provider. Result sets are generated whether or not your query includes a SELECT statement.

So, if your SQL statement simply executes an UPDATE SQL statement, a result set, but no rowset, is returned. The UPDATE result set simply contains the number of rows affected. But if your query executes a SELECT statement that fetches rows from the data source, the result set contains a rowset. Although this rowset might not contain any rows, it does include the Data Description Language (DDL) schema information from the table(s) referenced. If ADO finds a rowset in the result set, ADO generates a Recordset object to manage it—even if there are no rows.

For example, you can code the following routine to fetch the schema of a selected table. (This is one of the few times when SELECT * is okay.)

```
rs.Open "select * from titles where 1=0", cn
Debug.Print rs.State, adStateOpen, rs.EOF
For Each fld In rs.Fields
    Debug.Print fld.Name, fld.Type, fld.DefinedSize
Next fld
```

Unbeknownst to the MSDN documentation, a Recordset is not simply a cursor. A Recordset is a COM object either defined in your code, or manufactured by an ADO method that might contain a rowset and quite a bit of DDL information about the origins of the data. This schema description describes where the data came from (the query, table, and field names), as well as including a bevy of other properties used to describe the data. The set of rows returned (the rowset) can be returned in the form of a cursor—a mechanism used to logically (and physically) manipulate the rowset. However, the default mechanism implemented to return the rowset is a cursorless result set, because it supports neither scrolling nor updatability. So, a Recordset object can return far more than just a cursor.

What's in a Result Set

Throughout the book I refer to a number of terms that might need clarification. While I've been known to make up terms from time to time, these terms are (mostly) from the textbooks I read many years ago when working with mainframe databases.

When you execute a query against any relational database provider, it responds by sending back a *result set*.[2] A result set can contain:

- 0 to 1 rowsets. These are sets of rows returned by a SELECT statement in the query.

---

2. Result set: This is why we called the RDO object that handled result sets the Resultset object.

- 0 to 1 rows affected value. This is returned by an action query, such as an INSERT, DELETE, or UPDATE SQL statement.

If you execute a stored procedure, your result set can also return multiple result sets, which can each contain a rowset or rows affected values but can also contain:

- 0 to 1 return status value. This is the integer returned when you execute the RETURN TSQL statement in a stored procedure.

- 0 to n OUTPUT parameters. The upper limit of these parameters is about 1000.

- 0 to n COMPUTE or COMPUTE BY rowsets and aggregate totals.

- 0 to n PRINT messages.

- 0 to 1 RAISERROR messages and error codes.

A result set can be as simple as a single rowset or it can be highly complex, with many different structures, depending on the logic in the query.

Development Strategies

The first question you should ask at this point is, "Do I need to create a Recordset at all?" The answer is maybe. Recordsets are *only* needed if the answer to your question must take the form of a rowset. If I were to ask you, "How many bathrooms does your house have?" you would not provide me with a detailed list of the locations of those rooms and the color of towels hanging in each—unless you were Martha Stewart. You would probably just answer "two."

The same principle applies when asking the server for information. You don't always need to return the answer to your SQL questions in the form of rows. If you have situations where the query can be answered with a Boolean (True or False), a number (2), a string "none", or even a set of values, you can pass these back to your application or component using OUTPUT parameters or a variety of other techniques—especially if you are communicating with the database through an intermediate middle tier. Just remember that the Recordset mechanism is relatively expensive to create and manage, so its use should be weighed against the resources it consumes.

Creating Recordsets is not that hard. Too many times, however, I've seen queries that bring perfectly healthy systems to their knees. No, it's not usually one query that does the job. It's more likely to be a dozen poorly written queries that are run too frequently that cause the most degradation. While a lot of emphasis is placed (correctly) on the Recordset CursorType and LockType properties, more attention needs to be paid to what gets shoved into the Source property.

Basically, the Source property or Source argument of the Recordset Open method is the "question" you need to get answered by the data provider. It can be the name of a table, stored procedure, or SQL query. Constructing this query can be a challenge. Remember that each provider requires its own dialect of SQL—it's like someone from Minnesota talking to someone from Alabama. Although they speak the same language, there are times where "you betcha" doesn't come across in quite the same way.

Visual Basic has tried to make construction of SC (Syntactically Correct)[3] SQL queries easier. However, my experiments have resulted in a couple of frustrating experiences that I won't share with you here. Instead, to make a long story short, it seems that what the Visual Database Tools thinks is an efficient Jet query is not what Access would construct for the same query against the same database—and I, for one, agree with Access' approach. Then again, the queries that Visual Database Tools generate for SQL Server seem to be fine—not only are they SC, but they adhere to the new ANSI JOIN syntax. I encourage you to try the four-paned Query Builder window (see Figure 6-1). This interactive graphical user interface (GUI) tool permits you to drag tables from the Data View window, select columns, criteria, and other filters, and see the generated SQL—as well as the rows returning from the query.

You can leverage this generated SQL in an ad hoc query or in the AS clause of a stored procedure. These queries can use parameters—simply reference a parameter marker "?" in the query (in appropriate places in the WHERE clause). While the Data Environment Designer can construct a Data Environment Designer object to execute the

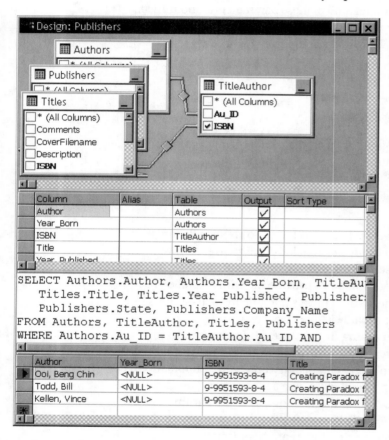

Figure 6-1: VDT Query Designer

---

3. SC queries are designed to not offend the query processor's sensibilities (it's so sensitive!)—just as politically correct comments are designed to not offend the reader.

query, the problems associated with the Data Environment Designer keep me from recommending it for most serious development.

You can also use Microsoft Access' query Design window to drag-and-drop your SQL queries. After the query is constructed to spec, simply copy the query from the SQL window. I would not depend on the Visual Database Tools to construct these queries, as they do not use optimal SC SQL; they use common joins instead of the ANSI JOIN syntax.

However, being able to code a SC query is not the complete path to a scalable, high-performance application. In this case, it's not always *how* you say it; it's *what* you say. The query processor is not easily offended, so you don't have to worry about hurting its sensibilities.

Working with the Biblio Sample Database

All of the examples used in this book access either the SQL Server 7.0 Biblio database or the two Jet 4.0 databases. All three databases are supplied on the companion CDCD.

The Biblio database has been saved and written to disk using SQL Server 7.0's new sp_detach_db stored procedure, which releases control of the .MDF and .LDF (data and log) files. These two files must be "reattached" to your SQL Server 7.0 database to use them. Sorry, there is no Oracle, Jet, or DB2 version of the Biblio sample data.

To reattach these files, follow these steps:

1. Copy the two files (workdata.mdf and worklog.ldf) from the CD to a convenient place on your hard disk. These two files are located in the \Databases directory on the CD. (The code example just below uses "C:\ADO\Databases" as a target directory.)

2. Make sure you don't already have a Biblio database on your SQL Server If you do, you'll have to rename the existing Biblio database (recommended), drop it, or rename the new version (not recommended).

3. Run the SQL statement to attach the database files to the server, thus installing the Biblio database. The file attachbiblio.sql contains this SQL statement:

```
sp_attach_db biblio ,'C:\ADO\Databases\workdata.mdf',
C:\ADO\Databases\worklog1.ldf'
```

After the database is installed, you'll discover it comes with only one UserID, Admin with the password pw. You can add yourself as a user (recommended), but if you do, you also need to configure the Biblio database permissions to let you have access to the database. You'll also want to modify the sample applications to use your UserID. No, I do not recommend using the SA UserID. The CD also contains an SQL script that can be used from Query Analyzer or ISQL to grant all permissions to your new UserID. Log on to QA, select the target database (Biblio), and execute the following stored procedure with your new user ID:

```
sp_GrantAllPermissionsTo <your UserID>
```

Constructing Recordset Objects

Depending on the technique you choose to execute the query, ADO will either manufacture a default Recordset object for you or will expect you to have one constructed and ready to go prior to executing the query. Frankly, I prefer the latter, because building my own Recordset gives me the greatest flexibility in how the rowset is managed once it arrives. However, because ADO's default Recordset is extremely efficient, having ADO manufacture it for me is not that big a deal. The default Recordset object is set up as RO/FO (read-only/forward-only) with its CacheSize property set to 1. This is generates a "firehose" or cursorless result set to hold the rowset returned from the query.

Before we start discussing the benefits of cursorless result sets, let's visit the techniques used to declare the Recordset in the first place. It's really pretty simple.

```
Dim rs As ADODB.Recordset
```

And somewhat later in your code (just before you need the Recordset):

```
set rs = New ADODB.Recordset
```

No, I don't recommend use of the seemingly easier:

```
Dim rs As New ADODB.Recordset
```

If you use the "Dim xx as New yyy" syntax, you won't face the wrath of God. However, you will pay a performance penalty *each* time the Recordset object is referenced. You'll also discover that the NextRecordset method no longer returns *Nothing* when there are no further result sets. But I talked about this in Chapter 2.

Understanding the Field Object

A Recordset contains from one to (almost) any number of Field objects—one for each column in the row. The answer to your question (your query) is stored in the

Field object—more specifically, in the Value property of the Field object. This is also where you place new or changed data to be transmitted back to the data provider. Basically, the Field object corresponds to the term "column" in relational database terms, rows being composed of one or more columns, just as Recordset objects are composed of one or more Field objects.

The Field object itself describes the data's size, origin, precision, numeric scale, source table, and column, and includes a whole series of bit flags that are stored in the Attributes property. These bit flags are all read-only unless you are constructing a Field object using the Recordset Append method. Table 6-1 shows the enumerated values for the Attributes property. I discuss the remaining Field object properties later in this chapter.

ATTRIBUTES PROPERTY ENUMERATION	BIT	DESCRIPTION
adFldCacheDeferred	0x1000	Indicates that the provider caches field values and that subsequent reads are done from the cache.
adFldFixed	0x10	Indicates that the field contains fixed-length data.
adFldIsChapter	0x2000	Indicates that the field contains a chapter value, which specifies a specific child Recordset related to this parent field. Typically, chapter fields are used with data shaping or filters.
adFldIsCollection	0x40000	Indicates that the field specifies that the resource represented by the record is a collection of other resources, such as a folder, rather than a simple resource, such as a text file.
adFldIsDefaultStream	0x20000	Indicates that the field contains the default stream for the resource represented by the record. For example, the default stream can be the HTML content of a root folder on a Web site, which is automatically served when the root URL is specified.
adFldIsNullable	0x20	Indicates that the field accepts null values.
adFldIsRowURL	0x10000	Indicates that the field contains the URL that names the resource from the data store represented by the record.

(continued)

adFldKeyColumn	0x8000	Indicates that the field is the primary key of the underlying rowset. Also can indicate that the field is part of a compound primary key.
adFldLong	0x80	Indicates that the field is a long binary field. Also indicates that you can use the AppendChunk and GetChunk methods.
adFldMayBeNull	0x40	Indicates that you can read null values from the field.
adFldMayDefer	0x2	Indicates that the field is deferred, that is, the field values are not retrieved from the data source with the whole record, but only when you explicitly access them.
adFldNegativeScale	0x4000	Indicates that the field represents a numeric value from a column that supports negative scale values. The scale is specified by the NumericScale property.
adFldRowID	0x100	Indicates that the field contains a persistent row identifier that cannot be written to and that has no meaningful value except to identify the row (such as a record number, unique identifier, and so forth).
adFldRowVersion	0x200	Indicates that the field contains some kind of time or date stamp used to track updates.
adFldUnknownUpdatable	0x8	Indicates that the provider cannot determine whether you can write to the field.
adFldUnspecified	-1	Indicates that the provider does not specify the field attributes.
adFldUpdatable	0x4	Indicates that you can write to the field.

Table 6-1: Field Attributes Property enumerations

> **TIP** *ADO does not really understand one of the primary reasons for creating Views—to protect the database. That is, we construct a View with permissions granted to access a subset of the underlying tables. However, if you use client-side cursors, ADO bypasses the View and attempts to access the root tables directly when you attempt to update the data. This is because when ADO constructs the meta-data to perform an UPDATE, DELETE, or INSERT, it has no idea that it's really accessing a View. So, when it comes time to perform the action query, it knows just where to go—to the root table.*

Working with Recordset Objects

After the Recordset object is constructed, you can set its properties and execute its methods. As long as the Recordset object remains "unopened," you can continue to make changes to its properties. You can even build your own Fields collection, thus describing the data structure itself. However, once the Execute or Open method opens the Recordset based on your design or constructs the Recordset for you (as with the Execute method), all of the Recordset properties except Value are frozen, so it's too late to code changes. A key point here is that the Execute method manufactures a brand new Recordset on its own, using the default Recordset configuration. While many design strategies make efficient use of the default cursor, there are occasions when you must change the base configuration. This is when you must use the Open method or one of the other methods I describe later that leverage an existing Recordset to define the desired Recordset behavior.

Let's look at the Recordset properties and methods and how to make best use of them by discussing them in the following functional groupings:

- Query Management—How the query is specified and executed against a specific data provider.

- Cursor management—How the Recordset cursor is specified prior to execution and how it's manipulated after the rowset is returned.

- Current row management—How the rowset is accessed and how the current row pointer is changed, saved, and moved.

- Update management—How the changes are made to the Recordset object's rowset.

- Concurrency management—How the cursor impacts other competing user's attempts to access and update the data.

- Transaction management—How you can initiate and commit o rollback transactions from your application or deal with transactions managed elsewhere.

- Status management—How ADO informs you of the condition (state) of the Recordset.

- Recordset persistence—How you can save your Recordset to a file, stream, or retrieve it once it has been saved.

Building Efficient Recordset Objects

All too often, we ask for more than we need when building Recordsets. The default ADO Recordset is very efficient, so ADO's behavior helps you construct a high-performance application or component. Each option you choose that varies from this default behavior costs time and resources to implement.

For example, asking for a scrollable Keyset, Static, or Dynamic cursor forces ADO to spend more time preparing keysets and the mechanisms to scroll around in the result set. All of the "complex" bound controls already know how to scroll through the result set, and you don't have to bind to them to get this functionality. Asking ADO to (try to) create an updatable result set against a complex or stored procedure-based query is simply a waste of time—it can't do it. And all too often, your SA doesn't want you to make direct changes to the underlying tables. These changes are reserved for stored procedures that can run business logic, more carefully guard secure data, and maintain referential integrity.

Using the Recordset Open Method

The ADO Recordset Open method is probably the most flexible of all ADO methods. It opens a connection (if you provide a valid connection string instead of a reference to a Connection object), and it executes any given Source string be it the name of a table (really inefficient) or a complex parameter-driven query. You can even execute parameter-queries with the Open method. Here's an example:

```
Set rs = New Recordset
rs.Open "Select title, Year_Published from titles " _
        & "where title like '" & txtParm1 & "'" _
        & "and year_published between " & txtParm2 & " and " _
            & txtParm3, cn, , , adCmdText
Set MSHFlexGrid1.Recordset = rs
```

In this example, I concatenated parameters into the query string passed to the Open method's Source argument.

As I mentioned in Chapter 5, the Open method's Source argument can contain anything that the Command object's CommandText property can contain:

- A SQL query as shown in the preceding code example. This is basically a SELECT (row returning) SQL query.

- The name of a table. This is converted by ADO to a SELECT * FROM <table> query.

- The name of a stored procedure, assuming that the stored procedure does not use input or output parameters.

- The name of a file containing a structure that can be converted to a Recordset, such as an XML, ADTG, or Stream file.

- A URL pointing to a page that can construct a Recordset and pass it back.

By default, ADO goes a long way toward choosing an efficient strategy to fetch your rows. Its default Recordset object is created as a read-only (RO), forward only (FO), cursorless (or firehose) result set.

The Open method assumes your Recordset is already instantiated and ready to go. So, before you use the Open method, you can set the Recordset LockType, CursorType, MaxRecords, CacheSize, and other pertinent properties to optimize the operation.

```
Set rs = New Recordset
SQL = "Select title, Year_Published from titles where title like 'Hitch%' "
rs.ActiveConnection = cn
rs.Source = SQL
rs.CursorType = adOpenStatic
rs.LockType = adLockOptimistic
rs.Open Options:=adCmdText
rs.Open SQL, cn, Options:=adCmdText
```

> **TIP** *Before you call the Recordset Open method, make sure that ADO and the Recordset are not "busy" managing the results of a previous query—even one that does not return a rowset. For example, if you execute the Open method using an INSERT statement as the Source argument, and then follow this execution immediately with another Open, ADO would still be busy dealing with the first Recordset and would not permit another operation. In any case, it does not make sense to use the Open method **unless you expect to get a rowset**. If the query does not return a rowset, simply use the Execute method.*

If all you want to change is the lock type or cursor type, you can pass these property settings as arguments to the Recordset object's Open method. The following example illustrates setting Recordset properties and using the Open method. However, the Source, CursorType, LockType, and CommandType (options) can all be set as Open method arguments, so setting individual properties in this manner is not particularly efficient.

```
Set rs = New Recordset
SQL = "Select title, Year_Published from titles where title like 'Hitch%' "
rs.Open SQL, cn, adOpenStatic, adLockOptimistic, adCmdText
```

If you construct an ADO Command object (declared as cmd) and simply want to create a Recordset based on the query specified in its properties, you can simply execute:

```
rs.Open cmd
```

> **TIP** *Using the Recordset object's Open method has one side effect—an ADO Command object is constructed behind the scenes to manage the query from the Recordset properties and options you provide in code before using the Recordset object's Open method. As far as I'm concerned, this means that you won't gain any COM efficiency by trying to avoid constructing an ADO Command object—it's created anyway.*

When you use the Recordset object's Open method, be sure to set the last argument (Options) to match the type of command in the Source argument. Choose from one of the CommandType enumerated options. For example, if you are executing a stored procedure, use:

```
rs.Open MySPNoParms, cn, adOpenStatic, , adCmdStoredProc
```

You might want to use the named argument approach, which helps eliminate problems associated with not being able to count commas at 3:00 a.m.

```
rs.Open MySPNoParms, cn, adOpenStatic, Options:=adCmdStoredProc
```

> **NOTE** *You can't use named arguments with Visual Basic Script (as in ASP). At least not until ADO 2.6. Stick with the commas and count carefully until SQL Server 2000, which is when ADO 2.6 arrives.*

Specifying the command type in the Options argument eliminates the need to ask the provider (or server) to identify what you are passing in the Source argument. This simple addition will make a measurable difference in your query's performance. And, no, ADO is not heuristic. It does not "learn" or "remember" that the last 200 times you ran this query it ended up being a stored procedure or a table reference. ADO still goes through the steps of trying to figure out what you're doing. It's better to give ADO's query processor a hint.

> **NOTE** *If your query fails to recognize one of your tables, but you know that the query works, you might have forgotten to set the initial catalog (the default database). If your SA didn't set the correct default, you might be pointing at the MASTER database. You need to either set it yourself in the ConnectionString or send your SA a dozen roses and ask to have this fixed.*

You can also execute parameter queries with the Open method. All you have to do is build a query containing the needed parameters—one way or another. This might seem to save you time because you don't have to create a Command object. However, in this case, you do have to manage the framing quotes yourself, and ADO will create a Command object behind the scenes anyway. For example, try this query:

```
strS = "Select Author from authors where year_born = " & txtYearWanted
rs.Open strS, cn, Options:=adCmdText
```

Now inspect the Visual Basic IDE *Locals* window. Notice that the rs.ActiveCommand property is set, pointing to a constructed ADO Command object built to manage the query. The locals window is a good way to debug your query, because you can see what options ADO set for your constructed Command object.

Accessing the Jet Table Object

When you create a Jet-based (.MDB) database, you often lean toward using the Jet Table object. This approach simply permits Jet to access a base table with one of the predefined Jet table indexes. Because Jet is especially good at fetching rows using this technique, it was a shame that you could not get at this technology until ADO 2.1. The downside to this approach is that there is no equivalent operation in SQL Server. This means that if you plan to scale to SQL Server at some point in the future, it is probably best to figure out another approach.

Using the Table object won't work unless you have both a Jet 4.0 database and the OLE DB Jolt 4.0 data provider. When you have these basic ingredients, accessing base tables via a selected index is easy. First, create a new Recordset object against the Jet 4.0 .MDB using the new ADO 2.1 version of the Jolt provider. In this case, you need to create a server-side cursor that Jet will manage for you. The Source property points to the table. Use the Recordset Open method with the adCmdTableDirect option flag. Now point to one of the table's indexes. Each time you use the Seek method, the Recordset is repositioned to the first row matching the Seek argument based on pointers in the selected index.

In the following example, I pass the index name in via a TextBox control:

```
Dim cn As Connection
Dim rs As Recordset
Private Sub Form_Load()
Set cn = New Connection
cn.Open "Provider=Microsoft.Jet.OLEDB.4.0;
Data Source=C:\My Documents\Beta V Corporation\Articles\ODBC API\Jet
Direct\New40.mdb;"

Set rs = New Recordset

With rs
    .CursorLocation = adUseServer
    .ActiveConnection = cn
    .Source = "Customers"
    .CursorType = adOpenKeyset
    .LockType = adLockOptimistic
    .Open Options:=adCmdTableDirect
End With

End Sub
Private Sub SeekButton_Click()
Dim intAP As Integer
With rs
    .Index = txtPK.Text
```

```
        .Seek txtSearch.Text
    End With
    intAP = rs.AbsolutePosition
    If intAP > 1 Then
        With MSHFlexGrid1
            Set .Recordset = rs
            .Row = intAP
            .RowSel = intAP + 1
            .Col = 0
            .ColSel = .Cols - 1
        End With
    Else
        MsgBox "No hits"
    End If
End Sub
```

> **TIP** *If you find that the Recordset Index property does not seem to be exposed, remember to set your Visual Basic project reference to ADO 2.1 or later.*

Creating and Opening Recordsets in Memory

ADO introduced a concept never before seen by DAO or RDO developers—the capability to create a Recordset entirely in memory. That is, you can create an almost fully functional Recordset object, populate the Field objects, and add, change, and delete records as necessary without using a database. You can also create a Recordset object from a database but disconnect it from the ActiveConnection (by setting it to Nothing) and keep it in memory as long as necessary.

You can also save (persist) this Recordset to disk, stream, XML, or binary Advanced Data Tablegram (ADTG) format. Be sure to visit Chapter 8, which discusses marshaling Recordsets from tier to tier.

The following code example illustrates the construction of an in-memory Recordset. The application is designed to capture the mouse events that occur on Form1 and record them to a Recordset. When the user clicks a stop button on the form, the Recordset is persisted to a file—in both ADTG and XML formats.

```
Private Sub Form_Load()
Set rs = New Recordset
rs.Fields.Append "Time", adDBTimeStamp, , adFldRowID + adFldKeyColumn
rs.Fields.Append "Delta", adInteger
rs.Fields.Append "Button", adInteger
rs.Fields.Append "Shift", adInteger
rs.Fields.Append "X", adSingle
rs.Fields.Append "Y", adSingle
rs.Open
ts = GetTickCount
bolDoor = True
varFields = Array("Time", "Delta", "Button", "Shift", "X", "Y")
End Sub
```

The next section of code illustrates two techniques for adding rows to the Recordset, using variations on the AddNew method. The first technique passes two Variant arrays to the AddNew method. The first argument is a Variant array that simply contains the Field names of the columns whose data is to be added. The second argument is another Variant array containing the values associated with each field name in the first array. In the following code example, when an incorrect value is passed to the Field object's Value property, ADO returns the message "–2147217887 Multiple-step operation generated errors. Check each status value." to warn us that one of the fields is incorrect. We'll have to check the Status property of each field to see which Field object is in error, and that can be a real pain to code. Incidentally, this error message occurred in the sample application as I tried to assign a string value to a Field object declared as single.

The second technique does the same thing and is also shown in the following code, but it's commented out. This approach uses a more traditional approach and does not depend on COM having to "look up" the names of the fields. However, recent tests show this approach is actually slower than the array technique. And not only that, but your Value property validation for each Field object is somewhat simpler—at least the errors occur when the field is referenced.[4]

```
Private Sub Form_MouseMove(Button As Integer, Shift As Integer, X As Single,
Y As Single)
If optStart And bolDoor Then
    bolDoor = False
    ' Technique one: Using Variant arrays.
rs.AddNew varFields, Array(Now, GetTickCount - ts, Button, Shift, X, Y)
```

---

4. This example is in the ..\samples\Recordset objects\memory based Recordsets directory on the CD.

```
'     ' Technique two: Using Field-by-Field referencing
'       rs(rsFld.Time) = Now
'       rs(rsFld.Delta) = GetTickCount - ts
'       rs(rsFld.Button) = Button
'       rs(rsFld.Shift) = Shift
'       rs(rsFld.X) = X
'       rs(rsFld.Y) = Y
        rs.Update
        i = i + 1
        txtEvents = i
        DoEvents
        bolDoor = True
End If
End Sub
```

One dramatic difference between DAO, RDO, and ADO is how ADO handles pending changes. That is, in both DAO and RDO you have to use the Update method after an AddNew or Field object change, or your changes are lost when you navigate to another row. In ADO, your changes are *saved* when you navigate to a new row, start another AddNew, or close the Recordset, and, of course, when you execute Update or UpdateBatch. For example, the following code adds two rows to the ValidStates table:

```
Option Explicit
Dim cn As Connection
Dim cmd As Command
Dim rs As Recordset
Dim varStateFlds As Variant
Private Sub Form_Load()
Set cn = New Connection
cn.Open "dsn=localserver", "admin", "pw"
varStateFlds = Array("State", "StateCode")
Set cmd = New Command
Set rs = New Recordset

rs.Open "ValidStates", cn, adOpenStatic, adLockOptimistic, adCmdTable

rs.AddNew varStateFlds, Array("Unknown", "UK")
rs.AddNew varStateFlds, Array("Not Specified", "NS")
rs.Close

End Sub
```

After the data has been captured, we save the Recordset to disk to two separate files, but just to illustrate a point. The ADTG file format is less than half the size of its

XML equivalent. Notice that the Save method does not know how to deal with a file that already exists, so we have to use the Kill function to remove any existing file.

```
Private Sub optStop_Click()
On Error Resume Next
Kill "c:\MouseDroppings.adg"
Kill "c:\MouseDroppings.xml"
On Error GoTo 0
rs.Save "c:\MouseDroppings.adg", adPersistADTG
rs.Save "c:\MouseDroppings.xml", adPersistXML
End Sub
```

But what if you wanted to create a stand-alone version of a Recordset but have it clone a data structure derived from a data provider—such as a database? You can still open the Recordset using a SELECT statement that returns the schema desired but no rows. Simply use a WHERE clause that returns no rows.

```
SELECT … WHERE 1=0
```

After this empty Recordset is opened, you can dissociate it from the Connection by setting the ActiveConnection property to Nothing and begin to use it as you would any other Recordset.[5] You'll have to specify adUseClient for the CursorLocation to get this to work.

Using Command Objects with the Recordset Open Method

Remember that I said that the Open method was one of the most flexible ADO methods? Well, it can also accept a preconstructed Command object as its Source argument. In this case, ADO takes the Connection and CommandText from the Command object and uses the properties of the Recordset to construct the cursor. Just remember to preset the Command parameters before you use the Open method. The CursorType and LockType properties can also be set as arguments in the Open. Note, however, that the Connection and CommandType is set through the Command object—ADO won't let you override it with Open arguments.

```
cmd(0) = txtYearWanted
cmd.Parameters(0).Value = txtYearWanted
Set rs = New Recordset
rs.CursorLocation = adUseServer
rs.Open cmd, , adOpenKeyset, adLockOptimistic
```

---

5. Actually, it's faster to assign the ActiveConnection property Nothing, not Set it.

Setting the Connection in the Open Method

Not only can the Open method set the Source argument (the query) on the fly, but it can also specify the connection. The ActiveConnection argument of the Open method can be set to:

- A valid Connection object

- A valid Connection string

However, you don't need to set the ActiveConnection argument, assuming that the Connection is specified elsewhere, as in the Source argument's reference to a Command object. If you specify a Command object as the Open method's Source argument, you can't override the Command object's ActiveConnection with the Open method's ActiveConnection argument.

This means that our Recordset Open method sample that we used in the previous example or two can be boiled down to one line:

```
rs.Open "select title from titles where title like 'Hi%'", "dsn=localserver",
    Options:=adCmdText
```

This approach does not really cause any serious problems. It constructs the default (firehose) Recordset against the trusted ODBC connection localserver.

Setting Other Recordset Properties before Using Open

If you don't want to accept the default Recordset, you'll have to set some properties using Open method arguments or by setting Properties before the Open method is executed. These control how, where, and when Cursors are created, how ADO handles concurrency issues, how data binding is handled, and how much data is fetched.

The Source Property

The SQL query you want to execute can be placed in the Source property before you use the Open method or can be found there afterwards. That is, if you execute a query using the Recordset.Open method and pass in the SQL to execute as a method argument, the Source property is populated by ADO from the method argument. Because you're working with a Recordset, ADO assumes that the query returns a rowset that will be exposed as an ADO Recordset object, so using action query commands in the Source property (or the Open method's Source argument) does not make sense.

ADO does not care what you put in the Source. It simply passes this through to the data provider as a string to be processed. The data provider might think your query's syntax is incorrect or it might fail to run it as expected for a bazillion other reasons.

We give ADO a hint about what's in the Source argument by setting the CommandType property or by using the Options argument in the Open method. This helps ADO determine whether the Source argument is a SQL command (adCmdText), the name of a table (adCmdTable), the name of a stored procedure (adCmdStoredProc), or a letter to your mom (adCmdUnknown). No single property does more to determine how scalable or fast your application or component is than the Source. It's critical that you make sure you're using the most efficient query possible. I revisit this property repeatedly in this book; for more information review the "Development Strategies" section earlier in this chapter.

Here's a simple example of how you can code the Recordset Open method using a preset Source property:

```
With rs
    .CursorLocation = adUseClient
    .Source = "select author, title from titles t, title_author ta, authors a"_
        "where a.au_id=ta.au_id and t.isbn=ta.isbn order by t.type"
    .Open , cn, adOpenStatic, adLockOptimistic, Options:=adcmdText
End With
```

> **TIP** *If your query or code has to reference table or field names with embedded spaces, enclose the names in brackets.*

```
rs.Open "Select [long field name] from [long table name] ", cn
Debug.Print rs(0).Name
Do Until rs.EOF
    Debug.Print rs("long field name")
        ' No, I don't approve of this technique
    rs.MoveNext
Loop
```

The CursorLocation Property

We discussed the CursorLocation property in Chapter 4, which discussed Connection objects (see the "Setting the CursorLocation Property" section). Each

Recordset you create inherits the CursorLocation from the Command object associated with it, and yes, you can change it after the Connection is open. Of course, if your Recordset Open method opens a *new* connection, creating a new Connection object in the process, the new Connection object's CursorLocation is set from the Recordset CursorLocation property. Make sense?

The CursorType Property

The CursorType property tells ADO how to manage and update the rows returned to your Recordset. The default Recordset behavior is a cursorless (RO/FO) result set, so if you want ADO to manage updates, concurrency, and scrollability, you have to choose an appropriate CursorType.

ADO has a number of limitations on the type and complexity of the cursors its providers can create, based on where the cursors are created. For example, client-side cursors (CursorLocation set to adUseClient) only support Static cursors (adOpenStatic), regardless of what you set the CursorType to. This is expected because, according to the ADO specification, if you set the CursorType to an unsupported value, the closest supported CursorType is used instead—ADO changes the CursorType property to reflect the type of cursor supported by the provider.[6] So, if a provider does not support the requested cursor type, the provider returns a similar type that it *does* support. If a different cursor type is returned, the CursorType property temporarily changes to match the *actual* cursor type in use once the Recordset object is open. After you close the Recordset, the CursorType property reverts to its original setting. Confusing?

So, how do you know what's supported by your provider? It's easy. Use the Supports method to determine whether the provider knows how to support specific functions with the returned cursor. For each of the cursor types in the following list to be supported by the provider, the Supports method must return True for all of the Supports method constants that follow:

- **adOpenKeyset:** adBookmark, adHoldRecords, adMovePrevious, adResync

- **adOpenDynamic:** adMovePrevious

- **adOpenStatic:** adBookmark, adHoldRecords, adMovePrevious, adResync

- **adOpenForwardOnly:** none

---

6. I wrote a program to construct all of the cursor types using the ODBC, native SQL Server, and native Jet 4.0 providers. The program and a table constructed from the results are provided on the CD and in the Appendix.

> **NOTE** *Although Supports(adUpdateBatch) might be True for Dynamic and Forward-only cursors, you should use either a Keyset or Static cursor for batch updates. Set the LockType property to adLockBatchOptimistic and the CursorLocation property to adUseClient to enable the Cursor Service for OLE DB, which is required for batch updates.*

So, what's the difference between the various types of cursors? Let's look at each in turn.

adOpenForwardOnly

The adOpenForwardOnly cursor is the default CursorType. In a FO cursor, database rows are fetched serially—basically, one at a time from the data source (but in CacheSize groups, at the provider level). As with a Static cursor, the actual data rows are fetched, but with a FO cursor, you can't reposition the current row pointer in any direction except forward (thus forward-only), and only one row at a time. Some providers simply reexecute the query and start over if you attempt to reposition to the first row. You can use the GetRows or GetString method against FO cursors to fetch all of the rows in a single operation.

FO cursors have a fixed membership. That is, rows added to the database after the cache is constructed are not returned as Recordset members. Changes (additions, updates, and deletions) made to the database after the cursor is populated are not reflected in the membership. Changes made to the Recordset by your client affect the locally cached membership and can be posted to the database—depending on the updatability of the Recordset.

Client-side cursor providers do not support FO cursors.

adOpenStatic

For adOpenStatic cursors, as with FO cursors, ADO copies database records into client Static cursor memory in CacheSize groups. However, Static cursors are fully scrollable. That is, after the Recordset is open, you can use any of the Move methods to reposition the current record pointer to any row in the result set.

Static is the *only* type of cursor supported by the client-side cursor location providers. It is also supported on server-side providers.

adOpenKeyset

The adOpenKeyset option generates a Keyset cursor. In this case, ADO copies only enough key information to the cursor for ADO to fetch specific records based on a WHERE clause generated from the key. Keyset cursors are fully scrollable and updatable. Most server-side providers support Keyset cursors.

> **NOTE** *Sybase drivers don't support Keyset or Dynamic cursors—only Static cursors are supported.*

adOpenDynamic

The adOpenDynamic option generates Dynamic cursors that behave very much like Keyset cursors, except for dynamic membership (discussed next). They are fully scrollable but do not support Bookmark positioning. This type of cursor is not supported on more complex result sets. For example, a three-table join prohibits creation of a Dynamic cursor.

If you want to order a Dynamic cursor, you have to do so with an existing index—the data provider can't reorder using an on-the-fly sort because it uses TempDB in a rather non-dynamic way.

Examining Recordset Properties after Opening

When you set a Recordset property and use the Open method, ADO passes these properties along as parameters to low-level OLE DB calls to the data providers. However, the provider might not be capable of implementing the requested option. In this case (and it's pretty typical), the provider usually does not complain (unless it's had a bad day); instead, it substitutes a supportable alternative. These "corrections" are applied to the Recordset properties after the Open method returns the Recordset. If you want to know what was implemented, check the property after opening the Recordset.

For example, if you ask for a Dynamic (adOpenDynamic) CursorType and the provider can't implement this type of cursor (many can't), it might substitute a Keyset cursor instead. In this case, the Recordset object's CursorType property is set to adOpenKeyset after the open. No, a trappable error is not (generally) tripped in this case. However, if you set the CursorType in the Recordset *property* before opening the cursor, ADO opens whatever cursor it can, based on the provider's capability, and when the Recordset is subsequently closed, the Recordset CursorType property reverts back to the original value.

Using the Supports Method

There are a number of ways to see how ADO constructed the Recordset you requested through the Recordset properties or Open method arguments:

- Inspect the individual Recordset properties after opening the Recordset.

- Inspect the Recordset Properties collection. These properties are referenced (only) by name. The number of properties and their names vary somewhat from provider to provider. I discuss a number of the most interesting Property objects when I discuss situations where they are needed.

- Use the Recordset Supports method. In this case, ADO exposes a number of clearly defined enumerations that the provider returns as Boolean values. For example, you can ask the provider if the Recordset "supports" updatability or scrollability.

The Supports method accepts the ADO cursor option enumerations shown in Table 6-2 and in Table 6-3. The first set of enumerations (Table 6-2) helps determine how the Recordset will handles changes. For example, you can see if the Recordset is updatable (adAddNew or adUpdate) or supports optimistic batch updates (adUpdateBatch).

CONSTANT	VALUE	DESCRIPTION
adAddNew	0x1000400	Supports the AddNew method to add new records.
adUpdate	0x1008000	Supports the Update method to modify existing data.
adDelete	0x1000800	Supports the Delete method to delete records.
adUpdateBatch	0x10000	Supports batch updating (UpdateBatch and CancelBatch methods) to transmit groups of changes to the provider.
adResync	0x20000	Supports the Resync method to update the cursor with the data that is visible in the underlying database.
adHoldRecords	0x100	Retrieves more records or changes the next position without committing all pending changes.
adNotify	0x40000	Indicates that the underlying data provider supports notifications (which determines whether Recordset events are supported).

Table 6-2: Determining what data modification features your provider "supports" using Supports method constants

The next set of enumerations (Table 6-3) lists the supported scrolling and repositioning features.

CONSTANT	VALUE	DESCRIPTION
adApproxPosition	0x4000	Supports the AbsolutePosition and AbsolutePage properties.
adBookmark	0x2000	Supports the Bookmark property to gain access to specific records.
adFind	0x80000	Supports the Find method to locate a row in a Recordset.
adIndex	0x100000	Supports the Index property to name an index.
adMovePrevious	0x200	Supports the MoveFirst and MovePrevious methods, and Move or GetRows methods, to move the current record position backward without requiring bookmarks.
adSeek	0x200000	Supports the Seek method to locate a row in a Recordset.

Table 6-3: Determining what scrolling and positioning features your provider "supports" using Supports method constants

In the next few pages, I illustrate how to use the Supports method in several useful ways.

Using the Recordset Clone Method

If you want to maintain a separate copy of your Recordset, you can use the Clone method. This technique is used to create multiple, duplicate Recordset objects and is especially valuable when you want to maintain more than one current record in a given set of records. Using the Clone method is more efficient than creating and opening a new Recordset object with the same definition as the original. The current record of a newly created clone is set to the first record.

Changes you make to one Recordset object are visible in all of its clones, regardless of cursor type. However, after you execute Requery on the original Recordset, the clones are no longer synchronized with the original. Closing the original Recordset does not close its copies, nor does closing a copy close the original or any of the other copies.

You can only clone a Recordset object that supports bookmarks. (See the preceding discussion, "Using the Supports Method.") Bookmark values are interchangeable; that is, a bookmark reference from one Recordset object refers to the same record in any of its clones.

Using the Recordset Close Method

You use the Close method to release the Recordset object's result set. This does not destroy the object, but clears out any pending fetches that might still be going on. You won't be able to close the Recordset if there are pending Update operations. In this case, use the Cancel or CancelUpdate method to clear these out before trying to use the Close method. You also won't be able to use the Close method if the Recordset is already closed or when the Recordset is set to Nothing. Closing the Recordset changes its State property from adStateOpen to adStateClosed.

> **TIP**   *If you're trying to fetch the Return status integer or OUTPUT parameters from a stored procedure, you have to use the Close method before referencing the Command object.*

Managing Cursor Membership

Any time you execute a query that includes a SELECT statement, ADO knows that you're going to need a Recordset to manage the rowset returned from the provider. Remember, the default configuration is a firehose (RO/FO, CacheSize=1) cursorless Recordset. Every layer of the data-access interface treats firehose Recordsets differently—they bypass virtually all of the routines needed to provide updatability, scrollability, and caching. On the other hand, if you need to create a true cursor to support scrollability, updatability, or caching, ADO fires up a number of routines to make it happen.

When the data provider receives a SELECT query to execute, it searches for rows that qualify based on the query's WHERE clause. If you create a cursor against a table, all of the rows currently in the table qualify as members. As qualifying rows are located, they are frozen in time using a "share" lock to prevent updates from changing them before the row can be copied to the client. This means an entire table can be locked while its rows are fetched in CacheSize sets. In more recent versions of SQL Server and Jet, the query processor might lock individual rows instead of the entire page where the row is stored. However, as the number of rows involved increases, the chances that the query optimizer (QO) will escalate locks to higher granularity increases—to the point where the entire table is share locked.

As the client accepts rows by populating its cursor or result set, the share locks are gradually released. The last locks are released as the last qualifying row is sent to the client, and not until then. Delaying rowset population can impede other database operations. While other clients can fetch rows with share locks, no client is permitted to change rows while share locks are in place on the row, page, or table. These clients are blocked for CommandTimeout seconds, waiting for the locks to be released.

As the server passes through the result set looking for qualifying rows, the query processor adds any rows it locates to the result set membership list. After the process has begun, if a row is added to the database that would have qualified, but the server has passed where it would have fit in the result set order, the row is not included as a member. However, if a row is added to the database in time to qualify in its correct place, it is added to the Recordset.

After the process of locating the qualifying rows is complete, the membership is frozen for Static and Keyset cursors. This means that rows added to or deleted from the *database* by other users are not reflected in the frozen cursor membership. Changes to your Recordset are saved in your client's Recordset cache and in the database, if you aren't using batch mode. However, other frozen cursors do not see these changes—not even other Recordsets in your own client. That is, if another user has opened and populated (frozen) a cursor containing the same rows, they won't see your changes until they reference the specific row again. Because Static cursors do not refetch from the server to get the most current data, they won't see your changes at all.

> **NOTE** *All client-side cursors are Static. You have to use server-side cursors to get the providers to implement Keyset, Forward-only, or Dynamic cursors.*

Rows are fetched in CacheSize sets, so cached rows have a tendency to lose currency with the membership in a rapidly changing database. That is, rows in the cache might include rows deleted from the database and would not include rows added after the cursor was opened.

For Dynamic cursors, Recordset membership is never frozen because the query is reexecuted each time a new CacheSize set of rows is required, making it very costly to implement and maintain Dynamic cursors.

> **IMHO** *IMHO cursors are fundamentally **evil**. They cause more problems than any other single feature of ADO (or DAO and RDO, for that matter). Generally, this is because cursors are created incorrectly, either with too many rows or with options that only degrade system scalability and performance.*

Recordset Row Order

I saw an interesting comment on one list I monitor that made me realize that some people don't know the order in which rows are returned to the client. Remember that the DBMS writes new rows to a table in the order in which they are written, unless you define a clustered index for the table. When it comes time to return the rows, unless you specifically sort the result set using an ORDER BY clause, Recordset rows are returned in the order they are located in the table.

If you told the DBMS to create a clustered index, the physical order in the DBMS table would be determined by that index. However, an "ordinary" (nonclustered) index does not affect how rows are stored in the table—simply how they are retrieved. When the QO builds a query plan to fetch rows to satisfy your query request, the QO might (just might) use one of the indexes to fetch the rows if it makes sense. For example, if you fetch too many rows, the QO might decide that navigating the tables through the indexes is more expensive than simply dumping rows from the table. If you just access an indexed table, the order should be based on that index, or on the clustered index, if you have specified one. But fetching rows based on a join (without an ORDER BY clause) can result in rows being returned in pseudo-random order.

When you add rows to your Recordset, the rows are added to the membership and appear at the *end* of the Recordset—not necessarily where the rows would fit in a sorted order, regardless of any clustered or "ordinary" indexes. Once you refresh your Recordset (reexecute the query), the newly added rows will appear in the correct sequence.

Managing the Recordset Cache Size

When ADO goes out for data from the provider, it does not come back until its bucket is full or until the data can all be fetched at once. You can change the size of that bucket by changing the CacheSize property. This value specifies how many rows are to be managed in the in-memory cache buffer. That is, the providers fetch CacheSize rows from the data source into memory before returning to ADO and your program. This makes ADO and the data provider more efficient.

However, ADO's default CacheSize setting is 1, which would seem to fly in the face of efficient data transfers. But the characteristics of the firehose cursor (FO/RO/CacheSize=1) cause the data provider to bypass ADO's cursor management schemes that take advantage of cache management; thus, the CacheSize setting of 1 has no role in the fetch operation.

> **TIP** *Your application is blocked (frozen) while the first CacheSize rows are fetched—even if you execute asynchronously. If the server spends considerable time filling the cache, you might consider using a smaller CacheSize setting and asynchronous queries to keep from blocking your application.*

As you move the current row pointer through the Recordset object, the provider returns the data from the local memory buffer. As soon as you move past the last record in the memory cache, the provider retrieves the next CacheSize records from the data source into the cache. If there are fewer than CacheSize records to retrieve, the provider returns the remaining records. If you position to rows previously fetched but no longer in the cache, the provider might have to refetch rows from the server, depending on whether you're using client-side or server-side cursors.

The CacheSize can be adjusted during the life of the Recordset object, but changing this value only affects the number of records in the cache for subsequent retrievals from the data source. Changing CacheSize does not change the current contents of the cache.

Records retrieved from the cache don't reflect concurrent changes that other users made to the source data. That is, if another user in the database deletes a cached row, you won't know until you try to refresh this row from the source table. To force an update of all the cached data, use the Resync method.

Tuning CacheSize

There have been a number of questions on the lists I monitor (internally and externally at Microsoft) concerning how ADO caches rows fetched from the database. When building a client-side cursor (not the default behavior), ADO caches as many rows as the client system can hold. Once the cache is full, the overflow is written to disk. This means that if you are using client-side cursors, after ADO exhausts allocated RAM, it will fill all available disk space on the drive accessed through the \TEMP environment variable.

Frankly, if you are fetching enough rows to fill your disk, you have already made a fundamental mistake. Adjusting the CacheSize property has no effect on this behavior because ADO uses the Recordset CacheSize property to determine the number of rows to fetch and cache from the data provider. While the currently requested row pointer is within the range of cached rows, ADO and the provider just return data from the cache. When you scroll out of the range of cached rows, the cache is released when the next CacheSize rows is fetched. So what CacheSize should you use in your application?

Unfortunately, there isn't a single optimal CacheSize that is appropriate for all applications. You should tune your application with different CacheSize values and use the one that offers the best performance. Using a small CacheSize value significantly improves performance for fetching data from an Oracle data store. Many ADO gurus recommend just leaving the CacheSize set to its default value: 1.

> **TIP** *You can use the Resync method to flush and refresh the cache.*

Setting the MaxRecords Property

Whenever you fetch rows, your query's WHERE clause should limit the scope of the query to a manageable number. However, you can't always predict how many rows will return. The ADO MaxRecords property can play an important role in limiting the size of result sets as well as the time it takes to fetch them. MaxRecords simply tells ADO to stop fetching rows once *n* rows have arrived. There might be more rows that qualify, based on your SELECT statement, but no more than MaxRecords will be fetched from the data provider. In some cases, ADO simply passes the MaxRecords value to the provider, so it limits the number of rows to fetch. For example, setting MaxRecords to a nonzero value (e.g., 10) adds the following statement to your query (at least when using the SQL Server data provider):

```
SET ROWCOUNT 10
```

> **NOTE** *The Jet providers do not recognize the MaxRecords property. The MDAC team recommends that you add a TOP clause to your SELECT statement to limit the number of rows returned.*

Using Cached Data Pages

Not only does ADO manage the physical transportation of data rows from the provider to the client data cache, it also can break up the cache into *logical* groups, that is, pages. You determine the logical page size by setting the Recordset PageSize property. The PageCount property then returns the number of pages in the Recordset. It's computed by dividing the number of rows by PageSize. If your provider does not support the PageSize property, ADO returns –1 for PageSize.

After you set up the PageSize, you can use the AbsolutePage property (1-based) to reposition the current row pointer to a specific set of rows—*n* pages into the result set. Cool? Well, almost.

What we *really* need is logical page management deeper in the query-generation process. The current implementation of logical pages assumes the cursor (evil) is so large (double evil) that your client will want to fetch it in logical sets. That is, for this technology to work, your Recordset has to be large enough to page. This means that the query processor on the server has constructed this large result set and has started sending it to the client. I think a better approach is to have the server's query processor locate the *nth* page of qualifying data rows. Perhaps in a later version of SQL Server.

Using the Resync Method

Suppose you just added to or updated your Recordset, or you simply want to make sure the data in your Recordset contains the most current information for the current row. Or perhaps you find that records retrieved from the cache don't reflect concurrent changes that other users made to the source data. To force an update of all the cached data, use the Resync method. The Resync method is also useful if you are using either a Static or Forward-only cursor, but you want to see changes in the underlying database. (With Keyset cursors, as you position to specific rows in the result set, ADO refetches current information from the database or the cache. Static and Forward-only cursors don't attempt to keep in sync with the database.)

Unlike the Requery method, the Resync method does not reexecute the Recordset object's underlying command. New records in the underlying database are not visible, so the Recordset membership is unchanged. If the attempt to resynchronize fails because of a conflict with the underlying data (for example, a record has been deleted by another user), the provider returns warnings to the Errors collection and a runtime error occurs. Use the Filter property (adFilterConflictingRecords) and the Status property to locate records with conflicts. Resync is only available for updatable (non-RO) Recordset objects with client-side cursors.

> **NOTE** *Support for the Resync method on server-side cursors was dropped after ADO 1.5. Resync is only available for client-side cursors on ADO 2.0 and later.*

If the Unique Table and Resync Command dynamic properties are set, and the Recordset is the result of executing a JOIN operation on multiple tables, the Resync method will execute the command given in the Resync Command property only on the table named in the Unique Table property. Table 6-4 shows how you can modify the Resync method behavior using the optional arguments.

CONSTANT	DESCRIPTION
adResyncAllValues	Default. Overwrites client-side Value property data and pending updates are canceled.
adResyncUnderlyingValues	Does not overwrite client-side Value property data and pending updates are not canceled.

Table 6-4: Resync method optional arguments

Managing the Current Row

When you run a query that returns a rowset, ADO constructs a Recordset to manage it—even if there are no qualifying rows. That is, a SELECT statement might return no qualifying rows, but ADO still constructs a Recordset to manage the rowset. However, there are a number of situations unique to ADO that you should be aware of. For example, many of the status properties of ADO can't be tested *unless* the Recordset contains rows, and then they can be tested only if the current row pointer is addressing one of these rows.

The following routine simply tries to test to determine whether an edit is in progress. Because the routine cannot be sure that a valid Recordset exists when it begins, it has to jump through a number of hoops before testing the EditMode property. This was simpler in DAO or RDO.

First, we test to determine whether the Recordset object even exists, by testing it for Nothing. Note that this syntax won't work if you declared your Recordset object variable (rs) using the Dim rs as New Recordset technique.

```
Private Sub cmdSearch_Click()
If rs Is Nothing Then
```

Next, because we know that the Recordset exists, we test the State property to make sure the Recordset is open—we can't test the EOF or BOF properties until the Recordset exists and is open. Note use of positive instead of double-negative logic here. It's a lot less confusing for old eyes.

```
ElseIf rs.State = adStateOpen Then
    If rs.EOF Or rs.BOF Then
```

Okay, we know that the Recordset object exists and that it's open and not at EOF (or BOF). Now we can test the EditMode property. Whew!

```
ElseIf rs.EditMode = adEditInProgress Then …
```

When working with Recordset objects, you need to be prepared for the occasional empty rowset and other invalid current row situations. This means you might have a Recordset object variable point to:

- A Recordset set to Nothing

- A closed Recordset—its State property is adStateClosed

- An open Recordset, but have the current row positioned beyond the data rows (either side of BOF or EOF)

- A deleted row—either you or another user deleted the row

It's up to your code to manage the current row pointer (CRP); and ADO makes it fairly easy to do. You can move the CRP using any of these techniques:

- Use the Move methods—MoveNext and MovePrevious to move forward or backward one row; MoveLast and MoveFirst to move the CRP to the last or first row of the Recordset. There is also a Move method to move forward or backward *n* rows.

> **TIP** *Once you are positioned at BOF, using MovePrevious causes a trappable error, just like using MoveNext when EOF is true. If you permit your users to navigate through a Recordset, be sure to code the error traps to prevent errors associated with navigating off the ends of your Recordset.*

- Use the BookMark property to save a CRP and reset it later.

- Use the AbsolutePosition property to move to the *nth* row of the *populated* Recordset—but only on client-side cursors.

- Add a new row to the Recordset using the AddNew method. This moves the CRP to the last row in the Recordset. The row is added to the target table in the appropriate sequence, as determined by the data source indexes.

- Use the CancelUpdate method after using AddNew. This moves the CRP to the CRP setting before the AddNew operation. For example, if the CRP is at row 10 of 15 and you add a new row, the CRP is moved to row 16 (to the new row). CancelUpdate returns the CRP to row 10.

Managing Recordset Inserts

Adding rows to an existing Recordset implies that when the Recordset is persisted, these new rows should become part of the existing data store. This might mean that ADO will write the row to a specific table, or that it will simply add the row to a memory-resident Recordset that's persisted to a file, XML, binary stream, or other data store. No, ADO won't update or add data to more than one table at a time, so if the query is the result of a join, you have to be careful about which columns you change, how you construct new rows, and how ADO deals with these changes on the data provider.

To get ADO to add a new row to your cursor, simply use the Recordset's AddNew method. This method creates an empty Recordset (with no Value properties set). After it is created, you can address the individual Field object values, one by one. Another (faster) approach is to pass the new Field values in a Variant array to apply to the Field values. ADO is different than DAO and RDO when it comes to the AddNew and Update methods. In these older technologies, you had to use the Update method to persist the new row or other changes to the Recordset—if you moved off the row, you lost the changes. ADO takes a radically different approach—you have to purposefully cancel the changes if you don't want ADO to save new or changed rows to the Recordset and the database. If you move the CPR to another row, or close the Recordset, the effect is the same as using the Update method. This means that if your user changes his or her mind, you have to use the Cancel or CancelBatch method to flush the current row's changes or all changes made to the batch.

The following example shows the use of this Variant array technique. Sure, you can reference the individual Recordset Field objects one-by-one to fill in the Value properties, but the Variant array technique seems awfully easy—and the engineers tell me it's faster.

```
Option Explicit
Dim cn As Connection
Dim cmd As Command
Dim rs As Recordset
Dim varFields As Variant
Dim varValues As Variant

Private Sub Form_Load()
On Error GoTo FLEH
```

```
Set cn = New Connection
cn.Open "dsn=localserver", "admin", "pw"
```

The following code opens the Recordset with the intent to simply add rows, so only the DDL information is fetched, not any rows.

```
Set rs = New Recordset
rs.Open "Select Title,type,price,pubid, ISBN from titles where 1=0", _
    cn, adOpenKeyset, adLockOptimistic, adCmdText
```

In the code shown next, we fill in the two Variant arrays used to pass in the Field names and Values. Don't worry about putting quotes around the numbers—Visual Basic and ADO coerce these to the right datatypes when moving the values into the arguments sent to the data provider. ADO uses these arguments to construct an update cursor statement. ADO does not use a constructed INSERT statement for this operation—it uses the sp_cursor ADO system stored procedure.

```
varFields = Array("Title", "type", "price", "pubid", "ISBN")
varValues = Array("New title", "MI", 90.99, 90, "bogus")
```

Okay, now we're ready to add the first new row. We could get an error here (before the Update) if there is a collision with the primary key or if the Field values don't match the Field property constraints.

```
rs.AddNew varFields, varValues
rs.Update
```

Next, we add two more rows using the same technique, but we'll try to fool ADO with incorrectly formatted values. ADO rejects this next AddNew because the price is not a number.

```
varValues = Array("Another New title", "MI", "bad", 90, "bogus2")
rs.AddNew varFields, varValues
rs.Update
```

The next row will be rejected as well; the Type column is constrained in the database with a foreign key. It has to match one of the known ValidTitleTypes table entries—it doesn't.

```
varValues = Array("A third New title", "XX", "-86", 90, "bogus3")
rs.AddNew varFields, varValues
rs.Update
rs.Close
```

Next, we clean up the mess we made in the Titles table by deleting any of the bogus ISBN rows. We can make sure this does not affect more than the single row that actually worked by wrapping the whole operation in a transaction. We could have wrapped the whole set of AddNew operations in a transaction, but that would have confused what you saw in the Profiler—assuming you were watching.

```
cn.BeginTrans
cn.Execute "Delete titles where ISBN like 'bogus%'", intRecordsAffected
If intRecordsAffected > 3 Then
    cn.RollbackTrans
    MsgBox "Nope, something went wrong with the delete!"
Else
    cn.CommitTrans
End If
rs.Close
Quit:
    Exit Sub
FLEH:
    Debug.Print Err.Number, Err.Description
    Select Case Err
        Case -2147217873 ' Violation of PRIMARY KEY constraint 'aaaaaTitles_PK'.
        'Cannot insert duplicate key in object 'Titles'.
            ' or ... [Microsoft][ODBC SQL Server Driver][SQL Server]INSERT
            'statement conflicted with COLUMN FOREIGN KEY constraint
            'FK_Titles_ValidTitleTypes'. The conflict occurred in database
            'biblio', table 'ValidTitleTypes', column 'Type'.
            MsgBox "Can't insert a duplicate row into titles table " _
            & or invalid title type. "
            & Mid(Err.Description, InStrRev(Err.Description, "]") + 1)

            rs.CancelUpdate
            Resume Next
        Case -2147352571 'Type mismatch.
            MsgBox "Field type(s) not correct."
             rs.CancelUpdate
            Resume Next
        Case 3219, 3704: Resume Next
        Case Else
            Stop
            Resume
    End Select
End Sub
```

> **NOTE** *Note that the Error.Number returned is the same for a Primary key violation (when a duplicate record already exists) as for when the primary key/foreign key is incorrect. You have to parse the string to figure out which occurred. Remember that these error messages are translated to French, German, Spanish, and a bunch of other languages, so this might be an issue for those trying to create an application that might have to run on a number of localized ADO platforms.*

Working with System-Generated Primary Keys

Adding rows to a Recordset is almost as easy as Updating existing rows. In this case, the collisions can occur because other clients have added rows with the same primary key (PK). Using a system-generated primary key easily prevents this. SQL Server, Jet, and Oracle all have ways to do this using columns defined as Identity, AutoNumber, and so forth. For more information on SQL Server Identity columns, look up "Auto-Numbering and Identifier Columns" in MSDN.

There are a couple of best practice approaches for adding records that you need to consider when handling system-generated primary keys. First, you need to decide whether the generated keys must be unique on a single server or across an indeterminate number of servers. If it's the latter, you'll need to define the table column to use a GUID instead of an integer. This guarantees that the key is unique regardless of where or when it is created. What's cool about the GUID technology is that GUIDs can be traced back to their origin—conventional identity integers can't.

After you've chosen a unique row identifier strategy, you need to figure out how to retrieve this new system-generated PK after new rows are added. If you use Recordset cursors, consider using the Resync method to get the latest identity value for the new row. ADO can do this automatically if you set the right arguments on the Update Resync property. Remember that new rows are always added to the end of your Recordset, regardless of their correct order in the Recordset membership. Using the Resync method does not affect the order of the rows in the database or the Recordset.

If you use a SQL Server stored procedure to do the INSERT, the procedure can return the new identity value by using the @@IDENTITY global variable—assuming that no other INSERT statement reset the value. Remember that the TSQL RETURN function can only return an Integer—not a GUID—so you have to use an OUTPUT parameter to return the latest GUID value.

However, this approach is also dangerous. If the stored procedure maintains referential integrity by adding rows to other tables, the @@IDENTITY value is reset by any operation that adds a row to a table *with or without* an Identity column. For instance, suppose your stored procedure adds a row to Table1 using a TSQL INSERT statement. In turn, the INSERT Trigger on Table1 might add a row to Table2, which also has a system-generated identity value. This second identity value is applied to the current @@IDENTITY value. If the second table had no identity column, SQL Server would have set @@IDENTITY to zero.

> **TIP**   *One of the problems here is that ADO can't find the new row in the database because it does not have its primary key and won't have it until the cursor is rebuilt. That is, when you add a row and the system generates the PK, it's recorded in the database table, but not in the cursor. That's because ADO simply uses an INSERT statement to add the row, and there is no built-in mechanism to return the new row's PK.*

The problem here is that you want to be able to reference newly added rows (new customers or new order items, for example) at the client without having to completely requery the database, which is always an option. That is, the newly added rows are fully populated on the server, including the new PK values. In the 1960s, when my hair was longer and my pockets emptier, I tried to sell Electrolux vacuum cleaners door-to-door. While I only sold one (to my mother), I did meet some nice people who simply couldn't afford to buy the machine and I didn't have the heart to con them into it. But I digress. In the process of selling these machines, I used a preprinted multipart sales book. Each page of the book had a number, and no other salesperson (there were no PC "sales people" back then) had the same set of numbers. When sales were completed, the customer got one copy of the form and I submitted the carbon to the home office to be filled. All further references were made with that unique customer number. I'm sure you've used similar forms in your office for expense accounts or other office automation operations.

Okay, so how does this apply to your problem? Well, what if you followed the same practice with your applications? What if your application for managing customers, orders, and order items created empty customer records ahead of time, along with empty order and order item records? When it came time to add a new customer, all you would do is update an existing customer record that was preassigned to your application, and do the same for the orders and items. The downside here is that the database would be stretched somewhat by empty records. But this need not be a problem if you use VarChar datatypes that start out small and stretch to accommodate new data rows. You would also not have to worry about collisions. The empty customer records already "belong" to your application, and no other application has the right to alter them—at least not until they are populated the first time. When you run out of empty records, you simply execute a procedure that returns another set. You can also use a status field to show whether or not the customer is empty.

Managing Recordset Updates

There always seems to be any number of ways to accomplish your goals. Some are faster, some easier, some illegal. Using ADO to update your database is no exception—while some approaches are kinda silly, most aren't illegal (except in parts of Cleveland). You have (at least) these options:

- Create an updatable cursor using one of the valid LockType settings.

- Create a stored procedure to perform updates to one or more tables.

- Code a Command object that executes an Update statement.

- Hard-code an SQL statement that executes an Update statement.

While you can't always use all of these options, you usually have several to choose from. However, you'll find it a little tricky using two or more techniques at the same time. For example, suppose you use an updatable cursor to fetch a row, and try to use a stored procedure or UPDATE statement to perform the update. You'll discover that the Recordset can block your own UPDATE.

To illustrate the sum of the Update techniques, I wrote a rather long example program (see ...Recordset Objects\Updating\Handling Errors on the CD). Let's step through some of the code. While some of the concepts have not been discussed yet, the code raises some interesting points that are clarified later in this chapter.

Walking Through the Update Example Application

The example application illustrates *basic* update error handling and permits you to simulate multiple users and how their interaction either blocks or permits updates. Once the application is started, the connection is opened in Form_Load and the valid ISBN list is populated. At this point, you need to select an ISBN from the ISBN Wanted drop-down list and click Fetch. The row matching the selected ISBN will be displayed in the Fetch frame. After a few seconds, a background event fires and uses the Resync method to fetch the database state of the row to show what changes other users have made. If another instance of the application (or another application, for that matter) changes the row, the lower "Underling" frame reports this activity. The application determines whether a row has changed by examining the TimeStamp field. Comparing TimeStamp datatyped columns proved to be a little harder than I anticipated.

You can select the CursorLocation (server or client) and the LockType (Optimistic or Pessimistic) by using the option buttons. If you choose Pessimistic locking, the application enables a slider bar to let you specify how long to wait before the application releases the row being edited. This is done with a "watchdog" timer routine that is enabled when the fetch is executed. A progress bar reminds you how much time is left to complete the change.

When you have made a change to the row in the Fetch data frame, you need to click either the Update or Cursor Update buttons—or Abandon Change. These buttons work as follows:

- Update—runs an ADO Command to perform an update on the fetched row. This routine cancels the pending update, closes the updatable Recordset, and executes the UPDATE statement through the Command object. If you don't close the updatable Recordset, the Update command (in Pessimistic mode) can't update the row. (Technically, they are two separate transactions because they happen on separate connections, so the Command UPDATE will have to wait until the cursor releases its locks.)

- Cursor Update—simply uses the Recordset Update method.

- Abandon Change—undoes the change to the row and releases the fetched row in Pessimistic mode.

Let's look at the code. First, notice that I manage the TimeStamp columns in Variants. I tried both Byte arrays and Variants, and settled on Variants, but both worked equally well.

```
Dim varTimeStamp As Variant
Dim varTimeStampDB As Variant
```

The Form_Load event sets up two Command objects, as well as a couple of Recordset objects to be used later. The first, shown next, is a simple parameter query that returns a single row from the Titles table based on a specific ISBN.[7]

---

7. The International Standard Book Number (ISBN) is a unique number, assigned in blocks to publishers who assign individual numbers to their books, CDs, and other publications.

```
...
With cmdSelect
    .Name = "TitleByISBN"
    .CommandText = "Select Title, Year_Published, ISBN, TimeStamp" _
        & " from Newtitles where ISBN = ?"
    .CommandType = adCmdText
    .Parameters.Append .CreateParameter("ISBNWanted", adVarChar, adParamInput, 20)
End With
```

The second Command object is used to submit a stand-alone UPDATE statement using the current row's Field object values as parameters.

```
With cmdUpdate
    .Name = "UpdateTitle"
    .CommandText = "Update NewTitles set Title = ?, Year_Published = ? " _
        & " Where ISBN =? and TimeStamp = ?"
    .CommandType = adCmdText
    .CommandTimeout = 5          ' Don't wait long...
    .Parameters.Append .CreateParameter("NewTitle", adVarChar, adParamInput, 255)
    .Parameters.Append .CreateParameter("Year", adSmallInt, adParamInput)
    .Parameters.Append .CreateParameter("ISBNWanted", adVarChar, adParamInput, 20)
    .Parameters.Append .CreateParameter("TimeStamp", adVarBinary, adParamInput, 8)
End With
```

The routine to open the database connection is handled outside of the Form load event to give the application an opportunity to switch between client-side and server-side cursors. This routine, shown next, also populates the drop-down ISBN list. The complete code for this routine is included in the sample on the CD.

```
Private Sub cmdOpenDB_Click()

cn.CursorLocation = intOptCursorLoc
cn.Open "provider=sqloledb;data source=(local);default catalog=biblio", "Admin", "pw"


cmdSelect.ActiveConnection = cn
cmdUpdate.ActiveConnection = cn
```

When the user clicks the Fetch Command button, the following routine executes the TitlesByISBN Command object, based on the ISBN row selected from the drop-down list of valid ISBNs. The State property determines whether there are pending edits that would be lost if the query were reexecuted.

```
Private Sub cmdFetch_Click()
tmrResync.Enabled = False

If rs.State = adStateOpen Then
    If rs.EditMode = adEditInProgress Then
        i = MsgBox("Abandon your changes? Click OK to fetch a new record.", _
        vbOKCancel, "Edit in progress...")
        If i = vbCancel Then GoTo Quit
    End If
    rs.CancelUpdate
    rs.Close
End If
```

If the LockType is set to pessimistic, we can't just fetch and sit on the row, so the application starts a watchdog timer to release it in *n* seconds.

```
If intOptLockType = adLockPessimistic Then
    tmrWatchDog.Enabled = True
    lblUpdateWarning.Caption = "Warning... less than " & sldDelay.Value _
        & " seconds to complete the change"
Else
    tmrWatchDog.Enabled = False
    lblUpdateWarning.Caption = ""
End If
```

In any case, we run the fetch Command and dump the row to the TextBox controls.[8]

```
Set rs = New Recordset
rs.LockType = intOptLockType
rs.CursorType = adOpenStatic
cn.TitleByISBN cmbISBN.Text, rs
ShowRsRow (Rows)
```

If the user changes one of the field values shown in the TextBox controls, the Validate event fires (when focus is lost). This routine, shown next, illustrates simple client-side field-level validation. Most of the emphasis here is on the Year_Published column. The client simply checks to see if the value is a number between 1900 and the current year. Note that the database rule for this database table column specifies no values outside of 1930 and 2000.

---

8. Actually, instead of a TextBox control, this application uses a custom control I wrote myself that's a combination of Label and Textbox. Yep, the source for this control is also on the CD.

To test how ADO handles rule violations, try to set the year value to 1928, which is valid as far as the client code is concerned, but invalid as far as the server-side rule is concerned. If you set up this test and click the Update button, the server returns an error to ADO. Note that a *different* error message *number* is returned when you use Update method, as opposed to the UPDATE SQL command. Both return the same error description that reports the rule and column that caused the error.

```
Private Sub ltbText_Validate(Index As Integer, Cancel As Boolean)
    Select Case Index
        Case enuTB.ISBN
            ' don't permit changes to primary key...
            Exit Sub
        Case enuTB.Title
            rs(enuTB.Title) = ltbText(Index).Text
        Case enuTB.Year
        ' Note these criteria do NOT match the DB Rule criteria
            With ltbText(enuTB.Year)
                If IsNumeric(.Text) Then
                    If .Text >= 1900 And .Text <= Format(Now, "YYYY") Then
                        Else: MsgBox "Invalid year"
```

The update routine is invoked when any Update button is clicked. It updates the row either by using a direct UPDATE command or by simply using the Update method on the Recordset.

The first routine (Case 0) executes the ADO Command object set up to execute the UPDATE SQL statement. In this case, we have to release the row held by the Recordset cursor or our UPDATE statement won't succeed—at least when we use Pessimistic cursors. This really isn't necessary for optimistic cursors. Because this technique does not support automatic Resync, we simply reexecute the single-row query.

```
Private Sub cmdUpdateButton_Click(Index As Integer)
On Error GoTo cmdUEH
Select Case Index
    Case 0                ' Update Command
        rs.CancelUpdate     ' The rs is holding the row
        rs.Close
        cmdUpdate.Execute intRecsAffected, Array(ltbText(enuTB.Title).Text, _
                ltbText(enuTB.Year).Text, _
                ltbText(enuTB.ISBN).Text, _
                varTimeStamp), adExecuteNoRecords
    '   Update sucessful...
        cmdFetch = True        ' Refetch the row (including the TimeStamp)
```

The second routine (Case 1) simply updates the Recordset using the Update method. If the Recordset object supports the Resync method, we activate it before the update. This saves us from doing extra work later to fetch the rows.

```
    Case 1                ' Recordset Update method
        If rs.Supports(adResync)
        Then rs.Properties("Update Resync") = adResyncUpdates
        rs.Update
        ShowRsRow (Rows)
    …
```

The update error handler is programmed to deal with a number of basic contingencies. An "Optimistic concurrency" failure is returned if some other user changed the row using either another application or another instance of this application.

The timeout error occurs if some other user has the row held. We set the CommandTimeout to five seconds, so this error occurs rather quickly—perhaps too quickly for the backend to resolve multiple update and select hits on the same row.

The two cases of error numbers (Err.Number) are returned if the server-side rules are violated. You will want to fully populate this error handler with other similar conditions on your own database. For example, when adding rows, you'll want to trap primary key violations or primary key/foreign key violations.

```
cmdUEH:
    Debug.Print Err, Err.Description
    Select Case Err
        Case -2147217864
            ' Optimistic concurrency check failed. The row was
            'modified outside of this cursor.
            MsgBox "Some other user has changed the record" _
            & since you fetched it. The values stored" _
            & in the database can be seen below."
            rs.CancelUpdate
            Resume Quit
        Case -2147217871 '        Timeout expired
            MsgBox "Some other user has the record locked.
            "Update did not take place.",
            vbCritical, "Update timeout."
            Resume Quit
        Case -2147217900, -2147467259
            ' A column insert or update conflicts with a rule imposed
            'by a previous CREATE RULE statement.
            MsgBox Err.Description, vbCritical, "Update failed—rule violation"
            Resume Quit
        Case 3704        ' Invalid rs state... just quit
            Resume Quit
```

Note the debug code that follows. I use this technique to stop execution of the application while it's being worked on, so I can easily insert new error case numbers and their resolutions. No, don't leave this handler in your production application.

```
        Case Else
            Stop
            Resume
    End Select
...
```

If the user chooses to abandon the update and release the row, the following routine tells ADO of the user's decision by executing the CancelUpdate method.

```
Private Sub cmdCancelUpdate_Click()
If rs.State = adStateOpen Then
    rs.CancelUpdate
    rs.Close
    ShowRsRow (Clear)
End If
cmdCancelUpdate.Enabled = False
```

```
End Sub
```

The next routine runs every few seconds to refetch the server-side values.[9] If we are using client-side cursors, we can simply use the Resync method to accomplish this. The server-side values are returned in the Field object's UnderlyingValue property. If we choose server-side cursors (CursorLocation = adUseServer), then we must run a new query with another, separate Recordset object.

```
Private Sub tmrResync_Timer()
If cn.CursorLocation = adUseClient Then          ' client-side cursors use
    Resync
    cmdFetch.Enabled = False
    ' Just bring in new underlying values
    rs.Resync adAffectCurrent, adResyncUnderlyingValues
    With rs
        If .EOF Then
            lblError.Caption = "The ISBN you are working with has been deleted by
            another user. (or ISBN has changed)"
            Beep
        Else
            ltbTextDB(enuTB.Title).Text = .Fields(enuTB.Title).UnderlyingValue
            ltbTextDB(enuTB.Year).Text = .Fields(enuTB.Year).UnderlyingValue
            ltbTextDB(enuTB.ISBN).Text = .Fields(enuTB.ISBN).UnderlyingValue
            varTimeStampDB = .Fields(enuTB.TimeStamp).UnderlyingValue
```

The routine also compares the server-side TimeStamp column with the TimeStamp fetched initially, as shown next. If they aren't the same, the database row is different (somehow) from the client-side version.

```
            If IsEmpty(varTimeStamp) Then
                ElseIf (CStr(varTimeStamp) = CStr(varTimeStampDB)) = False Then
                    lblError.Caption = "The current ISBN has been changed…"
                    Beep
                End If
            End If
        End With
```

---

9. By "server-side" I really mean the values stored in the database, wherever it is—on a server down the hall or in a database file on your system.

If we're using server-side cursors, we have to run a separate stand-alone Recordset. This Recordset is FO/RO for minimum impact and best performance.

```
Else                 ' Server-side cursors require manual requery.
    If intOptLockType = adLockPessimistic Then
    Else
        cmdFetch.Enabled = False
        If rsDB.State = adStateOpen Then rsDB.Close
        cn.TitleByISBN rs(enuTB.ISBN), rsDB
        With rsDB
            If .EOF Then
                lblError.Caption = "The ISBN has been deleted by …."
                Beep
            Else
                ltbTextDB(enuTB.Title).Text = .Fields(enuTB.Title)
                ltbTextDB(enuTB.Year).Text = .Fields(enuTB.Year)
                ltbTextDB(enuTB.ISBN).Text = .Fields(enuTB.ISBN)
                varTimeStampDB = .Fields(enuTB.TimeStamp)
                If IsEmpty(varTimeStamp) Then
                    ElseIf (CStr(varTimeStamp) = CStr(varTimeStampDB)) = False
Then
                        lblError.Caption = "The ISBN has been changed…."
                        Beep
…
```

When using pessimistic locking, the user won't be permitted to camp on the row. After the row is fetched, the user has only *n* seconds to either change it or abandon the fetch. If the user waits longer than that, the watchdog timer releases it for the user, as seen in the following code:

```
Private Sub tmrWatchDog_Timer()
Static intCount As Integer
Exit Sub
intCount = intCount + 1
If intCount > intWatchDogDelay Then
    lblUpdateWarning.Caption = "You have waited too long to change this record."
    "Changes discarded."
    Beep
    cmdCancelUpdate = True
    lblError.Caption = "Record released."
…
```

NOTE *This application fetches a single row and locks it using either optimistic or pessimistic locking. When using optimistic locking, other users are permitted to fetch and update the row; however, with pessimistic locking other users are locked out of the row (and all of the rows in the cache) as long as the cursor is open. That's why we cannot permit the user to dawdle while deciding what to change.*

Understanding Update-Related Properties

If you want ADO to manage updates for you, you have to choose the right property settings. Many of the combinations of CursorLocation, CursorType, and LockType don't yield updatable Recordsets. Even those that do might degrade to RO if the query is too complex—if ADO can't figure out how to address specific rows in the result set or the source table to be changed. Check out the chart in the Appendix, which lists all of the combinations for SQL Server (both ODBC and OLE DB providers) and Jet databases. The program that generates this chart is on the CD, so you can run the application against your own data provider.

ADO might do more than you expect, as far as update management is concerned. DAO, RDO, and ADO differ significantly in (at least) one respect. When you change a Field object's Value property in an ADO Recordset, the changes are persisted in a temporary buffer and are not written to the database. That much you know. However, in ADO, when you move the current row pointer to a new row (without using the Update or UpdateBatch method), ADO saves that changed row to the database in immediate mode[10] or commits the row to the persisted Recordset in batch mode. This means when you use MoveNext, MoveFirst, any of the other Move methods, or any other method that changes the current row position in the cursor, you trigger an update operation. The update also fires if you close the Recordset.

If you want to undo a change made to the Recordset, you can execute the Cancel or CancelUpdate methods, which backs out the changes—assuming they have not already been posted to the database.

When you execute the Update method, ADO moves the current Recordset changes from a temporary buffer to the Recordset itself. If the LockType property is set to Optimistic or Pessimistic locking, ADO submits a command to the data provider to persist the change to the database. If the LockType is set to adLockBatchOptimistic, ADO does nothing further and the database remains unaffected. If no changes are pending when you use the Update method, a

---

10. When updating with ADO, you either use Optimistic Batch updating, which defers database updates until you execute UpdateBatch, or immediate mode, which saves changes to the database immediately upon execution.

trappable error occurs. Executing the UpdateBatch method in either immediate or batch mode flushes all changes in the Recordset to the database.

Updating Newly Inserted Rows

If you insert a new row, ADO won't be able to find it to make changes or to delete it unless you set the Change Inserted Rows property to True. If this is not set, ADO reports that it has lost the cursor position for the current row.

LockType

ADO spends considerable time trying to figure out how to update your Recordset. It might even submit extra DDL queries to capture additional information about the tables involved in the query. You can alter the way ADO performs updates by setting the LockType property. By default this value is set to adLockReadOnly, which prevents ADO from worrying about updating the Recordset. That's not to say you can't construct UPDATE, DELETE, or INSERT statements on your own to execute changes, or to call a stored procedure to do so—these techniques usually are more efficient than having ADO construct the needed overhead mechanisms to manage updates.

Not all ADO providers support all lock types. If you ask for a LockType your provider doesn't support, it switches to a type that it does support. To check whether your provider can provide specific update services, check the Supports method for True settings on adUpdate and adUpdateBatch. You'll find that pessimistic locking (adLockPessimistic) is not supported on the client-side ADO data provider.

There are three locking strategies supported by ADO—four, if you count adLockReadOnly:

- **adLockBatchOptimistic:** This lock type is only available on the client-side provider. It enables deferred or batch updates.

- **adLockOptimistic:** This lock type instructs ADO to create an updatable cursor (if possible) and to handle the updates without persistent locks.

- **adLockPessimistic:** This option instructs ADO to create an updatable cursor and to lock the current CacheSize rows while changes are made.

The three locking strategies are all very different in their approach to data update management.

Batch Optimistic Updates   When using client-side cursors (CursorLocation set to adUseClient), you must set your LockType to adLockBatchOptimistic if you want ADO to manage updates for your cursor. In this case, ADO constructs a

Recordset and persists any changes that you make in the Recordset itself, but it does not send these changes to the database. When you're ready to post the changes to the database, ADO "batches" all persisted changes together and transmits them to the data provider as a block.

This approach to ADO Recordset update management was first introduced in RDO. It has been enhanced in ADO and now provides the core functionality for "disjoint" or "disconnected" Recordsets. Consider this scenario: Suppose you open a Recordset in Batch Optimistic mode using the client-side cursor provider. You can then dissociate the Recordset from the connection by setting the ActiveConnection to Nothing. At this point, the Recordset object is fully populated and is a stand-alone object. You can persist it to a file or to an XML stream and pass it to another layer. You can also update the Recordset wherever it's sent, using conventional AddNew/Update, Delete, or change/Update strategies (I discuss these a little later in this chapter). Once you reassociate the ActiveConnection to a valid connection, the UpdateBatch method can be used to post any changes made to the database. Cool? I think so.

The real point here is that depending on whether or not you use the disconnected technique, the Update method changes its behavior. That is, when you make a change to the Recordset in Batch Optimistic locking mode and use the Update method, the changes are recorded in the Recordset, but *not* sent to the database. These changes are simply made a part of the Recordset structure. When you finally use the UpdateBatch method against your Recordset, ADO gathers up all of these change requests and applies them to the source tables.

> **TIP** *In ADO 2.5, the Field object also exposes a new Status property. No, this is not used to indicate Field-by-Field object update status. It's used when working with the new Record object. However, in ADO 2.6 this functionality is expanded to include Field-by-Field object status.*

Updating with Optimistic Locking The *adLockOptimistic* LockType setting is ADO's most common update strategy. You can use this LockType when working with either server-side or client-side cursors. Typically, when the Update method is executed, ADO and the data provider construct a suitable UPDATE, INSERT, or DELETE SQL statement and submit it to the data engine for processing.

> **NOTE** *To see exactly how these cursors behave, I wrote a sample application that permits setting each of the CursorLocation, LockType, and CursorType properties, as well as a variety of query and update options. Look for ..\Sample Applications\Recordset\Updating on the CD.*

The type of update operation used by ADO depends on the type of operation used to fetch the rows. Remember the command strategy techniques we discussed in Chapter 5? For example, when we use the Recordset Open method to execute a Command object, ADO uses the (proprietary) system procedure sp_cursor to fetch the rows. In this case, ADO also uses the sp_cursor stored procedure to make changes. When I updated the Year_Published Field of the Recordset (I touched no others), ADO submitted the following sp_cursor call to SQL Server:

```
sp_cursor 531914844, 33, 1, N'titles', 1994
```

When I touched two columns, both were updated through the same mechanism. Notice that the cursor is referenced by number, but we don't really know what the other parameters are.[11]

```
sp_cursor 531914844, 33, 1, N'titles',
'High Integrity Compilation : A Case Study (New)', 1999
```

Let's walk through the query types (shown in Table 6-5) again, and see what mechanisms are used to update the rows—starting with Server-side CursorLocation. I set the LockType to adLockOptimistic and the CursorType to adOpenKeyset.

COMMAND SYNTAX	GENERATED UPDATE QUERY
Cn.GetTitles	sp_cursor 532619356, 33, 1, N'titles', 1901
rs.Open cmd	sp_cursor 544628828, 33, 1, N'titles', 1901
rs.Open strSQL	sp_cursor 532643932, 33, 1, N'titles', 1901
cmd.Execute	sp_cursor 544751708, 33, 1, N'titles', 1901
Cn.GetTitlesByYear	(Not updatable)

Table 6-5: Update Queries: Server-side, optimistic locking

---

11. The sp_cursor functions are Microsoft proprietary, and Microsoft is hesitant to publish how they work because they are not intended for direct access by the developer community. I'll try to work out this issue and publish a separate white paper on this in the months to come—another postretirement project.

Notice that each of the generated queries is basically the same as the other generated queries, regardless of the technique used to fetch the data in the first place. Now let's switch to client-side cursors and the adLockBatchOptimistic LockType, as shown in Table 6-6. In this case, we have to use Static CursorType—that's the only type supported with client-side cursors.

COMMAND SYNTAX	GENERATED UPDATE QUERY
Cn.GetTitles	sp_cursor 532619356, 33, 1, N'titles', 1901
rs.Open cmd	sp_cursor 544628828, 33, 1, N'titles', 1901
rs.Open strSQL	sp_cursor 532643932, 33, 1, N'titles', 1901
cmd.Execute	sp_cursor 544751708, 33, 1, N'titles', 1901
Cn.GetTitlesByYear	sp_cursor 544751708, 33, 1, N'titles', 1901

Table 6-6: Update Queries: Client-side, batch optimistic locking

The stored procedure query is updatable when accessed through the client-side optimistic batch cursor provider; it is not updatable when accessed through the server-side provider.

I also tried making changes using the optimistic batch Recordset, and I used MoveNext to trigger the Update method (behind the scenes). When I finally executed UpdateBatch, ADO transmitted the following script to the server. This was sent as a single TSQL query.

```
sp_executesql N'UPDATE "biblio".."titles" SET "Year_Published"=@P1 WHERE
"ISBN"=@P2 AND "Year_Published"=@P3;
UPDATE "biblio".."titles" SET "Year_Published"=@P4 WHERE "ISBN"=@P5 AND
"Year_Published"=@P6;
UPDATE "biblio".."titles" SET "Year_Published"=@P7 WHERE "ISBN"=@P8 AND
"Year_Published"=@P9', N'@P1 smallint,@P2 varchar(13),@P3 smallint,@P4
smallint,@P5 varchar(13),@P6 smallint,@P7 smallint,@P8 varchar(13),@P9
smallint', 1901, '0-1338103-9-9', 1900, 1991, '0-2015983-0-2', 1995,
1992, '0-4448922-4-9', 1991
```

The syntax ADO used to construct this query is determined by the Update Criteria property, which I discuss shortly in the "Building an Update WHERE Clause" section.

Updating with Pessimistic Locking   Someone came into the room when I started this section and thought I was writing a book on positive mental attitudes. I assured her I wasn't. Pessimistic locking is not the opposite of optimistic locking—it's just different. The choice of one or the other must be made with careful consideration of the impact on other users and system scalability. Far too many developers choose pessimistic locking without really knowing how it works and the impact it has on the system. Because of this problem, I tell my students that they need a note from their mom before using it. One of these days I'll get one in the mail.

While optimistic concurrency control works on the assumption that resource conflicts between multiple users are unlikely (but not impossible), and that transactions execute without locking any resources, pessimistic locking attempts to lock resources as required and holds the locks for the duration of a transaction.

Only some server-side CursorLocation data providers support pessimistic locking—SQL Server providers do. When your application sets the Recordset LockType property to adLockPessimistic, the data provider attempts to place a *lock* on the underlying database rows at the time they are read into the cursor result set. If the cursor is opened in a transaction, the update locks are held until the transaction is either committed or rolled back. If the cursor is opened outside of a transaction, however, the lock is dropped when the next row is fetched. Therefore, a cursor should be opened inside a transaction any time full pessimistic concurrency control is wanted.

An update lock prevents any other task from acquiring an update or exclusive lock on the locked row (page or table), which prevents any other task from updating the row. An update lock, however, does not block a shared lock, so it does not prevent other tasks from *reading* the row unless the second task is also requesting a read with an update lock.

> **TIP** *SQL Server supports locking "hints" that instruct the server to manage the locks in specific ways. These hints can be used with a modicum of discretion with ADO.*

Cursor and Lock Types Available for Different Providers The *Hitchhiker's Guide to Visual Basic and SQL Server* includes a comprehensive table that lists several combinations of data sources and lock types to show which options resulted in updatable RDO Resultset objects. To create an equivalent and far more comprehensive table for this book, I wrote a new sample application, and the results are shown in the "Appendix—Supports Analysis."

This appendix clearly shows how the Supports method returns vital information about what features the provider is capable of implementing. For example, you can see that the client-side provider can only implement Static CursorType cursors. Note that when the application requests an unsupported CursorType or LockType, the provider switches to an implementation it *can* support.

Building an Update WHERE Clause

To uniquely identify a specific row to be fetched or updated, ADO depends on its capability to construct a WHERE clause that identifies one, and only one, row. If ADO cannot figure out how to locate specific rows, it degrades the cursor LockType to read-only and you'll have to use your own devices to change the database. You have significant control over how the WHERE clause is constructed, and it makes sense to alter the default behavior to match the schema of your base tables.

In addition, ADO needs to determine whether the row has changed since it was last fetched. If you set the CursorLocation to adUseClient and the LockType property to adLockBatchOptimistic, ADO adds additional criteria to the WHERE clause to compare initial client-side columns or time stamp values (before changes) with their server-side values. If columns don't match up when the update is attempted, the update process fails.

The Update Criteria Recordset property is used to instruct ADO how to figure out if the data has changed since it was fetched. You can choose to have ADO identify the specific row using combinations of the primary key, a time stamp, or the PK and selected columns. If the column values or time stamp value changed since the data was first fetched, the update operation fails because the data provider cannot locate a matching row.

For example, if the Update Criteria property is set to adCriteriaTimeStamp, ADO generates an UPDATE statement that simply tests to see whether the specified database row, based on the primary key (ID), contains the same time stamp value that it did when first fetched (passed in argument @P3). If this row is located and the time stamp values are unchanged, the row is updated—otherwise an error is returned to ADO. A typical UPDATE statement could look like this:

```
UPDATE "biblio".."students"
SET "FirstName"=@P1
WHERE "ID"=@P2 AND "timestamp"=@P3
```

If the row has been deleted, the primary key won't be located and the UPDATE fails. If the row is found, but the tested columns don't match up, ADO can fetch the current database data values for you. This way you can decide if the current values in the table can be used instead of the values your user wants to use. If you set the Update Resync property in the Recordset object's dynamic properties to adResyncConflicts, ADO fetches the data-side values for you. When the update fails because someone else changed the data, the latest and greatest data appears in the UnderlyingValue property for each of the Field objects in your Recordset. The OriginalValue property is populated with the data values prior to the client changes.

Two warnings: First, I haven't tried this in a scenario where deletions are involved, for example where an update fails because the row was deleted, a deletion fails because the row was modified, or a deletion fails because the row was already deleted.

And second, ADO uses the newly retrieved data in the WHERE clauses the next time you try to update this row. Why is this a warning? Many people may have bad error-handling code and may attempt to update the same row again without realizing they're about to overwrite the changes made by another user—changes that caused the conflict in the first place.

Remember that if you want ADO to manage updates using the Update Criteria property, ADO requires that you set the CursorLocation property to use client cursors—adUseClient. This also means you'll be using Static cursors. The Update Criteria property can be set *before* the Open in ADO 2.0 or anytime in ADO 2.1. Valid settings for the Update Criteria property are:

- **adCriteriaUpdCols**: (The default) This setting constructs an UPDATE WHERE clause that includes the primary key as well as (just) those Field objects whose values have been changed or reset by your code. This approach assumes you don't care if other table columns changed while you were editing your Recordset. So, if you don't want ADO to include a Field object's name in the WHERE clause, don't touch it—don't even reset it to the same value, because that constitutes a change.

  ```
  UPDATE "biblio".."students"
  SET "FirstName"=@P1
  WHERE "ID"=@P2 AND "FirstName"=@P3
  ```

- **adCriteriaAllCols**: In this case, the WHERE clause includes *all* Fields object names in the Recordset (including any time stamps), whether they have changed or not.

  ```
  UPDATE "biblio".."students"
  SET "FirstName"=@P1
  WHERE "ID"=@P2 AND "FirstName"=@P3 AND "LastName"=@P4 AND "timestamp"=@P5
  ```

- **adCriteriaKey**: This option instructs ADO to construct the WHERE clause based solely on the PK. This option ignores changes in the server-side columns and simply updates the row if it still exists in the table. This table has a time stamp field, which is also ignored.

  ```
  UPDATE "biblio".."students"
  SET "FirstName"=@P1
  WHERE "ID"=@P2
  ```

- **adCriteriaTimeStamp**: This option has ADO construct the WHERE clause using the PK and the TimeStamp column. If there is no TimeStamp column, ADO reverts to adCriteriaCols—ah, excuse me, there is no such property setting as adCriteriaCols. The OLE DB SDK document is in error. This should be adCriteriaAllCols.

> **NOTE** *Specifying adCriteriaTimeStamp may actually use the adCriteriaAllCols option to execute the Update if there is not a valid TimeStamp field in the table. Also, the TimeStamp field does not need to be in the Recordset itself.*

> **TIP** *There's a lot of good detailed ADO information that is, for some reason, left out of the "standard" MSDN searches. However, it can be found in the OLE DB SDK's OLEDB.CHM.*

Update Method Options

The Update method is used to post changes either to the database in immediate mode or to the in-memory Recordset in batch mode. As we discussed earlier in this chapter, when looking at the AddNew method, you can take either of two approaches to change the Field.Value properties in the Recordset row. You can address and modify selected Field objects one at a time, or you can pass an array of Field objectnames and new Field object values to change the record. Remember to only change those Field objects whose values have changed if you want to keep the update simple. Changing the Field object's Value property back to its initial setting can slow down the update process.

For example, the following code updates the current Recordset row—changing the Title and Year_Published columns. The Field name array does not have to include any columns that have not changed. The initial Field names array can also be constructed early in the application and reused as necessary later in the application.

```
rs.Update Array("Title", "Year_Published"), Array("New Title's Title", 1990)
```

This Update statement caused ADO to execute the following query—notice how ADO doubled up the single quote embedded in the new title:

```
sp_executesql N'UPDATE "biblio".."titles" SET "title"=@P1,"year_published"=@P2
WHERE "title"=@P3 AND "year_published"=@P4 AND "ISBN"=@P5', N'@P1 varchar(255),@P2
smallint,@P3 varchar(255),@P4 smallint,@P5 varchar(20)', 'New Title''s Title',
1990, 'High Integrity Compilation : A Case Study (New)', 1901, '0-1338103-9-9'
```

You can also reference a single Field object in the Update statement. The following code might go in the Validate event if the input data passes muster.

```
rs.Update "Price", txtBoxPrice.Text
```

> **TIP**   *It's not a good idea to update the primary key. If you do, ADO won't be able to locate the record to perform subsequent operations. If you think about it, changing the primary key really constitutes a delete and subsequent insert.*

Dealing with Complex Query Updates

Just as when client-side cursors are created against a single table, when client cursors are created from multiple base tables (for instance, in a join operation), data manipulation performed by the ADO Cursor Service can keep the cursor consistent with each base table referenced while generating the result set. ADO can provide explicit update control to ensure that updates applied to the base tables preserve referential integrity restrictions—that is, primary key/foreign key relationships.

When the Unique Table ADO property is set, ADO Row Fix-up mode is implemented. The primary key of the table identified by Unique Table becomes the primary key of the entire cursor, and the columns holding the primary keys of all the base tables are read-only. Updates and inserts are restricted to columns of the unique table. The Unique Table property must be set for Row Fix-up to occur.

When you execute a complex query, the Recordset object is often the result of a JOIN operation executed on multiple base tables. The rows affected depend on the AffectRecords parameter of the Resync method. The standard Resync method is executed if the Unique Table and Resync Command properties are not set.

The command string of the Resync Command property is a parameterized command or stored procedure that uniquely identifies the row being refreshed, and it returns a single row containing the same number and order of columns as the row to be refreshed. The command string contains a parameter for each primary key column in the Unique Table—otherwise, a runtime error is returned. The parameters are automatically filled in with primary key values from the row to be refreshed.

When you execute a query using the adUseServer CursorLocation (the default), ADO simply asks the backend to create and manage the cursor and all aspects of updatability through the use of the aforementioned system stored procedures.

Update Error Handling

So, what happens when you can't update? For example, when another process has a row or page locked, your application is blocked until the row is free of all locks. If there is a lot of activity on the database, the SQL Server can hold off additional Share locks to prevent your UPDATE, INSERT, or DELETE from waiting forever. However, if these locks can't be freed in CommandTimeout seconds, your Update method will trip a trappable error reporting the timeout—not the fact that another user locked the row. If the Update fails because some other user changed the row since you last read it, then errors are handled through more traditional means.

UpdateBatch Method Options

When you are working with Optimistic Batch cursors, database updates are deferred until you use the UpdateBatch method. When you're ready to post changes back to the database, make sure your connection is reestablished (if you disconnected it).

You have several options when posting your changes. The UpdateBatch method accepts an argument that specifies how the update operation is to be handled. Table 6-7 lists the options.

UPDATEBATCH ARGUMENT	DESCRIPTION
adAffectAll	(Default) Affects all records in the Recordset.
adAffectAllChapters	Affects records in all chapters of the Recordset.
adAffectCurrent	Affects only the current record.
adAffectGroup	Affects only records that satisfy the current setting. You must set the Filter property to one of the valid predefined constants to use this option.

Table 6-7: UpdateBatch arguments

> **TIP**   *The adAffectAll enumeration is "hidden." Visual Basic statement completion won't show it unless you tell the object browser to show hidden elements.*

If the attempt to change the tables in the database fails for any or all records because of a conflict with the underlying data (for example, if a record has already been deleted by another user), the provider returns *warnings* to the Errors collection and a runtime error occurs. Use the Filter property (adFilterAffectedRecords) and the Status property to locate records with conflicts.

If the Unique Table and Update Resync dynamic properties are set, and the Recordset is the result of executing a JOIN operation on multiple tables, the execution of the UpdateBatch method is implicitly followed by the Resync method. That is, ADO automatically requeries the database row to determine the current values, including the new TimeStamp. You can use these values to help decide how to respond to the failed update.

Remember, you have three copies of the data setting of each Recordset Field object:

- The value first read from the provider. Original data values are maintained in the Field object's OriginalValue property.

- The value set by the client. Current data values are maintained in the Field object's Value property.

- The value set by another client and saved to the database. Current data values are maintained in the Field object's UnderlyingValue property.

Your application needs to arbitrarily choose one of these values, make a choice based on business rules, or, as a last resort, involve the user in which to choose. This final choice is often the most expensive as far as scalability is concerned—especially if you have pending transactions or pessimistic locks in place. If the user is involved, the database might change again before a decision can be made—especially if the user leaves for the Bahamas on her honeymoon before deciding.

Once someone or your code decides which version of the data to accept, there are several ways to make the changes:

- To accept the data in the database, you don't have to submit another update, but you might want to requery the database to see what changed. This can be done automatically as described earlier or by rerunning the query.

- To force your changes through, you simply resubmit the Update statement. ADO constructs the WHERE clause using the newly refreshed values. However, you face the same risk of someone else changing the data either since you last tried to update or after your changes succeed.

- To force your changes through more forcefully, you might consider changing the Update Criteria property to change the update strategy. That is, instead of having ADO construct a WHERE clause that requires certain known values or a specific time stamp, you can simply update the row based on the primary key.

- To undo the changes made by another user, you can construct and submit an UPDATE statement from the OriginalValue property settings.

These options enable you to closely control modifications to a particular base table in a Recordset that was formed by a JOIN operation on multiple base tables.

Recordset Status

If errors occur in the process of executing the Update method, you can check the Recordset object's Status property to see what went wrong. To see just rows that failed to update, set the Filter property to adFilterAffectedRecords. Visit each row in the Recordset; if there are no rows, your batch update succeeded. If your batch update did not succeed, you can determine why the update failed or what operation was performed by using the constants listed in Table 6-8. Incidentally, these constants are bit settings, so when filtering, ADO may set multiple status values at once.

CONSTANT	VALUE	DESCRIPTION
adRecOK	0	Record updated successfully.
adRecNew	0x1	Record is new.
adRecModified	0x2	Record modified.
adRecDeleted	0x4	Record deleted successfully.
adRecUnmodified	0x8	Record not modified.
adRecInvalid	0x10	Record not saved: bookmark is invalid.
adRecMultipleChanges	0x40	Record not saved: multiple Records affected.
adRecPendingChanges	0x80	Record not saved: refers to a pending insert.
adRecCanceled	0x100	Record not saved: operation canceled.
adRecCantRelease	0x400	New Record not saved: existing Record locked.
adRecConcurrencyViolation	0x800	Record not saved: optimistic concurrency in use.
adRecIntegrityViolation	0x1000	Record not saved: integrity constraints violated.
adRecMaxChangesExceeded	0x2000	Record not saved: too many pending changes.
adRecObjectOpen	0x4000	Record not saved: conflict with an open storage object.
adRecOutOfMemory	0x8000	Record not saved: out of memory.
adRecPermissionDenied	0x10000	Record not saved: insufficient user permissions.
adRecSchemaViolation	0x20000	Record not saved: violates database structure.
adRecDBDeleted	0x40000	Existing record already deleted.

Table 6-8: Recordset Status constants

Filtering Out the Failed Rows

Okay, so you don't want to visit each Recordset row one-by-one to see which rows failed to update. You don't have to; you can use the Recordset object's Filter property to make rows that don't match the Filter criteria invisible. No, rows are not removed from the Recordset when you set a Filter—they are simply hidden. The Filter property can be set on either client-side or server-side cursors. Table 6-9 lists the Filter constants.

FILTER CONSTANT	ALLOWS YOU TO VIEW RECORDS:
adFilterAffectedRecords	*Affected by* the last Delete, Resync, UpdateBatch, or CancelBatch call.
adFilterConflictingRecords	*Failed* in last batch update.
adFilterFetchedRecords	In the current cache—that is, the results of the last call to retrieve records from the database.
adFilterPendingRecords	Changed but not sent to the server. Batch update mode only.
adFilterNone	All records in the Recordset—clears filter.

Table 6-9: Filter enumerations to support Recordset updates

When you first use the UpdateBatch method, the Filter property can be used to show only those rows that had update problems. However, after you set the Filter property to adFilterNone to show all of the records, you can't ask to see the affected records again—that status information is cleared.

The Filter property can play an important role in the middle tier when it comes time to decide how to manage update collisions. There are a couple of things to remember, though. If you want to get a disconnected Recordset from a business object, make changes to the disconnected Recordset, and send it back to the business object, and you also want to see which records were deleted, you need to set the Recordset object's MarshalOptions property to adMarshalAll. If you set the MarshalOptions property to adMarshalModifiedOnly, you'll only see new and edited rows, not the deleted rows.

The following is a Microsoft Transaction Server business object that fetches the rows for the Recordset, detaches it, and returns it to the client:

```
Function GetRS(TitleWanted as String) As Recordset
    Dim conn As Connection
    Dim rs As Recordset
    Set conn = New Connection
    Set rs = New Recordset
    conn.Open "provider=sqloledb;data source=(local);initial catalog=pubs;", _
"Admin", "pw"
```

```
        rs.CursorLocation = adUseClient
        rs.Open "select Tc1, Tc2, Tc3 from TestTable" , _
            conn, adOpenKeyset, adLockBatchOptimistic
        Set GetRS = rs
        rs.ActiveConnection = Nothing
        Set rs = Nothing
        conn.Close
    End Function
```

The following routine accepts the Recordset as changed by the client and posts the changes to the database:[12]

```
Function ProcessUpdates(rs As Recordset) As String
    Dim strReturn As String
    rs.Filter = adFilterPendingRecords
    strReturn = "Rows changed = " & rs.RecordCount & vbCrLf
    Do Until rs. EOF
        If rs.Status = adRecDeleted Then
            strReturn = strReturn _
            & "That row deleted, OriginalValues " & vbCrLf _
            & rs(0).OriginalValue & vbTab  _
            & rs(1).OriginalValue & vbTab  _
            & rs(2).OriginalValue & vbTab  _
            & rs(3).OriginalValue & vbCrLf
        Else
            strReturn = strReturn  _
            & "That row changed, OriginalValues " & vbCrLf _
            & rs(0).OriginalValue & vbTab _
            & rs(1).OriginalValue & vbTab _
            & rs(2).OriginalValue & vbTab  _
            & rs(3).OriginalValue & vbCrLf  _
            & "Here are the new values: " & vbCrLf _
            & rs(0).Value & vbTab & rs(1).Value & _
            & rs(2).Value & vbTab & rs(3).Value & vbCrLf
        End If
        rs.MoveNext
    Loop
ProcessUpdates = strReturn
End Function
```

---

12. This code is not exactly coded to "best practice" standards. It overuses the string cocontation operator (&), which can materially affect performance. However, since this is an exception routine, it should not be executed very often..

The following code is the client code. We modify two rows, delete one, and add one.

```
Sub main()
    Dim rs As Recordset
    Dim obj As Object
    Set obj = CreateObject("RowsChanged.CheckStatus")
    Set rs = obj.GetRS("Data")
    Debug.Print "Rows in recordset before changes = " & rs.RecordCount
    rs.MoveFirst
    rs.Update Array(77,88,"Fred")
    rs.MoveNext
    rs.Delete
    rs.MoveNext
    rs.update Array(7,8,"George")
    rs.AddNew Array(100, 200,"New Row Added"
    rs.MoveNext
    Debug.Print "Rows in recordset after changes = " & rs.RecordCount
    rs.MarshalOptions = adMarshalModifiedOnly
    Debug.Print obj.ProcessUpdates(rs)
End Sub
```

The following is the return string from ProcessUpdates when MarshalOptions is set to adMarshalModifiedOnly.

```
Rows in Recordset before changes = 6
Rows in Recordset after changes = 6
Rows changed = 4
That row changed, OriginalValue
1   1   1   One
Here are the new values:
1   77  88  Fred
That row deleted, OriginalValue
2   2   2   Two
That row changed, OriginalValue
3   3   3   Three
Here are the new values:
3   7   8   George
That row changed, OriginalValue
Here are the new values:
    100 200 New row added
```

Helping ADO Know What and How to Update

To help ADO know what specifically named table to update (add, change, or delete), the data provider fills in the source owner, database, and table names after the query is executed. If these cannot be determined, it's unlikely that ADO can construct a valid Update statement. Several properties are added to the client-side Recordset Properties collection to store this query-dependent information. You can set these properties in code to make a decision about what to update if it gets confused:

- **Unique Catalog** specifies the catalog or name of the database containing the table.

- **Unique Schema** specifies the schema or name of the owner of the table.

- **Unique Table** specifies the name of the base table upon which updates, insertions, and deletions are allowed. This value is based on the catalog and schema (user) settings already set.

When the SELECT statement has data from many tables and ADO decides it can build an updatable Recordset, each Field object in the Recordset carries the source database and table.

Update Resync Property—Dynamic (ADO)

Do you want to save yourself the trouble of coding another fetch to determine the current contents of the database tables involved in your successful or failed update operation? If so, you can set the Update Resync property to one of the enumerated values listed in Table 6-10. However, the Update Resync property is only available if the Unique Table dynamic property has already been set. Update Resync instructs ADO to automatically follow the UpdateBatch method with a Resync method call. The settings in Table 6-10 determine the scope of the operation.

UPDATE RESYNC PROPERTY ENUMERATIONS	DESCRIPTION
adResyncAll	Invokes Resync for each row with pending changes.
adResyncAutoIncrement	(Default.) Attempts to retrieve the new identity value for columns that are automatically incremented or generated by the data source, such as Microsoft Jet AutoNumber fields or Microsoft SQL Server Identity columns.
adResyncConflicts	Invokes Resync for all rows in which the update or delete operation failed because of a concurrency conflict.
adResyncInserts	Invokes Resync for all successfully inserted rows. However, primary key column values are not resynchronized. Instead, contents of newly inserted rows are resynchronized based on the existing primary key value.[13]
adResyncNone	Does not invoke Resync.
adResyncUpdates	Invokes Resync for all successfully updated rows.

Table 6-10: Update Resync property enumerations

The following constants can be used in combination:

- adResyncAutoIncrement *and* adResyncConflicts

- adResyncAutoIncrement *and* adResyncInserts

- adResyncAll, adResyncUpdates, adResyncInserts, *and* adResyncConflicts

Submitting and Managing Multiple Operations

When working with more sophisticated backend operations, you'll often need to run more than one operation at a time. These operations can be SELECTs, action queries, or combinations of the two in any order. Not all providers support multiple operations. For example, the Jet provider can't accept more than one operation at a time, but SQL Server, Oracle, and others can. While it's not at all

---

13. If the primary key value has changed, Resync won't retrieve the contents of the intended row. For automatically incrementing primary key values, first call UpdateBatch with adResyncAutoIncrement to retrieve the data source-generated primary key value.

unusual to submit several SELECT, INSERT, DELETE, UPDATE, or other TSQL statements together (what we call *scripts*), these multiple operations are more likely to be the result of executing stored procedures.

There is nothing in the ADO rule book that says you can't submit multiple action or SELECT queries in a single CommandText property or Source argument string, as long as you do it right. The limitation lies with the provider. This means that if your provider supports multiple operations, you can bundle together 2, 12, or 1,200 SQL operations at once. The upper limit is a function of the size of the provider's command buffer.

It's easy to construct these command scripts. All you have to do is concatenate the commands together into a single string and use the string as you would any SQL query or action. Be sure to maintain the "white space" between operators. That is, when you concatenate two strings that should be separated by a space, include the leading (or trailing) space in the concatenation expression. However, if you're doing this for performance reasons, you won't want to use the Visual Basic concatenation operator (&). Using the MID$ function is faster, as I illustrate in the next code sample.

> **TIP**   *When constructing the query string, be sure to avoid inserting (or leaving) any binary zeros in the string. If you do, ADO executes up to the zero and stops.*

Once you execute the command, and after ADO returns control to your application, you can begin to parse the returning rowsets and result sets that are generated. Generally, all commands sent to the backend for processing return a result set. No, not all result sets contain rowsets, and you don't have to process all of the rowsets, or even all of the result sets generated by ADO; you can simply close the Recordset, set it to Nothing, and forget about it.

The following code illustrates a couple of techniques you might find useful. First, I construct a TSQL Create Table command to construct a new Sales test table. Note the use of *fixed-length* strings instead of ordinary variable-length strings.

```
…
Dim strSQL As String * 32767      ' About 32K of ram
Const strINSERT As String = " INSERT INTO Sales (SalesRegion,SalesAmount, ISBN)
VALUES ("
…
```

Next, I use the Execute method to execute two TSQL commands as a script. The first tests for the existence of the table about to be created. If it exists, the backend drops it. The next command creates the table. This step illustrates use of a batch or script to construct a new Sales table. Notice how there are really two parts to this query. One tests the existence of the table and executes a DropTable if it already exists and the second creates a new Sales table.

```
cn.Execute "if exists(select * from sysobjects where type = 'U' and name =
'Sales')" _
    & "  begin drop table sales end " _
    & " CREATE TABLE Sales (SaleID INT IDENTITY(100,1) , " _
    & " SalesRegion CHAR(2), " _
    & " SalesAmount smallmoney," _
    & " ISBN VarChar(20)" _
    & " CONSTRAINT ID_PK PRIMARY KEY (SaleID) )"
```

The next section of code fills in the fixed-length query string with 200 INSERT statements, each containing a random ISBN and other randomly generated values. Note the use of the MID$ function instead of the Visual Basic concatenation (&) operator—this approach dramatically increases performance and is explained in more detail shortly. The MID$ lines insert (as opposed to concatenate) the insert values into the target query string. I left the concatenate operation (a single line of code) in the loop to illustrate how it's done. Also, note that the fixed-length string is initialized to spaces. This eliminates the chance that misaligning the MID$ insertions will leave an orphaned zero byte.

```
strSQL = String(intLenstrSQL, " ")
For i = 1 To 200
    intRegion = Int(Rnd(1) * 9)
    strCurAmount = Format((Rnd(1) * 100), "####.##")
    intRnd = Rnd(1) * 99
    strISBN = "'" & vaISBNs(0, intRnd) & strInsertEnd
'   '  simple but slow VB concatenation is commented out here
'     strW = strW & strINSERT & intRegion & "," & strCurAmount & "," & strISBN
    strWork = String(intLenStrWork, ",")
    Mid$(strWork, 1, Len(intRegion)) = intRegion
    intTLen = Len(intRegion) + 1
    Mid$(strWork, intTLen, Len(strCurAmount)) = strCurAmount
    intTLen = intTLen + Len(strCurAmount) + 1
    Mid$(strWork, intTLen, Len(strISBN)) = strISBN
    intTLen = intTLen + Len(strISBN)
    Mid$(strSQL, intLenSQL, intLenInsert) = strINSERT
    intLenSQL = intLenSQL + intLenInsert
    Mid$(strSQL, intLenSQL, intTLen - 1) = Left$(strWork, intTLen - 1)
    intLenSQL = intLenSQL + intTLen
```

To execute the query line-by-line, comment out these next three lines:

```
'    cn.Execute Left$(strSQL, intLenSQL)
'    intLenSQL = 1
'    strSQL = ""
Next i
```

After the string is populated with our 200 INSERT statements, it's ready for execution. I simply set the string length and pass the script (strSQL) to the Recordset Open method. ADO passes this string straight through to the server for execution. Check out the Profiler to see!

```
intLenSQL = intLenSQL - 1
rs.Open Left$(strSQL, intLenSQL), cn, Options:=adCmdText
```

Each of the INSERT statements returns a result set, and we can loop through them all. However, ADO does not expose the Records Affected return value from the INSERT statements, so the following part of the example is really for naught. However, if you had embedded SELECT statements in stored procedures, you could use this routine to step through those rowsets and output parameters. It would probably make sense to add a Set NOCOUNT ON to the query, to completely eliminate the overhead generated by the INSERT result sets.

```
i = 0
Do Until rs Is Nothing
    For Each er In cn.Errors
        Debug.Print "Recordset"; i, er, er.Description
    Next er
    Set rs = rs.NextRecordset
    i = i + 1
Loop
Debug.Print i; " Recordsets found"
```

> **NOTE** *This example, along with virtually all other examples in this book, is provided on the book's CD. To find this one, search for Sample Application\Recordset Objects\Multiple Operations.*

Constructing SQL Statements Without the Concatenation Operator

Because Visual Basic is brutally clumsy about concatenating strings, it makes sense to try to avoid use of the ampersand (&) concatenation operator whenever possible.

However, trying to abstain from the & operator is tough. A number of clinics here in Redmond specialize in treating & addicts, but with limited success. I know I have trouble refraining from & on the podium, but I'm taking it one demo at a time.

I also recommend that you avoid "roll-your-own" SQL queries because of & expense. If your SQL is simply constructed by substituting parameters into a SQL WHERE clause, you can use the following techniques to cut 30 percent from your query setup time. Because this is an operation performed every time you execute your query, this 30 percent improvement can multiply into significant savings.

If you use this technique, *you'll* have to make sure the parameters don't contain any single quotes—ADO won't do it for you. Consider using the new Visual Basic Replace function to find embedded single quotes. Replace each single quote with two single quotes.

```
strParm = Replace(strParm, " ' ", " ' ' ")
```

To get the best performance when you construct your own SQL statements, you'll want to use the Mid function to insert the parameters instead of using & concatenation. This is easy if the length of the parameters is fixed, as when you pass numbers, but still doable if you pass variable-length arguments.

The following code example compares several "traditional" argument-management techniques with a more efficient approach using the Mid function. In this case, we set up the query ahead of time, much in the same way that we construct Command objects. I plan to use this approach in the middle tier where query construction time is critical and where I don't like to use a Command object (unless I expect to manage *return* parameters from the provider).

The first part of the code uses the & technique that I (and everyone else) have been illustrating for years as the way to insert parameters into SQL WHERE clauses.

```
SQL = "SELECT Name, Address "
    SQL = SQL & "FROM Authors "
    SQL = SQL & "WHERE Name like '" & txtParameter & "' ;"
```

Unfortunately, this technique costs us dearly in lost time, as Visual Basic allocates and reallocates memory (several times) to handle the strings.

The Mid technique eliminates the need for & concatenations by first figuring out ahead of time where to insert the parameter. It also uses a *fixed-length* string instead of a normal variable-length string declaration to manage the SQL query. After this preliminary step is done, we can easily reference the specific bytes in the query to change on each execution. This technique is about 30 percent faster than the preceding example.

```
'   Set up the operation. This is done once-early in the application
'   Note that flSQL is declared as a fixed length string…
Dim flSQL as String * 128
flSQL = "SELECT Name, Address FROM Authors WHERE Name like '"
j = InStrRev(flSQL, "'") + 1    ' Find the last single quote
k = Len(txtParameter) + 1       ' Compute the parameter length
'   Fill in the parameter. This is done just before execution
    Mid(flSQL, j) = txtParameter    ' Insert the parameter in the query
    Mid(flSQL, j, k) = "';"         ' Close the framing quote
```

Simply reducing the number of & operations can help improve performance. You save about 10 percent by simply using a Visual Basic constant for the preamble SELECT statement.

```
SQL = strSQL & "WHERE Name like '" & txtParameter & "' ;"
```

Remember that the line continuation character can help make code more *human* readable, but it hurts performance by about five percent each time it's used to break up a quoted string that has to be reassembled at runtime. No, the compiler does not preconcatenate these strings to save time later.

```
SQL = "SELECT Name, Address " _
    & "FROM Authors " _
    & "WHERE Name like '" & txtParameter & "' ;"
```

Canceling, Undoing, and Rolling Back

Oops, you made a change to your Recordset and you don't want to commit those changes to the database. Relax. ADO has lots of options to choose from. You can undo changes to just the current record or all of the changes made so far to the Recordset. Basically, you have these options:

- To undo changes, but only to the current record, use the CancelUpdate method with the adAffectCurrent option.

- To undo the entire set of changes made to a Recordset since the last time you committed changes, use the CancelUpdate method with the adAffectAll option (the default). After you use Update (or UpdateBatch), you can't undo the changes.

- To undo changes, but only to rows in the current subset of the Recordset based on the Filter criteria, use the CancelUpdate method with the adAffectGroup option.

- To undo an entire series of changes made since you executed BeginTrans, you can use the Connection object's RollbackTrans method. However, once you use CommitTrans, the changes can't be rolled back—unless you're using nested transactions.

After you execute the CancelBatch method, ADO might not be able to determine the current record in the Recordset. That's why it's a good idea to force the current row pointer to a specific location after using CancelBatch. For example, you could use the MoveLast method to move to the last valid row in the Recordset. If you are adding a new row when you use the CancelUpdate method, the current row is repositioned to the row that was current before the AddNew call.

If the attempt to cancel the pending updates fails because of a conflict with the underlying data (for example, a record has been deleted by another user), the provider returns warnings to the Errors collection but does not halt your program. A runtime error occurs only if there are conflicts on all the requested records. Use the Filter property (adFilterAffectedRecords) and the Status property to locate records with conflicts.

Using the Recordset Save Method

Let's look a little more closely at the Recordset object's Save method. Any open Recordset can be saved—not just ones created in memory. Once a Recordset is saved, it can be reopened by referencing the filename in the Open method.

The following example opens a Recordset from the filename specified by the CommonDialog control. The Open method uses the filename as the Source argument—not as the Connection argument. While it's possible to create a Connection object and set the Connection string to "File Name=" & .Filename, the simple Open method expects the syntax shown here:

```
With CommonDialog1
    .ShowOpen
    Set rs = New Recordset
    rs.Open .FileName
    Debug.Print rs.RecordCount
End With
```

If the Filter property is in effect for the Recordset, only the rows that qualify based on the Filter criteria are saved. (I discuss the Filter property in Chapter 7.) If the Recordset is hierarchical, the current child Recordset and its children are saved, but not the parent Recordset. If Recordset membership population is not complete, the Save method blocks until the asynchronous population is complete. This ensures that all member rows are included.

> **NOTE**   *An interesting issue: When using server-side cursors (adUseServer), the Save method saves all rows for the statement, regardless of the MaxRecords setting specified for the Recordset.*

Once the Recordset is opened against a file, the Save method resaves the Recordset to the same file by default. If you save to a new filename, the original file is left open. While the Recordset is open, other users have read (only) access to the file.

After using the Save method, the current row pointer is positioned to the first row of the Recordset. At this point, you can continue to work on the Recordset—it remains open until you use the Close method or set the Recordset to Nothing.

If you try to use the Save method in an Internet Explorer Web page, remember that, for security reasons, the Save method is only allowed in zones with "low" and "custom" security settings. For a more detailed explanation of security issues, see the white paper titled, "Security Issues in the Microsoft Internet Explorer," at http://www.microsoft.com/data/techmat.htm.

CHAPTER 7

Manipulating Your Recordset

IN CHAPTER 6, WE DISCUSSED HOW, when, and why to construct a Recordset. Once you decide to create a Recordset to handle the rowset generated by your query, you will want to manipulate it. You'll think about binding it to data-aware controls (I suggest you don't), and think about sorting, filtering, and finding rows in the rowset (I suggest you do). When you paid up to seven some-odd megabytes of RAM for ADO, you mostly bought sophisticated Recordset management routines. Knowing how to use these routines efficiently and effectively will go a long way toward making your application a success.

Data Binding Your Recordset

I'm not a fan of data binding. IMHO, the expense of coding and managing data-bound controls seems to be higher than the benefits gained. Yes, data binding and Visual Basic's capability to manage it have improved in Visual Basic 6.0. But there are also fewer reasons to use it. While the data-bound (and unbound) controls have improved, the problems associated with connecting and result set management have not. For example, you don't need to data bind to fill a grid with rows from a Recordset—the MSHFlexGrid object's Recordset property can be set to any Recordset. Yes, bound controls can automatically update records based on changes in the control. You can do the same in one line of code in a grid click event. But as you'll see, trying to trap errors can be a serious drawback that can cripple any production application.

Sooner or later, you'll discover that when working with more sophisticated applications, you still have to code routines to validate the control cells before committing them to the Recordset—not to mention the error handlers needed regardless of the technique used. Beyond that, the bound control approach seems best suited for smaller table-based systems and not for procedure-based systems, where access to base tables is either limited or prohibited. I won't spend a lot of time on this. Other books and the documentation do a fine job of that. Data binding does not constitute a best practice.

Fetching Techniques

Some of the data access code I've seen in the past 25 years seems quite fetching—other code is downright ugly (sorry 'bout that). But we do need to touch on techniques that, at least on the surface, seem like good ways to quickly populate and offload Recordset objects. For example, fetching Recordset data row-by-row often seems expensive and downright unnecessary. However, offloading rows into a Variant array or delimited string can also be costly. As a means to pass data from tier to tier, the Variant array can be especially costly. We'll discuss this more completely in Chapter 8, but consider that Variant arrays transmit their data in padded Unicode data structures. These behemoth arrays take considerably longer (almost three times as long) to move from tier to tier when compared to Recordsets.

As I see it, there are two parts to the fetching operation. (There are probably three but I can't think of a third.) First, fetching completes membership population. This, in turn, releases share locks on the server. This is good—good for scalable applications and for those other clients waiting to perform updates on the rows and pages (and perhaps tables) that you have share locked. Second, fetching can "offload" the Recordset to another control, to a file, to a stream, or to a named memory area. This is often necessary to display, transport, or persist the Recordset. But it's not always needed. Sometimes we can leave the data in the Recordset, make changes, and send the whole Recordset (or just the changes) to another layer.

Basically, there are many techniques used to populate and unload Recordsets:

- Use the MoveNext method until EOF changes to True, or use the MoveLast method. While these techniques do not unload the Recordset, they do complete population.

- Use the GetRows or GetString method. These methods both unload and populate in a single operation.

- Assign the Recordset to a "complex"[1] bound control. The control completes population as you scroll.

- Assign the Recordset to a "smart" unbound control, such as the MSHFlexGrid.

---

1. Complex bound controls handle multiple rows of a Recordset. For example, a Grid control is a complex bound control. Simple bound controls handle only one row, such as a TextBox control.

- Let ADO self-populate.

- Assign the ActiveConnection property to Nothing. ADO ensures Recordset population is complete before cutting off the connection.

Remember that ADO self-populates if left to its own devices. That is, after the first set of rows arrives and control returns to your application (whether or not you're running asynchronously), ADO continues to populate your Recordset behind the scenes on its own thread.

> **NOTE** *Recordset population should never be a problem, as long as you don't fetch any more than a few CacheSize rows (a couple of hundred). Any more than that and you have to start worrying about membership population to free server-side locks, memory consumed on the client, and whether your client will run out of patience with you and your application.*

ADO begins (and tries to end the population process) by prefetching a set of rows before returning control to the client. By default, this initial set contains 50 rows. You can control the number of records in the initial fetch by setting the "Initial Fetch Size" property in the ADO Recordset Properties collection.

Displaying Rows with the MSHFlexGrid Control

One of the easiest and fastest ways to get the Recordset values in front of the user is to set the MSHFlexGrid control's Recordset property. I've been using this approach for some time now, and it seems to work fine—except in one situation. When using server-side cursors, you cannot inspect the Recordset object's EOF (or almost any other) property[2] before assigning the Recordset to the grid. If you do, you'll get a 30023 error from the grid. (Sigh.) I submitted a bug report on this issue, but they aren't going to fix it. You'll have to switch to client-side cursors for this to work—or don't touch the EOF property.

After the data is displayed in the grid, as shown in Figure 7-1, you'll notice that the headings are filled in for you, but the column widths will usually need to be adjusted to match your Recordset data. To fix this, I usually loop through the grid

---

2. David Sceppa and Rick Nasci fought for some time to get this "bug" fixed. The ADO folks sent back a long paragraph describing how this was a "by design" feature.

when it's used for the first time and assign appropriate widths. After you set the ColWidth property for each column, setting the Recordset property has no further effect on the column width settings. I use the TextWidth function in Visual Basic to return the correct number of twips to assign to the ColWidth property. This function accepts a string whose width is translated into twips. I use a variable-length string of M characters because the M character is a maximum width character, and when using proportional fonts, this can make a big difference. For example, the number of twips is far less if you use a string of period or space characters than it is when using a wider character. Using a string of M characters makes it easier to estimate the number of twips needed for an appropriate number of characters in each field.

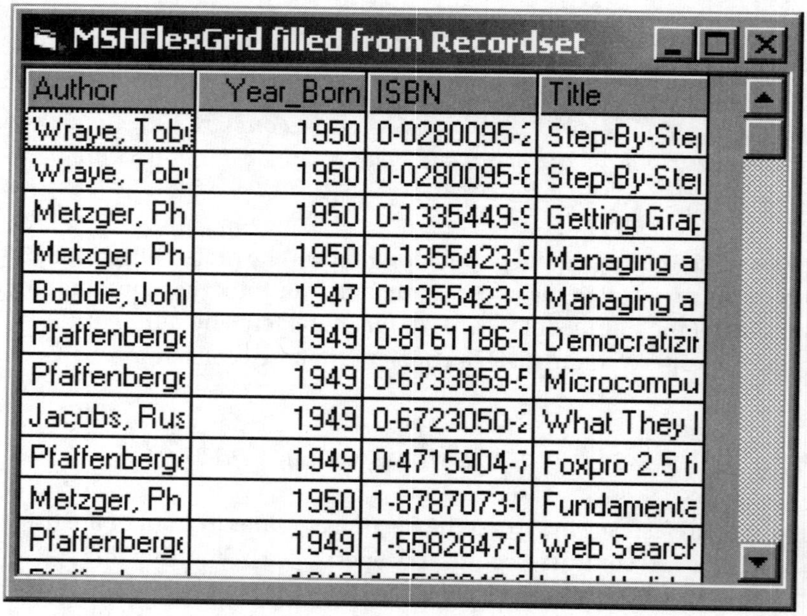

Figure 7-1: Set the MSHFlexGrid1.Recordset to your Recordset to display the rowset.

The Choose function in the following example returns an appropriate number of M characters based on the width of each Field in the Recordset.

```
i = 0
With MSHFlexGrid1
    .Row = 0
    For Each fld In rs.Fields
        .ColWidth(i) = TextWidth(String(Choose(i + 1, 12, 7, 10, 7, 80), "M"))
        i = i + 1
    Next fld
End With
```

Displaying Rows Using the Immediate Window

Another way of seeing the Recordset data while debugging the application is to dump the rows to the Immediate window, as shown in Figure 7-2:

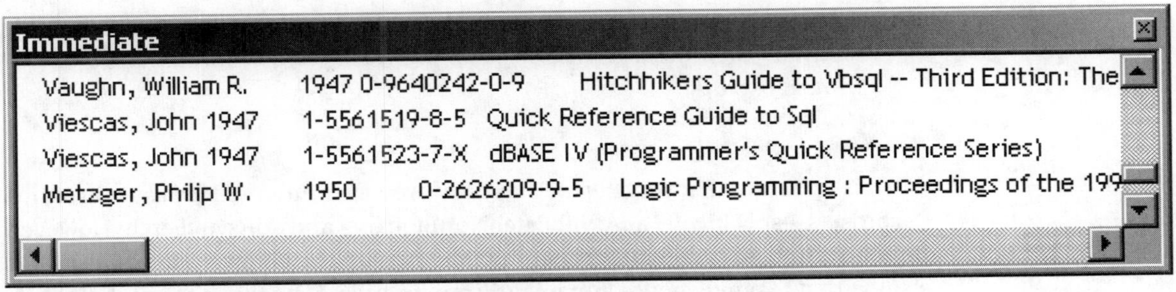

Figure 7-2: Use Debug.Print to display the Recordset field names and values in the Immediate window.

I use the following routine to show the Field names followed by individual row values. While this is pretty intuitive, it might be handy to dump the Recordset while debugging.

```
For Each fld In rs.Fields
    Debug.Print fld.Name,
Next fld
Debug.Print
Do Until rs.EOF
    For Each fld In rs.Fields
        Debug.Print fld.Value,
    Next fld
    Debug.Print
    rs.MoveNext
Loop
```

Asynchronous Fetching

If you use the adAsyncFetch option as an Options argument on the Open method, ADO continues to fetch rows behind the scenes after synchronously fetching the initial set. This wasn't implemented in ADO until version 2.5, despite being an acceptable Options argument for some time. However, if you execute the MoveLast method on a scrollable cursor, you disable the asynchronous operation—your code blocks while ADO dutifully fetches the rowset.

> **IMHO** *The Move methods (all of them) should include an option to support asynchronous operations, to prevent blocking no matter what. Perhaps someday.*

It is apparent that server-side cursors were never intended for asynchronous Recordsets—specifically adAsyncFetchNonBlocking and adAsyncFetch. However, server-side cursors do work (meaning they free up the client to do something else) with adAsyncExecute and a Static cursor type. However, they still block, because you cannot reference the data in the Recordset until the cursor is fully populated.

In ADO, you can get an asynchronous operation through the ADO Connection or Command objects. To enable this option, use one of the following enumerations with the Open or Execute methods:

- **adAsyncExecute** creates a second thread and begins executing the command on that thread. When the provider finishes executing the command, ADO uses notification (it fires an event) to inform your code that the query has completed executing.

- **adAsyncFetch**, when using client cursors, fetches the results on a second thread in the background after the execution of the command completes. A notification occurs (an event fires) when the entire result set has been fetched.

The event handlers are activated if you declare the ADO Connection and Recordset variables using the WithEvents option, as shown in the following code:

```
Dim WithEvents Cn as ADODB.Connection
Dim WithEvents Rs as ADODB.Recordset
```

Once you declare the Connection object and Recordset object using WithEvents, Visual Basic adds the objects to the object drop-down list in the IDE (as shown in Figure 7-3) and exposes the event handler prototypes. The asynchronous operations fire the ConnectComplete and ExecuteComplete events on the Connection object when the asynchronous operation is done.

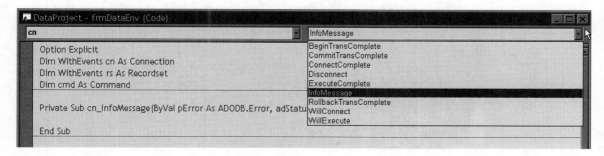

Figure 7-3: The Visual Basic IDE exposes the Recordset Events.

When you request events on the Recordset object, asynchronous operations fire the following events:

- **FetchProgress:** This method is called periodically during a lengthy asynchronous operation to report how many more rows have currently been retrieved (fetched) into the Recordset.

- **FetchComplete:** This method is called after all the records in a lengthy asynchronous operation have been retrieved (fetched) into the Recordset.

When you haven't set up event handlers, use the State property to indicate completion of asynchronous operations—check the adStateExecuting and adStateFetching State property bit flags to determine whether the asynchronous operations are still progressing.

Do Until RS.EOF Loops

Quite a few programs use Do Until or Do While loops to fetch and offload the data rows until RS.EOF returns True. This is not one of the 7 deadly computer sins (a topic for another time), but it is one of the top 20 sins. Sometimes you don't have a choice, but consider what's going on in the loop:

- Are you moving the first row to a set of controls on the form and waiting for the user to press Next so that you can execute MoveNext? This is not a good idea—at least not until you have completed population. If you can, execute a MoveLast and then a MoveFirst[3] after opening the Recordset. This completes population. If this seems to take a long time, you've fetched too many rows.

---

3. If your code executes a MoveFirst just after the Recordset opens, you might trigger another execution of the query for no purpose.

- Are you testing each row for a specific value and on selected (or each) row performing some sort of update operation? Again, this is not a good idea, especially if you are running against SQL Server, Oracle, or any intelligent backend. These systems can filter and process sets of rows much faster than your client can. Just read up on stored procedures.

- Are you simply dumping rows to a delimited string, XML structure, or Variant array? This is a waste of time, as there are built-in functions to do this for you.

- Are you dumping the Recordset to a grid control record-by-record? Again, this is not necessary, because the MSHFlexGrid control and many other third-party controls support Recordset properties that can be set to your Recordset object. Even if they don't support a Recordset property, they might support a Clip property that can accept a delimited string as constructed by the GetString method (which is discussed next).

Fetching Recordsets with GetRows and GetString

ADO supports two methods for offloading the entire contents of, or a subset of, the Recordset to either a Variant array or a delimited string. When I first started working with RDO (which supports similar functionality), these methods seemed very cool—fast, easy, and powerful. However, the bloom is off the rose with these methods, as far as I'm concerned, now that I know their impact and how they were implemented.

GetRows extracts some or all of the Recordset rows and sends the rows to a Variant array. The following code uses the default settings to extract the entire Recordset:

```
vaArray = rs.GetRows
```

In much the same way, the GetString method extracts some or all of the Recordset rows, but GetString constructs a "pseudo" delimited string. I say pseudo because IMHO a delimited string includes quotes around the string elements of the string; GetString, however, does not put quotes around the strings—it simply separates them with the field delimiter (such as tabs or commas). This makes it harder to deal with the delimited string when it arrives. For example, you'll find it tough to construct correct delimited strings from fields that contain quotes. You can specify the interfield delimiter and the interrecord delimiter, but if you want to pass the delimited string to a control that supports a Clip property, you can leave the syntax as is—the default settings are fine.

```
strDelimited = rs.GetString
```

In RDO, you had to provide a very large number (well beyond the number of rows expected) to extract all of the rows from your Recordset using the GetRows and GetClipString methods; but by default, ADO extracts all rows. You can fetch a few rows at a time with either method by using the Rows argument. However, only the GetRows method lets you select a starting position in the Recordset using the Start argument.

Here are some additional examples. First, we create a Recordset with three Fields. Then, we move down five rows and capture a bookmark. And then we reposition to the top of the Recordset.

```
rs.Open "select title, year_published, ISBN from titles where title like 'H%'", cn
rs.Move 5
vaBookmark = rs.Bookmark
rs.MoveFirst
```

In the next part of the code, we dump all fields from the 100+ rows into the array. If you use −1 for the Rows argument, ADO fetches all remaining rows, starting at the current record pointer.

```
vaArray = rs.GetRows
rs.MoveFirst
```

In this next case, we start at the first Recordset row and extract 10 rows, but just the Title field.

```
vaArray = rs.GetRows(10, , "title")
rs.MoveFirst
```

The Start argument is not a starting row number, but it can tell ADO to start at various points in the Recordset, assuming the Recordset supports bookmarks. The Start argument can take the following values in addition to a normal Bookmark value:

- **adBookmarkCurrent**—start at the current record.

- **adBookmarkFirst**—start at the first record.

- **adBookmarkLast**—start at the last record, thus returning only one record.

- **A bookmark** Reposition to a previously saved bookmark.

This next code example extracts five rows starting at the bookmarked row (which is row 5), and dumps just the Year_Published field.

```
vaArray = rs.GetRows(5, vaBookmark, "Year_Published")
rs.MoveFirst
```

The next line extracts just the ISBN and Title fields from all rows.

```
vaArray = rs.GetRows(Fields:=Array("ISBN", "Title"))
```

To reposition the CRP to the beginning of the Recordset, I used the MoveFirst method before fetching the rows. However, you don't have to do this, and if the Recordset is opened as forward-only, you won't be able to—at least not without rerunning the query.

GetRows does not "remove" rows from the Recordset, nor is the method affected by the Sort property, but it *is* affected by the current Filter property setting. That is, if you set the Filter property before using GetRows (or GetString), you get just the rows in the Recordset that satisfy the Filter criteria.

Using the RecordCount Property

If you want to know how many Records met the criteria in your query's WHERE clause, you can check the RecordCount property. However, RecordCount is *not* implemented for the default Recordset (RO/FO) or for *any* forward-only cursor—it always returns –1. If RecordCount does not seem to work on your scrollable cursor, try using MoveLast to force population, but be prepared for a wait while all rows are fetched. Remember, you can also examine the array boundaries of the Variant array constructed with the GetRows method if you want to return a valid row count.

> **TIP** *In some cases, ADO executes the MoveLast method to fully populate the cursor when you reference the RecordCount property. This means that if you open the View Locals window, the RecordCount property is referenced and ADO might execute the MoveLast method. If you aren't ready for a long wait while the Recordset is being populated, don't check the RecordCount property.*

Switching to a scrollable cursor just to get the RecordCount does not make sense, because of the considerable overhead imposed by ADO to manage scrolling. On the other hand, some folks recommend adding a SELECT COUNT(*) to the query to return the number of qualifying rows. However, this makes the server work twice as hard on the query—once to get the count, and again to fetch the rows. COUNT(*) is not necessarily accurate anyway, because the row count can change between queries. If you surround the two queries (the COUNT(*) and the row-returning query) in a transaction, you prevent changes to the database while you're fetching, but this imposes additional scalability problems. If you use adUseClient for the CursorLocation, ADO creates a Static cursor, which supports the RecordCount property without problems.

If you use Return @@ROWCOUNT or return the @@ROWCOUNT in the Return status or OUTPUT parameter, these also require that the cursor be populated before the parameters are returned. That is, ADO needs to have read the last row from the server. If there are not very many rows in the cursor (50 or less), ADO will have completed population by the time you get control and you'll be able to pick off the OUTPUT parameters or Return status (an integer). However, if there are more than CacheSize rows to return, you have to wait at least until population is complete before accessing the OUTPUT parameters or Return status. In any case, remember that the return status and OUTPUT parameters are not available with some providers until you close the Recordset. This seems to throw another monkey wrench in this strategy.

> **TIP** *When using Forward-only cursors, ADO can run a tally of records visited, but only if you set the CacheSize property to something greater than 1. As you move forward through the Recordset, RecordCount reflects the current tally. When you reach the end, it equals the number of rows fetched.*

Working with Variant Arrays

For those of you not familiar with Variant arrays, here are a couple of tips. First, the UBound function can be very helpful. It returns the dimensions of the array; but remember that Variant arrays are indexed by columns and rows, not by rows and columns as you might expect. When you use the UBound function to see how many rows and columns resulted from your GetRows method call, use this syntax:

```
lngRowsInArray = UBbound(vaArray,2)
intColumnsInArray = UBound(vaArray,1)
```

After you know the dimensions of the Variant array, you can extract the data, like this:

```
Sub DumpRows(lrs As Variant)
Dim i As Integer, j As Integer
For i = 0 To UBound(lrs, 2)
    For j = 0 To UBound(lrs, 1)
        Debug.Print lrs(j, i),            ' Note col, row
    Next j
    Debug.Print
Next i
Debug.Print String(25, "-")
```

If you're not sure about how the array elements are numbered, you can simply check out the Locals Window in the Visual Basic IDE—it dumps the entire array for you, as shown in Figure 7-4. Notice how the array boundaries are shown. Figure 7-4 shows three columns (0, 1, and 2), and 1 row (0-based).

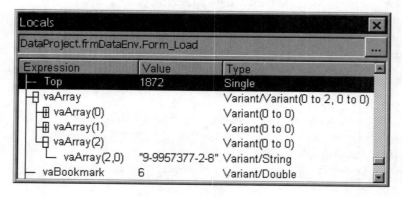

Figure 7-4: Examining the Locals Window GetRows Variant Array

When using these techniques, remember that executing GetRows on an empty Recordset will result in a trappable error being raised.

```
3021
ADODB.Recordset
Either BOF or EOF is True, or the current record has been deleted. Requested
operation requires a current record.
```

In these cases, it is a good idea to assign Empty to the variant variable. So, whenever you are expecting data in a variant, check to see if it is Empty before referencing array elements.

Sorting, Filtering, and Finding

When you have a Recordset open, you can manipulate its contents. For example, if you populate a grid control and want to manipulate the rows, you can:

- Set the Sort property to one of the Recordset Field names to reorder the rows in either ascending or descending sequence.

- Set the Filter property to a valid criteria string to hide all rows not meeting the criteria.

- Execute the Find method to locate rows based on a criteria string.

To help you check out the Sort and Filter properties and the Find method, I wrote a small sample application. The full source is on the CD, and we'll walk through the code here, pointing out some critical points along the way.

Before we get started, though, I want to point out that you can sort, filter, and find quite easily on the server. That is, you can make things smoother and more efficient for everyone if you leave the rows on the database where they belong. Passing rows in bulk to the client to manipulate can be expensive. However, that said, these client-side techniques can be a great way to reduce the dependency on the server for sorting, filtering, and finding once the Recordset is constructed and transmitted to the client.

Now, let's step through our sample application. First, we set up the variables. Notice that we'll save a few bookmarks to help find our way around the Recordset.

```
Option Explicit
Dim cn As Connection
Dim cmd As Command
Dim rs As Recordset
Dim i As Integer
Dim intWidth As Integer
Dim varBookMarkStart As Variant
Dim varBookmarkTop As Variant
```

Next, we open the connection and run a query to return selected columns from the data provider. We help the process by sorting the data before it arrives. The sample sets the ActiveConnection to Nothing, but you don't have to. However, this is not a bad idea if you expect to spend some time tinkering with the Recordset. We close the Connection, because we don't expect to need it again. There's a little more code used to make the grid a tad more presentable, but you can check that out on the CD.

```
…
rs.Open "SELECT Name, City, State, Zip, " _
    & " (SELECT COUNT(*) From titles WHERE_
&titles.pubid = publishers.pubID) AS Titles " _
    & " From Publishers Where zip Is Not Null ORDER BY Name", cn
rs.ActiveConnection = Nothing
cn.Close
varBookMarkStart = rs.Bookmark          'Save first row position
varBookmarkTop = rs.Bookmark
Set MSHFlexGrid1.Recordset = rs  ' Pass in the initial Recordset
…
```

When the user clicks one of the grid control headings, we figure out which column was clicked and determine whether the user has already chosen this column to sort before. If so, we assume they want the opposite sort order—descending or ascending. Otherwise, we set the Recordset object's Sort property to the selected Field name.

```
Private Sub MSHFlexGrid1_Click()
Dim strCol As String
With MSHFlexGrid1
    If .Row > 1 Then Exit Sub               ' Only worry about clicks on the headings
    strCol = rs.Fields(.ColSel).Name
    Select Case rs.Sort
        Case "", strCol & " DESC"
            rs.Sort = strCol
        Case strCol
            rs.Sort = strCol & " DESC"
        Case Else
            rs.Sort = strCol
    End Select
    Set .Recordset = rs
End With
End Sub
```

The form, shown in Figure 7-5, has a few TextBox controls to capture the Filter and Find criteria strings, as well as a couple of Command buttons to start the Filter and Find routines.

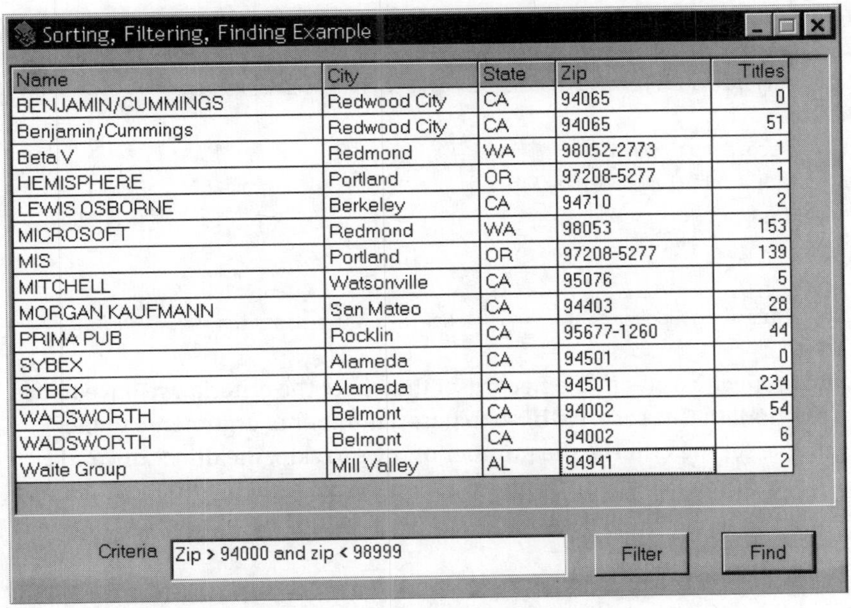

Figure 7-5: The Sort, Filter, and Find example user interface

The following code gets run when you click on the Filter Command button. It simply passes the filter criteria in the TextBox to the Filter property.

```
Private Sub cmdFilter_Click()
On Error GoTo cmdFEH
rs.Filter = txtFilterCriteria.Text
' Note txtFilterCriteria alone did not work
Set MSHFlexGrid1.Recordset = rs
```

When the user clicks on Filter, we take the criteria string and apply it to the Filter property, as seen in the following code segment. When we set the grid to the filtered Recordset, only rows that meet the Filter criteria are shown. The rest of the rows are still in the Recordset—they're just hidden.

> **TIP**   *You can't set the Filter property from a TextBox control without fully qualifying the Text property. That is, you have to code Rs.Filter = txtFilter.Text. If you leave off the .Text property qualifier, ADO gets confused as to how it's supposed to use the property.*

```
Private Sub cmdFind_Click()
On Error GoTo cmdFEH
rs.Find txtFindCriteria.Text, 1, adSearchForward, varBookMarkStart
If rs.EOF Then
    MsgBox "Record not found"
    varBookMarkStart = varBookmarkTop
    rs.MoveFirst
    Exit Sub
End If
varBookMarkStart = rs.Bookmark            ' New Starting position
```

To locate specific rows in the Recordset that meet the criteria, we have to use the Find method. In this case, we have to pass a number of arguments to the method. These set the criteria, the number of rows to skip, the direction, and a bookmark indicating the starting point. I coded the routine to keep looking until EOF is True and then start again at the top of the Recordset.

> **TIP** *As with the Filter property, you can't simply set the Find property to a TextBox control's default property. You must fully qualify the Text property; otherwise, ADO gets confused.*

If no records qualify, based on the criteria, the Recordset is positioned past the valid rows and EOF is set to True. Otherwise, the current row pointer is reset to the first matching row. In this example, I used the AbsolutePosition property to pass the current row number to the MSHFlexGrid control's Row property. We then reset the starting position bookmark so that subsequent searches will begin at the "found" row plus one. Note that all searches begin one row past the starting bookmark position. This initial bookmark is set to point to the first Recordset row.

Constructing Filter Strings

It seems there are a few difugelties (aka bugs) in the ADO string parser when it comes to dealing with Filter (and Find) criteria strings. While these issues are addressed in ADO 2.6, they might cause you a degree of grief before it arrives or on systems that don't have it installed. If you have problems with embedded quotes (single or double), pound signs (#), or exclamation points (!) characters, you may have found the bug.

> **NOTE** *To include single quotation marks (') in the Filter Value, try to use two single quotation marks to represent one. For example, to filter on O'Malley, the criteria string should be 'O''Malley'. To include single quotation marks at both the beginning and the end of the Filter Value, enclose the string with pound signs (#). For example, to filter on '1', the criteria string should be '#'1'#'. ADO has a number of bugs logged against the criteria string parser. Don't be surprised when various combinations of embedded single quotes, double quotes, commas, and pound signs confuse ADO.*

There is no precedence between AND and OR operators in the criteria strings, but Boolean clauses can be grouped within parentheses. However, you *cannot* group clauses joined by an OR and then join the group to another clause with an AND, like this:

```
(LastName = 'Smith' OR LastName = 'Jones') AND FirstName = 'John'
```

Instead, you would construct this filter as:

```
(LastName = 'Smith' AND FirstName = 'John') OR (LastName = 'Jones' AND
FirstName = 'John')
```

ADO uses either the asterisk (*) *or* the percent symbol (%) as its wildcard characters. In a LIKE expression, you can use a wildcard at the beginning and end of the expression (LastName Like '*mit*'), or only at the end of the pattern (LastName Like 'Smit*'). However, in a regular expression, the wildcard character can only be placed at the end of the expression.

Disconnecting Recordsets

A popular and very powerful feature of ADO is its capability to "dissociate" a Recordset from its parent Connection. Once you break off a Recordset from its Connection, you can pass it to another ADO-aware tier where it can be manipulated at will. You can scroll through the rows, add new ones, and delete and update rows. All of these changes are saved in the Recordset object itself. You can save the Recordset locally using the Save method, as we discussed previously, or send it to another tier for processing.

There are a few requirements that you must satisfy to get the disconnected Recordset to work. You must:

- Set the Connection object's CursorLocation property to adUseClient. The client-side cursor library implements this functionality.

- Open the Recordset setting LockType to adLockBatchOptimistic.

- Assign the ActiveConnection property to Nothing. I used to say "Set" the ActiveConnection property to Nothing, but this is not necessary.

That's it. When you're ready to post the changes to the database, you can reassociate the Recordset with a valid Connection object and use the UpdateBatch method to post the changes.

Choosing Read-Only vs. Read-Write Recordsets

In a general sense, there has been significant debate about whether or not one should ask ADO to construct Recordsets that can be updated through the ADO mechanism more or less directly. That is, should you create a cursor that knows how to make changes to the underlying data? As we progress through this chapter, there will be more discussion about this subject, but the bottom line tends to favor creating and using read-only Recordsets and managing the update operations yourself in code. Even if you only compare the sheer volume of data passed when requesting a RO vs. a read-write (RW) Recordset, you'll see why this recommendation is made so often. Use the Recordset.Save method to save each Recordset to a file and compare the sizes.

Working with Field Objects

The definition of Field objects is usually done for you. That is, when you construct a Recordset from a data provider, it's the responsibility of the provider to fill in the Field properties, including the name, datatype, size, and all of the other properties, such as the Status and Attributes. You can also choose to define most of these yourself by constructing an in-memory Recordset, as we discussed in the "Creating and Opening Recordsets in Memory" section in Chapter 6.

In any case, once the Recordset is open, only the Field object's Value property can be changed, and then only under ADO's careful scrutiny. You can try to change the Field Value property using the AddNew or Update methods, which accept Field names and Value settings, or you can directly address the Value property in code. However, if you try to apply an incorrect value to the Value property, ADO informs you by tripping a trappable error. Often it's "–2147217887

Multiple-step operation generated errors. Check each status value." However, in my case, the Status value was 0, so it wasn't much help.

> **NOTE** *The error that tripped up my program was one generated by ADO when I tried to set an adVarChar field to "She said, ""Hi there!"" ". Apparently, the embedded exclamation point confused ADO—it didn't seem to mind the embedded quotes or commas. Interesting.*

It's not a good idea to change the Field Value property willy-nilly. That is, don't change it if it hasn't changed. Setting the Value property to a value that's the same as the existing value is still a change as far as ADO is concerned. This causes extra overhead on ADO's part, as it tries to include the changed fields in the UPDATE statement's WHERE clause.

The other Field properties were discussed in Chapter 5, when I described the ADO Command object Parameters collection:

- **ActualSize and DefinedSize:** A Field object with a declared type of adVarChar and a maximum length of 50 characters returns a DefinedSize property value of 50, but the ActualSize property value it returns is the length of the data stored in the field for the current record.

- **Name:** The name used to reference the field in the database. This is the human interface to the Field object, not the computer interface.

- **Type:** The datatype of the Value property. The types used here are set when the table is first defined or fetched by the data source provider. See the discussion of the Type property in Chapter 5.

- **DataFormat:** This property is an object that specifies how the field is formatted when displayed on a data-bound control. MSDN has orphaned it but it is discussed a little later in this chapter.

- **Precision and NumericScale:** These properties are used to describe numbers that have decimal points or varying degrees of accuracy. For numbers capable of storing a fractional value, the NumericScale property reports how many digits to the right of the decimal point are used to represent values. The Precision property indicates the maximum number of digits to be stored for any number—integer or floating point.

- **OriginalValue:** This property returns the state of the Field object as it was before you made changes.

- **UnderlyingValue:** This property returns the state of the Field object as it is in the database after a Resync. It's the value some other user assigned to the column in the source table.

- **Value:** This is the only Field object property that you are permitted to change. It contains the value as initially read from the data source and it can be set to any valid character or binary state, depending on the constraints defined by the other properties.

- **Properties:** This addresses a collection of provider-specific properties that further define what the Field object is capable of doing, or other special attributes.

- **Status:** This property is not interesting for the Recordset Field object because it returns only one value—adFieldOK. It has more meaning for the ADO Record object.

The Mysterious DataFormat Property

The DataFormat property has apparenly slipped through the cracks—at least to some extent. While it appears as a property in the ADO type libraries, it's not listed as such in MSDN. Perhaps this will be fixed by the time you read this—or perhaps not.

The DataFormat property is similar to the DataFormat property on simple bound controls, such as textboxes. If you set the DataFormat property on a field to Currency and check the Recordset object's Value property, you'll receive a string formatted as currency.

In the following sample code, notice that the UnitPrice field displays the data as currency after using the DataFormat property. If you bind controls to the Recordset, the setting of the DataFormat property on the Field objects does not apply. I'm guessing this is because the bound controls don't access the Field's contents via the Value property. To use the StdDataFormat object, you'll need to set a reference to Microsoft Data Formatting Object Library. (Thanks to David Sceppa for this insight.)

```
Dim cn As ADODB.Connection
Dim rs As ADODB.Recordset
Dim strConn As String, strSQL As String
Dim objDataFormat As StdFormat.StdDataFormat
strConn = "Provider=SQLOLEDB;Data Source=Myserver;Initial Catalog=Northwind;"
strSQL = "SELECT UnitPrice FROM Products Where Category = 'Seafood'"
Set cn = New ADODB.Connection
cn.CursorLocation = adUseClient
```

```
cn.Open strConn, "Admin", "pw"
Set rs = New ADODB.Recordset
rs.Open strSQL, cn, adOpenStatic, adLockReadOnly, adCmdText
MsgBox "Unformatted: " & rs(0)     ' UnitPrice

Set objDataFormat = New StdFormat.StdDataFormat
objDataFormat.Type = fmtCustom
objDataFormat.Format = "Currency"
Set rs.Fields("UnitPrice").DataFormat = objDataFormat
MsgBox "Formatted as currency: " & rs!UnitPrice
rs.Close
cn.Close
```

Field Methods—The Chunk Brothers

There are only two Field methods: GetChunk and AppendChunk. These two methods are used to manipulate Binary Large Objects (BLOBs) fields. Before I bore (you) into how these methods work, I would like to talk you *out* of using them. IMHO, BLOBs don't really belong in the database. Yes, some developers have come to me with successful BLOB column implementations, but more often than not, these were the result of many, many hours, weeks, or months of complex development.

Consider what happens when you define a BLOB column, such as TEXT or IMAGE in SQL Server, or as MEMO or OLE Object in Jet. The database engine sets aside a pointer in the column to point to a data area in which it will store the binary information when it arrives. The database does not grow appreciably when a BLOB column is defined. However, when you pass a BLOB to the database for storage, the DB engine has to allocate memory to store it temporarily (thus shoving out other data rows from the cache), allocate disk space to store it (thus stretching the size of the database), and consume CPU resources to process it (thus slowing down other operations). The ADO and low-level interfaces used to transport the data to the database are also forced to fragment the BLOB into chunks, or smaller pieces, to accommodate the limitations of the transport mechanism. Each of these packets is sent, one by one, to the server for storage.

When the database is backed up, the BLOBs stored therein are included (thus making the backup slower and consuming more media), even if the BLOBs are read-only. And all too often, that's the case. For example, employee pictures don't change very often—if ever. Archived documents, blueprints, and maps also don't change very frequently. Even document templates and forms are static until they are filled in. Working text documents or in-process graphic files are also BLOBs and can change quite frequently, but without a specially adapted retrieval system, they are hard to work with when stored in a database column. Yes, you can write your own retrieval system if you've a mind to. But consider that this might have already been done.

Retrieving a BLOB column reverses the process used to store it. You write a query that includes a BLOB column in the Recordset, the DB engine locates that row (along with others), and the BLOB is temporarily saved to the DB engine's data cache. Other rows are forced out, along with procedures and other recently discarded but reusable data and query plan pages. The BLOB is then rechunked and transmitted over the wire to your client, where it gets written to local RAM, overflowing to the \TEMP area on the client's hard disk. Your code then uses the GetChunk method to retrieve the data into yet another local memory area.

Once it's there, you have to decide what to do with it. If you're fetching a picture, you might try displaying it with a Visual Basic Picture or Image control, or with a third-party graphics control. Virtually all of these know how to deal with graphics resolved from *files,* not memory variables, so in most cases, you'll have to write the BLOB to a temporary file and use the Visual Basic LoadPicture function to display it. If the BLOB is a document, such as a Microsoft Word .DOC file, you'll also have to save the memory variable to a file and tell Word to open the file. However, Edward (my tech editor) tells me that one can also pass the contents of a PropertyBag element to the LoadPicture command. There's an example of doing this below.

Because we end up reading files to store the BLOBs and then writing files to manage them after retrieval, doesn't it make sense to leave the BLOBs in files? You can still store the path to the file in the database, and that makes sense. When you fetch the row, you get back the path. Microsoft Word, or your graphics processing program, or the LoadPicture function can all take that path directly and get the document, graphic, or picture—perhaps from a client-side CD or a server-side CD jukebox. This technique makes system maintenance easier (backups are faster and smaller), and for RW files, these can (must) be backed up separately as they are no longer part of the database.

SQL Server 7.0 has done quite a bit to make this process of storing BLOBs in the database work more efficiently. However, SQL Server still treats BLOB data pretty much like other data in that it lets a single 200MB BLOB flush its combined data and procedure cache. IMHO, a better choice for storing documents that need to be searched and retrieved using SQL is Index Server. See www.microsoft.com/NTServer/web/techdetails/overview/IndexServer.asp for more information.

Using ADO to Fetch BLOBs

Actually, you don't always have to use the Chunk methods to fetch or save BLOBs. Some ADO providers are pretty smart about handling BLOBs without any special code. As a matter of fact, I was able to extract pictures out of the database with only a few lines of code when I used the SQL Server OLE DB provider. However, your mileage may vary.

In the following code example, the vbiChunk variable is defined as a Byte array. When you use Byte arrays, Visual Basic doesn't try to convert the ANSI data to Unicode, which can be a problem with binary files. Because the LoadPicture method only accepts data from file, the BLOB data has to be saved to a file first, so we'll write the Byte array to a Binary file and use the LoadPicture function against that file.

```
vbiChunk = rs.Fields(enFields.Cover)
Put #1, , vbiChunk
imgFromGetChunk.Picture = LoadPicture(strTempName)
```

or:

```
pb.Contents = rs.Fields(enFields.Cover)
img.Picture = pb.Readproperty("img")
```

ADO informs you when you *can* use the Chunk methods (not when it makes sense to use them—that's up to you). If the adFldLong bit in the Field object's Attributes property is True, then you can use the GetChunk method for that field. Personally, though, I wouldn't go to the trouble if I can get away with the syntax shown above.

The GetChunk alternative looks similar to the code shown next. This shows how the query to fetch the desired row (and just one row is fetched), how the temporary file was set up, and how GetChunk was used to pick off 8192-byte chunks, one at a time. (This sample is on the CD at Samples\Recordset Objects\BLOB Sample.)

```
strTempName = "C:\temp\" & fso.GetTempName
Open strTempName For Binary As #1
If rs.State = adStateOpen Then rs.Close
cn.GetCoverByISBN cmbISBNs.Text, rs
```

Once the Recordset has been opened with the preceding code, we loop through the GetChunk method with the following code, fetching a portion of the binary bits, with each loop fetching the next set of bits. When the returned chunk is smaller than the selected chunk size, you've reached the end.

```
Do
    vbiTemp = rs.Fields(enFields.Cover).GetChunk(intChunkSize)
    Put #1, , vbiTemp
```

```
Loop Until UBound(vbiTemp) < intChunkSize - 1
imgFromGetChunk.Picture = LoadPicture(strTempName)
'
```

If the Recordset column does not have a BLOB, the GetChunk method returns a null. The preceding code does not check for this, and it should.

> **TIP** *Visual Basic can generate a unique temporary filename for you, so you don't have to worry about colliding with another filename somewhere. The trick is to figure out that the Microsoft Scripting Runtime contains this FileSystemObject function.*

This example brings up another key point. When working with BLOBs, it's very important to fetch *just* the Record containing the BLOB and no more. Don't fetch a hundred rows at a time unless you are ready to wait and bring your system to its knees.

> **NOTE** *When you save a picture in a Jet database with Access, it wraps the picture in a custom OLE wrapper. You'll have to decode that wrapper to access the picture in Visual Basic.*
>
> *You say you saw us (maybe me) demonstrating how easy it was to fetch pictures from Jet databases? The demonstrators faked it. They copied the pictures to a Visual Basic-based Jet database.*

Each subsequent GetChunk call retrieves data starting from where the previous GetChunk call left off. However, if you are retrieving data from one field, and then you set or read the value of another field in the current record, ADO assumes you have finished retrieving data from the first field. If you call the GetChunk method on the first field again, ADO interprets the call as a new GetChunk operation and starts reading from the beginning of the data. Accessing fields in other Recordset objects that are not clones of the first Recordset object does not disrupt GetChunk operations.

Using AppendChunk to Save BLOBs

Just as with GetChunk, ADO is smart enough to deal with most BLOB issues all on its own. You shouldn't need AppendChunk to save your BLOBs unless there is some other issue you are dealing with such as a tight memory situation.

ADO won't accept AppendChunk operations unless the adFldLong bit in the Attributes property of a Field object is set to True.

The first time you use the AppendChunk method on a Field object, ADO asks the data provider to write data to the field, overwriting any existing data. Subsequent AppendChunk calls add (append) to the existing data. If you are appending data to one field and then you set or read the value of another field in the current record, ADO assumes that you are finished appending data to the first field. If you call the AppendChunk method on the first field again, ADO interprets the call as a new AppendChunk operation and overwrites the existing data. Accessing fields in other Recordset objects that are not clones of the first Recordset object will not disrupt AppendChunk operations.

The following example illustrates how to use AppendChunk to pass chunks of data to the IMAGE field in the Covers table. I was lazy and didn't fetch the specific row in the Covers table to change—which would have been a better idea.

```
Private Sub cmdPutChunk_Click()
Dim strDataIn As String * 8192
Dim lngFPointer As Long
Dim strFileName As String
CommonDialog1.ShowOpen
strFileName = CommonDialog1.FileName
Open strFileName For Binary As #2
If rs.State = adStateOpen Then rs.Close
rs.Open "Covers", cn, adOpenStatic, adLockOptimistic, adCmdTable
Get #2, , strDataIn
rs.AddNew
rs.Fields(enCoverFld.FileName) = strFileName
rs.Fields(enCoverFld.BType) = "XXX"
rs.Fields(enCoverFld.Version) = "00000"
rs.Fields(enCoverFld.ISBN) = cmbISBNs.Text
Do
    lngFPointer = lngFPointer + intChunkSize
    rs.Fields(enCoverFld.Cover).AppendChunk (strDataIn)
    Get #2, lngFPointer, strDataIn
Loop Until lngFPointer >= FileLen(CommonDialog1.FileName)
rs.Update
quit:
rs.Close
Close #2
End Sub
```

Working with Stored Procedures

I've folded some discussion of stored procedure handling into the preceding discussions, so you should have a pretty good idea of how stored procedures are executed. This section summarizes those points and adds a few new ones that I haven't yet touched on.

First, ADO was designed from its inception to execute stored procedures—at least simple ones. While there are a few disconnects here and there, ADO does a great job of handling stored procedure invocation and the stuff that stored procedures return, including the return status, output parameters, and both single and multiple result sets, along with their rowsets.

You don't have to do much to get ADO to invoke your stored procedure. You no longer have to hard-code the call statement as you did in RDO, and for simple stored procedures, you can simply reference them as methods of the Connection object. I'll show you how to construct a call statement for those situations where either you want to know what's going on behind the scenes or you want to get closer to the inner workings of ADO.

When you want to capture more than just the rowsets from a stored procedure, such as the return status or OUTPUT parameters, you must construct a Command object to handle them for you. I've discussed how to construct a Command object before, so I won't discuss it again. Just keep these tips in mind:

- Set the CommandText to the name (just the name) of the stored procedure. Yes, there are a couple of other options, which I'll discuss in a minute.

- Set the Name property to the stored procedure's name (optional). The CommandText and Name properties should match.

- Set the Command type to adCmdStoredProc to tell ADO the CommandText contains the name of a stored procedure.

- Set the ActiveConnection to the target server capable of executing the stored procedure.

- Fill in the Parameters collection. As was discussed in Chapter 5, ADO can do this by using the Refresh method or by hand using the Append and CreateParameter methods.

- Set the correct direction for each noninput Parameter, regardless of how the Parameters collection is populated. This ensures that ADO understands how and when to handle the parameter.

- Set the Value property to assign a default setting for each parameter.

Executing Stored Procedures

After you've set up a Command object, executing a stored procedure is just a process of setting the execution-time parameter values and executing the Command object. Simple? Well, actually, there are other, even simpler ways to execute stored procedures—even those stored procedures that require input arguments. Sure, you have to use a Command object if you expect to capture Return Status or OUTPUT parameters; but if that's not the case, you can get away with a lot less. In any case, you should be familiar with the techniques to execute Command objects.

What you have to be careful about is the impact of your choice of ADO syntax. As I said, ADO was designed from the outset to execute stored procedures. Because of this, and because the ADO team wanted to support legacy code from RDO and ADO, a number of antiquated techniques will work.

Performance Considerations

Before we look at the examples, note that the execution times for all of these techniques were almost identical—after the second execution. That is, the first time these commands were executed, ADO took about 0.5 seconds (half a second) to run on my computer.[4] The second time took about half of that time (0.28 seconds), but all subsequent executions took (roughly) between 0.038 and 0.007 seconds to run. Apparently, there is some setup time that is not necessary when the query is reexecuted. I suspect the data and query plan being cached on the server is part of this difference, as well as connection-pooling overhead.

When the system is left idle for a while or the server is restarted, these cached structures are flushed and the timings return to their initial state. Other techniques (Open method vs. stored procedure as method) seem to require initial setup as well, but the server-side of the equation seemed to help any query that executed the same stored procedure.

Let's look at example code for the top four techniques: stored procedure as Connection method, Recordset Open method, Connection Execute method, and Command Execute method. Yes, there are other methods, but they don't really buy you anything except a reputation for obscure code.

Using the Stored Procedure as a Connection Method

The technique in this first example seems to be missing from most documentation. It's the simplest of all and seems to work more elegantly and

---

4. I also had the Profiler running, which would impact performance. See the sample application in ...\Sample applications\Recordset Objects\Stored Procedures\Simple Example.

efficiently than most, if not all, other techniques. It takes advantage of the fact that ADO exposes all stored procedures as methods of the Command object. This means you can simply code the stored procedure as shown in the following code, followed by the input arguments (no, you can't specify return status or OUTPUT arguments), followed by the preinitialized Recordset to receive the first rowset. ADO does not construct a Command object, but it does set the Source property to the appropriate ODBC Call statement, just as we would do in RDO.

```
cn.Au42 1950, 1960, rs
```

When this code executes, the SQL Server 7.0 profiler simply shows the stored procedure being executed with its input parameters. There are no "preparation" steps, no use of sp_executesql, no nothing—just the stored procedure call. Cool.

```
Profiler: Au42 1950, 1960
```

Using the Recordset Open Method

This approach passes a string containing the stored procedure, along with the parameters, to the Recordset Open method.

```
strSource = "au42 " & txtParm1.Text & ", " & txtParm2.Text
```

In some tests, however, I found ADO (sometimes) passed the arguments as quoted strings to the server. For example, sometimes ADO sent this to the server to execute:

```
Profiler: Au42 '1950', '1960'
```

This did not seem to bother the server, but if it does, you can cast the Text property to an integer using the CInt function:

```
strSource = "au42 " & CInt(txtParm1.Text) & ", " & CInt(txtParm2.Text)
rs.Open strSource, cn, Options:=adCmdText
```

This approach enables you to set up the Recordset ahead of time, so you can choose the type of cursor and locking desired, along with other appropriate Recordset properties.

Using the Connection Execute Method

We discussed the Connection Execute method in Chapter 4, so you should be familiar with its use. Remember that you can get the RecordsAffected value back from action queries, but not from SELECT queries. However, you also have to settle for the default firehose (RO/FO/CacheSize=1) cursor, because the Execute method manufactures the Recordset for you.

We pass in the same source string as constructed in the previous example.

```
Set rs = cn.Execute(strSource, intRA)
```

Using the Command Execute Method

We discussed using the Command object in Chapter 5. Executing a stored procedure with the Command object is no different than the other techniques, in respect to what gets executed on the server. In this case, however, you have to provide the parameters either by using a Variant array containing the parameters, or by passing in the parameters using direct references to the Command object. Both techniques are shown below.

Providing the parameters in a Variant array:

```
Set rs = cmd.Execute(intRA, varParams)
```

Setting each parameter individually:

```
cmd.Parameters(1) = txtParm1.Text
cmd.Parameters(2) = txtParm2.Text
Set rs = cmd.Execute(intRA)
```

Dealing with Stored Procedure Result Sets

The tricky part, which is the handling of the stuff that returns (but it isn't that tricky), comes after the stored procedure is executed. Remember that data providers return one or more result sets from the data provider, whether or not you're executing a stored procedure. An individual result set contains:

- **No or one Rowset:** Stored procedures return no rowset to any number of rowsets. These must be captured using ADO syntax that specifies a Recordset, unless you simply want to discard the results.

- **A rows affected value:** When you execute an action query and don't use the SET NOCOUNT ON, the provider returns the number of rows inserted, deleted, or updated.

- **A row count:** After the provider completes processing the query, it returns a tally of the rows processed. If the cursor supports it, this value is assigned to the RecordCount property once it arrives.

- **A Return Status integer:** All stored procedures send back a return status, but unless you or ADO constructed the Parameters collection to capture this integer, it falls in the bit bucket.

- **OUTPUT parameters:** Stored procedures can and should return OUTPUT parameters whenever possible—especially when it can eliminate one or more rowsets.

When you examine the Recordset ADO returns after executing your stored procedure, but before you start wondering where the rows are, consider the nature of a stored procedure. Stored procedures are *programs*—plain and simple. These programs can return no rowsets at all, and perhaps not even return status or output parameters. On the other hand, they can return any number of rowsets, rows-affected values, and output parameters (within the limitations of the data provider). And as I said, the set of rowsets, rows-affected values, and output parameters is called a *result set*. So it's easier to simply say stored procedures can return from one to any number of result sets.

To effectively use stored procedures, you must understand what they do (duhh). Some stored procedures return a different combination of rowsets and rows-affected values based on the logic, and thus a different number of result sets. Suppose you have a procedure that runs once a month to generate sales totals. The procedure runs one section of code on an "ordinary" month, but additional sections of code run at the end of the quarter, midyear, and at the end of the year. Because of this, your application needs to be prepared for *n* result sets.

> **NOTE** *INSERT, UPDATE, and DELETE statements all return rows-affected values. ADO does not make it easy to fetch these unless you execute a stored procedure using the Execute method, and then only if there is one statement. It does not work for batches.*

Okay, so you ran the query and examined the Recordset. You discovered that the Recordset object is not Nothing[5] (it's instantiated), but it's also not open (State = adStateClosed). What's the deal? Well, it could be that your first result set did not contain a rowset. For example, if the first statement in the stored procedure is an UPDATE statement (or any action operation), a result set is generated and ADO is informed that the first data is available. ADO subsequently constructs a Recordset to hold the result set and discovers there is no rowset, so it cannot open the Recordset. However, if your stored procedure executes a SELECT statement that returns no rows, an empty rowset is generated and ADO returns the instantiated Recordset with EOF=True.

A technique you can use to reduce overhead in complex stored procedures is to ignore the rows-affected value. That is, you can use the SET NOCOUNT ON TSQL statement in the stored procedure to tell SQL Server to not bother generating result sets just for the rows-affected values. Doing so saves time and can improve the execution speed of your code—it's another best practice.

As a point of reference, ADO 1.5 executed SET NOCOUNT ON automatically. This behavior was changed in ADO 2.0, which means that if you upgrade to ADO 2.0 or later (on purpose or not), your stored procedure handlers will now receive extra action query result sets—and will probably break. A fix for this problem is to add the SET NOCOUNT ON command to the stored procedures in question.

> **WARNING**   *If you use the SET NOCOUNT ON TSQL statement outside the scope of a stored procedure, the setting is persisted in the connection. This means all subsequent use of the connection uses this option—even those clients inheriting the connection from the connection pool. Be sure to turn this option off, by using SET NOCOUNT OFF, when you're done.*

Capturing RecordsAffected Values

When your result set executes an action query, it returns a rows-affected value—unless you disable this functionality using SET NOCOUNT ON. For example, if you execute an Update statement that affects all rows in the Animals table where Type = "pig", the rows-affected value should return 70 if there are 70 qualifying pigs in the table.

The rows-affected value can be captured using two methods—the Connection.Execute method or the NextRecordset method. Both of these ADO

---

5. I hate double negatives, but there is no ADO or COM notation for Something. Wouldn't it be nice if we could say, "If RS is Something Then...." Wouldn't that be something?

methods support returned arguments to capture the rows-affected value. If you don't turn off the rows-affected values using SET NOCOUNT ON when executing a stored procedure that has several action queries, ADO can expose each action query's rows-affected value using the NextRecordset method.

```
Set rs = rs.NextRecordset(intRA)
```

Accessing OUTPUT Parameters

One of the most important components of a result set can be the set of OUTPUT parameters passed back from stored procedures. OUTPUT parameters can be used instead of rowsets for singleton operations—operations that return only a single set of values. More importantly, OUTPUT parameters can be returned by stored procedures *instead* of a rowset, thus avoiding the (considerable) expense of constructing a Recordset. The OUTPUT parameter can be set up to return any provider datatype, from integers to BLOBs. You can also return computed or aggregate information in OUTPUT parameters drawn from complex multitable queries. While your data provider limits the number of OUTPUT parameters (SQL Server 7.0 limits stored procedure parameters to 1,024), you can still send a large number of values back to the ADO client.

OUTPUT parameters are easy to manage in ADO. While ADO itself stumbles a bit when constructing a Parameter object to deal with individual OUTPUT parameters, you can easily overcome this difugelty. Basically, the problem lies in the fact that the data providers don't differentiate between OUTPUT and INPUT/OUTPUT parameters, so ADO assumes that all OUTPUT parameters are INPUT/OUTPUT. All you have to do is change the Direction property to adParamOutput before executing the query.

> **NOTE** *If you return a rowset and OUTPUT parameters or a Return status integer, you have to close the Recordset before they are visible. I discuss this in detail a little later in this chapter.*

Let's walk through an example of a routine that calls a stored procedure that *only* returns OUTPUT (and return status) parameters, but no rowset. This means we won't need a Recordset at all, and the OUTPUT parameters will be available as soon as the query is executed.

```
Create PROCEDURE OutputTitleByISBN
    (@ISBNWanted varchar(20) = '0-0233058-8-6',
    @Title VarChar(250) OUTPUT,
```

```
    @Author VarChar(50) output,
    @TypeDescription varchar(30) output,
    @Price money  output)
AS
Select @Title = Title,
    @Author = Author,
    @Price = Price,
    @TypeDescription = v.Description
from Titles t, Title_Author ta, Authors a, ValidTitleTypes v
Where t.ISBN = @ISBNWanted
and a.au_id = ta.au_id
and ta.isbn=ta.isbn
and v.type = t.type
```

The Visual Basic code that executes the preceding stored procedure is fairly straightforward, as shown next. The routine for constructing the Command object is in the Form_Load event, where it is executed but once.

```
With cmd
    .CommandText = "OutputTitleByISBN"
    .Name = "GetTitle"
    .CommandType = adCmdStoredProc
    .Parameters.Append .CreateParameter("ReturnStatus", adInteger,
adParamReturnValue)
    .Parameters.Append .CreateParameter("ISBNWanted", adVarChar, adParamInput, 20)
    .Parameters.Append .CreateParameter("Title", adVarChar, adParamOutput, 250)
    .Parameters.Append .CreateParameter("Author", adVarChar, adParamOutput, 50)
    .Parameters.Append .CreateParameter("Type", adVarChar, adParamOutput, 30)
    .Parameters.Append .CreateParameter("Price", adCurrency, adParamOutput, 200)
    .ActiveConnection = cn
End With
End Sub
```

The following routine parses the returning OUTPUT parameters and paints them on the form. Notice that the Command object is executed using the adExecuteNoRecords option to prevent the construction of a Recordset. This helps performance.

```
Private Sub cmbISBNs_Click()
Dim parP As Parameter
Dim intRa As Integer
If cmd.ActiveConnection Is Nothing Then Exit Sub
picPrint.Cls
```

```
With cmd
    .Parameters(1) = cmbISBNs.Text
    .Execute intRa, , adExecuteNoRecords
    picPrint.Print "Records affected:"; intRa
    For Each parP In cmd.Parameters
        picPrint.Print parP.Name, Tab(15), parP.Value
    Next
End With
End Sub
```

Managing Multiple Result Sets

One question that comes up often (I've raised it myself) is, "*When* are the OUTPUT parameters available to the client if I combine OUTPUT parameters with rowsets?" Well, that's an interesting question. It only comes up in cases where the stored procedure returns *both* output parameters and a rowset that's transmogrified into a Recordset. A very interesting point came up when I tried this with a dual-purpose stored procedure—I discovered that if you touch the Parameters collection before closing the Recordset, all values are lost. That is, once the query is executed, you must fetch the rowset from the Recordset prior to even attempting to view the Parameters collection (as in the Locals window). If you don't fetch the Recordset first and close it before you peek at the Parameters, they are set to empty. Isn't that *special?*

The following example parses the rowset and the OUTPUT parameters returned from a dual-mode (OUTPUT and rowset) query. Notice how the Recordset object must be closed (but not necessarily set to Nothing) *before* attempting to access the Parameters collection. The OUTPUT parameters are sent in the final packet returned to the client once the query is complete.

```
Dim parP As Parameter
Dim intRa As Integer
If cmd.ActiveConnection Is Nothing Then Exit Sub
picPrint.Cls
Set rs = New Recordset
With cmd
    .Parameters(1) = cmbISBNs.Text
    Set rs = .Execute(intRa)
    Set MSHFlexGrid1.Recordset = rs
    rs.Close
    picPrint.Print "Records affected:"; intRa
    For Each parP In cmd.Parameters
        picPrint.Print parP.Name, Tab(15), parP.Value
```

```
      Next
End With
End Sub
```

The following code walks through each of the returned Recordsets. It uses the NextRecordset method to flush the current Recordset and enable the next. This is repeated until the retrieved Recordset is set to Nothing.

```
… Process first Recordset
Do
     Set rs = rs.NextRecordset
     … Process next Result set
Loop Until rs is Nothing
```

The NextRecordset method closes the existing Recordset and repeats the process of Recordset construction. At this point ADO either replaces the existing Recordset with the next result set or returns a Recordset set to Nothing. Remember that subsequent Recordset objects might (just might) contain rowsets, so be prepared for instantiated, but *closed*, Recordset objects when there is no rowset—as when an action query is in the script or stored procedure. A closed state (adStateClosed) Recordset is returned when there is another result set, but it contains no rowset—as when you execute an action query.

Apparently, ADO handles multiple result sets differently than earlier data access interfaces. In the past, the server did not process each subsequent result set until the client dealt with the preceding result set. That is, unless you canceled the query or canceled the whole operation (both are options in DB-Library and RDO), the server would not continue to process the stored procedure once the cancel command was received. However, despite what the MSDN doc says, the spec says that the provider might choose to process all result sets in the stored procedure as a unit, one after another, sending the individual result sets back to the client one-at-a-time. This seems to be what ADO is doing. Because of this, you cannot expect the Cancel method to have much effect on the processing of a stored procedure—even on one that returns multiple result sets.

The NextRecordset syntax shown in the previous code example overlays an existing Recordset object with the next result set. While you can assign the next Recordset to another Recordset variable, you won't be able to reference the previous Recordset once NextRecordset has executed. However, there's nothing to stop you from persisting each Recordset to a Stream as it arrives. This way you could manipulate each one at your leisure.

> **NOTE**   *The Command object's InfoMessage fires a "No more results" message when all Recordsets have been processed. This is another way to determine when all Recordsets have been visited.*

To illustrate the use of multiple result set stored procedures, I wrote an example application (on the CD, see ..\sample applications\Recordset object\ stored procedure\multiple result sets). The stored procedure parser in this application is pretty typical of a simple multiple result set handler, but before I show you this code, take a look at the code used to populate the two drop-down ListBox controls that contain the valid types and valid ISBNs used in the program. This code calls the stored procedure that returns two separate rowsets—one for each drop-down. The parser simply walks through the rows and populates the lists from the rowsets. The stored procedure looks like this:

```
CREATE Procedure GetValidTypesAndISBNs
    (@ISBNRange varchar(20) = 'H%' , @MaxRows integer = 50)
As
    Select Type, Description from ValidTitleTypes
Set Rowcount  @MaxRows
    Select  ISBN from Titles where Title like @ISBNRange
Set RowCount 0
    return @@Rowcount
```

The code in Visual Basic that runs and parses this stored procedure is also pretty simple:

```
Set rs = New Recordset
cn.GetValidTypesAndISBNs "H%", 50, rs
```

```
Do Until rs.EOF
    cmbValidTypes.AddItem rs(0) & " : " & rs(1)
    rs.MoveNext
Loop
cmbValidTypes.ListIndex = 0
Set rs = rs.NextRecordset
Do Until rs.EOF
    cmbValidISBNs.AddItem rs(0)
    rs.MoveNext
Loop
cmbValidISBNs.ListIndex = 0
rs.Close
```

The routine used in the run procedure is a little more complex, but it covers most of the bases when accessing multiple result set stored procedures. In this case, we test the Recordset State property for adStateOpen to see if the result set has a rowset, and the EOF property to see whether there are rows in the rowset. If there are rows, we display them in the grid. If not, we simply step to the next Recordset using the NextRecordset method until this method returns a Recordset set to Nothing. I laid out this logic in a flowchart (takes me back to my IBM 360 days) that should make this process clearer. The flowchart is shown in Figure 7-6, and the code looks like this:

```
Do
    If rs.State = adStateOpen Then
        If rs.EOF Then Else Set MSHFlexGrid1.Recordset = rs      'No rows?
    End If
    Set rs = rs.NextRecordset
    If rs Is Nothing Then
    Else
        i = MsgBox("Next recordset? Press Cancel to end.", _
        vbOKCancel + vbInformation)
        If i = vbCancel Then Exit Do
        MSHFlexGrid1.Clear
    End If
Loop Until rs Is Nothing
```

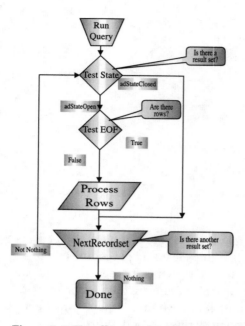

Figure 7-6: Handling multiple result sets returned from stored procedures

Handling Complex Result Sets

Stored procedures return rowsets, return status values, and OUTPUT parameters, and they can also return:

- Extra result sets, including rowsets generated by COMPUTE statements

- Strings generated by TSQL PRINT statements

- Values and "error" messages returned by RAISERROR statements

Remember that the RAISERROR function in TSQL does not necessarily indicate a fatal error. For years, RAISERROR has been used to signal logical conditions that need extra attention at the client. For example, when an application sells a pair of green high-heel shoes and calls a stored procedure to record the sale, an UPDATE statement is executed that affects the quantity-on-hand value for that shoe type. The stored procedure might also check to see whether the current quantity-on-hand is lower than a specified reorder trigger amount. If that's the case, the stored procedure could use a RAISERROR function to signal that the update succeeded, but the quantity of green high-heel shoes is low. It's the responsibility of your application to deal with this extra chunk of information passed back to your client or component.

Handling Compute Statements

The TSQL COMPUTE statement generates totals that appear as additional summary columns at the end of the result set. When used with BY, the COMPUTE clause generates control-breaks and subtotals in the result set. You can specify COMPUTE BY and COMPUTE in the same query. ADO returns all of this extra data as additional Recordsets.

Ideally, COMPUTE statements are handled in hierarchical Recordset structures. While this example does not do that, it is possible to set this up using ADO. I discuss hierarchical techniques in Chapter 10.

The following stored procedure is an example of COMPUTE and COMPUTE BY TSQL statements. These provide summary information on grouped rowsets in the form of additional aggregated totals and subtotals. Each time a group is segmented by the stored procedure, an additional rowset is generated for the COMPUTE totals. I show you how to process this stored procedure next. This code can also be found on the CD under \Sample Applications\Compute By.

```
Create procedure ComputeAvgPriceByPublisherAndType
    (@statewanted varchar(2) = 'WA',
    @CompanyWanted varchar(20))
as
SELECT substring(Company_Name,1,20)Company, type, price
FROM titles t, publishers p
WHERE t.pubid = p.pubid
and state = 'wa'
and Company_Name like @CompanyWanted + '%'
and price > 0
order BY t.pubid,type
COMPUTE avg(price) BY t.pubid, type
COMPUTE avg(price) BY t.pubid
COMPUTE avg(price)
```

There are three levels of COMPUTE BY result sets in this procedure, in addition to multiple sets of detail rows—one set for each type and publisher:

- Average price by publisher and type

- Average price by publisher for all types

- Average price for all publishers and all types

The code that executes and processes the result sets returned by this stored procedure is fairly simple. We start by setting up a form to capture the state and company wanted. The Form_Load event handler creates a Command object and its parameter collection to manage the two input parameters.

```
Private Sub Form_Load()
Set cn = New Connection
Set cmd = New Command

cn.Open "dsn=localserver", "SA", ""

With cmd
    .CommandText = "ComputeAvgPriceByPublisherAndType"
    .Name = "ComputeTest"
    .CommandType = adCmdStoredProc
    .Parameters.Append_
    .CreateParameter("StateWanted", adVarChar, adParamInput, 2, "ca")
    .Parameters.Append_
    .CreateParameter("CompanyWanted", adVarChar, adParamInput, 20)
    .ActiveConnection = cn
End With
```

The cmdRun button click event, shown next, executes the Command object, passing in the arguments from the TextBox controls. The initial Recordset contains the first set of detail rows from the query. This Recordset is applied to the MSHFlexGrid control to be displayed.

```
Private Sub cmdRun_Click()
Set rs = New Recordset
cn.ComputeTest txtStateWanted.Text, txtCompany.Text, rs
Set MSHFlexGrid1.Recordset = rs
```

To fetch the next set of detail rows or COMPUTE aggregate, we simply use the NextRecordset method to fetch the next Recordset in the stream of data being returned from the server. When no further result sets are available, the NextRecordset method returns Nothing.

```
End Sub
Private Sub cmdNext_Click()
Set rs = rs.NextRecordset
If rs Is Nothing Then
    MsgBox "No more results..."
    Set MSHFlexGrid1.Recordset = Nothing
Else
```

```
      Set MSHFlexGrid1.Recordset = rs
End If
End Sub
```

Handling PRINT and RAISERROR Statements

ADO handles the PRINT and RAISERROR TSQL statements similarly. Both
fire the InfoMessage event, which returns the message text specified in the
TSQL statement. This text string is returned in the ADODB.Error object's
Description property.

```
Private Sub cnn_InfoMessage(ByVal pError As ADODB.Error, _
adStatus As ADODB.EventStatusEnum, ByVal pConnection As ADODB.Connection)
Debug.Print "A message arrived: ",_
pError.Description, pError.NativeError,  pError.Number
End Sub
```

However, there are a few caveats:

- RAISERROR statements in SQL Server must have a severity level of 11 to 18.
  Lower severity errors are ignored. Unfortunately, a single RAISERROR
  message terminates the query being executed, so subsequent result sets
  are tossed. (Sigh.)

- PRINT statements in SQL Server can also populate the ADO Errors
  collection. However, PRINT statements are severity level 0, so at least one
  RAISERROR statement greater than severity 10 is required in the stored
  procedure to retrieve a PRINT statement with ADO through the Errors
  collection. (Double sigh.)

- RETURN status values in a stored procedure must be associated with at
  least one result set. (Triple sigh.)

All this means that although you can process RAISERROR and PRINT
statements, many (many) will be ignored unless your stored procedures are
revised to conform to these restrictions. This implementation is a giant step
backward for ADO when compared to DB-Library, which supported far more
functionality with RAISERROR.

If you don't enable the Connection object's InfoMessage event, the PRINT
and RAISERROR messages and error number values are lost, and your application
proceeds as if nothing happened. That is, unless the RAISERROR severity number

is high enough to tell ADO that something serious has occurred while executing the stored procedure. This is because ADO returns only severities 11 to 18 as "informational" events. PRINT statements are treated as severity 0 errors.

> **NOTE** *To retrieve a RETURN value in ADO with a stored procedure, there must be at least one result set. To work around this problem, when no result sets are specified (in the ADO sample code), the stored procedure executes a SELECT NULL to return a null result set to ADO, thereby populating the RETURN value. In addition, to working around the issue of specifying no RAISERROR statements and a combination of PRINT statements, default RAISERROR statements are generated in order to provide a context for returning the PRINT statement via ADO.*

The RAISERROR and Messages Dilemma

I also discovered that there's a dramatic difference in the way that the OLE DB provider for ODBC and the native OLE DB provider for SQL Server manage RAISERROR and PRINT statements. The ODBC provider seems to return all messages generated by the server, including simple informational messages. However, it does not return *any* RAISERROR messages. In my test, only the "No more results" message was returned when I stepped past the last result set after having executed a multiple result set stored procedure. In contrast, the OLE DB native provider returns very few messages, but it *does* return the *first* RAISERROR message, although this terminates the query. Both providers simply ignore any RAISERROR message with a severity less than 11.

I queried the SQL Server internal support alias on campus and got a detailed explanation of what's going on. While I don't completely agree with the implementation, I can see why it has evolved into what we're seeing. According to the gurus, handling the messages and errors raised by SQL Server in OLE DB and ODBC-based environments has always been difficult because of two fundamental factors:

- The way SQL Server returns errors and messages at the TDS level

- The way OLE DB providers handle messages and errors

The first of these issues has to do with how SQL Server returns errors and messages. Because DB-Library was SQL Server's first low-level interface, much of the confusion has to do with mapping functionality that was available when DB-Library was fully supported. DB-Library expects applications to have separate error and message handlers, each exposing a callback function. We implemented this in Visual Basic from the earliest days using special API calls. These error and message callbacks fired events that we could trap to manage all errors and messages (regardless of severity).

Although this architecture was considered for ODBC 1.0, it was dropped in favor of the more generic ODBC mechanism, where the ODBC function returns codes that indicate the presence of errors or messages. These messages and errors could be subsequently retrieved using SQLGetDiagRec, but there was no event support for this. This means that the developer has to code an error-polling routine to regularly check to see whether an error (or message) has arrived.

To work with this approach, when the SQL Server ODBC driver detects items that would have gone to a DB-Library *message* handler, it returns SQL_SUCCESS_WITH_INFO to the ODBC function call. The ODBC driver only sets SQL_ERROR if it gets an item that would go to the DB-Library *error* handler. When this happens, items such as the output of a PRINT or RAISERROR statement with a low severity only generate a SUCCESS_WITH_INFO return. If the provider ignores these, the error or message is ignored and lost.

On the OLE DB side of the problem, the architecture attempts to further distance the data provider (SQL Server) from the application. Because the OLE DB spec says that a provider cannot return DB_S_ERRORSOCCURRED if there are only *warnings* (such as low-severity RAISERROR calls), when SQLOLEDB (the native SQL Server OLE DB provider) gets messages back (as opposed to errors), it exposes the messages as *error* records. However, OLE DB still has to return S_OK to the OLE DB consumer. SQLOLEDB consumers have to be coded to test for the presence of OLE DB error records containing messages, even when they get S_OK. Because this coding is in ADO itself, there's little that you as an ADO developer can do about capturing messages and low-severity errors.

A few more information points to clarify the situation:

- The OLE DB Provider for ODBC does not always check for messages when a driver returns SQL_SUCCESS_WITH_INFO. If ADO is not always returning messages from the SQLOLEDB provider, ADO cannot always populate an error collection if a provider returns S_OK. This means ADO applications have difficulty getting any PRINT statements, and don't get any RAISERROR statements with a low severity, as many OLE DB applications using the OLE DB Provider for ODBC are layered over the SQL Server ODBC driver.

NOTE *Other statements, such as DBCC statements, SET SHOWPLAN, and SET STATISTICS, also use the same mechanism as PRINT and low-severity RAISERROR statements. These are also ignored.*

- The fact that the ODBC-based SQL Server utilities, such as Query Analyzer and OSQL, return the output of these statements shows that it can be done properly.

The problem facing the SQL Server provider developers keeps getting increasingly complex as they tinker with the provider clockworks. If they "fix" this problem, lots of applications might fail, because they would now get errors and messages for operations that were simply ignored in the past. The Microsoft developers are looking for better solutions.

Handling Automatic Parameter Population in Transactions

I noticed something interesting about using the Parameters collection's Refresh method when working with stored procedures. If Refresh is called within a transaction, the data provider locks some of the system tables. After a Refresh call, and while this transaction is still active, calling Refresh from another application hangs. This also hangs SQL Enterprise Manager if the server node is expanded. This behavior can be seen with ADO 1.5, ADO 2.0, and MSDASQL provider with SQL 6.5. However, it does not seem to affect SQLOLEDB provider with SQL Server 6.5/SQL Server 7.0 or MSDASQL provider with SQL Server 7.0.

The reason for this behavior is that ODBC (when implemented through the use of the MSDASQL provider) returns the metadata associated with the Parameters collection via the SQL Server TempDB database. If this process is wrapped in an uncommitted transaction, any other process that tries to insert a row into the TempDB sysobjects table (say, by trying to automatically populate another Parameters collection) hangs until the transaction is rolled back or committed.

Remember that this happens only when the Parameters collection is automatically populated from *within* a transaction. If the client application manually populates the Parameters collection, no round-trip is made to the server to get the parameter information, and no locks are implemented in the TempDB database. Another workaround is to use automatic population, but use it outside the scope of the transaction. In that case, executing the Command object within the transaction will not cause excessive locking in TempDB.

I'm a big fan of avoiding automatic population whenever possible, because the application will take a pretty noticeable performance hit while it makes the round-trip to the server to obtain the metadata associated with the parameters collection.

Providing Stored Procedure Parameters by Hand

Those of you who are migrating from RDO might be tempted to roll your own Call statements and fill in the parameters by hand. I'm afraid I don't see why one would still want to do this, but for those who want a clearer path when migrating from RDO, here it is.

Instead of setting the CommandType to adCmdStoredProc, try adCmdText. In this case, you have to pass either a correctly formatted Call statement or the name of the stored procedure concatenated to any parameters. This seems pretty silly to me, as it takes more code and more work on the part of the providers and server to decode what you're trying to execute. The Call statement is formatted in the same way as was done in RDO.

Your query's parameters can be provided using a variety of techniques, each of which has advantages and drawbacks that include (or don't include) the capability to leverage your procedures and scale your applications. Although using the Command object is the preferred best practice technique, you might find the need to call stored procedures using the Call statement or simply by rolling your own CommandText. You can pass parameters to stored procedures (or to ordinary ad hoc queries) in the following ways:

- **As hard-coded arguments in an SQL query string.** In this case, ADO can't really help manage the parameters for you, and other people can't use the query either, even if they are performing the same search. The real disadvantage here is that to change the parameter you have to recode, recompile, retest, and redeploy your application.

```
MySPFindTitleByState 'CA'
```

- **Using a question mark (?) parameter placeholder in an SQL statement.** In this case, you enable ADO's capability to manage the parameters for you. Simply setting a Command object's CommandText property to this query string gives enough information to ADO and the data provider to build a rough Parameters collection. Your code doesn't have to deal with embedded quotes in the parameters passed, or any framing quotes, because ADO and the data provider handle these for you.

```
MySPFindTitlesByState  ?"
```

- **As the question mark (?) parameter placeholders in a stored procedure call that accepts Input, Output, or Return Status arguments.** We have now reached the next (but not the highest) level of sophistication when building parameter queries. When you execute a stored procedure with this Call syntax, ADO manages the query and its parameters for you. Because ADO is handling the parameters for you, you don't need to worry about embedded or framing quotes. The following quoted string is assigned to the CommandText property.

```
"{Call MySPFindTitlesByState(?)}"
```

- **As the question mark (?) parameter placeholders in a DataEnvironment object.** You can also build parameter queries using the Data Environment Designer. The Data Environment Designer performs most of the complex tasks that you would have to duplicate in code and also provides a shareable way to build the fairly complex SQL statements required by parameter queries. That is, after you create a DataEnvironment object that references a stored procedure (or other query), you can share it among the other developers who also need access to this query. This approach also assumes you haven't read Chapter 12 on the Visual Database Tools. In that chapter, I detail the plethora of problems, oversights, and bugs you get when using the Data Environment Designer.

How to Use Parameter Markers

Each query parameter that you want to have ADO manage must be indicated by a question mark (?) in the text of the SQL statement. To execute a query that takes a single input parameter, your SQL statement would look something like this:

```
Select Publisher from Publishers Where State = ?
```

Multiple parameters can be salted throughout the query, as required. You need to follow a few rules, though, and I get to those in a minute. But you can pass parameters to several queries at once when building multiple result set queries. For example, you could provide the following SQL statement for execution and expect it to manage all three parameters:

```
Select Title from Titles
Where Description between ? and ?
Select Author from Authors where Author Like ?
```

Here are those multiple parameter tips and rules I promised:

- Parameter queries can use question marks as placeholders for both the input and output parameters.

- Stored procedure calls are surrounded by braces ({}), as shown in the following code. This string is applied to the CommandText property. Failure to use correct call syntax might not prevent the procedure from being executed, but the ADO might not be able to identify the parameter positions or markers.[6]

```
{ ? = Call MySP }
```

- Passing Nulls: Many stored procedures require or permit you to pass NULL as an input Parameter. When you do, the stored procedure can substitute its own default value or take other logical action based on an unknown value being passed. There's no real mystery to passing a NULL—simply assign the Parameter Value property with the vbNull constant.

ODBC Call Syntax

Table 7-1 summarizes the ADO[7] Call syntax that you have to include in your queries unless you use the UserConnection Designer, which creates this Call syntax for you. You need to include a question mark (?) for each parameter, regardless of direction.

QUERY PARAMETER CONFIGURATION	ODBC CALL SYNTAX
No parameters	{Call My_sp}
All parameters marked—input, output, both	{Call My_sp (?, ?)}
Some parameters marked	{Call My_sp (?, 'Y')}
Query returns just a return status argument	{? = Call My_sp}
Query with the works	{? = Call My_sp (?, ?, 'Y')}

Table 7-1: Handling parameters using the Call syntax

---

6. Remember that ADO can generate the correct call syntax for you.

7. This "ADO" call syntax was originally developed for ODBC applications. It's used now for both ODBC and OLE DB interfaces.

Acceptable Parameters

The types of data that are acceptable as parameters depends on the provider. For example, you can't always use a TEXT or IMAGE datatype as an output parameter—although the newer drivers are more tolerant of this option. In addition, if your query doesn't require parameters, or if it has no parameters in a specific invocation of the query, you can't use parentheses in the query. For example, for a stored procedure that does not require parameters, you can pass the following quoted string to the CommandText property.

```
"{ ? = Call MySP }"
```

Thus, when executing a stored procedure that needs no input parameters, we still build a Parameters collection, but we use it to capture the return value parameter.

Here are the rules I mentioned earlier, having to do with what, when, and where parameters can be used—but only if you're rolling your own Call statements:

- When you submit queries that return output parameters, these parameters must appear at the end of the list of your query's parameters.

- While it is possible to provide both marked and unmarked (inline) parameters, your output parameters must still appear at the end of the list of parameters. This means that your stored procedure must be coded to place all output parameters at the end of the parameter list.

- ADO versions 2.5 and earlier don't support named parameters for stored procedures. You can use named parameters when calling stored procedures using adCmdText, but ADO can't manage them for you. This is supported in ADO versions 2.6 and later.

- For some (including the SQL Server) providers, all inline parameters must be placed to the right of marked parameters. If this isn't the case, ADO returns an error indicating "Wrong number of parameters." An inline parameter is one that you hard-code or provide yourself in lieu of using a parameter marker.

- ADO supports BLOB data types as parameters, and you also can use the AppendChunk method against the Parameter object to pass TEXT or IMAGE datatypes as parameters into a procedure. When passing BLOBs in parameters, set the datatype to adLongVarChar.

> **TIP**   *Be sure to specifically address stored procedures that don't reside in the current (default) database.*

> **NOTE**   *All stored procedures return a "return status" value, whether you ask for it or not. The value isn't exposed in the Parameters collection if you don't ask for it, but it's generated by the stored procedure nonetheless. I like to pass back some useful information from the stored procedure in this argument—for example, @@ROWCOUNT.*

Accessing Deprecated Recordsets

When you upgrade to ADO 2.1 or 2.5 from an earlier version, you might discover that your old applications don't seem to work correctly. In some cases, you get unresolvable errors, especially when working with the Data Environment Designer, the ActiveX Data Control, or the Data Form Wizard

All of these Visual Basic 6.0 tools were left behind when the MDAC team changed the interfaces (basically the structure) in the Recordset object.

While Visual Studio Service Pack 4 (SP4) is supposed to correct these Visual Basic 6.0 tool problems, you might have a need in your own applications to code around these changes. Well, you're in luck. ADO's type library includes "deprecated" interfaces for older versions of the Recordset object. These can be seen, along with other interesting behind-the-scenes interfaces, if you set the Visual Basic 6.0 Object Browser to show hidden members. Simply right-click on the object browser (click on View..Object Browser or press F2 to make it appear) and click "Show hidden members." Once set, the Recordset, Recordset15, Recordset20, and Recordset21 interfaces are all visible, as shown in Figure 7-7. To use these older (outdated) interfaces, declare your Recordset object as one of these deprecated interfaces.

Another use for deprecated Recordsets is the capability to marshal them to older clients. For example, if you have a client that's running

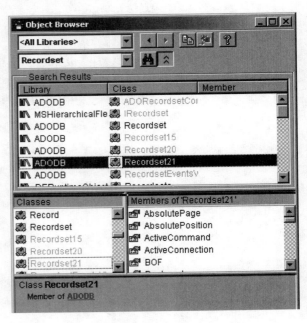

Figure 7-7: Right-click the Object Browser and select "Show hidden members" to see deprecated objects such as Recordset21.

ADO 2.0 and your server is running 2.5, you can send the client a Recordset20 deprecated Recordset. Here's an example of a routine that can be coded to return the ADO 1.5 version of the Recordset:

```
Public Function ReturnRS(strConnect As String, _
                         strQuery As String) As ADODB.Recordset15
    ' Or, Use this syntax for ADO 2.0 or 2.5
    ' Public Function ReturnRS(strConnect As String, _
                         ' strQuery As String) As ADODB.[_Recordset15]
    Dim adoCon1 As New ADODB.Connection
    Dim adoRs1 As New ADODB.Recordset
    ' Set the CursorLocation to adUseClient to return an ADORecordset.
    adoCon1.CursorLocation = adUseClient
    adoCon1.Open strConnect
    adoRs1.Open strQuery, adoCon1, adOpenStatic, adLockBatchOptimistic
    ' Cannot close the ADO Recordset object here,  but it can be disassociated.
    Set adoRs1.ActiveConnection = Nothing
    ' Return ADO Recordset object to Client.
    Set ReturnRS = adoRs1
  adoCon1.Close
End Function
```

NOTE *The code path used to implement the Recordset does not change when you choose a deprecated interface. This technique simply exposes the selected version's properties, methods, and events, and hides the full implementation.*

CHAPTER 8

Passing Resultsets Between Layers

AFTER YOUR QUERY IS DONE, THE various techniques discussed in the last chapter (such as ADO Command objects and the ODBC API) still need to pass back the results to the routines that initiated the query in the first place. This chapter explains how to pass the rowsets back (and forth) between the layers.

I'm of the opinion that less is more when it comes to passing data between layers. Because you wrote the query in the first place, and because you also defined the database and its tables (or at least understand the schema), you know how the data should be returned. You don't usually need to be told in any degree of detail how many columns were generated, the datatypes of each column, the updatability of individual columns, or which tables were used to retrieve the data. While this information is interesting to clients who don't have an intimate knowledge of the data layer, it's just overhead that describes schema information you're already very familiar with.

The other aspect of this DDL overkill is that the typical ADO Recordset repeats the same DDL information *each* time you run the query—not just the first time the query is run. It's sorta like packaging individual potato chips in tiny plastic bags that have the size, weight, and composite ingredients printed on the outside. Wouldn't it be great if we could requery and just get the data—and not all the extra DDL? Perhaps someday.

On the other hand, some developers ask for more metadata, and to be able to use "spandex"[1] properties, and to bind complex validation rules, etc. If you are going to compile and forget your application, less metadata is good for the network. However, for adaptable apps, DDL is crucial. Granted, the OLE DB layer has no thought of optimizing the transfer and caching of metadata. Perhaps someday…

I just came back from VBits 2000 (San Francisco) where I witnessed another preview of Visual Basic/Visual Studio 7. I mention this here because Visual Basic 7.0, like SQL Server 2000, is embracing XML as if it's the answer to the universal question, "What's the meaning of life?" For those of you who don't accept "42" as the answer, you probably won't accept XML as the answer either.

---

1. By spandex, I mean the ability to add additional properties to the Field to further qualify, clarify, and extend the metadata.

However, XML is a very powerful new paradigm. Will it replace ADO or COM someday, or peanut butter and jelly sandwiches? Although it might prove to be a viable way to cross-communicate between clients and data providers, I doubt if it will replace COM or PBJ on whole wheat. Remember when us old folks looked somewhat askance at HTML and ASP-based Visual Basic Script applications? Well, XML has the potential to be even more important. Stay tuned.

Delivering Pizza with a Dump Truck

Developers trying to move data from one place to another are confronted with a variety of choices. Usually the "places" include a component run on a server somewhere and a remote client application. As I see it, developers face a number of problems when trying to solve this problem.

The first is what delivery vehicle should be used. All too often, we choose an oversized delivery vehicle for the situation—like delivering pizza with a giant truck. It works, but it scares the customers, not to mention the neighbor's dog.

The second problem is that we tend to return far more data than the customer can consume before it starts getting cold. This is like delivering the pizzas you anticipate the customer will order next week.

The third problem relates to the others, but is a little more complex. Developers, and the interfaces we choose, have started packaging the data in wrappers that describe the information down to the finest detail. This is like getting our pizza in a package that describes the crust and each mushroom, pepperoni, and anchovy, and explains how the ingredients were gathered, processed, and prepared. This technique is most useful when you need to deliver pizza to space aliens who might not know what they are getting, and who need to know how to consume it.

So, let's take a longer look at these problems and your choices for solving them. First, consider the type of data you want to move. If you simply want to pass something simple back to the client, consider a simple approach. That is, if you only want to pass back a string of characters, a "yes," a "no," or a number, then you don't really need a complex data structure to do so. Yes, more complex data structures are handy if the client needs to know how to deal with the data and does not really know what to expect. They are also handy if you want the other end to handle the updating of the data for you. For example, if your customers tell you to deliver something hot and Italian, you might want to include a description and reheating instructions, as well as legal disclaimers—unless you send out a sweaty tenor.

So, if you need an ADO Recordset object to define the data being transmitted, use a Recordset. But you also have other alternatives that might be far easier to construct, transmit, and parse on the other end. For example, Visual Basic has a number of new extensions that know how to deal with delimited strings. A typical Recordset can take 100K to store a few rows, while a delimited string contains very little overhead—one to three extra characters per field, and two extra characters per row.

Transmitting a Recordset means that your client can use ADO to move around in the rows, and to filter, sort, and find specific rows in the data after it arrives. But these approaches begin to smack of the second problem. Why return data that the customer will discover is cold and stale when the customer finally gets to it? When working with static data (with a long shelf life), sending out extra data can seem like a good idea, but if the client never uses it, you have wasted network, server, and client resources gathering, packaging, and transmitting it. Many more successful applications have found that transmitting rows "just in time" and "only as needed" works better than simply dumping 100 boxes of hot pizza on the doorstep.

The following text is an example of a delimited string result set. I replaced the tab characters with the text "<tab>" for readability. As you can see, all we get here is data. This approach assumes you know what the data you asked for is going to look like.

```
3<tab>Boddie, John<tab>1947<tab>0-1355423-9-1<tab>1996<tab>0-1355423-9-
1<tab>Managing a Programming Project : People and Processes
244<tab>Vaughn, "Wm"<tab>1947<tab>1-5561590-6-4<tab>1995<tab>1-5561590-6-4
  <tab>Hitchhiker's Guide to Visual Basic & Sql Server
```

When "Hold the Anchovies" Isn't Enough

Sometimes the client needs to be able to change the data and sometimes (but not nearly always) an updatable cursor is called for. In this case, the ADO Recordset seems to fit the bill. In many respects, the ADO Recordset object is really quite sophisticated. It contains a wealth of information about the data and where it came from. Some of this information can be essential when it comes time to update the data in the original source. RDO (rdoResultset) and ADO Recordset objects also support the concept of "multiple" resultsets, so you can execute a complex stored procedure and return 1, 2, or 20 resultsets, and use an automorphing Recordset object to refer to the first and to each subsequent result set. The ADO Recordset object also supplies a bevy of properties that describe a number of complex aspects of the data structure, often making it possible to identify the root source of the data.

However, some applications need something even more generic and less binary than an ADO Recordset, especially when updatability is not that important. That's where XML comes in. XML is touted as the new universal format for data on the Web. XML allows developers to describe and deliver rich, structured data from any application in a standard, consistent way. XML is an internationally recognized format for result set (schema + data) persistence. Not only does XML define the data and its structure (even hierarchical or multiple rowset data), but it can persist changes to the data as well. Well-formed XML can be read by anyone, in any language, anywhere in the world—perhaps even on other worlds. Simply put, XML is yet another way to pass data from one point to another and carry with it some of the information you need to know about the dataset to view it, change it, and manage it. You don't need ADO to decipher an XML data structure, just an XML parser. No, there's nothing built-in in an XML data structure that tells you *where* the data came from, just what it looks like, so it is tough to create an update statement based simply on an XML dataset. In addition, you can't tell that the data was drawn from Table X or Stored Procedure Y.

When working with ADO, you can save Recordsets to an XML stream (in ADO 2.5) or to a file (in ADO 2.1 or later). ADO's adPersistXML format, aka XMLData is also referred to as a canonical format. So, the XML structure could look like the data shown below or any other well-formed XML. However, ADO understands how to read well-formed XML—regardless of the source.

XML data structures are broken into sections that first define the data rows—at least the names of the fields (columns) and their datatypes. This is the </s:Schema> section. The following section, </rs:data>, contains the data itself. Each and every field is tagged, so the data structure repeats the field names over and over—once in each row as shown here:[2]

```
<rs:data>
<z:row Au_ID="244" Author="Vaughn, William" Year_Born="1947" ISBN="1-5561590-6-4"
Year_Published="1995" Expr1="1-5561590-6-4" Title="Hitchhiker's Guide to Visual
Basic & Sql Server - Fourth Edition (Book and Disk)" />
<z:row Au_ID="5386" Author="Viescas, John" Year_Born="1947" ISBN="1-5561519-8-5"
Year_Published="1989" Expr1="1-5561519-8-5" Title="Quick Reference Guide to Sql" />
<z:row Au_ID="5386" Author="Viescas, John" Year_Born="1947" ISBN="1-5561523-7-X"
Year_Published="1990" Expr1="1-5561523-7-X" Title="dBASE IV (Programmer's Quick
Reference Series)"
</rs:data>
```

This permits a degree of flexibility in that you can define an XML dataset that could potentially contain different fields for each row, but multiple resultsets are not (yet) supported by Visual Basic or ADO.

It is important to note that in the schema section, ADO stores enough information to build the right UPDATE statements for an UpdateBatch—this enables you to modify the Recordset and, if necessary, send it back to the server to

---

2. While this may seem scandalous regarding the amount of network traffic generated, XML's main transport is intended to be HTTP, which, since version 1.1, has native compression that greatly reduces the overhead of these repeated tags.

have the changes committed, after setting the ActiveConnection back, of course. In reality, an XML-persisted Recordset is still a Recordset with nothing left out.

My point is that we developers need to build solutions using the right packaging, with the right contents, with the right amount of useful information. Don't send more than is needed—no more fields or DDL or rows than the customer can consume at a sitting. This means that you should use a bicycle when the pizza place is close, and hold the anchovies.

Understanding Recordset Marshaling

When you want to transport data from one tier to another, or when you are sharing ADO objects among threads, it's best to understand what COM and ADO do behind the scenes. This can also help you understand your options, and the limitations of using ADO in the middle tier.

COM marshaling involves two concepts:

- Passing data from one process or thread to another

- Synchronizing threads accessing a COM object

When passing Recordsets from place to place, ADO behaves very differently depending on whether or not you're asking it to move data between threads or parts of your own application (within a single process), or between two separate processes via a COM (or DCOM) link. Let's examine the various flavors of ADO marshaling and see how they behave in these two environments—in process and between processes.

ADO General Marshaling

By default, ADO provides standard COM marshaling. This means that ADO uses standard OLE automation types for its arguments, and interface pointers can be passed across processes without any special custom marshaling code. For example, a COM server can return a Connection or Recordset object to a client, and the ADO object's interface pointer can be passed across processes (in other words, you can pass a reference to the object). Any calls to methods of the interface cause a call from the client back to the existing server-side ADO object.

For the in-process case, ADO specializes the marshaling of its objects by using the COM Free-Threaded Marshaler (using CoCreateFreeThreadedMarshaler). This means that while ADO is marked for apartment-model threading by default, ADO skirts the apartment rules with the free-threaded marshaler and will have direct pass-through of any ADO object interfaces from one thread to another. No COM synchronization takes place, as ADO is thread-safe and does all of the necessary synchronization. Overall, this means that ADO does not use COM marshaling for the in-process scenarios.

Beyond Standard Marshaling

ADO's standard marshaling is sufficient for many, but not all scenarios. For example, standard marshaling across processes can hurt performance because for each call to the ADO object, an application makes a call across process. It would be better for performance if all of the data of a Recordset were returned to the client. Any subsequent calls such as fetching would be made locally in the client rather than back to the COM server where the Recordset was created.

ADO already provides such a mechanism for the Recordset object. To return a Recordset object from a server and have the data of the Recordset marshaled to the client, specify adUseClient for the Recordset object's CursorLocation property. The adUseClient value tells the Recordset object to use the Client Cursor Engine, which caches all of the records of the Recordset. Whenever a Recordset is sent across process boundaries with adUseClient set, a Recordset object (which also uses the client cursor engine) is constructed in the receiving process and it is populated with the sent records. At this point, the Recordset is said to be "disconnected" or "disassociated" from a database connection. The database connection is not carried along with the Recordset data when adUseClient is specified.

So, to make sure ADO knows that you plan to pass the Recordset to another tier, be sure to set the ActiveConnection to Nothing, just as we discussed in Chapter 6. By setting the ActiveConnection property to Nothing, we signal ADO to complete population so all qualifying rows become members before the Recordset is released to you and before it gets sent anywhere.

With adUseClient set, you always pass the data of the Recordset when sending the Recordset across process boundaries. This is typically called "passing by value." Without adUseClient, you will always get standard marshaling, and only a reference to the ADO Recordset object is passed across process boundaries—this is typically called "passing by reference."

Limitations of Marshaling Recordsets "By Value"

When ADO Recordset objects are passed by value, the client cursor engine marshals the Recordset data across the process boundaries. The newly created ADO Recordset object in the receiving process simply attaches to the Recordset stored in the client cursor engine cache.

However, there are a number of important issues here. Because the underlying OLE DB *rowset* (the data and metadata) is being marshaled, instead of the ADO Recordset, the properties of the Recordset object do *not* get marshaled. This means that properties such as Filter, Sort, and ActiveConnection are not carried from one process to the next. So, for example, a common pitfall is to set the Filter property of a Recordset and expect only the filtered records to be passed across the process boundaries. Instead, all of the original records of the query are passed. Furthermore, the cursor location is set to the beginning of the Recordset when it is marshaled—a new ADO Recordset is created in the receiving process and is attached to the marshaled rowset, causing the cursor to be positioned at the first record. The current cursor pointer is lost.

So, as a general rule of thumb, do not expect Recordset properties to be marshaled across process boundaries. The advantage to this is that ADO Recordset marshaling is lightweight, passing only the metadata (table name(s), column name, and data types, and some flags) and record data.

Marshaling Out of Process

When one tier modifies a Recordset object, it often makes sense to marshal back just the changes, instead of the whole rowset. However, it also makes a difference whether or not your code is marshaling across process boundaries. Remember that when you test a component that's coded as a class within your Visual Basic application, it's running in process. When it's running in another executable somewhere, it's running out of process. This section focuses on the situation where you're passing a Recordset to another tier—way out of your process.

If you pass an ADO Recordset in process, you are passing a reference to an object in memory, regardless of the setting of the CursorLocation property. When you pass an ADO Recordset out of process, the ADO libraries are loaded in both processes.[3] The ADO libraries pass the information stored in the Recordset from the one process to the other. In the process, ADO converts the Recordset to ADTG format, thus reducing network overhead. Each process then has its own copy of the Recordset object, rather than just a reference to the initial object. This means that the other tier's copy of the data does not reflect changes on either end of the wire.

Let's look at a couple of examples. The first example passes the data from a server to a client. This is accomplished by having the client call an MTS component's method that returns a Recordset. This could also be a Web page that returns a Recordset (or an XML string or Stream—which we discuss in Chapter 9).

---

3. Just make sure that both ends of the transfer (client and server) are loaded with compatible versions of ADO (2.0 to 2.0 or 2.1 to 2.5).

```
Public Function GetAuthorsByISBN(ISBN as String) as Recordset
Dim rs as ADODB.Recordset
' Do what it takes to fetch the rows for the Recordset …
Set GetAuthorsByISBN = Rs
End Function
```

Suppose you call this method *out of process* using this VB client code:

```
Dim rs as Recordset
Set rs = oServer.GetAuthorsByISBN(txtISBN.Text)
' Display and manipulate (add, change, delete) the rows for the Recordset …
```

In this case, the server-side Recordset is left unmodified.

At this point, we're ready for phase two. We need to send the changes back to the server so it can reconnect the Recordset to the data source and post the changes. This is the Microsoft Transaction Server component that posts the changes to the data source.

```
Public Sub SaveAuthor (ByVal Rs as Recordset)
On Error GoTo ErrorHandler
Dim Cn as ADODB.Connection
Set Cn = New Connection
Cn.Open "provider=sqloledb;data source=(local);initial catalog=mydb", _
"admin", "pw"
Set Rs.ActiveConnection = Cn
' And the UpdateBatch posts the changes to the database—or tries to…
Rs.UpdateBatch
Exit sub
ErrorHandler:
 ' Yada yada yada…
End Sub
```

Of course, unless you have a "Yada" processor, you'll need to stick in robust collision-management error handlers here.

So what if I send 50 rows and the client only changes 1? Does ADO have to send back the whole megillah? Actually no—you can tell ADO to send just the changes back to the server to post to the data source. This saves processing time and network bandwidth. So, how do you do it? The ADO Recordset object exposes the MarshalOptions property. If you use adMarshalModifiedOnly, ADO only copies over the updated and new records. If you use adMarshalAll, all of the data is copied. It's that simple.

The bookmark, filter, and sort information are not used in determining what records are passed across process boundaries. All rows of the Recordset are passed, regardless of the current setting of the Filter property. In the resulting Recordset, the first record is the current record, regardless of the bookmark set in the other process. The resulting Recordset does not receive the value of the Sort property from the other process.

Marshaling Performance

Limiting the amount of data sent in both directions is the primary means of effecting performance improvements when marshaling. The server should return just the rows and columns absolutely necessary, if we need to return rows at all. There are plenty of cases where rows are not really called for, and simply passing variables back will do just fine. When the client sends data to the server for posting, it's essential that it send just the changes. Otherwise, it's kinda like asking your wife for a phone number and, in response, she throws the yellow pages at you.

Let's explore different options to send and receive data between tiers. The first scenario assumes you want to send more than a single set of values. In this case, you usually want to send a Recordset as it's designed to deal with multiple rows (sets) of related values (columns). The second scenario we examine focuses on passing single sets of data values such as those returned by OUTPUT parameters from a stored procedure.

Passing Sets of Data

The ADO Recordset object gives you a lot of functionality on the client side, but it needs to bring in all the metadata (DDL) to the client to recreate itself. When you remote a Recordset to the client, you automatically get access to an advanced object model that enables you to do rich data manipulation, such as data shaping (and reshaping), off-line sorting, and filtering, as well as automatic updating to the backend when the metadata is rich enough. Metadata includes column names and aliases, datatypes, precision or scale, primary key and foreign key info, base table info, updatability info, and more. Let's walk through some of the guiding principles that hobble or enhance marshaling performance. Sure, some of these points have been made before, but, as you've guessed, these are all intertwined in the fabric of a high-performance application or component.

- If your application needs the flexibility and depth of structure provided by the Recordset, then by all means pass a Recordset. For example, if your application needs to morph to evolving data structures, the metadata in a Recordset always reflects the latest structural and schema changes. Your application can be coded to adapt automatically to these changes. However, if you don't expect changes or you want a lighter-weight approach that depends on stable (inviolate) schemas, passing the metadata is an unnecessary luxury you can do without.

- The best way to pass efficient Recordsets is to construct small, focused Recordsets. To make sure your Recordsets contain just the rows and columns you need, write your SELECT statement carefully. SELECT *, as I said earlier, is a pariah—it is to be avoided. Choose just the columns you need for this particular query and no more. Make sure your WHERE clause focuses your query on just the rows you need *now*, not 10 minutes from now, and generally never more than a few hundred rows.

- Remember to set the MarshalOptions property to ensure that just modified rows are sent back from the client to be posted.

- Don't pass BLOBs from tier to tier unless you can't avoid it. In any case, only pass BLOBs for specific pictures or objects when called for—avoid including a BLOB column in a multirow Recordset. Examine alternative transport mechanisms for BLOBs, such as intranet or common file shares.

- To avoid the metadata overhead of a Recordset, you can choose one of the other data formats, including CSV, Variant array, or arrays of user-defined types (UDTs). Each has varying degrees of pseudo-metadata handled by Visual Basic, but not nearly the rich DDL as persisted by the Recordset. For example, you'll be able to pick up a type definition out of a Variant, but it's a "fuzzy" definition. So, in most cases, you'll be depending on the discipline (you've heard of that, haven't you?) in your organization—the discipline that prevents one developer from changing a data structure without informing the rest of the team. If your organization is facing a lot of changes imposed by the client or the dictates of your business, perhaps this approach is problematic. In the "olden" days, this was standard operating procedure—no changes without the data committee agreeing.

When you marshal a CSV[4] or a safe array (another form of multiple set data), the Recordset metadata does not get marshaled, but there is not a whole lot you can do with that data on the client. You won't have any of the Recordset features available to display, filter, sort, or munge the data. But that might not be necessary for your requirements. For large Recordsets, marshaling is not very

---

4. CSV: A fancy acronym for a comma-delimited record. However, these are saved in Unicode, which doubles the amount of RAM (and disk) they require.

expensive, but for small Recordsets the metadata portion can be proportionally heavy when compared to the data and CSV/safe arrays.

When you use XML to marshal the data, the marshaling technique again depends on whether you need the metadata on the client or not. If you have to marshal all the metadata, XML actually uses more space than the binary protocol—but only about 50 percent more. Marshaling Recordsets using the ADO binary format and XML has been tested, but XML compresses well, so the difference is not really significant in size or performance.

Passing Disconnected Recordsets

ADO makes it easy to pass data between layers using the Recordset object. Unlike RDO and DAO, ADO can construct a totally stand-alone Recordset object. After the Recordset is passed to another layer (also running ADO), reconstituting the Recordset is done automatically.

To create a stand-alone (disjoint) Recordset in code, you need to do the following:

1. Create the Recordset object in the usual way, using the Client/Batch cursor library—set the CursorLocation property of the Connection or Recordset object to adUseClient before they are open.

2. Set the LockType property to batch-optimistic locking (adLockBatchOptimistic).

3. Run your query, and when the Recordset is open, set its ActiveConnection property to Nothing. This forces ADO to complete populating the Recordset and to release the Recordset from the connection. Any further action against the Recordset will not require access to the database. And no, you don't have to close the connection after having passed the Recordset object.

At this point you can pass the Recordset object from layer to layer, as long as the target layer has a compatible version of ADO (e.g., 2.1 SP2 and 2.5) installed. Because ADO is installed with Microsoft Office, Internet Explorer, Visual Studio, and a plethora of other applications, the chances of it being installed are pretty good. The target code can make changes to the Recordset in the usual manner (assuming the Recordset was updatable in the first place).

> **TIP**   *If you aren't sure if the Recordset is updatable, the easiest way to tell (in code) is to check using the Supports method.*

```
If rs.Supports (adAddNew) Then ...
```

> **NOTE**   *If Supports returns True, then you have an updatable Recordset. I kept getting a read-only Recordset despite setting all of the properties correctly, or so I thought. It turns out that I had omitted a comma in the Recordset.Open method. When I switched to named arguments, the correct argument was passed to the Open method and the Recordset was updatable.*

After you pass the Recordset back to the calling tier, the code there can work with the Recordset as if it were created there—up to a point. All of the additions, changes, and deletions are saved in the Recordset on the target. When (or if) you need to post changes to the underlying database tables, follow these steps:

1. Pass the altered Recordset back to a tier that has access to the database.

2. Reconnect the data source by resetting the ActiveConnection property to another open connection.

3. Use the UpdateBatch method.

The server-side and client-side code follow in the next two sections.

The Server-side Code

This code constructs a new Recordset without benefit of a Command object. It builds the query by concatenating the single input parameter that finishes the Like expression. Once constructed, the Recordset object's ActiveConnection property is "set" to Nothing to dissociate it from the Connection. No, we don't use the Set operator—it takes too long and it's not necessary. Just assign the ActiveConnection property to Nothing, as shown:

```
Public Function GetRecs(Author As String) As Recordset
Dim rs As Recordset
OpenConnection
Set rs = New Recordset
```

```
With rs
    .CursorLocation = adUseClient
    .CursorType = adOpenStatic
    .LockType = adLockBatchOptimistic
    .Open "select Au_id, Author, Year_Born " _
& " from authors where author like '" & Author & "' ", _
        cn, Options:=adCmdText
    .ActiveConnection = Nothing
End With
cn.Close
Set GetRecs = rs
End Function


Private Function OpenConnection()
Set cn = New Connection
cn.Open "Provider=SQLOLEDB.1;Integrated Security=SSPI;" _
& "Initial Catalog=biblio;Data Source=betav2"
End Function
```

The following simple code posts the changes to the Recordset. The changes made by the client are embedded in the Recordset itself. Notably missing from this code is the error handler to deal with collisions. That was discussed in Chapter 7.

```
Private cn As Connection
Public Function PostChanges(rs As Recordset) As Integer
OpenConnection
Set rs.ActiveConnection = cn
rs.UpdateBatch
cn.Close
End Function
```

The Client-side Code

The client-side code looks like the code below. This entire application, with both client-side and server-side code, is provided on the CD in the Passing Recordsets directory.

I use several enumerations to map the individual Recordset Field objects as well as the TextBox control arrays. These not only help readability for humans, but they also help performance as discussed earlier.

```
Dim rsLocal As Recordset
Enum fldRs
```

```
        AuID
        Author
        Year_Born
    End Enum
    Enum idxText
        Add
        Update
        Delete
    End Enum
    Enum idxTab
        Query
        Add
        Update
        Delete
    End Enum
```

The following routine is used to fetch the Recordset from the server-side or simply another component. Because we need to test to find out if there are pending changes before running the query (which would discard these changes), we have to go through a number of steps to see if the Recordset exists, if it is open, and if its edit mode is still unchanged.

```
Private Sub cmdQuery_Click()
If rsLocal Is Nothing Then
    ElseIf rsLocal.State = adStateOpen Then
        If rsLocal.EditMode = adEditNone Then
        rc = MsgBox("If you requery now, changes will be lost. " _
& "Press OK to continue or Cancel to keep current records.", _
vbOKCancel + vbCritical, "Request to requery")
        If rc = vbOK Then
        Else
            Exit Sub
        End If
    End If
    End If
End If
```

If we know there are no pending changes (or we don't care to keep them), we run the query, passing the filter string that will be inserted in the query at the server, as follows:

```
Set rsLocal = GetRecs(txtFilter)
```

After the Recordset is returned, we can then pass it to the MSHFlexGrid, which knows how to display it. We do have to tune the columns a little, as the grid does not set the widths correctly, but that's easy using the TextWidth function. The following code does this:

```
If rsLocal.EOF Then

    MsgBox "No rows returned"
    Set MSHFlexGrid1.Recordset = Nothing
Else
    Set MSHFlexGrid1.Recordset = rsLocal
    MSHFlexGrid1.Col = fldRs.AuID
    MSHFlexGrid1.ColWidth(fldRs.Author) = _
    TextWidth(String(Len(rsLocal(fldRs.Author)), "M"))
End If
```

If the Recordset is updatable, we enable the portions of the tab control containing the buttons and dialogs that control changes to the Recordset, as follows:

```
If rsLocal.Supports(adAddNew) Then
    fraAdd.Enabled = True
…
```

The change routines ensure that the row selected from the grid is deleted or updated, or that a new row is added. They also change the color in the grid to reflect the changes as they are made. This reminds the user that these changes are temporary—not saved to the database.

The following delete routine confirms the operation and simply uses the Delete method against the Recordset. Deleted grid rows are marked in red to show that they are no longer available.

```
Private Sub cmdDelete_Click()
rc = MsgBox("Press OK to confirm deletion of this record or Cancel to abort.", _
vbOKCancel + vbCritical, "Request to delete record")
If rc = vbOK Then
    rsLocal.Delete
End If
Setcolor (255)
End Sub
```

The add routine, shown next, validates the new data and uses the AddNew method to initiate an Add operation. The new data is posted from the text boxes, and the Update method saves the new row in memory. No changes are posted to the database until the Recordset is passed back to the server, and we're not ready to do that yet.

```
Private Sub cmdAdd_Click()
Dim rc As Integer
If ValidateAuthor(idxText.Add) Then
    fraAdd.Enabled = False
    rsLocal.AddNew
    rsLocal(fldRs.Author) = txtAuthor(idxText.Add)
    rsLocal(fldRs.Year_Born) = txtYear_Born(idxText.Add)
    rsLocal.Update
    txtAuthor(idxText.Add) = ""
    txtYear_Born(idxText.Add) = ""
    fraAdd.Enabled = True
End If
```

In the following code, a new row is added to the grid and painted green. Because we don't know what the primary key will be, we simply show it as "??".

```
With MSHFlexGrid1
    .Rows = .Rows + 1
    .Row = .Rows - 1
    .Col = fldRs.AuID: .Text = "??"
    .Col = fldRs.Author: .Text = rsLocal(fldRs.Author)
    .Col = fldRs.Year_Born: .Text = rsLocal(fldRs.Year_Born)
    .Setcolor (&HFFFF00)
End With
End Sub
```

Remember that this sample application is driven from a tabbed dialog control. This next set of code is embedded beneath the Update on that control. When the user selects the Update tab, the selected row is shown in a couple of text boxes. Changes made to these boxes are posted to the local Recordset when the cmdUpdate button is clicked, but only after the contents of the text boxes are validated.

```
Private Sub cmdUpdate_Click()
Dim rc As Integer
If ValidateAuthor(idxText.Update) Then
    fraUpdate.Enabled = False
    rsLocal(fldRs.Author) = txtAuthor(idxText.Update)
    rsLocal(fldRs.Year_Born) = txtYear_Born(idxText.Update)
    rsLocal.Update
```

```
      fraUpdate.Enabled = True
'     Make grid look like Recordset
```

After the Recordset is changed, we copy the changes back to the selected row in the grid so the grid matches the current (RAM-based) Recordset, as shown in the following code. We paint the row yellow to show that its values are transitory and not posted to the database yet.

```
With MSHFlexGrid1
      .Col = fldRs.Author
      .Text = txtAuthor(idxText.Update)
      .Col = fldRs.Year_Born
      .Text = txtYear_Born(idxText.Update)
    End With
    Setcolor (&HFFFF&)
End If
End Sub
```

Posting the Recordset Changes to the Database

When the user decides to post the changes to the database, the following routine bundles up the Recordset and passes it to the server-side component discussed earlier. Yes, we need collision-detection code here, too. We discussed this in Chapter 7—remember?

```
Private Sub cmdPostChanges_Click()
rc = PostChanges(rsLocal)
cmdQuery_Click       ' Refetch rows to sync grid
End Sub
```

Passing Strings and String Arrays

A tempting alternative to Recordsets can be as simple as passing a string back from the server. However, this alternative makes it harder to perform updates on the underlying data—harder, but not impossible. In cases where updating is not done through cursors, it does not matter. For example, when the query is complex—too complex for ADO to manage updatability on its own—you'll have to fall back on a "manual" update strategy anyway. This is typically the case when the result set is generated from stored procedures, especially those with complex or multiple result sets. Situations like this are often handled through stored procedures designed to process the updates. To get these to work, you'll have to construct the parameters to pass the primary key on your own—ADO can't do it for you as it does when working with Recordsets.

> **NOTE** *When considering this strategy, remember that the Data Object Wizard can generate the Visual Basic code needed to execute canned procedures (stored or ad hoc), as well as the code needed to create custom controls to display and capture user changes. The Data Object Wizard can make the implementation of this design painless.*

When working with string-based result sets, you also need to consider that Visual Basic is notoriously clumsy at handling strings, as we discussed earlier. If you have to have Visual Basic parse the strings field by field, you'll lose ground to a Recordset approach, where field management is done for you. You won't be able to simply cram a multirow string into a grid unless you first format it correctly.

Filling a Grid with a Clip String

To get around Visual Basic's limitation in parsing strings, you can construct a clip-format delimited string that you can pass directly to a control supporting the Clip property (such as the MSHFlexGrid), but setting up the grid to accept it is a little tiresome. The following example shows how to do it, for those who want to try. Another subtle point here—you might want to include the column names as the first row of your delimited string, so the grid control has its headings filled in. This code expects that to be the case. I set the FixedRows property to 1 and the Rows property to 5 for this example:

```
Sub FillGrid(strParm As String)
With MSHFlexGrid1
    .Clear
    .Row = 0
    .ColSel = 1
    .RowSel = 4
    .Clip = strParm
    .Row = 1
    .ColWidth(0) = TextWidth(String(Len(.Text), "M"))
    .RowSel = 1
End With
End Sub
```

If you want ADO to construct a delimited string from the data in your result set, you can use the GetString method—it's similar to the GetClipString method in RDO. The GetString method is more flexible than RDO's version, but it has a fairly serious shortcoming—it does not know how to properly frame the strings. That is, GetString does not put quotes around the string elements; it simply separates them with a selected delimiter. This means that if your string has embedded delimiters (embedded tabs by default), ADO becomes confused and does not construct the delimited string result set correctly. This limitation aside, GetString (according to some tests done by the MDAC team) is about five times faster than performing the same operations yourself in code.

You'll also find that ADO does not attempt to "stringify" binary fields. That is, if you have selected a column containing your customer's picture, ADO will simply return a null when it tries to convert it to a string. When we look at XML, we'll find that ADO does convert binary fields to their Unicode equivalent.

Here's an example of constructing a clip string in code. In this case, we run a query to return the authors for a selected ISBN.

```
Public Function GetAuthors(ISBN) As String
Const Headers As String = "Author" & vbTab & "Year Born" & vbCr
Dim strData As String
Dim i As Integer
OpenConnection
Set rs = New Recordset
rs.Open "SELECT Authors.Author, Authors.Year_Born " _
        & " FROM Authors INNER JOIN Title_Author_
        & ON Authors.Au_ID = Title_Author.Au_ID " _
        & " WHERE (Title_Author.ISBN = '" & ISBN & "' )", _
cn, adOpenForwardOnly, adLockReadOnly, adCmdText
If rs.EOF Then
    GetAuthors = ""
    Exit Function
Else
    strData = rs.GetString(adClipString, -1, , , "<null>")
    GetAuthors = Headers & strData
End If
cn.Close
End Function
```

Note that the "strData =" line (in bold, a few lines up) executes the GetString method using the default (tab) delimiter for fields and vbCr (0x0D) for rows. We also pass in the string "<null>" whenever the value is not provided, as when the year born data is not known.

My tests show that once you get past the first dozen or so rows, passing strings gets to be increasingly expensive, in terms of time, memory, LAN, and patience consumption. Most of the time seems to be lost in handling the delimited string itself, if you have to process the string element by element. You also have to deal with embedded framing quotes and other string-delimiter details, such as when strings contain the character you're using as a framing quote. This is the typical 'O'Malley' problem.

Consider that when working with the Web and ASP (Visual Basic Script), you don't really work with strings at all—you have to deal with Variants containing strings. These can be even slower.

In the end, you'll find it's far faster to pass single-row result sets via a simple delimited string than it is to pass a single-row (or few-row) Recordset. If all you need in response to your query is a simple "yes" or "no," then it's silly to construct a full-blown Recordset to pass the data.

Passing Output Parameters instead of Rowsets

Suppose there was a technique that did not require the construction of a Recordset, but still let you pass back arguments that ADO could manage for you? Well, if you submit a query that returns OUTPUT parameters instead of rowsets (as generated by SELECT statements), you don't need to have ADO construct a Recordset at all. However, you will need to write a stored procedure to generate the OUTPUT parameters, and an ADO Command object to manage them for you.

The drawback here is that this approach doesn't really fit when there is more than one qualifying row. That is, if the query returns a *set* of results, you have to map the results into a single set of OUTPUT parameters in the stored procedure—either that or fall back on a rowset—and then construct a Recordset or a user-defined or Variant array to handle the rowset.

If you can make do with a single row, as with a specific key query, keep reading. The code examples in the following two sections show how to construct an ADO Command object that accepts both input and output parameters and that can be passed back to another tier, just as a Recordset was in the previous example of passing strings and string arrays.

The Server-side Code

On the server tier, we provide two routines: one to fill the client-side pick-list of ISBNs, and another to execute a query based on the chosen ISBN.

In the first case, we construct a firehose cursorless result set and pass it back to the client where its rows are used to fill a common ComboBox control.

```
Private cn As Connection
Dim rs As Recordset

Public Function GetISBNs() As Recordset
OpenConnection
Set rs = New Recordset
rs.CursorLocation = adUseClient
rs.Open "select top 50 ISBN from Titles", cn, adOpenStatic, _
adLockReadOnly, adCmdText
Set rs.ActiveConnection = Nothing
Set GetISBNs = rs
cn.Close
End Function
```

The second routine constructs an ADO Command object to execute a stored procedure that takes a single input parameter and returns two output parameters. We construct the Command.Parameters collection manually (with some difficulty) to improve runtime performance (not developer performance in this case). This code is tied to the stability of the stored procedure—if the stored procedure changes arguments (either in number, position, or datatype), then the code is broken.

After the query is executed, the Command object is passed back to the client tier. Edward (my technical editor) threw a hissy fit when I used this technique, and I tend to agree with him. Passing Command objects between tiers is ugly. Yes, you can do it—it just isn't particularly efficient, and Edward won't help you when you call developer support. The following code uses adExecuteNoRecords to prevent the construction of a Recordset object. Once passed, the local Command object is discarded—it has to be constructed each time, unless we can maintain state on the server (which is not likely if we expect to scale this component).

```
Public Function GetRecs(ISBN As String) As Command
Dim cmd As Command
Dim RecordsAffected As Integer
OpenConnection          ' Our own routine to open the connection
Set cmd = New Command
With cmd
    .CommandText = "FetchTitleByISBN"
    .CommandType = adCmdStoredProc
    .Parameters.Append .CreateParameter("ISBNWanted", adVarChar, adParamInput, 20)
    .Parameters.Append .CreateParameter("Title", adVarChar, adParamOutput, 255)
    .Parameters.Append _
    .CreateParameter("Year_Published", adSmallInt, adParamOutput, 2)
    .ActiveConnection = cn
```

```
        .Execute RecordsAffected, ISBN, adExecuteNoRecords
End With
cn.Close
Set GetRecs = cmd
End Function
```

A second variation on the preceding approach is to pass back a user-defined type that defines two variables to return the title and year published. The following version has considerably less overhead than passing back the entire Command object:

```
Public Function GetRecs(ISBN As String) As udtParms
Dim cmd As Command
Dim RecordsAffected As Integer
Dim outParms As udtParms
OpenConnection
Set cmd = New Command
With cmd
    .CommandText = "FetchTitleByISBN"
    .CommandType = adCmdStoredProc
    .Parameters.Append .CreateParameter("ISBNWanted", adVarChar, adParamInput, 20)
    .Parameters.Append .CreateParameter("Title", adVarChar, adParamOutput, 255)
    .Parameters.Append _
    .CreateParameter("Year_Published", adSmallInt, adParamOutput, 2)
    .ActiveConnection = cn
    .Execute RecordsAffected, ISBN, adExecuteNoRecords
cn.Close
outParms.Title = .Parameters(1)          ' title
outParms.YearPublished = .Parameters(2)          'Year published
End With
GetRecs = outParms
End Function
```

The Client-side Code

On the client, we have two very simple routines. The first fills the pick-list ComboBox. This control eliminates the errors generated when users type in ISBN numbers. In this case, we call GetISBNs, a server-side component that returns a firehose cursor (FO/RO, CacheSize=1) with ISBNs from the first 50 rows of the Titles table. These are used to select valid ISBNs from the Titles table.

```
Private Sub cmbISBNs_GotFocus()
Dim rsLocal As Recordset
If cmbISBNs.ListCount = 0 Then
```

```
    Set rsLocal = GetISBNs
    Do Until rsLocal.EOF
        cmbISBNs.AddItem rsLocal(0)      ' ISBN
        rsLocal.MoveNext
    Loop
    cmbISBNs.ListIndex = 0
End If
End Sub
```

The second routine calls the GetRecs server-side component, passing in the chosen ISBN. In this example, shown next, we pass back the entire Command object and pick off the two output parameters in the client code. Why didn't we just pass back the two arguments? It would make more sense in this case....

```
Private Sub cmbISBNs_Click()
Dim cmdLocal As Command
Set cmdLocal = GetRecs(cmbISBNs.Text)
txtTitle = cmdLocal.Parameters(0)        ' Title
txtYearPublished = cmdLocal.Parameters(1)    ' Year Published
End Sub
```

However, it seems to me that the preceding approach is also less efficient than simply passing back the two values as a user-defined type. The following variation of the example shows how that's done using a commonly defined Type structure (udtParms):

```
Private Sub cmbISBNs_Click()
Dim inParms As udtParms
inParms = GetRecs(cmbISBNs.Text)
txtTitle = inParms.Title
txtYearPublished = inParms.YearPublished
End Sub
```

Passing Variant Arrays

Because ADO also knows how to generate Variant arrays from Recordsets, just as it can generate delimited strings, it *might* make sense to construct an array containing the rows we need to fetch. However, the results of my (and Edward's) tests were very disappointing. Consider these facts:

- Variant arrays return Unicode strings. That is, each string is converted at the server to a 16-bit-per-character form before transmitting it to the client.

261

- Many packets returned to the user are padded for some reason with the text "User."

- The number of raw packets returned is almost three times the number returned for a disconnected Recordset containing the same data. Part of this difference is due to the Recordset VarChar fields being marshaled as 8-bit characters instead of as 16-bit characters.

The raw numbers for this test tell the story. The Variant array cost 87 frames and 94,888 bytes, while the Recordset cost 34 frames and 23,406 bytes.

If you decide you have to pass back a Variant array despite the results from our tests, I won't stop you—in fact, I'll show you how. The Recordset GetRows method is used to construct a Variant array from your data rows. However, as with a delimited string, you won't get the field names unless you tack them on to the array or pass them separately. You will get better element handling as the individual array elements (the Recordset fields) are populated with some DDL information that helps Visual Basic understand what each element contains. You can also tell how many rows and fields are in the array by using the UBound and LBound functions against the array—assuming you don't already know.

While Variant arrays initially take less overhead than a Recordset, they also consume more resources than strings or string arrays. Variant arrays do, however, expose string, numeric, and binary fields. This can be useful in cases where you want to figure out what to do with a binary value in an array element. For example, you could try to pass back a picture in a Variant array element, but once it arrived in your Visual Basic program, what would you do with it? The Image and Picture controls don't know how to present anything except file-based pictures (or PropertyBag elements). You'll have to figure out how to get the binary bits saved to a file and go from there. On the other hand, if you're clever, you could figure out what a Data Source control (like the ADO data control) does to solve this problem. It seems to me it's easier to store the picture in a file in the first place.

Another point: When I did the tests to see how many packets were generated by the various data access techniques (Recordsets vs. Variants vs. delimited strings vs. user-defined types vs. PropertyBags), I discovered that Variants consumed almost three times as many network resources as Recordsets. No serious architectural choice should be made without considering network transmission burdens.

The Server-side Code

The following code processes the Recordset generated by a SELECT query. It tests to see whether any rows were returned because you can't use GetRows unless there are rows. The routine passes the Variant array back to the client tier. If no rows are returned, we set the Variant array to Empty.

```
If rs.EOF Then
    vData = Empty
Else
    vData = rs.GetRows(-1)
End If
GetAuthors = strData
```

The Client-side Code

This client-side code extracts rows from the Variant array and posts them to a grid. The UBound function is used to see how many rows and columns were returned. Remember that Variant array elements are referenced backwards. That is, the array is indexed: MyVariantArray(column, row). This example code also fills in the column headings manually.

```
Sub FillGrid(varParm As Variant)
Dim i As Integer, j As Integer
With MSHFlexGrid1
    .Clear
    .Cols = UBound(varParm, 1)
    .Rows = 5
    .Row = 0
    .Col = 0
    .Text = "Author"
    .Col = 1
    .Text = "Year Born"
        For i = 1 To UBound(varParm, 2) ' Loop through resultset returned
            .Row = i
            For j = 0 To UBound(varParm, 1) - 1
                .Col = j
                .Text = "" & varParm(j, i)
            Next j
        Next i
        .Row = 1
        .Col = 0
        .ColWidth(0) = TextWidth(String(Len(.Text), "M"))
    End With
End Sub
```

Passing User-defined Structures

Creating and passing a user-defined structure is another technique that can be used to transmit information back from the middle tier or between modules in your application. User-defined structures use the Type operator to describe the variables that are passed, and they use an identical Type declaration on the client end to mirror the same structure. Actually, the Type declarations should be declared as Public in a public class. This way both the client and other applications using the Type can see the definition. The advantage to using user-defined structures is that you transmit *just* the structure—not any extra DDL as you do with a Recordset or XML, or, to some extent, with Variant arrays.

As with similar approaches (such as using delimited strings), you have to construct your own update operations. This means you have to understand how to construct a WHERE clause pointing to the rows to be updated, or how to execute the appropriate stored procedure to do the job for you.

Another issue to be considered in the user-defined structure approach is how you will handle multiple rows. That is, an individual structure element stores the data from a single row, such as a single customer or part. To store multiple rows, you have to declare an array of the template structure described in the Type declaration. Once the data arrives, you have to unravel the structure, row by row, placing the right elements in the right columns of a grid or other control.

A typical Type statement looks like this:

```
Type objCustomer
     ID as Long
     Name as String
     Address as String
     Phone as String
     Photo as Variant
End Type
```

Setting the values of the individual customer objects is done in two steps. First you need to declare the Customer object using the Type-declared datatype.

```
Dim MyCust as objCustomer
Dim MyCustArray() as objCustomer
```

If you choose to create an array of the typed structure, you simply create an array declaration referencing the Type-declared datatype. However, the dimension (size) of the array—the number of rows—is usually set elsewhere. That is, the component that fills the array usually changes the size of the array to match the number of rows retrieved. Because of this you declare the client-side of the array without indicating the boundaries. The second step is to simply set the values in the object.

```
With MyCust
.ID = 22
.Name ="Fred"
    .Address="123 Silly Street"
    .Phone="Unlisted"
End With
```

When you're ready to retrieve the data on the client side, the called function can return either a single structure or an array of the typed structure.

```
MyCust = GetOneCustomer( )
MyCustArray = GetSetOfCustomers( )
```

Once the data arrives, it appears in a one-dimensional array. You can determine how many rows are available by using the UBound function, which returns the upper boundary of the array. For example, if your GetSetOfCustomers function returned 50 rows, the following RowsFound code would return 50 (or 49 if you start indexing the array at 0).

```
RowsFound = UBound(MyCustArray, 1)
```

The UDT Server-side Code

On the server, you use the same common Type declaration to describe the data, but in this case when you dimension the array (if you use one), you have to fix a size before referencing the array. However, if you build it larger than necessary, or not large enough, you can use the ReDim (Preserve) function to reset the size of the typed array. To make this clearer, let's walk through a sample application that uses user-defined structures to pass data from tier to tier.

The application is called User-Defined Types and is located on the companion CD. It is divided into two parts: client-side and server-side. The server-side code is responsible for executing several queries—each illustrates the use of passing user-defined structures back to the client. The client application manages input parameters and writes the returning data to list boxes and a couple of grid controls. We'll get to the client application in a few pages, but first let's first walk through the server-side code.

The first declaration, in the following code, describes the objAuthor structure. It's used to describe a single row of information gathered about a selected author. In this case, we'll use this structure to define a single row of an array of qualifying authors—but I'm getting ahead of myself.

```
Option Explicit
Public Type objAuthor
    Author As String
    Year_Born As Variant
End Type
```

The next section describes another structure. In this case, it's tTitle, which is used to describe a single title fetched by ISBN. The structure is a mix of strings, both fixed and variable-length. It could contain a combination of any other Visual Basic datatype—even arrays of types.

```
Public Type tTitle
    Publisher As String
    City As String
    ISBN As String * 20
    Year_Published As String
    Title As String
    Cover As String
End Type
```

In an effort to remove literal string references when fetching Parameter and Field object elements, I create item-by-item enumerations in the following section of code. These can dramatically improve performance. We discussed this earlier in Chapter 8.

```
Private Enum enuRSAuthor
    Author
    Year_Born
End Enum
Public Enum enuParms
    ReturnStatus
    ISBN
    Publisher
    City
    Year_Published
    Title
    Cover
End Enum
```

Okay, we're ready for the code—there are four functions to come. One to open the connection (for all of the other functions) and three others that fetch specific UDTs for the client—authors by ISBN, title by ISBN, and a list of appropriate ISBNs (that have related rows in the Covers table).

We start by constructing an ADO Command object in the following code. We don't have a choice in this case; we are executing a stored procedure that returns OUTPUT parameters. Okay, so I'm combining two examples in one module—sue me. The primary purpose of the Command object is to manage the query's Parameters collection for us.

```
Private cn As Connection
Private cmd As Command
Private rs As Recordset
Private i As Integer

Public Function GetTitle(ISBNWanted As String) As tTitle
Dim objRetTitle As tTitle
Set cmd = New Command
OpenConnection
With cmd
    .Name = "TitleByISBN"
    .CommandText = "TitleByISBN"
    .CommandType = adCmdStoredProc
    Set .ActiveConnection = cn
```

You'll find that ADO is somewhat challenged about how it maps the parameters in the target stored procedure. As we discussed earlier, we have a couple of choices here: construct the Parameters collection parameter-by-parameter (which is faster, but takes more code), or use the Refresh method (which is slower, but more reliable). In any case, when the Parameters collection is created, ADO and the layers expect the parameters to exactly overlay the parameter map exposed by the stored procedure. Messages complaining about missing parameters can be caused by too few parameters, by output parameters passed with no initial value (a bug), or by other confusion on your (or ADO's) part.

The parameter names you provide are meaningless. ADO only supports passing parameters to the data providers in order. That is, the first parameter must be created and passed first, the second after the first, followed by all other parameters in the order in which they are defined in the stored procedure. ADO does not support named parameters. That is, in ISQL or Query Analyzer, you can specify the stored procedure arguments by name in any order. This is what ADO does not support—until ADO 2.6[5] comes online for the first time. While the server identifies the parameters by name and the error messages indicate which parameter is in error by name, ADO references parameters positionally. Get them out of order, or don't define them correctly, and you are toast. The ADO Parameter object names have no bearing on the names used by the stored procedure, unless you use Refresh. In this

---

5. ADO 2.6 ships with SQL Server 2000 due out in July, 2000. There should also be a web release soon thereafter.

case, the parameter names match because they're generated and returned by the server along with the rest of the parameter properties.

```
    .Parameters.Append _
        .CreateParameter("ReturnStatus", adInteger, adParamReturnValue)
    .Parameters.Append _
        .CreateParameter("ISBNWanted", adVarChar, adParamInput, _
        20, ISBNWanted)
    .Parameters.Append _
        .CreateParameter("Publisher", adVarChar, adParamOutput, 20)
    .Parameters.Append _
        .CreateParameter("City", adVarChar, adParamOutput, 50)
    .Parameters.Append _
        .CreateParameter("Year_Published", adSmallInt, adParamOutput)
    .Parameters.Append _
        .CreateParameter("Title", adVarChar, adParamOutput, 255)
    .Parameters.Append _
        .CreateParameter("Cover", adVarChar, adParamOutput, 255)
End With
```

After the Command is created and its parameters set (we set the input parameter value when we created the Parameter object), we can execute the query.

```
cmd.Execute Options:=adExecNoRecords
```

You don't see a Recordset? That's right, there isn't one. That's the advantage of using (just) OUTPUT parameters instead of a rowset. In this case, we know that only one row (should) result from a hit on the Titles table, given a specific (unique) ISBN number.

The following code references our single-row objRetTitle object and fills in the individual elements. We use the enumerations to make this easier for the human coder to read and to reference the elements faster. After we've filled in the structure from the data row, we simply pass it back to the client. Sure, we close the connection, but it gets closed anyway when the module goes out of scope.

```
With objRetTitle
    .ISBN = ISBNWanted
    .Publisher = "" & cmd.Parameters(enuParms.Publisher)
    .City = "" & cmd.Parameters(enuParms.City)
    .Year_Published = "" & cmd.Parameters(enuParms.Year_Published)
    .Title = "" & cmd.Parameters(enuParms.Title)
    .Cover = "" & cmd.Parameters(enuParms.Cover)
End With
```

```
cn.Close
GetTitle = objRetTitle
End Function
```

This next function returns a set of authors that wrote a specific book (based on the ISBN). Unlike the previous GetTitles function, this function returns an array of the objAuthor structures.

```
Public Function GetAuthors(ISBNWanted As String) As objAuthor()
Dim objRetAuthors() As objAuthor
OpenConnection
Set rs = New Recordset
rs.Open "Exec AuthorsByISBN '" & ISBNWanted & "'", cn, , , adCmdText
```

We take a different approach in the preceding function (just for a little variety)—we don't create a Command object. All too often, Command object's a waste of time in the middle tier, especially if you don't have to deal with returning parameters. Instead, we create a concatenated query that calls the stored procedure. Because we know the parameter string won't contain single quotes (remember the 'O'Malley' condition?), we can safely construct the query string. Yes, even though this is a stored procedure, we still call it adCmdText. If we called it a stored procedure (adCmdStoredProc), ADO would try to manage the parameters on its own.

If the Recordset is returned with no rows, we have to fill in the structure with appropriate information as we do in the following code. This is why I defined the Year_Born element of the structure as a Variant—so I could set it to a string if there was no valid year.

```
If rs.State = adStateClosed Or rs.EOF Then
    'No author on file for this ISBN
    ReDim objRetAuthors(1)
    objRetAuthors(1).Author = "Not on file"
    objRetAuthors(1).Year_Born = "Unknown"
```

Okay, we got some rows. In the following code, we start by redimensioning the objRetAuthors array to hold the required number of rows. It now contains *n* structures defined by objAuthors. We know from experience that books are written by 1 to 4 authors—so 10 should be big enough for the array. We step through the Recordset, row by row, moving data from the Field objects (referenced by the enumerations) to the array of user-defined objAuthors (again, referenced by enumerations). If we find that one of the Year_Born fields is set to null, we pass a string back to the user to make sure that the user doesn't think the author was born 2000 years ago. Because the database doesn't have anything written by St. Paul (who was born before year 0), this should not be a problem.

```
Else
If Not (rs.EOF and rs.BOF) Then
    ReDim objRetAuthors(1 To rs.RecordCount    i = 1
    Do Until rs.EOF
        With objRetAuthors(i)
            .Author = "" & rs(enuRSAuthor.Author)                 ' Author
            If IsNull(rs(enuRSAuthor.Year_Born)) Then
                .Year_Born = "No year on file"
            Else
                .Year_Born = rs(enuRSAuthor.Year_Born)            ' Year Born
            End If
        End With
        i = i + 1
        rs.MoveNext
    Loop
ReDim Preserve objRetAuthors(1 To i - 1)
End If
```

After we have processed the rowset, we can clean up and pass the array of objAuthors back to the client, as shown next:

```
rs.Close
cn.Close
Set rs = Nothing
Set cn = Nothing
GetAuthors = objRetAuthors
End Function
```

This next function fetches a set of ISBNs that have pictures and authors on file. We only really care about the first 50 of these, so we limit the query accordingly.

```
Public Function GetISBNs() As Variant
OpenConnection
Set rs = New Recordset
rs.Open "select top 50 isbn from covers where isbn in" _
& (select isbn from title_author)", cn, , , adCmdText
GetISBNs = rs.GetRows
End Function
```

In this case, we return the rows as a Variant array. This approach makes the most sense in this case.

The final function simply opens the database connection for all of the other functions.

```
Private Function OpenConnection() as Connection
Set cn = New Connection
cn.Open "Provider=SQLOLEDB.1;Initial Catalog=biblio;Data Source=betav8", _
"Fred",""
Set OpenConnection = cn
End Function
```

The Client-side Code

Next, we need to see how to parse the user-defined structures once they arrive back at the client. Much of this code deals with building clip strings for the Grid control. We could have presented the data in a variety of other ways, including using TextBox controls or perhaps building a Web page. The client application looks like Figure 8-1 when it's running.

The application initially presents a list of valid ISBNs in the ComboBox at the bottom of the form. When the user selects an ISBN, the cmdQuery button is fired and we look up the information on the chosen ISBN. The resulting row is painted into the top grid control. We then perform a second query to populate the grid with the set of authors for the selected book. Yes, some books have many authors—not this one.

The code looks like this:

```
Private Sub cmdQuery_Click()
Dim objLocalTitle As tTitle
Dim objLocalAuthors() As objAuthor
Dim strGrid As String
objLocalTitle = GetTitle(ISBNList.Text)
```

At this point, we have captured the selected ISBN from the ComboBox control list and passed it to the GetTitle function (described previously). We get back a user-defined structure, as declared in our common module.

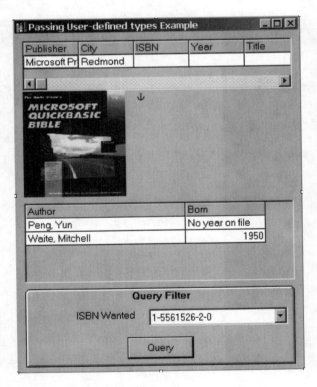

Figure 8-1: Presenting the rows on the client

The first task is to pass the filename of the picture to the Image control. The database has the IMAGE, but we fetched the filename and simply used that to fetch the data from one of the files stored at that path location on disk.

```
Image1.Picture = LoadPicture(objLocalTitle.Cover)
With objLocalTitle
strGrid = .Publisher & vbTab & .City & vbTab & .ISBN & vbTab & .Year_Published _
        & vbTab & .Title & vbTab & .Cover
End With

With MSHFlexGrid1
    .RowSel = 1
    .ColSel = .Cols - 1
    .Clip = strGrid
    .ColSel = 0
End With
```

Next, we step through the user-defined structure, creating a tab-delimited string as we go (as shown in the following code). This is passed to the grid control using the Clip property. This approach eliminates the need to step through the grid, row by row and column by column, referencing each cell—something to be avoided.

```
objLocalAuthors = GetAuthors(ISBNList.Text)
MSHFlexGrid2.Rows = UBound(objLocalAuthors, 1) + 1
strGrid = ""
For i = 1 To MSHFlexGrid2.Rows - 1
    With objLocalAuthors(i)
        strGrid = strGrid & .Author & vbTab & .Year_Born & vbCr
    End With
Next i
With MSHFlexGrid2
    .Row = 1
    .Col = 0
    .RowSel = .Rows - 1
    .ColSel = .Cols - 1
    .Clip = strGrid
    .ColSel = 0
    .RowSel = 0
End With
End Sub
```

Early in the application, we use the Form_Activate event to fill the ComboBox containing the valid ISBNs and set up the grid controls, as in the following code. We don't do this in Form_Load because we don't want the user to wait while this initial setup is done. This way, the form is painted immediately, and before the user has a chance to focus on the form (unless the user had too much coffee), the ComboBox is filled and the user can proceed to use the form. Because the list of valid ISBNs can (theoretically) change from time to time, this process is repeated each time the form is activated. You might consider moving intensive code and complex queries to a less frequently executed event.

```
Private Sub Form_Activate()
Dim varISBNs As Variant
Me.MousePointer = vbHourglass
varISBNs = GetISBNs
ISBNList.Enabled = False
For i = 0 To UBound(varISBNs, 2) - 1
    ISBNList.AddItem varISBNs(0, i)
Next i
ISBNList.Enabled = True
ISBNList.ListIndex = 0
Me.MousePointer = vbDefault
```

In the Form_Initialize event, we pass back a Variant array constructed by the query to fetch a set of valid ISBNs. It's easy to loop through this Variant array and fill the ComboBox. Too bad the ComboBox doesn't support a Clip property. If it did, we could have passed back a delimited string and applied it directly to the Clip property to populate the list, as we do with the headings in the Titles grid.

```
With MSHFlexGrid1
    .Rows = 2
    .Cols = 7
    .FixedRows = 1
    .Row = 0
    .Col = 0
    .RowSel = 0
    .ColSel = 6
    .Clip = "Publisher" & vbTab & "City" & vbTab & "ISBN" _
        & vbTab & "Year" & vbTab & "Title" & vbTab _
        & "Cover"
    .Row = 1
    .RowSel = 1
End With

With MSHFlexGrid2
    .Row = 0
    .Col = 0: .Text = "Author": .ColWidth(0) = TextWidth(String(20, "M"))
```

```
      .Col = 1: .Text = "Born": .ColWidth(1) = TextWidth(String(10, "M"))
      .Row = 1
      .Col = 0
  End With
End Sub
```

That's it. As you can see, passing user-defined types has a few challenges but is fairly easy to understand. It's also fast and easy on the net, because there is little DDL information being passed. However, as you can also see, it requires an intimate knowledge of what's getting built, sent, and received. It would be tough to decode the structure on the receiving end without the Type declaration. These Type declarations also must be cast in concrete before they are propagated through your development organization. If they change after you build your application, you are in the soup. However, in some cases (certainly not all), you can "simply" recompile and redeploy, assuming that the hard-coded assumptions on the data structures do not change.

Passing Property Bags

I attended one of Francesco Balena's (fbalena@softdes.it) talks at VBits in the fall of 1999. He discussed a number of ways to improve performance in Visual Basic applications, which was very enlightening. Many of his suggestions are incorporated in this chapter and others. After his talk, I cornered him to get his opinion on the fastest way to pass data between tiers. I suggested user-defined types and delimited strings. He listened patiently like one of those mountaintop monks. He then proceeded to describe a fairly obscure (to me) technique—PropertyBag objects. While I knew that these were not sacks kept backstage at a burlesque theater, I had never used them (intentionally). He told me that the PropertyBag was implemented for the first time in Visual Basic 5.0 and improved in Visual Basic 6.0 to support "persistable" objects by exposing the Persistable class attribute.

Basically, a PropertyBag is an object that can work as a repository for any type of (simple) data, which includes all public creatable numeric and string data, but does *not* include arrays and collections. This means that you have to store individual array items one by one. It also means that you'll want to use this approach to pass single-row values, such as the output arguments fetched from a stored procedure.

The PropertyBag object exposes only two methods and one property:

- The WriteProperty method stores an element into the PropertyBag. The WriteProperty method has three arguments: the first is the name of the property that you want to store; the second is the data value to be stored; and the third is the default value for the property, which is optional. This method will store your data value and the associated name you supply, unless your data value matches the default value. If you specified a data value that matches the default value, no value is stored, but when you use ReadProperty to find this entry in the PropertyBag, the default value passed on to ReadProperty is returned. If you don't specify a default value in your call to WriteProperty, the data value is always stored. Watch out, though—calling WriteProperty twice will write another copy of the data, it won't overwrite the previous value. Also, once a value is in a PropertyBag, there is no way to remove it.

- The ReadProperty method retrieves an element from the PropertyBag by name. If Visual Basic can't find it, the default value is returned. If there is more than one value with that name, it will return the next in sequence.

- The Contents property determines the internal state of the PropertyBag. This is exposed as a Byte array that "serializes" the current contents of the PropertyBag. What the documentation does not say out loud is that you can both read from and *write to* this property, but we'll talk about that later.

Each element of data in the PropertyBag is named so you can reference it later, either reading or writing. Both methods accept an optional argument indicating a default value for the element.

Initially, the PropertyBag object was designed as a mechanism to store any of your control's properties that were set in the VB IDE. That is, if you open a Visual Basic form file in a text editor such as Notepad, you'll see text that you wouldn't normally see on the code window in your application. This text describes the form, the controls, and all of their settings. This is where the PropertyBag stores the property settings of your control, with any binary information being stored in the equivalent FRX file.

When you run the Visual Basic Addin Visual Basic 6.0 ActiveX Control Interface Wizard, it creates PropertyBag code for each property you define in your custom control. If you need more details on how these work, consult MSDN help. The topic "Storing properties using the PropertyBag object" is a good information source.

Similarly, you can make your properties persistent by trapping the Visual Basic WriteProperties event. This event occurs less frequently, usually when the client form is unloaded after a property has been changed within the IDE. Runtime property changes are obviously not stored in this way. Ordinarily, you would not want them to be persistent.

Using the PropertyBag Object to Transport Stuff

Okay, so how can we use a PropertyBag to return data from another tier? Up to this point it seems that all the PropertyBag is good for is to manage Visual Basic form-based controls. Well, consider that the documentation does not really say that you can *write to* the Contents property. Given that, what if you created a property bag on the server, filled it with a number of named property arguments (even in a hierarchy), and passed the Contents property as a byte array back to the client? Cool? Sure. And fast. However, this approach is not faster than passing back just the variables. On the client end, we simply take the Byte array and apply it to the Contents property of our own locally instantiated PropertyBag object—easy. Of course, those of you using ASP code will not be able to manage byte arrays...

PropertyBag Server Code

Here's the server-side code. It's the same as the previous example except in this case, we pass a Byte array and construct a PropertyBag object to manage the row.

```
Public Function GetTitle(ISBNWanted As String) As Byte()
Dim pbRetTitle As PropertyBag
Set pbRetTitle = New PropertyBag
Set cmd = New Command
OpenConnection
With cmd
    .Name = "TitleByISBN"
    .CommandText = "TitleByISBN"
    .CommandType = adCmdStoredProc
    .Parameters.Append _
        .CreateParameter("ReturnStatus", adInteger, adParamReturnValue)
    .Parameters.Append _
        .CreateParameter("ISBNWanted", adVarChar, adParamInput, _20, ISBNWanted)
    .Parameters.Append _
        .CreateParameter("Publisher", adVarChar, adParamOutput, 20)
    .Parameters.Append _
        .CreateParameter("City", adVarChar, adParamOutput, 50)
    .Parameters.Append _
        .CreateParameter("Year_Published", adSmallInt, adParamOutput)
    .Parameters.Append _
        .CreateParameter("Title", adVarChar, adParamOutput, 255)
    .Parameters.Append _
        .CreateParameter("Cover", adVarChar, adParamOutput, 255)
    Set .ActiveConnection = cn
    cmd.Execute
End With
```

As I said, pretty much the same as the other approaches. Now comes the magic. The following code simply writes each Recordset Field value to named

PropertyBag elements. When it comes time to pass back the PropertyBag, we simply pass the Contents Byte array back.

```
With pbRetTitle
    .WriteProperty "ISBN", ISBNWanted
    .WriteProperty "Publisher", "" & cmd.Parameters(enuParms.Publisher)
    .WriteProperty "City", "" & cmd.Parameters(enuParms.City)
    .WriteProperty "Year_Published", "" & cmd.Parameters(enuParms.Year_Published)
    .WriteProperty "Title", "" & cmd.Parameters(enuParms.Title)
    .WriteProperty "Cover", "" & cmd.Parameters(enuParms.Cover)
End With
cn.Close
GetTitle = pbRetTitle.Contents
End Function
```

PropertyBag Client Code

Here's the client code that accepts the data row back from the server. There's nothing complicated about sending Byte arrays over the wire, unlike some of the more sophisticated interfaces we have seen. However, it's more complicated, less maintainable, and harder to code. Moreover, you lose the ability to use this approach from script clients. In a sense, a PropertyBag is conceptually similar to passing XML strings around—both are extensible property repositories that allow for rich or dumb structure but pass on the burden of the extra handling to you. The only difference is the format of the persistence buffer.

```
Private Sub cmdQuery_Click()
Dim pbLocalTitle As New PropertyBag
Dim objLocalAuthors() As objAuthor
Dim strGrid As String
Set pbLocalTitle = New PropertyBag
pbLocalTitle.Contents = GetTitle(ISBNList.Text)
Image1.Picture = LoadPicture(pbLocalTitle.ReadProperty("Cover"))
With pbLocalTitle
strGrid = .ReadProperty("Publisher") & vbTab & _
            .ReadProperty("City") & vbTab & _
            .ReadProperty("ISBN") & vbTab & _
            .ReadProperty("Year_Published") & vbTab & _
            .ReadProperty("Title") & vbTab & _
            .ReadProperty("Cover")
End With
```

```
With MSHFlexGrid1
    .RowSel = 1
    .ColSel = .Cols - 1
    .Clip = strGrid
    .ColSel = 0
End With
```

Once the Byte array arrives from the server, applying it to a new PropertyBag object permits you to access each of the properties by name. It couldn't be much easier.

Passing XML

XML is the most written about, most extolled, and most debated of all of the new technologies. ADO has implemented the capability to persist and construct Recordsets to and from XML since version 2.1. It is far more comprehensive a subject than can be treated here, but that won't keep me from expressing an opinion or two about it. I'm convinced XML is vitally important—for specific special cases. It should, in my opinion not be used as a *universal* data transmission media. However, the number of interesting (and useful) things you can do with XML is growing.

Unless you've been living in a cave in south Texas (they don't have a local ISP in Big Bend yet), you have been deluged with articles about how XML can solve all of the world's problems. And not all of this information is hype. Yes, XML is another OSFA[6] approach. However, XML makes a lot of sense when you need to transmit information from one application to another and the applications don't know anything about each other (as when talking to space aliens). XML is supported across browser (and operating system) boundaries, and it can be an important tool for moving information from tier to tier.

XML is also a very flexible way to express data structures in a universally understood paradigm for applications that **do** speak the same language. HTML provides ways to display information, but without context or dynamic behavior. In contrast, XML exposes data content and structure—even hierarchical structure. XML Recordsets can also be updated either directly or indirectly (through procedures) because they expose sufficient DDL source-table information (in some cases) to construct an UPDATE statement WHERE clause. In Chapter 9, I show you how to create an **updatable** XML-based Recordset.

---

6. OSFA: One size fits all. Like socks and airline seats, ODBC and OLE DB are OSFA data interfaces. A "universal" paradigm made to suit everyone—but no one in particular.

> **NOTE** *Conceptually, working with the Web is strangely similar to working with IBM 3270 terminals in the 1970s. That is, the central system generated coded instructions for painting text and crude graphics on the target terminal. The terminal had enough processing power to decode the instructions and paint the boxes and text on the screen at the specified coordinates. The user would see the text, position the cursor using the tab key or other function key, and change or enter new data. We found that the real bottleneck became the central system (what we called the "CPU" in those days). As more users were added, the screens were created increasingly more slowly. However, users were used to delays from 10 to 60 seconds, which most systems could support. HTML has brought us back to this world of simple display languages running remotely on "dumb" browsers. And we're back to waiting 10 to 60 (or more) seconds for the data to arrive and get painted.*

Using XML to pass data with ASP

This section discusses how to use XML to pass data from an IIS ASP to a generated HTML page. Chapter 9 discusses how to create updatable XML Recordsets.

You can easily persist a Recordset to an XML *file* using the Recordset.Save method, as shown below, in a normal Visual Basic program or in Visual Basic Script running in an ASP.

```
rs.Save filename, adPersistXML
```

The Save method's capability to persist to an XML file has been supported since ADO 2.1. This technique can be used to transport Recordset data, but you have to transport the whole file between layers to do so, which is not practical for many applications.

However, in ADO 2.5 (as first implemented in Windows 2000 and now available for download) you can construct an ADO *Stream* containing an XML Recordset—even a hierarchical version. A Stream object is simply an in-memory file, or at least it sure looks like it to your code.

```
Dim stmMyStream as ADODB.Stream
Set stmMyStream as New ADODB.Stream
rs.Save stmMyStream, adPersistXML
```

The other ADO 2.5 feature that makes all of this easy is ADO's capability to open persisted Recordsets over HTTP. In addition, the Stream object's ReadText method provides a simple way of extracting a Stream's contents and, when combined with Response.Write, ASP code can return an XML-encoded Recordset without saving anything to a file. The receiving end of this XML can be another Web page that knows how to paint the XML, or it can be your own Visual Basic application, which can reconstitute the XML into a Recordset.

We will spend quite a bit of time in Chapter 9 discussing persisting to Streams because it makes sense (in some cases) to pass the streams back and forth between Web pages (ASP to HTM), between Web pages and Visual Basic programs (Visual Basic to ASP), or even between layers of any of the above.

CHAPTER 9

Web-based Solutions

FOR MANY OF YOU, WEB DEVELOPMENT is either entirely new or a skill you want to acquire. Unlike Al Gore who apparently "invented" the Internet some time ago and knows all about it, I am in the group of people who had to learn about the Web the hard way—through trial and error and a lot of reading. This chapter assumes very little. It starts out with basic Web development architecture and tries to bring everyone up to speed on the terminology and how ADO functions differently in an ASP.

Microsoft is spending a lot of money on new Web development tools—almost as much money as it's spending on lawyers these days. We'll see Visual Studio 7.0 (someday) and how it leverages middle-tier code written in a Visual Basic-like language[1] that leverages HTML, XML, and XSL scripts. Hopefully after having read this chapter, you'll know how to make best use of ADO and these new evolving tools—at least you won't be blindsided by the innovations as they arrive.

Web Development 101

For those of you out there who have been working with the Web and are comfortable with its basics, skip down to the next section. I want to try to explain Web development to those who are just getting used to this new paradigm.

Basically, Web development is done in two forms. First, programs such as Front Page and others handle the *presentation* of information. They generate the backgrounds, buttons, and visual aspects of the Web page. All of this coding is stored in the form of HTM and other files on a Web server (usually managed by IIS). While there are ways for a "normal" Visual Basic Win32 program to access IIS-based applications, I'll focus (at least initially) on Visual Basic Script (VBScript) applications. Active Server Pages and other HTML pages you create can be coded in combinations of HTML and one of the scripting languages. I'm partial to VBScript, but the browser community does not universally support it. However, it's always supported under IIS, so that's where I'll execute my Web-based code.

The next form of development, seen in most substantial systems, executes code that runs on the central server—IIS. Interestingly enough, this is not typically binary compiled code (although it can be, if you use Web Classes), but

---

1. No, Visual Studio's version of Visual Basic won't be the same as what you're coding in now. Similar, but different enough to make you pause for a second or two.

interpreted Visual Basic or Java *Script*. This is not even "compiled" Visual Basic "P" code, but raw source that's stored in ASPs, loaded, interpreted, and executed on the fly.

VBScript is more like MBASIC 80 than Visual Basic—it's considerably less sophisticated. For example, using VBScript, you can't create ADO or other COM objects ahead of time, as you can in "regular" Visual Basic code. While an ASP can reference COM objects, even ADO COM objects, these have to be created in Visual Basic or another language that supports a binary compiler (so you can build the DLLs). To access ADO or any other COM object from a VBScript program, you have to use the CreateObject method to construct these objects at runtime. In addition, VBScript also works entirely with Variant variables (which may in turn contain strings, numbers, arrays, objects, etc.). This means that all VBScript COM references are "late" bound.

There's also a new set of restrictions, and many of these limitations derail a variety of the things we do to improve performance:

- Visual InterDev will help fill in VBScript method arguments, but only those fully enumerated (and not all are). This means you'll have to include a file containing all of the Visual Basic ADO constants. No, don't fall back on using the values instead of the constants. You can also put a reference to ADO in the Global.ASA file. This will help Visual InterDev autocomplete the ADO statements as you type. ADO ships with a file that can be included in your ASP page: \Program Files\Common Files\System\ado\adovbs.inc

- VBScript supports only the Variant data type—the AS clause in the Dim statement generates a syntax error. Thus, you can use Dim to declare your variables and arrays but not their datatype. If you follow good programming practice, you'll have an Option Explicit statement on your page that forces you to declare all of your variables and helps locate undeclared variables.

- VBScript doesn't support all of the features of the Dim, Public, and Private statements used to declare variables. You can continue to use variables with different data types—you can still create Date values, String values, and Double values, but they must be created according to the rules of the Variant data type.

- Data types aren't the only things missing. VBScript also lacks several statements. It's missing all of the statements related to file I/O, such as Open, Close, Read, and Input. The Scripting.FileSystemObject model replaces these basic I/O functions.

- Other statements that are not available are Write, GoSub, On GoSub, On GoTo, On Error (and all of the Resume operators), and DoEvents. Yes, that means you'll have to rethink your error-handling approach.[2]

VBScript Error Handling

One of the most limiting aspects of VBScript code is the error handler, or the lack of one. Yes, you can turn on error handling, but only to skip over any code that causes errors and ignore the error—On Error Resume Next. Most Web pages I've seen use this technique. This means that you'll have to add code to deal with the errors after *each* line of VBScript code that could potentially cause an error.

However, IIS5 (on Windows 2000) implements new technology that alleviates this problem by enabling you to configure an exception ASP page. This page is called whenever your script encounters an unhandled error. This means you can implement a "central error handler" based on this code.

The default exception page passed by IIS (%WinDir%\Help\iisHelp\common\500-100.asp) can be modified to handle your particular site's error issues. If you need a better user interface, better logging, or simply better error management, you can configure IIS and tell it which page it should go to on a Website, directory, or page-wide scope. This page has access to the ASPError object, which has properties that tell you all you want to know about the error. For example, was it a script syntax error or a runtime error? What page caused the error and what line and what description was passed?

The use of these exception pages may also alleviate problems associated with inadequate error handling and debugging information, as outlined later in the chapter. While the default error page doesn't show the error Description (for some obscure reason), you can edit it and insert the following in Line 65:

```
<h3><%= objASPError.Description %></h3>
```

This change will let you see the description of the error above all the rest of the information.

You'll also find that it won't be easy to send back error messages when things go wrong in the ASP. You don't want to let IIS or VBScript display an error page, so you'll want to trap the errors and deal with them. However, if you expect to send back an XML response, it can't have Response.Write "informational" messages embedded within. So, when your ASP expects to send back XML-formatted data

---

2. For more information on the specifics of Visual Basic Scripting Edition coding, see http://msdn.microsoft.com/isapi/msdnlib.idc?theURL=/library/partbook/egvb6/programmingwithvbscript.htm.

and an error occurs, you'll have to resolve these errors yourself (on the ASP) or use a couple of other techniques that I'll illustrate as we go on.

ASP code is a strange mix of executable (Visual Basic or Java) script source code intermixed with HTML commands. This threw me at first, because I did not get the gist of the "shift" characters that tell the compiler to compile some text and pass the rest to the browser to perform some function. Because of this, you'll sometimes find HTML interspersed with script code, using special tags to indicate the shifts in and out of the compiled code. However, most of my ASP pages that return XML don't try to send non-XML-formatted HTML back to the browser—not unless there's trouble.

> **TIP** *The tags used to switch in and out of VBScript code in an ASP page are "<%" and "%>". Anything inside these beginning and ending tags is considered script code to be compiled and executed when the page is loaded. You can switch in and out of "code" anytime you want. Anything **outside** of the code brackets is sent to the browser as raw text or HTML commands.*

The Browser's HTML Interpreter

The browser has its own interpreter that recognizes HTML commands for constructing tables, drawing lines or boxes, or simply moving the text cursor to the next line, and a lot more, just like in the 3270[3] systems. Well, sorta. Today's browsers also support 3D and vector rendering, drag and drop, and an event system that the 3270 never had. Yes, it's possible to tell the browser to interpret and execute script code, but keep in mind that only IE supports VBScript. All browsers support JavaScript, so you'll find a lot of code generators for this new OSFA[4] language.

Because all browsers support HTML, this provides a universal way to communicate to the browser from an ASP page running VBScript on the server. As the spring of 2001 gets closer, we'll see how Visual Basic 7.0 provides a way to create Visual Basic *binary* executables and extrude HTML (and XML) to pass content back to the client.

The browser expects you to pass "tags" that describe specific regions of the Web page. These tags are bracketed in less-than (<) and greater-than (>) symbols. For example, a tag used to capture user input in a text box would look like this:

```
Name wanted: <INPUT TYPE= "TEXT" NAME="txtName" VALUE= "Default" >
```

---

3. 3270: When I started working on mainframes in the 1970s, the 3270 was used as an "intelligent" terminal to display data passed from a mainframe. It used a rudimentary data display and editing language not unlike really basic HTML.

4. OSFA: One size fits all.

The tag here begins with the "<" symbol followed by the tag name—"INPUT" in this case. The tag ends with the ">" symbol. Between the "<" and ">" symbols are attributes, which are synonymous with properties. In this case, the TYPE, NAME, and VALUE attributes are specified to tell the browser how to treat this INPUT area and how to reference it from elsewhere on this page or on other pages we launch. The string "Name wanted:" appears on the Web page in front of the INPUT text box. Anything not embedded in the HTML tags appears on the page as text.

Running ActiveX Server Pages

There are many ways to run the code in your ASP. One common way is to simply reference it from an ordinary Web page. This could be manifested as a URL tag that points to the ASP file on the server. You can also use the Form tag and the Action attribute to do the same thing (as shown in the following code). The Form tag names a specific ASP file on the Web server, just as you would point to a remote file. In this case, I used the "Post" technique to pass an argument (the name wanted) to the ASP. This technique prevents parameters passed to the ASP from appearing on the URL invoking the ASP.

The code shown here is a simple (really simple) Web page used to capture a couple of parameters from a browser and to launch an ASP. See PostExample1.HTML in the sample Web (ADOBP) on the companion CD for the entire source.

```
<html>
    <meta NAME="GENERATOR" Content="Microsoft Visual Studio 6.0">
    <FONT SIZE="4" FACE="ARIAL, HELVETICA">
    <B>ADO Examples and Best Practices Example 1</B></FONT><BR>
    Passing arguments between an HTML form and an ASP<BR>
    using the Post method<BR>
    <body>
```

This next line is the FORM tag that references the SimpleASP.ASP page in a specific directory on the Web server. I'll discuss the operation of this tag a little later in this chapter.

```
<FORM action=..\asp\SimpleASP.asp method=post>
```

The next few lines display two INPUT boxes (basically browser-based TextBox controls) to capture keystrokes from the user. The NAME attribute for each control is used to identify the controls to the ASP. The VALUE attribute contains an initial (default) value that's passed if the user does not type anything into the control. The attributes of these controls are passed as members of the Request object's FORM property so they can be referenced by name on the ASP.

```
    Name: <INPUT NAME="txtName" VALUE="Vau%" > <BR><BR>
    Max Rows:<INPUT  NAME="txtMaxRows" VALUE=50
        style="HEIGHT: 25px; WIDTH: 31px" maxlength=2
        dataformatas=Numeric><BR><BR>
    <INPUT type="submit" value="Submit Query">
</FORM>
</body>
</html>
```

A little later in this chapter, I'll discuss the server-side ASP code. In that code, I extract the arguments captured by the Web page code shown above by examining the Request object's Form property. We'll get to the server-side code in a minute.

The Web page built with the HTML described above is shown in Figure 9-1:

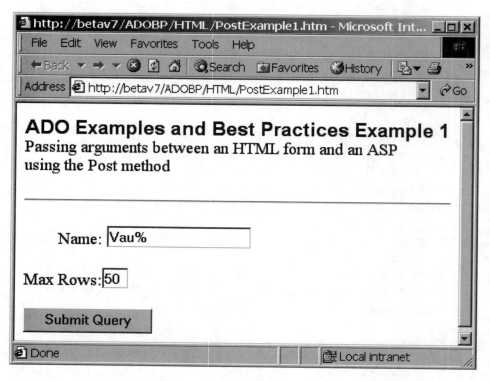

Figure 9-1: Capturing parameters from a Web page and invoking an ASP

Passing Parameters

Because the queries we run in the ASP usually need parameters, you'll have to collect parameters using Input tags (or some other HTML tag) or expect the parameters to be concatenated to the URL used to launch the Web page. For example, if you want to select a set of authors from the Biblio test database whose last name begins with a specified string, you could prompt the user with the previous code. Note the Input tag with its Type set to "submit" (shown again here). This constructs the command button that launches the ASP when clicked by the user.

```
<INPUT type="submit" value="Submit Query" >
```

At this point, the current page is pushed down in the stack, as it were. The user can navigate back to it, but the ASP typically generates the next page the user sees. However, if the ASP code takes too long to complete, the user is likely to either go elsewhere (give up) or click the Submit button again. If they click again, IIS launches yet another copy of the ASP and restarts the process—which only aggravates a bad situation. There's really no way to prevent this (as you can in Visual Basic).

The Form tag in the earlier code (shown again below) tells the browser to construct a Form object. When the Submit button is clicked, the browser passes the Form object to the ASP named in the Form Action attribute. The Form tag also specifies the method to be used to pass any captured INPUT values to the target page.

```
<FORM action=..\asp\SimpleASP.asp method=post>
```

In this case, we specified that the browser is to use the Post technique to pass the arguments in the structure behind the scenes to the ASP. This way the arguments do not appear in the URL. This prevents someone from simply editing the URL in the browser to change the parameters (which is possible if you set the Method attribute to Get).

> **NOTE** *A URL simply points to the "virtual" filename on the remote IIS server. It might point to an HTM, ASP, or other page recognized by the browser.*

If you set the Form object's Method attribute to Get (as opposed to Post) to pass parameters from your Web page to the ASP, the browser tacks the arguments to the end of the URL, separated with "?" characters. The end of each parameter is marked with a percent sign (%) as shown below (although it's not always used).

```
http://www.betav.testsite.getdata.asp/?txtName=Vau%
```

If you set the Form object's Method attribute to Get, the ASP can reference the individual arguments through the QueryString collection, as shown next:

```
Dim txtName
txtName = Form.QueryString("txtName")
```

Visual Basic vs. VBScript Development

The ASP or Internet paradigm illustrates a fundamental difference between writing interactive Visual Basic client/server applications and Web-based applications. In Visual Basic, we construct presentation controls that are basically static. That is, they are filled by code running on the client. In the VBScript ASP programming model, the client makes a data request and subsequently paints the contents of the result set in these static display controls. Generally, Visual Basic client/server developers don't construct a new form with data-generated controls for each query (but we could).

In Web-based development using ASPs, it seems that the new pages (or at least regions of the page) are reconstructed almost from scratch on each query. However, as I illustrate later in this chapter, we can call the same IIS-based server-side ASP code from "traditional" Visual Basic programs—and fairly easily.

Using XML to Return Data from Web Pages

In this section, we walk through a sample Web project that starts with a simple Web page used to capture the necessary query parameters. We'll use the Web page just discussed and walk through an ASP that returns the data in XML, based on the passed parameters. The second application we discuss (in the "Managing Recordsets Using XML Stream Objects" section of the chapter) uses a Visual Basic client/server-like application to launch ASP pages, update rows, and process the errors.

In the preceding example, we discussed how the Submit button launches an ASP that runs a query based on the input parameters. This ASP code returns an XML Recordset that's formatted and converted to HTML with an XSL template. This draws and populates a table filled with the Recordset data on the user's browser. In this case, the "table" generated is a series of boxes, headings, and content—not a database table.

The Server-side Active Server Page

The ASP code does most of the work in our application. It opens an SQL Server connection, runs a query, returns a Recordset, and constructs the XML to be sent back to the browser. It also formats the XML using an XLS script that formats the XML into an HTML table. The XSL style sheet is designed to morph to any XML structure passed, so it would be handy to use it for other generic XML applications.

The ASP code itself is stored as a file on the IIS server with its permissions and properties set up, so IIS recognizes this as an executable page. Without these settings, IIS won't do much with the page, but it will complain that you don't have sufficient permission to execute the ASP. One quick way to get these settings right is to put your ASP pages in a directory with ASP pages created by your Visual InterDev system. Yes, I used Visual InterDev to develop these samples—so sue me.

> **TIP** *When working with Visual InterDev, you'll see many method arguments being autoinserted for you as you type. That's cool. However, if you want to come up with nonenumerated options, you have to make sure that the application can recognize the ADO constants by adding the following line to the top of your ASP:*

```
<!- #INCLUDE FILE="../include/ADOVBS.INC" ->
```

> **NOTE** *Without this line, I kept getting an ADO error (0x800A0BB9) without further explanation. I suspect the Open method's adCmdText option setting threw the interpreter. However, once I inserted Option Explicit into the ASP code, the interpreter told me it did not understand adCmdText. Just make sure your project contains the Include file.*

Let's walk through the ASP server-side code. The first section sets up the variables used in the ASP code. We don't have the option to declare the datatypes here—everything's a Variant. The On Error Resume Next statement helps prevent the VBScript interpreter from simply passing an error page back to the client (browser), but I usually comment this out while developing, to help catch the syntax errors. Once you enable On Error Resume Next, all errors are ignored and you'll have to insert code to test for errors after each operation that is likely to cause an error. After that, the code should look very familiar. We build a perfectly ordinary ConnectionString to pass to the Recordset Open later in the ASP.

Note that the ConnectionString (sConn) hard-codes the user name, password, server name, and database into the ASP. Yes, we could have passed these in from the HTM page that launches the ASP and inserted them into the Visual Basic code using the Request.Form("variable name") technique, but this disables connection pooling—unless everybody types in exactly the same thing. But you don't need to worry about hard coding these values because changing them later is easy, and once the page is changed and resaved, all subsequent references use the new settings—instantly.

However, in secure production systems, you probably don't want to leave this username and password hard coded—especially because lots of other people are likely to work on the page and everyone who does will be able to see the password. A workable solution, as I have mentioned before, is to use a UDL file to contain the connect string. You can give read/write access for the UDL to the administrators and read-only access to users under which context this file will be used (usually the System, and IIS's IUSR_machinename and IWAM_machinename local users).

Let's walk through the ASP code. The first thing we do is tell IIS that the page uses VBScript as the script language. After that notation, the ASP code looks pretty much like any other Visual Basic application.

```
<%@ Language=VBScript%>
<%
Option Explicit
Dim sConn, sSql, rs, Query, MaxRows, stm
On error resume next
sConn = "Provider=SQLOLEDB.1;Password=xyzzy;User ID=ADOASP;" _
    & "Initial Catalog=biblio;Data Source=(local)"
```

The following code extracts the parameters by name from the Request.Form properties collection. These named properties correspond to the named INPUT controls tagged in the invoking client-side Web page. Each input argument is validated and forced to a default value if it is incorrect. Input validation could have been done on the client, but if business rules change, you have to keep the client-side code in sync, too. But this is not nearly as hard as it is when working with Win32 client/server applications. All you have to do is change the Web page HTML to prevalidate the INPUT values.

```
MaxRows=Request.Form("txtMaxRows")
if MaxRows > "99" or MaxRows < "1" then MaxRows = "50"
Query = Request.Form("txtName")
if Query ="" then Query = "A%"
```

The following code constructs a SELECT statement to return the desired rowset. No, I don't recommend use of "&" concatenation to build the string, but we have to use it here so my editors don't try to chop it up (it would stretch off the printed page). Next, we create an ADODB Recordset object the hard way—by using the CreateObject method. We open the Recordset using the SQL string and the ConnectionString constructed earlier. Note that we don't create a separate Connection object in this case—but ADO does, behind the scenes.

> **TIP** *The ASP Connection.Open method will be executed many, many times in quick succession—once by each client that references the ASP. That's why it's important to make sure connection pooling (as we discussed in Chapter 4) is working.*

Actually, to help manage connection errors, you might consider creating a separate Connection object and using it to open the database connection. This way you can trap errors independently of opening the Recordset. Once the Connection is open, you can pass the opened Connection object to the Recordset Open method.

```
sSQL="Select Top " & MaxRows & " Author, Year_Born " _
    & " from authors where author like '" & query & "' "
set rs = CreateObject("ADODB.Recordset")
rs.Open sSQL, sConn,,,adCmdText
```

> **IMHO** *Many (okay, almost all) example code samples I found did not set the CommandType option when using the Open method. This is simply lazy coding—it can make a big difference in how quickly a query is executed.*

The next line tests whether the Open method worked by testing the Visual Basic Err object for 0. If there are errors, we simply pass a message back to the browser using the Response.Write method. This logic also bypasses any attempt to return the XML.

```
if err then
    Response.Write "Error occurred:" & err.description & "<BR>"
    Err.Clear
else
    if rs.EOF then
        Response.Write "No authors found using " & Query & " filter.<BR>"
    Else
```

> **TIP** *When sending messages back to the browser, be sure to add the <BR/> tag at the end of each line. Unlike Visual Basic's Print function, no CRLF sequence is automatically added to the end of your string.*

Now it's time to construct the XML to return to the client. In this case, we persist the Recordset to an in-memory structure that was implemented for the first time in ADO 2.5—the Stream object. In this case, the Stream is persisted as an XML structure based on the Recordset. We then "write" the stream (containing the Recordset in XML) to the client browser as a Response. We follow this with an XSL-formatting style page. Both the Stream and the XSL (file) are sent back using the Response.Write technique, but notice that we set the Response.ContentType to "text/XML" so the browser knows how to deal with the data being passed back by the ASP. The ContentType attribute is formatted as *type/subtype* where *type* is the general content category and *subtype* is the specific content type. For example, "text/HTML," "image/GIF," "image/JPEG," "text/plain," and (for our example) "text/XML" are typical ContentType settings. Let's look at the code to do all of this magic.

> **WARNING** *If you set the ContentType to "text/XML" and you decide to write plain text (or HTML) later, the browser won't show it.*

```
Set stm = Server.CreateObject("ADODB.Stream")
    rs.Save stm,adPersistXML
    Response.ContentType = "text/xml"
    Response.Write "<?xml:stylesheet type=""text/xsl""
href=_""recordsetxml.xsl""?>" _
    & vbCrLf
    Response.Write stm.ReadText
    stm.close
    Set stm = Nothing
    end if
end if
%>
```

> **NOTE** *The final step (as shown above) concatenates a small XML Style file (XSL) to format the XML data. It's included on the CD, so you can look at it at your leisure. Developed by Andrew Brust[5], this illustrates another OSFA approach. That is, this template script knows how to break down the XML and create a browser-based table from the structure—as long as it's not hierarchical.*

The non-XML Response.Write messages are only sent back if something goes wrong during the Open (Connection or Recordset) and we *don't* switch to XML ContentType. If you do mix in human-readable messages in a XML document, you'll get strange errors about your Headers not matching. What's really happening is the extra Response.Write strings corrupt the carefully formatted XML generated in the next step.

> **IMHO** *As far as I'm concerned, error handling should be a top priority in your Web page development. We've all seen "professional" sites throw up meaningless messages when things go wrong. As your application does more and more things, the chances that an ASP page will fail go up dramatically. When the server can't support any more connections, your RAM is exhausted, or your system gets locked out by other operations, you need to provide more than a moronic (default) message—as would be generated by the code shown above.*

The next few lines of code close the VBScript tag and tell the VBScript interpreter to include the ADOVBS.INC file. I expect that some performance might be gained if only the specific constants contained in this (rather large) file were included—especially if you consider that the ASP is *interpreted* from source code each time it's run. More lines to compile means poorer performance.

```
<!— #INCLUDE FILE="../include/ADOVBS.INC" —>
```

---

5. I used a number of references to find examples of ASP coding. These included the book **Professional Active Server Pages** published by Wrox Press (Homer, Enfield, et al.) and several articles published in **Visual Basic Programmer Journal**, including a great article "ADO Enhances the Web" by Andrew Brust and William Wen (Progressive Consulting). I also got a lot of help from my friends and coworkers at Microsoft, including John Thorson and Carmen Sarro (and many others), and from my technical editor, Eduardo.

> **IMHO** *I used Visual InterDev to write and test these samples. When compared to Visual Basic and its interactive debugging, statement-by-statement execution, and support windows (such as the Locals window), Visual InterDev comes up really lacking. I found it very hard to figure out what was going on with my code and why it did or did not work. The error messages returned by ADO and IIS were cryptic at best.*

Managing Recordsets Using XML Stream Objects

After completing the preceding XML example, I started asking questions and found a few answers that really opened up a whole new paradigm using XML. While you might be tired by now of XML, I think you'll find this next sample to be well worth the time it takes to study it.

The preceding example used an ASP that generates a parameter-driven Recordset passed back as a formatted XML HTML table. The ASP page expected the client to be a browser-based Web page that captured the name parameter and maximum number of rows to pass. In contrast, this next example shows how to use Visual Basic as your frontend (hardly a radical concept) to execute the ASP code. But in this case, we create an updatable Recordset, make changes to it, and send the disjoint Recordset back to an ASP to be posted to the database using the UpdateBatch method. The tricky part (if that's not tricky enough) is to manage the errors. These errors are (or could be) generated at every phase—when we open a connection, run the initial query, construct the XML, send and receive the XML, post the changes back to IIS, and get the results of the UpdateBatch. The architecture of this new sample is shown in Figure 9-2.

The approach here is similar in many respects to other architectures that we have discussed. It leverages code executed on another platform—IIS in this case. However, unlike executing compiled stored procedures on SQL Server, which are written (just) in TSQL, this code is interpreted on the fly, which runs considerably slower than compiled stored procedures. On the other hand, VBScript is more flexible than TSQL, so there are advantages that might (just might) outweigh the lack of speed. One of these differences is the ASP code's capability to execute binary code developed in Visual Basic, C, or any other language. This binary code can also execute the same stored procedures you've been using all along—and so can the ASP VBScript code.

But there's still another issue here. While stored procedures communicate with the client (or component) through Tabular Data Stream (TDS) (through remote procedure call (RPC) protocol), our IIS ASP code sends us (and expects to receive) HTTP-formatted structures. This means a lot more packets are sent over the wire. But, as Edward (my technical editor) pointed out to me, this comparison

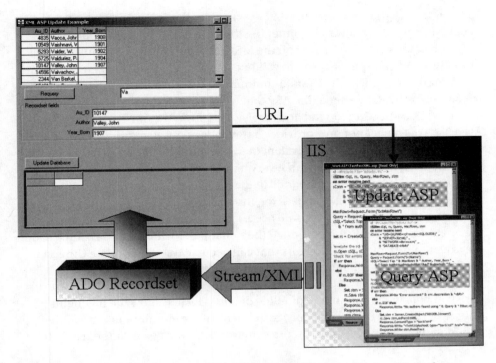

Figure 9-2: Returning XML from an ASP via URL reference to pass a Recordset

is not exactly apple vs. apple. The bottom line is that this newly emerging paradigm is very different, but far more flexible in many respects than those we have used and depended on for decades.

Examining the Visual Basic to ASP Code Example

Let's step through the three code modules one at a time. First, we examine the Visual Basic client application which captures our query filter to be passed as a parameter to the WHERE clause of the ASP that executes the query for us.

Basically, the Visual Basic client program works like this. We start the application and launch an initial query using the current value in the query criteria TextBox (txtQueryParm). To run the query, we simply use the Recordset Open method to address and run the query ASP (recordsetxml.asp), passing the query argument in the URL. The ASP returns XML, which ADO converts directly into a Recordset on the client (a feature implemented in ADO 2.1).

This is where the first little trick comes in. ADO expects a Recordset to be returned by the ASP, not an error message, but because this is not a Web page, we can't just execute a Response.Write on the ASP to tell the user what went wrong.

So, to pass back the error number and description, the ASP constructs a new Recordset and adds a row to it containing the error and its details. Cool? When the application gets a click event on the MSHFlexGrid control, it populates a set of TextBox controls that are used to validate any changes made.

After the user clicks the Update command button, we use another technique to send back the Recordset to the ASP that will do the UpdateBatch. This code uses the MSXML object to send and receive XML from the ASP—a new feature of ADO 2.5. This object not only provides a way to pass our Recordset (saved to a Stream containing the XML equivalent of the Recordset), but a way to retrieve the response from the ASP. This became very handy when I needed to pass back error information as comments embedded in the XML, because the MSXML object exposes the ResponseText as well as the ResponseXML.

If errors do occur (and errors *do* occur), the user is given an option to retry the operation or simply force through their changes. Included in the source code is a skeleton treatment of the errors that can occur. We set the Update Criteria property to force the changes through—or simply resubmit the query.

Incidentally, because this program is provided in source on the CD, I won't bore you here with many of the piddling details—I'll just show the highlights unique to this approach. You'll recognize many of the enumerations and other common techniques we have discussed before, so I won't go over them again.

> **TIP** *I found that it was easier to develop my prototype ASP code in the Visual Basic 6.0 IDE. Once it's working in Visual Basic, transporting the working code to the ASP was a snap.*

The Client-side Visual Basic Code

We start by creating a constant that points to the IIS server and our Web root. Nope, that server is not on the WWW, so don't bother looking. The txtField TextBox is populated when we get a click event on the MSHFlexGrid control.

```
Const WebHost As String = "http://betav7/testxml/myhtml/"
```

The following code runs when the user changes the criteria and clicks the Requery command button. It's also run when the application first starts. It invokes the ASP and passes the current criteria with the URL. The Recordset Open is either passed a rowset from the ASP or a new Recordset containing the error type (connection or query), number, and description. If the first Field is named EType, then we know we have an error embedded in the XML stream.

However, if there's no error, there's a rowset. In this case, we simply fill the grid
with the Recordset data.

```
Private Sub cmdRequery_Click()
On Error GoTo cmdEH
If rs.State = adStateOpen Then rs.Close
rs.Open WebHost & "recordsetxml.asp?Query=" & txtQueryParm
If InStr(rs.Fields(0).Name, "EType") Then
    ' The connection or query did not work.
    The XML has the error messages... not the rows
    Select Case rs.Fields("EType")          ' Error Type
        Case enuError.Connection
            MsgBox "The active server page could not connect to the server. "_
            & vbCrLf & _ rs.Fields("Description"), _
            vbCritical, "Error Connecting"    ' Description field
        Case enuError.OpenRecordset
            MsgBox "The active server page could not execute the query. " _
            & vbCrLf & rs.Fields("Description"), vbCritical, _
            "Error Opening"     ' Description field
        Case Else
            'huh
            MsgBox "Unrecognized error type. Programming error", vbCritical
    End Select
 Else
Set MSHFlexGrid1.Recordset = rs
End If
Quit:
    Exit Sub
```

The next section of the code runs when the user clicks the Update
command button. We construct an MSXML object to pass a Stream object
containing the Recordset (in XML) to the ASP where the UpdateBatch method
will be applied.

```
Private Sub cmdUpdate_Click()
Dim strMsg As String
Dim stm As ADODB.Stream
' Microsoft XML Version 2.0
Dim xml As MSXML.XMLHTTPRequest
Dim rsLocal As Recordset
```

```
Dim fld As Field
Dim stmXML As Stream

On Error GoTo cmdUpdateEH

Set xml = New MSXML.XMLHTTPRequest
Set rsLocal = New Recordset
rsLocal.CursorLocation = adUseClient
rsLocal.Properties("Update Criteria") = adCriteriaAllCols
RetryUpdate:
Set stm = New ADODB.Stream
rs.Save stm, adPersistXML                ' Save global RS to Stream
'
' Hit the page that can do the UpdateBatch we could send
' a flag to request either a rowset or an error
'
xml.Open "POST", WebHost & "UpdateXMLRS.ASP", False
xml.send stm.ReadText
```

The ASP tries to update the database, but stuff (usually) happens, so you can occasionally expect to get back an XML stream containing the "updated" (but with pending rows) Recordset to see which rows did not update.

After the Recordset arrives (remember, it only comes back if there were collision errors), we can use the Filter property to deselect the rows that were not affected. The Recordset still has all of the rows in it, so if you simply pass this filtered Recordset to the grid, you'll see them all. That's why I used another routine to fill the grid manually. The error number and description values are passed back from the update ASP through the comments tag in the XML. When we look at the update ASP code, we'll see how that's done.

```
If xml.responseText <> "" Then                ' Test for error text or rowset
    rsLocal.Open xml.responseXML              ' Open rowset
    rsLocal.Filter = adFilterPendingRecords
    If rsLocal.RecordCount > 0 Then
        DumpRsToGrid rsLocal
    If InStr(xml.responseText, "RSUpdate error") Then    ' Deal with the errors…
```

The Server-side ASP Query Code

This code illustrates a couple of new techniques. Sure, I leveraged the code used in the first XML example in this chapter, but in this case, we can't send back error information via HTML—we can only respond with a Recordset. That's because we're using the ADO Recordset Open method to fetch the rows. If something goes wrong with the connection or query, we have to report that fact to the client. Of course, we could just return nothing to the client and have it use the ADO "GuessWhatWentWrong" function, but that has not worked for me since I installed *Age of Empires* on my system. Again, for brevity, I'll leave off some of the code we already discussed.

Just as with earlier ASP pages, we construct the ADO objects by executing Server.CreateObject. We use a separate Connection object to make it easier to handle Connection errors. We also create a Recordset and a Stream object to pass the data from layer to layer.

```
' Initialize objects:
On error resume next
set cn = server.CreateObject ("ADODB.Connection")
Set rs = Server.CreateObject("ADODB.Recordset")
Set stm = Server.CreateObject("ADODB.Stream")
```

The next code builds a ConnectionString, and if the connection opens, it opens a Recordset based on the parameter concatenated to the end of the URL. We have no way to construct an HTML Form object in Visual Basic, so we have to set the Form Method attribute to Get". We also make sure the Recordset is constructed with optimistic batch locks so ADO can pass it back to the client in read-write mode. Remember, the default mode is RO.

```
cn.ConnectionString =  "file name=c:\biblio.udl"
cn.CursorLocation  = aduseclient
cn.Open
if err then
    BuildErrorRecord 0, err, err.Description
else
    Parm = Request.QueryString("Query")
    rs.Open "select Au_ID, Author, Year_Born " _
    & " from authors where author like '" & Parm & "%'"  Order By Author", _
        cn, adOpenKeyset, adLockBatchOptimistic, adCmdText
    if err then
        BuildErrorRecord 1, err, err.Description    'type 1 = OpenRecordset
    end if
End if
```

Okay, the Recordset is ready to be sent back. This next code persists the Recordset to the local Stream object in XML format. It then writes the Unicode-format information back to the sending "page" (our Visual Basic application). Yup, that's a lot of bits. Note that we didn't set the

Recordset ActiveConnection property to Nothing as we did when sending back Recordset objects in other middle-tier designs. Why? BHOM, but it works.

```
rs.Save stm, adPersistXML
Response.ContentType = "text/xml"
Response.Write stm.ReadText
```

If something goes wrong when opening the connection or running the query, we construct a new Recordset to save the error information. The following routine is executed when there are errors to report back to the Visual Basic layer. We construct a raw Recordset object with three fields to hold the error type (connection or query), the error number, and the error description. Remember, when building ADO Recordset Field objects, if the Field is not large enough to hold the value passed to it, ADO ignores the whole value. For example, if you create a 100-byte string field, and try to set its Value property to a 101-byte string, ADO simply ignores the operation without making a peep. I would have expected it to truncate at 100 bytes, but no, it just ignores the whole string. How rude!

```
Sub BuildErrorRecord (intType, intErr, strDescription)
    set rs = server.CreateObject ("adodb.Recordset")
    With rs
        .Fields.Append "EType", adInteger
        .Fields.Append "Error", adInteger
        .Fields.Append "Description",adVarChar,255
        .open            ' Create new Recordset just for errors
        .addnew              ' Add a new row
        .fields("EType") = intType
        .fields("Error") = intErr
        .fields("Description") = strDescription
        .UpdateBatch
    End With
End Sub
```

The Server-side ASP Update Code

The last of our three routines has one responsibility—post the changes made at the client to the database. As with the other ASP pages we've seen so far, we use On Error Resume Next to disable the VBScript error handlers.

```
<!--#include File="adovbs.inc"-->
<%
Dim rs, stm, srtoption, ErrorMessage
on error resume next

Set rs = Server.CreateObject ("ADODB.Recordset")
Set stm = Server.CreateObject("ADODB.Stream")
```

This ASP page is fairly simple. We only need a Recordset object and a Stream. We reconstruct the Recordset object from the Stream passed to the ASP. Note the Open method using the Request object as the Source argument. We then reassociate the connection string and tell ADO to post the changes to the database.

```
with rs
    .CursorLocation = adUseClient
    .Open Request
    .ActiveConnection = "dsn=LocalServer;uid=TestASP;pwd=Secret"
    .UpdateBatch
end with
```

If nothing goes wrong, the ASP ends and returns control to the Visual Basic app that invoked it—it sends nothing back. I guess we could send back some XML comments providing records affected or similar feedback.

However, if something does go wrong, then we have to construct an XML string that contains the error information and the Recordset—it now has new Status information for those rows that did not get updated for some reason. Simply sticking a comment into the XML stream, which gets returned in the MSXML ResponseText property does this.

```
if err then
        ErrorMessage =  "RSUpdate error: " & err.Description_
        & "[" & err.Number & "]"
        rs.Save stm,adPersistXML  ' See the tip below
    ' Set content type to xml, specify XSL for formatting,
    ' then push XML stream text to calling component:
```

```
                Response.ContentType = "text/xml"
                'The following is treated as a comment
                Response.Write "<!- " & ErrorMessage &  " ->"
                Response.Write stm.ReadText
end if
```

> **TIP**   *In Windows 2000 (thus ADO 2.5 and later) you can simply save directly to the Response object instead of saving to a stream first. Thus:*
>
> ```
> rs.Save Response, adPersistXML
> ```

As this example illustrates, there are a lot of innovative techniques to pass data between layers—between client and server, between Web client and IIS, and between middle-tier components and the rest of the layers. I expect several of these techniques will stabilize and grow easier to use as we get closer to shipping Visual Basic 7.0—when we'll start all over again.

CHAPTER 10

Getting Your Data into Shape

NO, THIS CHAPTER IS NOT ABOUT thinning the fat rows out of your cursors—which might not be a bad idea. It is about using the ADO Shape syntax to manage hierarchical data. But what is "hierarchical" data? Most of us work with hierarchical data most of the time without knowing it. For instance, when you work with a Customers table that is tied to an associated Invoices table, which has an associated Items table, *that's* a hierarchy. The difference between a normal query and a hierarchical query is that the relationships are embedded in the hierarchy. That is, the schema of the relationship is part of the hierarchical structure. This way, the tool used to reference the data "knows" that there can be from zero to *n* orders for each customer and the Order table's CustID should point back to a valid row in the Customers table.

For some time now, the FoxPro and ADO teams have been working on creating a mechanism to handle the construction and management of data hierarchies. The goal was to facilitate maintenance of the underlying hierarchy tables. In other words, the new ADO technology I'm about to describe is used to fetch data as well as add, change, and delete rows without having to jump through flaming hoops to do so. The result of their work is a new OLE DB provider integrated into ADO and designed specifically to handle this fairly common data structure. This new OLE DB provider—the Shape provider—seems to make it easier to deal with a number of common data access problems, but as we'll see, the provider has a specific targeted audience, and that might not be you.

The Shape Provider

As we discussed earlier, the idea behind OLE DB is that it is supposed to handle any kind of data—from flat, unstructured data, to relational data, to complex object-oriented data sources and everything in between. The Shape provider is one of the new features introduced in ADO 2.1 that extends OLE DB functionality. As we'll discover later, the Shape provider is used in much the same way we use a cursor library or other OLE DB "providers." As with a cursor provider, you still need a data provider to fetch the rows—this means the Shape provider can work with virtually any data source. Basically, the Shape provider manages hierarchical data for data sources that don't know how to do it, or for developers that don't know how to get their data providers to return hierarchical data. It fetches rows to the client, organizes them in related groups, and exposes them to display controls (such as the MSHFlexGrid) or to reporting engines (such as the Visual Basic 6 Data Report engine). The Shape provider, like a cursor provider, supports updatability when possible. It also supports a variety of aggregate functions to help summarize data or simply provide computed columns.

Who's using the Shape provider here at Microsoft? Well, a number of internal applications use it. As I'll discuss later, these applications use relatively small databases (one database fits on a floppy) and many use the Shape provider with Web applications. Some developers see the Shape provider being useful anywhere the user has data with hierarchical relationships and the native data store does not support hierarchies. That would include most relational data stores.

Hierarchies are useful in many places where joins are currently used. That is, while a join returns the related rows, no implied relationship is built into the structure that's returned. Developers have asked for a way to program against a hierarchical object model to expose their join relationships rather than having to crunch a flattened denormalized joined set of records. The Shape provider provides this capability by keeping data normalized on the client. It also provides a consistent programming model for doing this against any backend. The fabricated rowset capabilities in Shape also provide a powerful tool for creating temporary tables and hierarchies without reference to any permanent data store. If you want to see where Shape fits, talk to the Access and Data Page folks in Office 2000—they used Shape extensively.

> **NOTE** *When I started researching the Shape provider, I discovered that there were many articles written about it, but none seemed to address my issues. That is, most of the examples use unbound queries against tiny databases, such as SELECT * FROM Authors in the sample Pubs database. I did find a useful article "Shape Up Your Data Using ADO 2.0 Hierarchical Recordsets in ASP" on the MSDN CD that built parameter queries, but this article discusses a Web-based application, and I usually focus on client/server Visual Basic applications.*

The focus of this chapter is with the client/server and large database developer in mind. As I got deeper into the Shape functionality, it became clear that the provider was meant for smaller, table-based databases—especially if you use the default behavior. Too many of the Shape provider's functional assumptions (and defaults) made it unsuitable for sizeable databases—or databases that can generate complex hierarchical result sets on their own. SQL Server, for one, can easily return a Recordset based on a single or a set of parent rows and all associated child rows—to any depth necessary—with a single call to the server. However, not all OLE DB or ODBC providers are capable of this level of sophistication, and simpler providers have no way to return these hierarchies. However, the Shape provider is more than just a way to return Parent/child hierarchies. It can also be used to construct, compute, and manage more complex aggregate functions that are used when you create reports.

When I worked on Microsoft's Visual Studio Marketing team, I demonstrated the Shape provider any number of times. After about a minute of flashy clicking and dragging, I ended up with a three-table hierarchy that looked something like Figure 10-1. This is really pretty easy. Just drag the three tables from the Data View Window over to the Data Environment Designer window and set the Relation property (on the Properties page) to cross-reference the au_id and title_id fields. I dragged the parent object (the "authors" command in this case) over to a form and chose the MSHFlexGrid to display the rows. No, I'm not going to walk you through this again. That's because I want to show you an easier way that requires a few lines of code but gives you a lot better performance and far more control over your results. If you want to see the demo, stop me in the hall at VBits sometime.

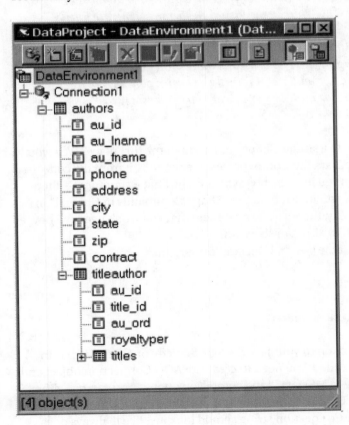

Figure 10-1: Hierarchy constructed by Data Environment Designer

Building a Simple Shape

Let's get started with the basics by creating a Visual Basic application that uses the Shape provider to do something simple. We'll use Visual Basic 6.0 Enterprise Edition for this exercise—I make no guarantees on the suitability of the Professional Edition. I also have SP3 installed, and the new ADO 2.5 (MDAC) library. I did, however, leave my references to the 2.0 type library—this prevents some problems with the Data Environment Designer caused by the newer versions of ADO. I accessed my local SQL Server 7.0 and the Pubs database to experiment with. I'm glad I did, because some of the sample applications would have taken all afternoon to run if they had a lot of data (more than 20 rows) to query. When you experiment, start with a set of small tables at first—graduating to a larger data store when you get comfortable.

> **NOTE** *Remember that the Shape provider's default behavior uses two (or more) SELECT * queries (with no WHERE clauses), so do most of the examples in MSDN. That is, the Visual Basic tools generate one open-ended query as the "Parent" command and one additional open-ended query for each "child" command. These are submitted to SQL Server as a single batch. This means that if you don't code otherwise, the Shape provider will return **the entire contents** of all 'n' tables to your client (or middle-tier server)—or at least try to.*

So, how do you create a simple Shape statement in the first place? Well, you can leverage it from the Data Environment Designer or copy it from my code shown below. I also won't go into the raw syntax of the Shape statement—there are a half-dozen MSDN articles for that. See "Shape Commands in General" in MSDN for starters. Frankly, there's quite a bit there that you won't need to know at all to run the examples I'm about to show you.

Start by setting up some General Declaration variables.

```
Dim cnn As ADODB.Connection
Dim rst As ADODB.Recordset
Dim rstTitleAuthor As ADODB.Recordset
```

Next, open a connection to your favorite SQL Server—one that still has the sample Pubs database loaded. You need to create an ADO Connection object and set its Provider property to MSDataShape before you open it. You can use either the default ODBC to OLE DB data provider or a straight OLE DB provider for SQL Server. This means your Connection string should look just like it always does. Mine references a DSN, but you can use a DSN-less connection.

```
Set cn = New Connection
cn.Provider = "MSDataShape"
cn.Open "Data Provider=sqloledb;data source=(local);"
initial catalog=pubs;", "admin", "pw"
```

Once you're connected, you can create a new Recordset and set the
StayInSync property to False to prevent extra queries from being generated. I'll
talk about this later.

```
Set rs = New Recordset
rs.StayInSync = False
```

In the next step, you'll have to provide the Shape provider with a correctly
constructed query using the Shape syntax. We pass this query to the provider
through the Recordset Source property just as we would any query, but consider
that the Shape provider does not really have much of a query processor, so stay
within the white lines. This does not mean you can't submit complex queries, as
the Shape provider simply passes these on to the backend for processing. It does
mean that some of the tricks we discussed in the Recordset chapters 6 and 7
won't work here.

```
rs.Source = "SHAPE {select au_id,au_lname, au_fname", _
            Address, city, state, zip from authors} " _
          & " APPEND ({select * from titleauthor}" _
          & " RELATE au_id TO au_id) AS chapTitleAuthor"
rs.Open , cn, Options:=adCmdText
```

In the first bracketed "{ }" expression after the Shape statement, you need to
provide an SQL SELECT statement (or a stored procedure) that returns the "parent"
result (row) set. In our example, we'll request all of the rows from the Authors table.

> **NOTE**   *Of course, selecting the entire Authors table is not that clever. No
> one in their right mind would request all the columns and all of the rows
> from a production table—unless the table has as few rows as the Pubs
> demonstration database. We'll fix this later.*

When the parent result set is created, the Shape provider returns it to your
application just like any other Recordset. However, the Shape provider tacks an
extra Field object on to the end of the Recordset. This means that if your table has
eight columns, nine Field objects return for each row. This extra (last) Field.Value
contains another Recordset, which contains the rows for the child rows

associated with the parent row. This way, each parent row contains not only its own data, but also all of the data for its children as well, and its grandchildren, and its great-grandchildren, ad nauseam. Figure 10-2 shows how each row returned from the Authors table contains an extra field pointing to the row(s) of the TitleAuthor table that correspond to this specific author.

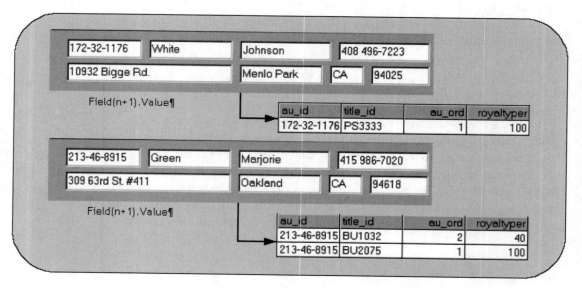

Figure 10-2: Author "parent" rows and associated TitleAuthor "child" rows

The next line in the SQL query to be passed to the Shape provider should be an APPEND statement that tells the Shape provider what rows should be fetched from the child table (TitleAuthor in the example) for each parent row in the Authors table. Here's where we concatenate the "APPEND ({select * from titleauthor}" into our query. Yes, you can have more than one APPEND statement in your Shape query, but let's stick with one child relationship for now. Here's the same SQL Shape statement again with the APPEND clause highlighted:

```
rs.Source = "SHAPE {select au_id,au_lname, au_fname", _
Address, city, state, zip from authors} " _
            & " APPEND ({select * from titleauthor}" _
            & " RELATE au_id TO au_id) AS chapTitleAuthor"
```

The last line in our SQL query is a RELATE statement that tells the Shape provider how to tie the two sets of rows together.

In this case, it's the au_id (author id) field in the two tables that have to match up. This means that for each row in the Authors table, the Shape provider will locate all rows in the TitleAuthor table having the same au_id and create a child Recordset with those rows. We name this relationship with the AS clause in the Shape statement. This name is assigned to the final (extra) Field object on the parent's Recordset so we can refer to it by name.

Once the Recordset returns, you can step through the records in the usual manner. Remeber that you need to immediately complete population of the Recordset. This frees up locks and permits other users to work with the data—especially because we used an open-ended query to build the parent result set.

For purposes of this example, I populated a TextBox control array with the values from the parent Recordset by binding the TextBox controls to an ADODC, which provides updatability and navigation through the parent Recordset. The TextBox controls and ADC were not initialized at design time; we'll set the required properties entirely in code.

```
'   Bind the root Recordset to the text boxes
For i = 0 To rst.Fields.Count - 2
        txtFields(i).DataField = rst.Fields(i).Name
Next I
```

We set the ADC's Recordset property to the parent Recordset returned by the Shape provider. This fills the TextBox controls and permits us to navigate up and down in the "Select * from authors" rowset.

```
Set Adodc1.Recordset = rst
```

As we arrive at each row, we reference the child rowset by extracting the Recordset from the extra Field object tacked on to the end of the Fields returned for each parent row. This Field object is named in the RELATE clause of the Shape statement.

```
Set rstTitleAuthor = rst.Fields("chapTitleAuthor").Value
```

> **NOTE** *Referencing a Field object by name, as shown above, is the slowest possible technique. It can be as much as six times slower than referencing the Field object by number. In a high-performance application, it is better to use an ordinal reference such as rst.Fields(rst.Fields.Count-1).Value. This small change, multiplied by the number of Field object references, can make a big difference in overall performance.*

For this example, I added a MSHFlexGrid to the form to display the child rows. This is easy to do—you simply have to assign the child Recordset to the DataSource property. Once assigned, the grid fills with the current set of child rows.

```
Set MSHFlexGrid1.DataSource = rstTitleAuthor
```

Couldn't we have just used the power of the MSHFlexGrid to display both the parent and child rows? Sure. I'll illustrate that technique later. But for now, let's take this a step at a time.

When we use the ADC to position from row to row, we have to remind the MSHFlexGrid about the Recordset to display. We do this in the MoveComplete event, as shown next:

```
Private Sub Adodc1_MoveComplete(ByVal adReason As ADODB.EventReasonEnum, ByVal
pError As ADODB.Error, adStatus As ADODB.EventStatusEnum, ByVal pRecordset As
ADODB.Recordset20)          ' Note we pass in Recordset20 instead of just Recordset.
' Use the faster technique here.
       Set rsTitleAuthor = rs(rs.Fields.Count - 1).Value
       Set MSHFlexGrid1.DataSource = rsTitleAuthor
End Sub
```

NOTE *After you add this code to the ADODC event handler, your application will fail to compile. Visual Basic reports "Procedure Declaration does not match procedure or event having the same name." This is a bug, but an expected one because we are using the ADO 2.5 (or 2.1) MDAC stack. Remember that the Recordset object changed from 2.0 to 2.1 so all later versions will exhibit this problem. We'll have to force the ADODC event handler to accept the ADO 2.0 version of the Recordset object to get around this problem. Notice how I did this by recoding the MoveComplete event handler to expect **Recordset20** instead of **Recordset**. If this is fixed in Visual Basic 6.0 SP4, this should no longer be a problem.*

What we end up with (as shown in Figure 10-3) is a form that shows a single parent row at the top in a number of bound TextBox controls, with the child rows shown below in the MSHFlexGrid.

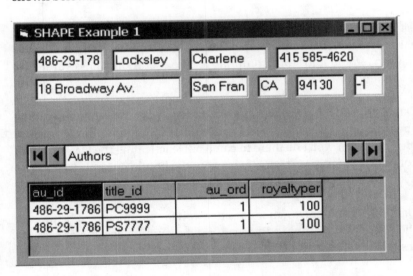

Figure 10-3: Using bound TextBox controls with the MSHFlexGrid

Why Not Use the Data Environment Designer?

We could have used the MSHFlexGrid to display the parents and all of the children. I didn't choose that approach for a variety of reasons:

- The grid is a PIA (that's a technical term) to set up in code, and because I didn't use the Data Environment Designer to create the parent-child relationships (I could have) I would have to wade into the grid's properties to set it up correctly. The grid properties don't seem to permit changing much at runtime anyway. For example, there's no (apparent) way to change the cell (grid column on a band) width at runtime (or design-time).

- The help topics for the grid assume you'll use it with the Data Environment Designer and don't really help to show how to interactively set it up through the grid's property page dialogs.

NOTE *I pressed F1 with the cursor focus on the MSHFlexGrid, expecting MSDN to show me help topics about the grid. It didn't. MSDN complained, "The compiled help (.chm) file does not contain context IDs." I guess that's because I'm using the most recent (July 1999) version of MSDN. Sigh. There's plenty of help on the grid—just do a "Search" for it in MSDN. I found 166 entries mentioning MSHFlexGrid.*

- Unless you tell it otherwise, the Data Environment Designer does not use the right (default) ADO connection or Recordset properties. This means you have to remind it to stop prompting for the user ID and password while opening.

- The Data Environment Designer (unless you code otherwise) launches itself before Form_Load time. This means that if something goes wrong, your error handler won't be there to catch it. Deactivating the Data Environment Designer isn't easy if you want the bound controls to autosynchronize at design time.

- The Data Environment Designer does not wait for parameters to be passed into the query you're running. Because we'll be running parameter-based queries (almost) exclusively, this simply won't work.

- Even if we trap the WillExecute event and pass in first-time parameters, we will still have to manually rebind (in code) any simple bound controls (like TextBox controls) to the newly created Data Environment Designer Recordset. While this is not a problem with the MSHFlexGrid (it's a "complex" bound control), it is an issue for many of my designs.

The Data Environment Designer approach does seem tempting. It makes a flashy demo and what you get is a codeless component that shows all parent rows with each child's rows tucked neatly underneath. For example, Figure 10-4 illustrates what the MSHFlexGrid looks like after having been populated from a Data Environment Designer-based query. Notice that the individual rows are already expanded. If you use the CollapseAll method, the grid will only show the parent rows. Clicking the + signs expands the child rows.

au_id	au_lname	au_fname	phone	address	city	state
⊟ 172-32-11	White	Johnson	408 496-722	10932 Bigge	Menlo Park	CA
	title_id	au_ord	royaltyper			
	PS3333	1	100			
⊟ 213-46-89	Green	Marjorie	415 986-702	309 63rd St.	Oakland	CA
	title_id	au_ord	royaltyper			
	BU1032	2	40			
	BU2075	1	100			
⊟ 238-95-77	Carson	Cheryl	415 548-772	589 Darwin l	Berkeley	CA
	title_id	au_ord	royaltyper			
	PC1035	1	100			
⊟ 267-41-23	O'Leary	Michael	408 286-242	22 Clevelan	San Jose	CA
	title_id	au_ord	royaltyper			
	BU1111	2	40			

Figure 10-4: An MSHFlexGrid populated from a Data Environment Designer-generated query

Granted, this is cool. And it did not take long to set up using the drag-and-drop techniques. But the impact it has on your system is substantial. To get the flexibility, performance, and scalability I'm sure you will demand, you will want a code-based approach.

TIP *If you insist on using the Data Environment Designer to build your relationships and bind to the MSHFlexGrid, be sure to reset the Data Environment Designer's Connection object's properties using its Visual Basic-based property page, as shown in Figure 10-5.*

Figure 10-5. Set the Run (and Design) PromptBehavior properties to "4 – adPromptNever." This gives your code a chance to capture the login ID failures instead of having ODBC (or OLE DB) expose login ID dialogs. These dialogs give the user an opportunity to reguess their login ID and password—over and over again—until they get it right—something I prefer to avoid.

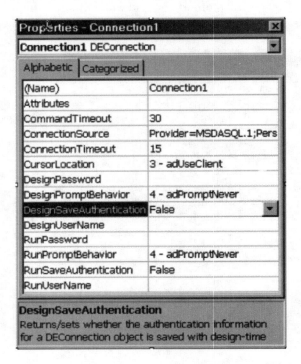

Figure 10-5: The Data Environment Designer Connection (Visual Basic) property page

Analyzing the Impact

Okay, so let's not get wrapped around the axle with the Data Environment Designer and the MSHFlexGrid. I discuss the strengths and weaknesses of the Data Environment Designer in Chapter 12, where we visit the Visual Database Tools.

Before we go on, let's see what impact the default (demo) program has on the server. We'll then compare that to the dent inflicted by the first example. Next, we'll try to see what can be done to Bondo over the dimples.

Remember that our initial query didn't use the Data Environment Designer—it used the same open-ended queries to return the rows: two "SELECT * FROM <table>" queries as generated by the Data Environment Designer. Using SQL Server 7.0's Profiler, we can see what impact these queries have on SQL Server. The Profiler displays the raw TSQL queries and other operations (such as opening connections), but you know that, we've discussed this before.

> **NOTE** *For some reason, when I was developing the data source-based samples (using the ADC and the Data Environment Designer), I noticed that the server eventually started returning connection errors for no apparent reason. The Profiler told me that ADO, the ADC, or Visual Basic had not bothered to close and release the connection(s) when I pressed the Stop button in the Visual Basic IDE or even ended the code normally. I tried to add code to explicitly close the Recordsets and Connection objects to no avail. I had to exit Visual Basic completely to get the Connections closed. Folks, this is the same problem I reported when I wrote my first book on VBSQL seven years ago.*

Let's take a look at the Profiler output for (part of) the example runs.

```
sp_prepare @P1 output, NULL, N'select * from titleauthor', 1 select @P1
select au_id,au_lname, au_fname, Address, city, state, zip from
authors;select * from titleauthor
```

The Profiler tells us that ADO told SQL Server to "prepare" a query plan for the *titleauthor* query and to then execute the two open-ended SELECT queries against *authors* and *titleauthor*. That's it. The Shape provider accepts all of the rows from both SELECT queries and passes the data back to the application to process. ADO makes no further trips to the server. This means that the Shape provider considers this data *static*—it does not attempt to get fresh data when it positions from row to row.

> **NOTE** *The queries generated by the Data Environment Designer using the drag-and-drop method are identical to those generated by our hard-coded example1 code shown above.*

Because the two tables are small (Authors has about 22 rows and TitleAuthor only about 25 rows), only about 50 rows are fetched—no big deal. So what if there were 16,000 authors and 50,000 titleauthor rows? Obviously, this approach would not work, or at least not very quickly. In addition, because these are open-ended queries, the negative impact on scalability would be easily apparent. In addition, consider that this is the simplest of shapes—it only has two family members: a parent and a single child. What if there were two or more children? The number of rows being sent back to the client over the network would start getting pretty ghastly before too long.

Finding a Better Way

Keeping this in mind, I wanted to find a way to get just the rows I wanted, but still let the Shape provider do its thing—providing the one-to-many relationship management in memory and still providing updatability for those (albeit rare) cases where I want to update through a cursor.

First, it was clear that I needed to limit the rows fetched by the initial "parent" query. Once this is done, we can selectively fetch the child rows on demand—or can we? Well, it turns out that you can, but you have to use another feature of the Shape provider that we'll talk about next—an index to cross-connect the parent and child.

So, limiting the initial parent query seems easy enough—just provide a WHERE clause. But, we also don't want to hard code a WHERE clause (in most cases), so I tried to create an ADO Command object that would generate the Shape Recordsets. Forget it, it didn't work. However, I did get the old-reliable "concatenate-on-the-fly" technique to work. By limiting the authors query to return only a single author, I forced ADO to refetch each time I wanted to see another author. You could also set up a query that returned only a selected group of parent rows—say, just the authors from California. We'll talk about using stored procedures to deal with this problem in a minute.

However, even when we fetch a single parent row, the child query is still returning all of the rows from the TitleAuthor table, not just those that match the parent. I figured the Shape provider *must* have a way to query the child rows only as needed, and it does. If you rephrase your Shape statement to pass a parameter from the parent query to the child query, ADO and the Shape provider change their strategy to fetch the child rows on demand. Here's how the parameter-based syntax looks:

```
rst.Source = "Shape  {select au_id, au_lname, au_fname, city, state, zip" _
          & " From authors where state ='" & txtStateWanted & "'} " _
             & " APPEND ({select * from titleauthor where au_id = ?}" _
             & " RELATE au_id TO Parameter 0) AS chapTitleAuthor"
```

> **NOTE** *The fetch-all-the-rows-at-once approach might be required for situations in which you can't depend on a persistent connection, as with Web pages or middle-tier components. But this does not mean you must fall back on the open-ended queries. There are still ways to write queries that only fetch "just enough" data.*

I capture the state wanted in a TextBox control (see Example3)[1] and concatenate it into the query when the user presses the Search button. The code ties the au_id in the parent query to a "?" in the child query in the RELATE clause.

Can you simply execute a stored procedure instead of the SELECT statement(s) in the parent and child queries? Sure. See Example4 for a working example.

```
rst.Source = "Shape {execute GetAuthorsByState '" & txtStateWanted & "'} " _
             & " APPEND ({select * from titleauthor where au_id = ?}" _
             & " RELATE au_id TO Parameter 0) AS chapTitleAuthor"
```

The Impact of the "Just Enough" Approach

Let's look again at what the Profiler reports about the parameter-based queries. I discovered something interesting here that probably will surprise you as much as it did me.

The TSQL statements being sent make a lot of sense—or they seem to at first.

First, ADO asks SQL Server to return (just) metadata for the titleauthor query.

```
SET FMTONLY ON
select * from titleauthor
SET FMTONLY OFF
```

Next, ADO performs the new parameter-based query using the concatenated parameter we supplied in code (from the TextBox on the form). This returns an initial rowset with just the California authors.

```
select au_id,au_lname, au_fname, phone, Address, city,
state, zip from authors where state ='CA'
```

Next, ADO makes a round-trip to find out what the metadata looks like for the key-based query against the TitleAuthor table. We're at three round-trips so far.

```
SET FMTONLY ON
select  au_id from titleauthor
SET FMTONLY OFF
```

At this point, ADO creates a temporary stored procedure used to fetch columns from the TitleAuthor table. This query fires whenever a specific Authors

---

1. All of the examples mentioned in this chapter are located on the companion CD. This chapter's examples are located under ..\Sample Applications\Hierarchy and Shape\Shape.

table row is selected. Because we select a whole series of author rows, we can expect this to be executed quite a few times—once for each row in the parent Recordset. Note that the final SELECT in this batch is simply returning the parameter @P1 from the sp_prepare statement.

```
sp_prepare @P1 output, N'@P1 varchar(11)', N'
select * from titleauthor where au_id = @P1', 1
select @P1
```

The final TSQL code reported by the profiler is the fetch (finally!) for our first parent row. That is, the Shape provider knows that the au_id for the first row is '172-32-1176', so it queries the server for any titles matching this author id.

```
sp_execute 1, '172-32-1176'       17:02:13.987
```

Well, we're not done yet. At this point, we have only positioned to the first row of the parent Recordset and fetched the first set of child (titleauthor) rows. As we fetch additional rows, we would expect ADO and the Shape provider to reuse temporary stored procedure #1 (as created above) to fetch additional rows from the TitleAuthor table. Sadly, this is not the case. As we can see in the Profiler dump, the Shape provider tells SQL Server to drop (unprepare) the preceding temporary stored procedure and create another just like it. Sigh. It then executes the new temporary stored procedure to return the next set of child rows.

```
sp_unprepare 1
sp_prepare @P1 output, N'@P1 varchar(11)', N'
select * from titleauthor where au_id = @P1', 1
select @P1    17:21:01.367
sp_execute 2, '213-46-8915'
```

Now this was a surprise to me. I would have expected the Shape provider to be able to at least leverage the work done to create the childrow queries already created. As you can see, this "just enough" approach has its problems. It requires several more round-trips per row than the "all-at-once" approach, which, frankly, looks like it has quite a bit of merit at this point. The "just enough" approach does fetch current data for each child row, but it depends on a static set of parent rows to drive the secondary query.

You can see how adding additional children to the hierarchy might be interesting. For example, customer-order-item queries would be fairly common. However, you can also see how any additional complexity in the hierarchy would be translated exponentially in increased overhead.

CHAPTER 11

Data Access Tips and Techniques

OVER THE LAST FEW YEARS, I'VE accumulated a lot of suggestions, tips, and reviews, as well as complaints about my treatment of Cleveland. Some of these came to me while writing examples or in the classroom as I taught my classes, while others were filtered from the mountains of e-mail I get on a daily basis. While many of these ideas have already made their way into earlier chapters, the ones described here have not. Instead of leaving out these orphans, I decided to bundle them together into their own chapter—so here they are.

Referencing Data on Other Servers

If you have a query that needs to include data joined from another server, you can easily do so by adding a reference to the server in your SELECT statement. As long as the server is preregistered, SQL Server (7.0) takes care of the details. Getting your remote server registered is easy. Start SQL Server Enterprise Manager and click on Security/Remote Server. You'll get a dialog that looks like Figure 11-1.

Using the dialog box, point to the remote server. Yes, this can be accomplished through system stored procedures too, but this is far easier. Next, you have to reconfigure the remote server so it knows to accept remote procedure calls from other servers. To do this, execute the sp_serveroption system stored

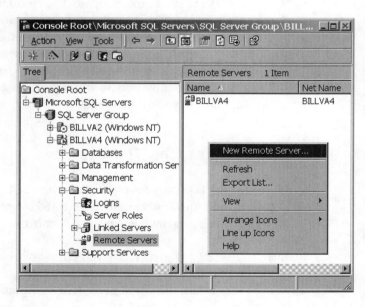

Figure 11-1: Using SQL Enterprise Manager to add a new remote server

procedure, as shown next. You only have to do this once, but you'll need SA permissions to do so.

```
EXEC sp_serveroption 'BETAV2', 'data access', 'true'
```

Okay, we're ready to try a multisystem join. For example, to join a table on BetaV2 (a server marked as *remote* on the server doing the join) with tables located on the server doing the join, code the following SQL Statement:

```
rs.Source = "SELECT Author, Year_Born " _
    & " FROM BETAV2.Biblio.dbo.Authors A, Title_Author TA, Titles T" _
    & " Where TA.au_id = A.au_id and ta.isbn = t.isbn and t.Title like  'Hi%' "
rs.Open , cn, Options:=adCmdText
```

Note how the name of the table is predicated with the server name, database name, and owner name, as in *server.database.owner.table*, this is documented in SQL Server Books Online. Of course, you can simply reference other databases on the same server by using the *database.owner.table* notation—but you knew that.

TSQL Tips

SQL Server 7.0 added a number of new operators and functions to the Transact SQL dialect to make returning what you wanted easier, and to give the SQL Server engine a better idea of what you were trying to accomplish. Here are a few tips to make your Transact SQL queries work a little smoother—and faster! Remember that the new SQL Server 7.0 features aren't turned on unless you're executing queries against a SQL Server 7.0 database *and* it's not in 6.5 Compatibility mode. If you import your SQL Server 6.5 database into SQL Server 7.0, the server starts out in 6.5 Compatibility mode, so you'll have to turn this off manually before the new syntax is activated.

Using the TOP Clause

The TOP clause is one of these new SQL Server 7.0 features that's designed to limit the number of rows returned by your query to the first *n* or *n* percent of qualifying rows. For example, return the top 120 rows of the Titles table like this:

```
SELECT TOP 120 Title From Titles
```

or return the top 15 percent of the Authors table like this:

```
SELECT TOP 15 PERCENT Author From Authors
```

If a SELECT statement that includes TOP also has an ORDER BY clause, the rows to be returned are selected from the ordered result set. The entire result set is built in the specified order and the top *n* rows in the ordered result set are returned. Using this technique, you can return the first *n* rows from the sales table in an attempt to show the best salesperson. But if you simply executed the following, you'd get the *lowest* 10 sales because the default sequence in an order by clause is ascending.

```
SELECT TOP 10 Sale, SalesPerson from Sales Order by Sale
```

To get the "top" (best) sales, you'll have to make a little change:

```
SELECT TOP 10 Sale, SalesPerson from Sales Order by Sale DESC
```

The other method of limiting the size of a result set is to execute a SET ROWCOUNT *n* statement before executing a statement. SET ROWCOUNT differs from TOP in these ways:

- The SET ROWCOUNT limit applies to building the rows in the result set before an ORDER BY is evaluated. Even if ORDER BY is specified, the SELECT statement is terminated when *n* rows have been selected. The *n* rows are selected, then ordered and returned to the client. Of course, if this is not done in a stored procedure, the setting is persisted on the connection and remains in place until the connection is actually closed—not just released back to the connection pool. This means other applications or components using this connection from the pool (even you) can inherit the SET ROWCOUNT (or any other SET value). Try to debug *that*!

- The TOP clause applies to the single SELECT statement in which it is specified. SET ROWCOUNT remains in effect until another SET ROWCOUNT statement is executed, such as SET ROWCOUNT 0 to turn the option off.

Using SELECT INTO Instead of Brute Force

When you find it necessary to move rows in droves from one server to another, you might find that SQL Server (or many other data providers) can do this far more efficiently than constructing INSERT statements and submitting them one at a time. This assumes, of course, that the data is already on the server. If the data is currently living elsewhere and your only portal to the data is your application, then by all means consider these options:

- The SQL Server Bulk Copy Program (BCP) excels at moving data from place to place—even fixed-length file data.

- With SQL Server Data Transformation Services (DTS), SQL Server can be set up to access anything with an ODBC driver or OLE DB provider or any other server that participates in standard data transformation services—most do.

- If all else fails, construct multiple INSERT statements into a batch and submit them all at once. I described how to do this in Chapter 8.

If, however, you merely want to move data from one table to another, use SELECT INTO. This operation is not logged (i.e., transacted), so it not only saves time, it's very easy to code.

```
Select Author, Year_Born into NewAuthorsTable from Authors
```

However, SQL Server won't let you do this until all of your duckies are in a row.

- You have to activate this option before you start. Get your SA to turn on "Select into/bulkcopy" using sp_configure or by selecting the bulk copy/select into option in the database property sheet.

- The statement shown above creates a NewAuthorsTable, so that table cannot exist before you run the query.

- Because the table does not exist, don't worry about indexes—these have to be created *after* the SELECT INTO is done.

- After a SELECT INTO, the Dump transaction operation will work only after you tell SQL Server to dump the database. Don't know how? Ask the SA.

Using UNION to Combine Identical Recordsets

If the multiple queries have identical column results and you want to process them as one Recordset, you could also look at using the UNION statement. It's not right for all situations, but does come in handy from time to time.

```
select X "FeedDesc" from mytable1
UNION
```

```
select Y "FeedDesc" from mytable2
UNION
select Z "FeedDesc" from mytable3
```

Assigning and Testing for NULL

Remember in ANSI SQL (TSQL, too) to *assign* a NULL to a variable, you code this:

```
SELECT @Variable = NULL
```

However, when testing for NULL, you need to use the IS NULL syntax:

```
WHERE YearDied IS NULL
```

The Visual Basic 6.0 Visual Database Tools have not picked up on this nuance, so you have to be careful when constructing your queries using the GUI tools.

Performance-Tuning Stored Procedures

A customer wrote that they had a performance problem executing a stored procedure. They had a table with serial numbers (about 500,000 records) and when performing the following query they got a timeout:

```
SELECT Title, Type FROM Titles where serialno like  '%a0332%' and type = 1
```

Now the problem is the wildcard *before* the *serialnumber*. They discovered with some help from us, that this approach causes SQL Server to execute a table scan, hitting all 500,000 rows. However, by keeping the % wildcard at the end of the expression, the performance is much higher.

Table scans can take a long time. If you think this is necessary, check whether there is a specific section of the serialno that users tend to want to search on—for example, the second through the sixth position of the key. It may make sense to break that portion of the serialno out into a separate indexed field if you're planning to do this type of search very often. If that's not an option, you might try selecting into a temp table using only the criteria that can allow the optimizer to use an index, and then search the temp table using the wildcard search. This should greatly reduce the number of rows that need to be scanned.

Remember that temp tables and SELECT...INTO are usually frowned upon because they place exclusive locks on the sysobjects, syscolumns, and sysindexes tables in TempDB, which can interfere with other processes going on at the same time. This can cause serious degradation in overall server performance, so this solution should be considered only as a last resort. Having said that, I should now say that I have had to resort to this solution a couple of times myself with no serious ramifications (so far). So, what you need to consider is how often will the SELECT...INTO #temp be performed, how many concurrent users will be running it, and how long does the actual SELECT...INTO #temp take? Keep these factors in mind when deciding whether or not to use this approach.

SET NOCOUNT Using OLE DB Providers

SET NOCOUNT is used to toggle the SQL Server Connection option that determines whether a result set is created when you execute an action query, such as INSERT, UPDATE, or DELETE. This result set contains the rows affected value. You can improve performance by eliminating unneeded resultsets, and SET NOCOUNT ON can accomplish this. The SQL Server ODBC driver does not provide information about the results of individual SQL statements within a stored procedure. The only result that comes back from a stored procedure execution is the results of the SELECT statement, if it has one.

SQLOLEDB has a new behavior, designed to provide more accurate information to the caller about what happened in the procedure. Each SQL statement within a stored procedure returns a result set, whether that is a count of rows affected a row set, OUTPUT parameters or any of about a dozen other structures. You can walk through these result sets in ADO using the NextRecordset method on the Recordset object. To get SQLOLEDB to behave as the SQL ODBC driver did, you can use SET NOCOUNT ON in the beginning of the stored procedure.

Granting Permissions

One of the most well-respected and talented trainers I've had the privilege of working with (and hiring at MSU) is Kimberly Tripp Simonnet. After repeated groveling on my part, she was kind enough to send me some code to handle the problem of creating new accounts in SQL Server and not being able to access the database because permissions were not set. The following stored procedure grants selective permissions on entire databases in one operation. You used to be able to do this through the user interface in SQL Server 6.5, but not with the new MCP version of SQL Enterprise Manager. This procedure is especially important because you won't be using SA as your UserID—will you? When you create a new UserID to test with, you probably want to start out with ALL permissions and cut these back as needed.

This SQL code creates the sp_GrantPermissions stored procedure in the Master database. The code is also on the CD as sp_GrantPermissions.SQL. It expects you to pass your UserName, ObjectType, and Permission. The ObjectType can be either U for User-defined tables, P for Stored Procedures, or V for Views.

The Permission argument lets you choose the type of permission to be granted. Choose SELECT, INSERT, UPDATE, DELETE, or ALL for Tables and Views, or EXEC for stored procedures.

> **NOTE** *The following code depends on SQL Server system tables. While the outward manifestation of these system tables has not changed for some time now, they have changed internally. For this reason, this approach should be used with caution as newer versions of SQL Server arrive.*

```
USE master
go
IF OBJECTPROPERTY(object_id( 'sp_GrantPermissions'),  'IsProcedure') = 1
    DROP PROCEDURE sp_GrantPermissions
go
CREATE  PROCEDURE sp_GrantPermissions
    @UserName      sysname = NULL,
    @ObjectType    nvarchar(2) = NULL,
    @Permission    nvarchar(6) = NULL
AS
SET NOCOUNT ON
IF @UserName =  ''
    SET @UserName = NULL
IF @ObjectType =  ''
    SET @ObjectType = NULL
IF @Permission =  ''
    SET @Permission = NULL
IF (@UserName IS NULL) AND (@ObjectType IS NULL)
    BEGIN
    RAISERROR( 'You must supply at least @UserName and @ObjectType.', 16, -1)
    RETURN
    END
IF (@ObjectType IS NULL)
    BEGIN
    RAISERROR ( 'You must supply an @ObjectType. Use  ''U'' for User-defined
tables,  ''P'' for Stored Procedures or  ''V'' for Views.', 16, -1)
    RETURN
    END
IF (UPPER(@ObjectType) NOT IN ( 'P',  'U',  'V'))
    BEGIN
    RAISERROR ( 'The object type supplied:%s is not valid. The @ObjectType
parameter must be either  ''P'',  ''U'' or  ''V''. Use  ''P'' for Stored
```

```
                  Procedures,  ''U'' for User-defined tables or  ''V'' for Views.', 16, -1,
                  @ObjectType)
                      RETURN
                      END
                  IF (UPPER(@ObjectType) IN ( 'U',  'V') AND UPPER(@Permission) =  'EXEC') OR
                  (UPPER(@ObjectType) =  'P' AND UPPER(@Permission) IN ( 'SELECT',  'INSERT',
                  'UPDATE',  'DELETE'))
                      BEGIN
                      RAISERROR ( '@Permission defaults to SELECT for Tables and Views and EXEC for
                  Stored Procedures. Possible values for @Permission are  ''SELECT'',  ''INSERT'',
                  ''UPDATE'',  ''DELETE'' or  ''ALL'' for Tables and Views or  ''EXEC'' for stored
                  procedures.', 16, -1)
                      RETURN
                      END
                  IF (@ObjectType IN ( 'U',  'V') AND @Permission IS NULL)
                      SET @Permission =  'SELECT'
                  IF (@ObjectType =  'P' AND @Permission IS NULL)
                      SET @Permission =  'EXEC'
                  DECLARE @ObjName      sysname,
                      @ObjNameStr      nvarchar(100)
                  BEGIN
                          DECLARE ObjNamesCursor CURSOR FOR
                          SELECT name FROM sysobjects
                          where type = @ObjectType AND status >= 0
                          ORDER BY name
                          OPEN ObjNamesCursor
                          FETCH NEXT FROM ObjNamesCursor INTO @ObjName
                          WHILE (@@fetch_status <> -1)
                          BEGIN
                          IF (@@fetch_status <> -2)
                          BEGIN
                          SELECT @ObjNameStr =  'Granting  ' + @Permission +  ' for object:' +
                  RTRIM(UPPER(@ObjName)) +  ' to  ' + @UserName +  '.'
                          PRINT @ObjNameStr
                          EXEC ( 'GRANT  ' + @Permission +  ' ON  ' + @ObjName +  ' TO  ' +
                  @UserName)
                          END
                      PRINT  ' '
                      FETCH NEXT FROM ObjNamesCursor INTO @ObjName
                          END
                      END
                  PRINT  ' '
```

```
DEALLOCATE ObjNamesCursor
go
```

More Recordset Secrets

It's possible to pass the contents of several Recordsets to a client from the middle tier. For example, if you combine a series of table-lookup queries in a multiple ad hoc SELECT, or execute a stored procedure that returns several result sets, you can combine the Recordsets into a single Variant array and transport them back to the client thusly:

```
EXE COM Server (running over DCOM):
Function GetData() As Variant
Dim rs(1 To 5) As ADODB.Recordset
Dim v As Variant
Dim i As Long, j As Long
    For i = 1 To 5
        Set rs(i) = New ADODB.Recordset
        rs(i).CursorLocation = adUseClient
        rs(i).Fields.Append "Now", adVarChar, 255
        rs(i).Open
        For j = 1 To 1000
            rs(i).AddNew "Now", GetTickCount()
        Next j
        Debug.Print rs(i).RecordCount
    Next i
    v = Array(rs(1), rs(2), rs(3), rs(4), rs(5))
    GetData = v
End Function
```

The client-side code looks like this:

```
Sub SimpleTest()
Dim objGet As GetMultiRS
Dim v As Variant
Dim i As Long
Dim rs As ADODB.Recordset
Set objGet = New GetMultiRS
    v = objGet.GetData
    Set objGet = Nothing     ' This releases COM EXE server.
    For i = 0 To 4
```

```
        Set rs = v(i)
        While Not rs.EOF
            Debug.Print rs.Fields(0).Value
            rs.MoveNext
        Wend
    Next i
End Sub
```

Increasing Recordset Performance

You can greatly improve ADO's insertion performance by doing insertions using
Arrays of variants instead of accessing the Field Value property Field-by-Field.
We've seen major performance increases, as much as 400 percent, using this
technique. Here is some code to demo the performance:

```
Public Sub ADOFastInsert()
Dim rs As ADODB.recordset
Dim sngStartTimer As Single
Dim i As Long, j As Long
Dim arrRecords() As Variant
Dim arrFieldList() As Variant
Const RECORD_COUNT = 1000
Const FIELD_COUNT = 20
    ' Build recordset.
    Set rs = New ADODB.recordset
    ReDim arrFieldList(0 To FIELD_COUNT - 1)
    For i = 1 To FIELD_COUNT
        rs.fields.Append "f" & i, adChar, 10
        arrFieldList(i - 1) = "f" & i
    Next i
    rs.Open
    ' Regular insert test.
    sngStartTimer = GetTickcount()
    With rs
        For i = 1 To RECORD_COUNT
            .AddNew
            For j = 0 To FIELD_COUNT - 1
                .fields(j).Value = "xxxxxxxxxx"
            Next j
            .Update
        Next i
        Debug.Print "Elapsed time for regular insert is " & _
```

```
GetTickCount - sngStartTimer & " seconds."
    End With


    ' Array insert test.
    sngStartTimer = GetTickCount
    With rs
        For i = 1 To RECORD_COUNT
            ReDim arrRecords(0 To FIELD_COUNT - 1)
            For j = 0 To FIELD_COUNT - 1
                arrRecords(j) = "xxxxxxxxxx"
            Next j
            .AddNew arrFieldList, arrRecords
        Next i
        Debug.Print "Elapsed time for array insert is " & GetTickCount -
sngStartTimer & " seconds."
    End With
End Sub
```

Fine-Tuning the Filter Criteria

A user wrote in with a (fairly typical) problem. When using the Filter property, some criteria settings cause an ADO error 3001. This doesn't work:

```
rsSchemaClone.Filter = "TABLE_NAME=" & Chr(34) & " 'Hello & World'$" & Chr(34)
```

but this does:

```
rsSchemaClone.Filter = "TABLE_NAME=" & Chr(34) & "'Hello&World'$" & Chr(34)
```

It turns out that ADO's Filter property syntax parser gets kinda confused when there are loose single quotes. To get around this problem, surround the entire string with pound (#) signs.

```
rsSchemaClone.Filter = "TABLE_NAME=#'Hello & World'$#"
```

Managing Errors from the Correct Source

When an error occurs, you might get a trappable error from Visual Basic, or ADO, or both. When working with an ASP, there are no error traps—at least not until Windows 2000 and ASP 3.0—so you'll have to test for errors yourself after each error-prone operations. I have seen cases where ASP gets an ADO error, but the VB description is empty. The following code tests for Visual Basic-generated trappable errors, as well as those errors generated by ADO and referenced in the Error object associated with the ADO Connection object.

```
StrTmp = StrTmp & vbCrLf & "VB Error # " & Str(Err.Number)
    StrTmp = StrTmp & vbCrLf & "   Generated by " & Err.Source
    StrTmp = StrTmp & vbCrLf & "   Description  " & Err.Description
     ' Enumerate Errors collection and display properties of
     ' each Error object.
Set Errs1 = Conn1.Errors
    For Each errLoop In Errs1
      With errLoop
          StrTmp = StrTmp & vbCrLf & "Error #" & i & ":"
          StrTmp = StrTmp & vbCrLf & "   ADO Error   #" & .Number
          StrTmp = StrTmp & vbCrLf & "   Description  " & .Description
          StrTmp = StrTmp & vbCrLf & "   Source       " & .Source
          i = i + 1
      End With
    Next
```

Working with the Schema Object

The ADO 2.0 exposes the Schema object to help you view and manipulate database schemas. The OpenSchema method returns self-descriptive information about the data source, such as what tables are in the data source, the columns in the tables, and the datatypes supported. However, it often makes more sense when working with SQL Server to simply query the sysobjects table to gather this information. Changes to the schema can be easily implemented in SQL Server using TSQL commands. On the other hand, not many providers are as flexible and powerful as SQL Server. This is where the Schema object comes into play.

The following example uses the OpenSchema method to display the name and type of each table in the Pubs database.

```
Public Sub OpenSchemaX()
   Dim cnn1 As ADODB.Connection
   Dim rstSchema As ADODB.Recordset
   Dim strCnn As String
   Set cnn1 = New ADODB.Connection
     strCnn = "Provider=sqloledb;Data Source=srv;Initial Catalog=Pubs; "
   cnn1.Open strCnn ,"admin", "pw"
   Set rstSchema = cnn1.OpenSchema(adSchemaTables)
```

```
    Do Until rstSchema.EOF
      Debug.Print "Table name: " & _
         rstSchema!TABLE_NAME & vbCr & _
         "Table type: " & rstSchema!TABLE_TYPE & vbCr
      rstSchema.MoveNext
    Loop
    rstSchema.Close
    cnn1.Close
End Sub
```

The next example specifies a TABLE_TYPE query constraint in the OpenSchema method Criteria argument. As a result, only schema information for the Views specified in the Pubs database is returned. The example then displays the name and type of each table.

```
Public Sub OpenSchemaX2()
    Dim cnn2 As ADODB.Connection
    Dim rstSchema As ADODB.Recordset
    Dim strCnn As String
    Set cnn2 = New ADODB.Connection
       strCnn = "Provider=sqloledb;Data Source=srv;Initial Catalog=Pubs;"
    cnn2.Open strCnn, "Admin", "pw"
    Set rstSchema = cnn2.OpenSchema_
    (adSchemaTables, Array(Empty, Empty, Empty, "VIEW"))
       Do Until rstSchema.EOF
         Debug.Print "Table name: " & _
            rstSchema!TABLE_NAME & vbCr & _
            "Table type: " & rstSchema!TABLE_TYPE & vbCr
         rstSchema.MoveNext
       Loop
    rstSchema.Close
    cnn2.Close
End Sub
```

Working with the Grid Control

In most of the examples you've seen in earlier chapters, I used the MSHFlexGrid as the target of choice. That's because it exposes a Recordset property that can accept the default firehose cursor. However, you can also use the Visual Basic Data Grid control to display your rows. Actually, it seems to handle headers better than the MSHFlexGrid control, so it might be a better choice if you are using a "bookmarkable" (ADO's term) Recordset. That is, if the Recordset object's

Supports method indicates that Bookmarks are supported (adBookmark), you can pass this Recordset directly to the DataGrid control's DataSource property. Here's an example:

> **TIP**   *To ensure that the DataGrid morphs itself to the Field name or data widths property, make sure you leave the DefColWidth property set to 0.*

```
Set rs = New Recordset
rs.CursorLocation = adUseClient
cn.au42 1900, 1950, rs
Set DataGrid1.DataSource = rs
```

Working with Strings

We already talked about how to make your applications (especially your Web pages) more efficient by not using the concatenation operator (&). The following two tips discuss a number of other string-related operations that can save you precious CPU cycles—especially when your application is sharing time with *Age of Empires* or other more important code.

Using Visual Basic's String Manipulation Operators

There are two types of string operators built into Visual Basic's runtime library—one type handles Strings and the other Variants. For example, the Left$, Mid$, and Right$ operators all handle (just) strings, while the Left, Mid, and Right functions handle Variants, which can be strings. If you know that the target operand is a string, use the string-specific functions.

Encrypting Strings

If you are uncomfortable saving sensitive text to a database or to an easily accessed document or text file, you might consider encrypting the data. Although the FBI can crack this pretty quickly, your cousin from Cleveland can't. The trick here is the XOR operator in Visual Basic, which functions at the bit level to manipulate the data values passed to it.

The following example illustrates use of the XOR operator to convert individual bytes of a string to make them unrecognizable without the use of a separate text key. The magic here is the formula that selects a byte from the key to

XOR against individual characters. This makes it even tougher for your cousin to crack the code, because he can't simply use hex FFFF as one would initially guess.

I don't profess to know how this little formula ((i Mod l) – l * ((i Mod l) = 0)) works, but it does. I checked out the MSDN article on data encryption for the formula, but it also failed to explain how it works. I suspect it permits you to use an encryption key of varying lengths to map to one of the characters in the password. That is, if you have a password of 10 characters, and an encryption key of 3 characters, the formula chooses one of the password characters to XOR against a selected byte of the encryption key. Make sense? Just don't forget the encryption key or you'll need the FBI to figure out your password.

The example takes a value from a TextBox control, encrypts it, and writes to a second TextBox. This is the value you should save to the database, Registry, or human-readable file. To retrieve the original value, simply pass in the encrypted text and the same password key. The same Encrypt routine repeats the process, but decrypts this time, which results in the original value. If you are working with NT, placing NT security on the right file or Registry key is *the* definitive way to prevent access—and the encrypting can be used to prevent files from being viewed.

```
Dim Char As Integer
Dim strPasswordIn As String
Dim strPasswordOut As String


Private Sub cmdDecrypt_Click()
    strPasswordIn = txtDataOut.Text
    txtDecrypted.Text = Encrypt(strPasswordOut, txtPasswordKey) 'Encrypt the string.
    Debug.Print "in:{" & strPasswordOut, "} out:{" & txtDecrypted.Text & "}"
End Sub


Private Sub cmdEncrypt_Click()
    strPasswordIn = txtDataIn.Text
    strPasswordOut = Encrypt(strPasswordIn, txtPasswordKey) 'Encrypt the string.
    Debug.Print "in:{" & strPasswordIn & "} out:{" & strPasswordOut & "}"
    txtDataOut.Text = strPasswordOut
  End Sub

Function Encrypt(secret As String, PassWord As String) As String
Dim strDataOut As String
    ' secret$ = the string you wish to encrypt or decrypt.
    ' PassWord$ = the password with which to encrypt the string.
    l = Len(PassWord$)
    strDataOut = String(Len(secret), " ")
    For i = 1 To Len(secret$)
       Char = Asc(Mid$(PassWord$, (i Mod l) - l * ((i Mod l) = 0), 1))
```

```
          Mid$(strDataOut, i, 1) = Chr$(Asc(Mid$(secret$, i, 1)) Xor Char)
      Next
  Encrypt = strDataOut
  End Function
```

Working with Graphics

If you want to design your own program or button icons, remember that an ICON is simply a bitmap. They are either sized 16x16 or 32x32 bits. Use Microsoft Paint or your own graphics program to construct these, and save the BMP format file with an ICO extension.

MDAC/ADO Setup Issues

We had a question from the field that went something like this: "My customer is developing a stand-alone app that uses ADO. They wish to make this app available for download, so it needs to be as small as possible. They are concerned about the 6.5MB size of the MDAC 2.1 SP2 download (ADO 2.5 MDAC_TYP.EXE is now 7.7 MB). My (the consultant's) advice to them was to incorporate MDAC 2.1 SP2 into their install." The note went on to say that the customer wanted to create a program that would work with any version of ADO starting at 1.5. Interesting problem.

One of the MDAC crew came back with this "Unofficial MDAC Redistribution/Setup Rude FAQ."

- If you want custom installs, MDAC setup is not for you.

- If you want integration into WMI, MDAC setup is not for you.

- If you want lightweight, Web-downloadable installs, or partial installs of only certain drivers, MDAC setup is not for you.

- If you want SMS integration, or push installs, MDAC setup is not for you.

- If you want to use a Microsoft database API with a Microsoft developer product with a Microsoft installer technology to produce a shrink-wrapped product with a setup program, MDAC setup is not for you.

- MDAC setup is a pioneer in the Windows 2000 "blast it all on there whether they need it or not" philosophy that is the future in a world of massive bandwidth and massive HDs.

- Then again, when MDAC is already installed, you have some assurance that the right ADO bits are already in place.

Basically, think of MDAC setup as a service pack (SP) setup. Like an SP setup, it cannot easily be integrated with anything. Remember having to reboot three times when installing Visual Studio 6? This is the kind of install to expect when using MDAC.

Like an SP, MDAC must be hand-installed on each machine by a computer user who knows what he or she is doing (i.e., the average end-user does not know that you need to shut down various NT services in order to install MDAC, etc.).

So, my advice to customers is to write a setup that checks whether MDAC is installed or not, and if not, throws up a warning message and tells the user to install MDAC. This is sort of the same scenario as VS6 refusing to install unless you have NT 4 SP3 installed first. If you are doing a Web install, you can just point the user to the MDAC installer on the Microsoft Web site.

Hooking Up Visual Basic/ADO Help

When you install ADO 2.*x*, the associated help files can't be found by Visual Basic 6.0 unless you put them in the Windows\Help directory.

CHAPTER 12

ADO and the Visual Database Tools

I'VE BEEN WRITING AND TALKING ABOUT the Visual Database Tools for several years now. Visual Basic version 5.0 really introduced the first of the tools—the User Connection Designer. The User Connection Designer was originally designed to make the process of creating an RDO application easier, and that it did. It reduced 40-some-odd lines of code to about 4. It had the capability to deal with most of the fundamental issues associated with executing SQL Server or Oracle stored procedures. However, the User Connection Designer stopped short of many of the features exposed in the Visual Basic 6.0 Data View window, Data Environment Designer, or the new data wizards. My *Hitchhiker's Guide to Visual Basic and SQL Server*[1] discusses these tools in the context of accessing SQL Server from Visual Basic in far more detail than does this chapter. The Visual Basic 6.0 Visual Database Tools are all capable of accessing more than just SQL Server. Because they leverage the latest providers exposed by OLE DB and ADO, they can be used to access Jet (3.5 and 4.0), Oracle, DB2, and many other data sources. While functionality varies dramatically from provider to provider, many support at least the basic functionality of the Visual Database Tools.

Visual Database Tools is reborn in Visual Studio 6.0, and instead of being installed and run as a separate application, the tools are now fully integrated into Visual Basic's user interface as the Data View window, Data Environment Designer, and Visual Query Designer. These tools appear in both Professional and Enterprise editions of Visual Basic. The Pro version does not have many of the more important features, so you probably won't be happy without the Enterprise Edition. Visual Database Tools also appear in one form or another in SQL Server 7.0, Visual InterDev, and most of the other Visual Studio languages. This chapter walks you through the Data View window, the Data Environment Designer, and the Data Object Wizard.

Visual Basic 6.0's Visual Database Tools were intended to revolutionize the way developers work with database tables and stored procedures. They were intended to make both developers and applications more productive and yield better performance. Whether they met that goal or not is an unanswered question. While the Visual Database Tools eliminated the need to use Microsoft

---

1. Now in its 6th edition (Microsoft Press, ISBN: 1-57231-848-1).

Access to build queries, and exposed a great deal of new, useful functionality, some of the implementation details leave something to be desired. In my opinion, the tools give the impression of being unpolished. After having worked with the tools and with customers trying to do the same, the development community and I have found too many uncompleted features, incompatibilities, problematic interfaces, and downright bugs. Because many of the Visual Database Tools were released in their "1.0" version, we have (sadly) grown to expect somewhat limited functionality.

This chapter is not intended to be a Visual Database Tools bash. On the contrary, this chapter is designed to help developers and their customers get the most out of what's there—to let them know what's working and what can make their job easier, without getting hung up on the rough edges.

Using the Data View Window

The Data View window is exposed by clicking on the yellow disk icon on the toolbar or by clicking View/Data View window. Opening the Data View window brings you directly into the Visual Database Tools world.

The Data View window is designed to help you construct and manage your data sources. You begin by creating a Data Link, which is simply a captured ADO connection string persisted to the Registry. A Data Link shares ancestry with the Universal Data Link (UDL) technology that persists connection strings to a file. However, you can't use a UDL to create a Data Link in the Data View window even though they both use the same ADO dialog boxes to create their links to your data source. Nor do UDLs appear in the list of known Data Links when you open your Data View window.

Creating Data Links

Creating a Data Link is intuitive. When Visual Basic starts, no Data Links exist—you have to create them yourself, even if you've registered ODBC DSNs or created OLE DB UDL files. Basically, you have to click the third icon from the left on the Data View window—Add a New Data Link (see Figure 12-1)—or right-click the Data Links folder and choose Add a Data Link. This opens the Data Link Properties page. This is where you specify the OLE DB provider and all of the other parameters needed to identify the server, database, and yourself to SQL Server. When you start Visual Basic 6.0, you should see all Data Links created in the past by whatever means, or you're supposed to. If you create a Data Link and Visual Basic crashes (or you crash it), Visual Basic won't have an opportunity to save your Data Link.

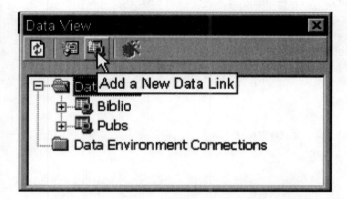

Figure 12-1: Visual Basic 6.0 Data View Window—adding a new Data Link

Once a Data Link is created, you can use it to explore what your data provider can expose. Not all data providers are created equally—many expose very limited functionality through the Data View window. Consider that ADOX, which was designed to support DDL operations, was not released until well after Visual Basic 6.0 and these tools were developed. It's the provider itself and its functionality that know how to respond to requests to expose underlying database functionality.

Working with Your Database Schema

Both the SQL Server and Oracle providers know how to expose database diagrams, but this is new for Visual Basic 6.0. The database diagrams permit you to map the database schema and primary key/foreign key relationships. As a matter of fact, if the database exists, you can construct tables and relationships using nothing but the Data View window. The design table dialog box supports a full range of table-column criteria, including identity columns, datatype, length, precision, scale, identity seed, GUID designation, and nullability. It also supports the rather startling capability to *insert* columns between other columns. This can be particularly problematic for existing applications that have hard-coded programs based on SELECT * queries, as they expect specific columns to be returned in a specific order. A misguided SA can really throw a wrench in the works by inserting columns between existing columns.

Adding a new table to a database can be done quite easily—assuming your UserID has sufficient permission. I added a table named Test to one of my sample databases by filling in the Data View design dialog box. The Data View window "table design" dialog box created the following script to be executed on demand. That is, no changes were made until the database diagram was saved. Notice how it manages the whole operation using transactions.

```
BEGIN TRANSACTION
SET QUOTED_IDENTIFIER ON
GO
SET TRANSACTION ISOLATION LEVEL SERIALIZABLE
GO
COMMIT
BEGIN TRANSACTION
CREATE TABLE dbo.TEst
    (
    Au_ID int NOT NULL,
    YearMarried varchar(50) NULL,
    Photo image NULL,
    Bibliography text NULL
    ) ON [PRIMARY]
     TEXTIMAGE_ON [PRIMARY]
GO
ALTER TABLE dbo.TEst ADD CONSTRAINT
    PK_TEst PRIMARY KEY NONCLUSTERED
    (
    Au_ID
    ) ON [PRIMARY]
GO
COMMIT
BEGIN TRANSACTION
ALTER TABLE dbo.Title_Author ADD CONSTRAINT
    FK_Title_Author_TEst FOREIGN KEY
    (
    Au_ID
    ) REFERENCES dbo.TEst
    (
    Au_ID
    )
GO
COMMIT
```

The schema diagram can be annotated to aid in documentation. It offers a great way to visualize the entire database or a selected subset of the tables and their relationships in a single glance. To establish or modify a primary key/foreign key relationship, simply drag from the primary key column of one table to the foreign key column of another. The Data View window takes care of the rest. A dialog box is exposed to verify the relationship, as well as to enable a number of update options.

The database diagram window indicates these relationships automatically by scanning the database's DDL information returned from the provider. Note the "key" symbol at the "one" end of the relationship line and the "infinity sign" at the "many" end of the relationship. For example, note that the Authors Au_ID column has a one-to-many relationship with the Title_Author.Au_ID column. This means there can be many titles for a specific author. The diagram also shows the Title_Author.ISBN column has a many-to-one relationship with the ISBN column of the Titles table—there can be many authors for a single ISBN (book).

Exploring Tables, Views, and Stored Procedures

One of the benefits of the Data Window is that it exposes the data interfaces of SQL Server. Once you click the + next to a Data Link, Visual Basic (and ADO) opens the connection and it queries for all of the DDL structures in the database. This exposes all of the database designs, tables, views, and stored procedures that are visible to your login ID. Yes, the database schemas you and the rest of your team create are all stored in the database where everyone can see them. As I said before, if you don't have permission to see portions of the database, they won't appear in the list—you won't even get connected unless you have permission to log on. Using the appropriate folder icons, go ahead and explode the lists one by one. I clicked on the Pubs folder. If you do, too, you should now see something similar to what is shown in Figure 12-2. Notice that I also (single) clicked on the Authors table and exploded the column names.

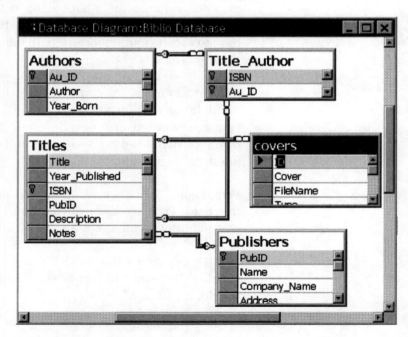

Figure 12-2: Visual Basic 6.0 Data View window—a typical database diagram

Each table can be explored to view its columns, and if you right-click on a specific column, you can view the column properties including the ADO datatype. If you right-click on the table name, you can enter the design mode or simply dump the table to a grid to edit.

If your provider supports it, the Views folder is also accessible. It exposes any views created on the database, or you can create your own views as needed, using a separate dialog box.

SQL Server and Oracle both use stored procedures quite heavily, and the Data View window provides basic support for viewing, authoring, and modifying stored procedures. While the "debug" function is basically crippled, you do have the ability to examine both returned and input parameters from stored procedures.

What's Missing

There are a few things missing in the Data View window dialog boxes that might make it hard to get started and maintain your production database. You'll find that there's no way to create:

- A new database. While the Data Link can make a connection to a data provider and select an initial catalog (default database), it provides no functionality to actually create the database in the first place. You'll have to use the tools that come with the database for that—assuming there are some.[2]

- A secondary index. You can specify a primary key—even a key with multiple columns for a new or existing table, and this operation creates a basic lookup index. However, there is no mechanism to create clustered or other secondary indexes to assist in locating or joining rows in a query.

- Permissions. The Data View window assumes you have authority to make the changes you're making and that you'll have other tools for delegating that authority to your users.

- UserIDs or passwords. Your ability to access the data might well be gated by the permission level of your UserID, and you should not be developing using SA.

---

2. MSDE is not shipped with any of the Visual Database Tools. You won't be able to create a database or perform any database maintenance functions unless you write TSQL queries or find another source of tools.

- Rules, defaults. While the queries you write depend on how these constraints behave, there is no mechanism for viewing or modifying them.

- Triggers. Although you can create stored procedures, there is no way to assign these stored procedures to trigger duty.

You'll have to use your own database tools to perform any of these basic database functions. To help get you over the hump with some packages, I've included a sample application on the CD that can be used to create SQL Server databases. You'll have to find a way to create your own non-Microsoft databases. Yes, this is basically the same application I posted on my Web site (www.betav.com) some time ago. I made another pass on this code and spruced it up a bit for the CD.

There are also a few issues that make the Data View window (in Visual Basic) seem unfinished:

- You can't use the Query Designer to help construct stored procedure code. While this is supported in the Visual InterDev version of this tool, it's not in Visual Basic, and it's sorely missed. Yes, you can type in the code by hand, but you're on your own when it comes time to code the joins.

- The stored procedure code window editor has a number of, shall we say, interesting problems. For example, it can be easily confused while performing simple edits, or while scrolling, or while typing.

- Although you can create a new DSN from the Data View window, you can't alter an existing DSN. This requires launching the ODBC applet from Windows.

- There's no way to control other ODBC behavior from the Data View window. For example, you can't disable or tune connection pooling as you can from the ODBC applet dialogs.

> **WARNING** *If you select a table in the database diagram or the Data View window and press the Delete key, the Data View window will delete the table from the database quite unceremoniously.*

Using the Data Environment Designer

The Data Environment Designer (shown in Figure 12-3) seemed to show a lot of potential—at first. However, as the development community and I waded into its functionality, the crooked seams started to show. I expect the Data Environment Designer was intended to replace and augment the functions and features of the User Connection Designer. Let's look at the Data Environment Designer's laundry list of features:

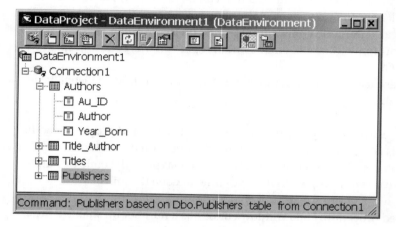

Figure 12-3: The Visual Basic 6.0 Data Environment Designer with Four Commands

- Provides a way to capture one or more OLE DB connection strings and automatically establishes appropriate connections at design and run time.

- Provides a way to easily author queries of all types at design time using an intuitive GUI.

- Persists these queries in a form that could be shared among an entire development team.

- Provides an interface to ADO that exposes underlying ADO Connection, Command, and Recordset objects and their properties.

- Exposes an event interface to map to underlying ADO events and helps manage synchronous as well as asynchronous operations.

- Manages input, output, input/output, and return status arguments passed to stored, as well as ad hoc, procedures.

- Manages the construction of ADO Shape statements, and displays hierarchical data structures.

- Acts as a "data source" control so that bound controls can access the data returned from the queries without writing code.

- Supports intuitive drag-and-drop functionality to make it easy to set up bound control forms and reports based on the DataEnvironment data source object.

Now let's take a closer look at the Data Environment Designer and how it manages (or at least attempts) to do all of this.

Data Environment Designer—Basic Techniques

There are several ways to use the Data Environment Designer. Many developers tell me that they find adequate functionality in the basic techniques, but that they stay away from the rest. Others say that the way the Data Environment Designer manages shapes and hierarchical result sets makes development of reports and complex shape operations far easier. I'll let you judge for yourself. The Data Environment Designer is also a "must-use" component of the Data Object Wizard, which constructs procedure-based applications and custom data-bound components based on Data Environment Designer Commands.

You can use the Data Environment Designer to create a persisted Connection object very simply—just drag a Table, View, or stored procedure from one of your existing Data Links (created with the Data View window) over to the Data Environment Designer window. This operation also creates a DataEnvironment Command object that returns the result set from the table, view, or stored procedure. However, you don't want to drag a table to the Data Environment Designer—not without clarifying the query—because the DataEnvironment runtime will construct an ADO Command object that will return all rows and all columns from the target table.

Using the Query Designer Window

To correct this problem, click on the newly created Command object and right-click to change its properties. Click on SQL Statement in the source of data frame and click on SQL Builder. This launches the four-paned query editor as shown in Figure 12-4.

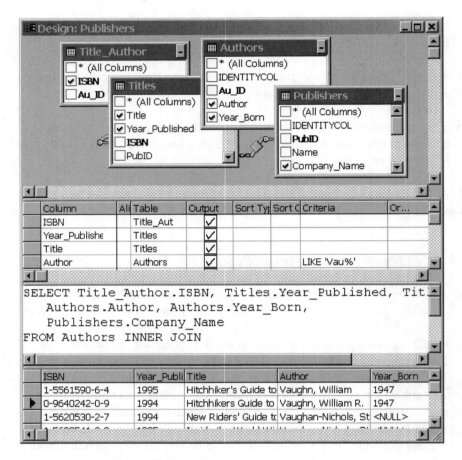

Figure 12-4: The Data Environment Designer's query editor

It's essential that you pare down the query to return just the required rows and columns from your table(s). It's easy to use the Query Designer window—just drag the tables needed from the Data Environment Designer or Data View window. The SQL query is created for you in the third pane, and you can select the required columns in the second. The top pane graphically shows the join relationships. If you right-click on the first pane and choose run, the Data Environment Designer will run the query and fill the fourth pane with the Recordset returned. Change any of the panes, and the changes are reflected in the other panes automatically. Very cool.

When you save your application, or just the .DSR file generated by the Data Environment Designer, the designer saves all of the parameters, properties, and other settings you provided when dragging and dropping and setting property page values. All of these values are stored in the binary (proprietary) DSR file and become a part of your project. The DSR file is processed again at runtime by the Data Environment Designer runtime engine, which reconstructs the DataEnvironment objects that you specified at design time. The DSR file can be shared with others in your development team. They can simply add the DSR to their project and then simply refer to the DataEnvironment object Connections and Commands as if they had constructed them on their own.

If you save the Data Environment Designer-generated .DSR file at this point and run your program, the Data Environment Designer runtime engine simply instantiates the DataEnvironment object and *nothing* else happens. The connection is not opened and the query is not executed. However, if you take the next GUI step and drag your Data Environment Designer Command object to a form, the designer creates a set of controls (right-click and you get to choose) and binds the Command object to these controls. However, there is no accommodation for input parameters for your query. In this case, when you run your program, the DataEnvironment object behaves (or misbehaves) like a Data control and starts to run before Form_Load—long before your error handlers get a chance to start (as if they did any good).

To run the DataEnvironment Command object against this connection without binding, you have to write a little code. To make it easier to code, I like to dereference the DataEnvironment object. Besides that, there's only one line of code required to run the query. Let's assume I have created a DataEnvironment Command object that executes a stored procedure called MySP. I created this Command object by dragging the stored procedure from the Data View window to the Data Environment Designer window. The MySP stored procedure requires three parameters, as shown in the following code, which executes this stored procedure at runtime:

```
Dim DE as DataEnvironment1
Set DE = New DataEnvironment1

DE.MySP "cat", 5, 32.5
```

The ADO Recordset resulting from this query is returned in an object exposed off of the DataEnvironment object and named after the query. In this case, the Recordset is returned in an object named rsMySP. However, to prevent losing it once we reference the Recordset, we have to create a separate Recordset variable to manage it.

```
Dim rs as Recordset
Set rs = DE.rsMySP
```

To rerun the query, close the Recordset and simply use the same code (DE.MySP...), as shown previously, with new parameters. No, there is no Refresh method.

```
DE.rsMySP.Close
DE.MySP "dog", 8, 45
```

Data Environment Designer Connection Error Handling

Note that none of this code explicitly opened the connection. This was handled behind the scenes by the DataEnvironment object runtime when the DataEnvironment Command is referenced for the first time. So, what if the connection cannot be established? Well, just as with ADO, you have to set up your own error traps to catch these not-so-unlikely errors. If the DataEnvironment gets in trouble when connecting, one of the first strategies it uses is to reprompt the user with a dialog box asking for the UserID and Password, along with options to change to another database. Unfortunately, this prompting behavior does not pay any attention to your Visual Basic error handler. This means that the user gets to guess at the password (if this is the problem) until they get bored or get it right. And the problem might not be the password at all. I simply paused the server and triggered this error scenario.

This is why it's essential that you tell the Data Environment Designer to let you handle the errors in your own code. It's not obvious how to do this, but it can be done:

1. Open the Data Environment Designer window.

2. Click the Connection icon in the Data Environment Designer window. You'll have to repeat this for each Connection in the designer.

3. Do *not* right-click to access the Connection properties—that's what most folks try, and it won't work.

4. Do press F4 to open up the VBIDE Property Page—the DataEnvironment object's Connection property page should appear (see Figure 12-5).

5. Change the DesignPromptBehavior and RunPromptBehavior to adPromptNever. Yes, you may be prompted several times in the process of changing this property. And no, you can't change it at runtime—it's too late then, and the property isn't exposed anyway.

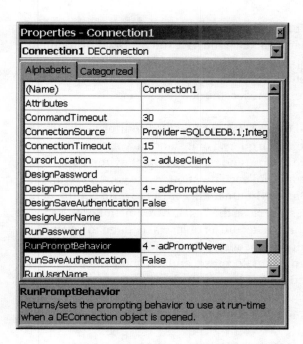

Figure 12-5: The Data Environment Designer Property page where you set prompt behavior

What's Missing in the Data Environment Designer

While the Data Environment Designer goes a long way toward addressing development problems, it seems to paint itself in a corner on many of these functions. Unless you go to a lot of trouble, you're likely to revert back to raw code. Let's look at what's missing or simply broken:

- There's no facility to "bind" the parameters—input or output. When you drag the DataEnvironment Command object to a form, the Data Environment Designer instantiates a grid or set of labels and text box controls for each Recordset Field that returns from the query. However, there are no controls created to handle the input parameters of your procedure, not to mention the output parameters or return status.

- Accessing the Command parameter collection is easy when executing the command as a method on the DataEnvironment object. However drilling down to a specific Command object's Parameters collection (somewhere in the DataEnvironment Commands collection) requires far more code than managing Command objects in ADO code.

- There's no refresh method on the DataEnvironment object or the Commands associated with it. This means that once you have run the DataEnvironment Command with one set of parameters (that you provide by hand), you can't simply change the parameters and reexecute the Command—at least not if you expect the bound controls to reflect the new Recordset.

- When using simple bound controls (such as TextBox controls) you also have to manually rebind on each query. For instance, if you try to run a parameter query, you have to close and rerun the DataEnvironment Command object from scratch for each iteration. While you can rerun the query from scratch, the DataEnvironment Recordset to form control data bindings are lost as soon as you close the DataEnvironment Recordset object, as the DataEnvironment Recordset object is required to rerun the query. This means the coded connection between the columns (Fields) returned in the DataEnvironment Recordset and the bound controls on your form are dropped and have to be reset for binding to work. Rebinding requires that you revisit each bound control and reset the DataSource and DataMember properties manually in code.

- When the Recordset returns from the DataEnvironment, it exposes a unique "touch-me-once" object. That is, once referenced, it cannot be referenced again. The rowset is dropped by the DataEnvironment runtime to prevent instance memory leaks. This means that you have to capture the DataEnvironment object's returned Recordset in a separate memory variable to prevent it from being lost after first reference.

- The Data Environment Designer was designed with and for ADO 2.0. Unless Visual Studio 6.0 SP4 corrects this problem, the DataEnvironment event handlers will no longer compile if you switch references to ADO 2.1 or later. This can be corrected by changing the events you expose to return Recordset20, but you won't be able to access any of the new ADO 2.1 or later Recordset object properties, methods, or events.

- The shape generator creates expensive SELECT * queries (with no WHERE clauses). While this works fine for small databases, it's a problem for databases with more than a few hundred rows. To get around this, you have to carefully construct the queries leading up to the Shape operation, as well as cross-link the queries manually in code.

- The Data Environment Designer is particularly sensitive about changes in stored procedures or database schema. Unless your stored procedures are frozen, accessing them with the DataEnvironment object is problematic.

- The default behavior of the Data Environment Designer is to create an expensive updatable, scrollable keyset cursor. In contrast, ADO's default behavior creates an efficient forward-only, read-only cursorless Recordset.

- The default behavior of the Data Environment Designer when it comes to table queries leads inexperienced developers into expensive locking situations. Dragging a table to the Data Environment Designer from the Data View window generates a SELECT * FROM <table> query.

- The default prompt behavior is exactly the opposite of ADO's prompt behavior. This means that the Data Environment Designer dialog boxes constantly and incessantly prompt the developer for the same UserID and password regardless of how many times it has been entered before.

- Trying to get the Data Environment Designer to correct this prompting behavior is about as hard as getting HAL to open the pod bay doors. There is no facility in the Connection dialog boxes to capture appropriate prompting behavior at design time, so it has to be repeated for each Connection object created in a separate properties window. We discussed earlier how to reset this behavior, but remember it can't be done in code—it must be done at design time.

- This default approach to connecting also causes the DataEnvironment runtime to ignore the Visual Basic On Error handling. This means the user can be confronted with data provider prompt dialog boxes regardless of the actual connection problem, requiring you to reset the prompting behavior before using the DataEnvironment object.

- While the Data Environment Designer exposes a property page to modify a number of critical aspects of the Connection and Command objects, these are not exposed to the developer at runtime. This means that you can't modify the prompting behavior, UserID, Password, or most other DataEnvironment object behaviors at runtime.

Using ADO Without the Data Environment Designer

ADO is really very flexible. There are a dozen ways to execute queries with very little code. For example, to open a connection and execute a parameter-based stored procedure can be as easy as this:

```
Set cn = New Connection
Set rs = New Recordset

cn.Open "dsn=localserver", "admin", "pw"
cn.AuthorsByYearBorn 1947, 1948, rs
```

When you code directly with ADO, you have full control over how and when the connection is opened, closed, and the object released. Because the prompting behavior is already correct, you don't have to worry about extra data provider prompts appearing out of nowhere. You can also provide runtime UserID and password values instead of using the values passed into the DataEnvironment object at design time.

Data binding with ADO is also not as problematic as you might think. However, what's missing from the ADO data control is the capability to define a Recordset and have it automatically construct pairs of label and TextBox (or other suitable) controls mapped to the Fields in the Recordset. However, you can use the Data Environment Designer to set up this query and manually substitute the ADODC as the DataSource on all of the bound controls, assuming you clear each bound control's DataMember property first.

But there's another option if you want to set up bound controls that do more than just extract data from unrestrained SELECT * queries such as parameter-driven stored procedures. You can use the Data Object Wizard.

Using the Data Object Wizard

The Data Object Wizard was created to address many of the more complex issues of data query and user interface design. Developers told Microsoft that binding to base tables did not usually make a lot of sense. In their real-world applications, they wanted to bind to more sophisticated parameter-based queries—especially to stored procedures. That's because the result sets generated from their queries were rarely derived from a single table. Results were generated from two to many table joins, based on parameters passed to the query.

This is where the Data Object Wizard comes in. It was designed from the outset by approaching the problem from a very different point of view, when compared to the Data Environment Designer or a traditional data source control. Because it is a "wizard," the design time code generates Visual Basic *source* code that developers can tune, cajole, or take as is. Because the wizard generates clearly understood (albeit voluminous) source code, the developer has the flexibility to add his or her own logic to any stage of the data query operation. In addition, because the process constructs a user control that can be compiled to binary, other developers can easily share the control or the source code to access it.

Phase One—Getting Ready

The first phase of Data Object Wizard data frontend development does not involve the Data Object Wizard. This is when you plan how to access the data in question and write the procedures to do so. In many cases, these procedures might already exist. For example, to update the Publishers table in the sample Biblio database, we created several queries:

- A parameter-based query to fetch the publisher(s) to manage.[3] In this case, I created a stored procedure that fetched publishers from a specific state. This rowset is used to populate a grid control in this example, but this query might return a single row to update.

- A parameter-based query to update a selected publisher by its unique PubID value. This routine is also implemented as a stored procedure that accepts the new column values and a PubID to locate the row to update. The procedure can handle collisions or other contingencies on its own, or it can leave this up to ADO if desired. You also have the option of indicating that updates are simply deletes followed by inserts.

- A parameter-based query to insert a new publisher. This routine is also implemented as a stored procedure that expects the new column values and a new unique PubID. You can also indicate that the inserted row has an Identity column to automatically provide the unique index. The routine also handles collisions or other contingencies on its own, or it can leave this up to ADO if desired.

- A parameter-based query to delete an existing publisher. This routine is also implemented as a stored procedure that expects a unique PubID to delete.

- A query to select all of the rows from the ValidStates lookup table. This is simply a Table-based query.

---

3. The Biblio database is included on the CD and it contains four stored procedures (described here) that manage the Publishers table. These are designed to be used with the Data Object Wizard.

After these queries are created, you have to make them visible to the Data Object Wizard through the Data Environment Designer. Yes, the Data Object Wizard depends heavily on the Data Environment Designer to open connections, execute the queries, and manage the Recordsets returned.

Phase Two—Creating the Recordset and DataSource Classes

After the queries are defined, it's time to run the Data Object Wizard for the first time. During this phase, you simply point the Data Object Wizard at the procedures we have already defined. You also indicate the primary key that's used to uniquely identify the specific row to insert, update, or delete. You can also provide pointers to "lookup" procedures to aid your user when selecting coded fields such as the state code. When this phase is done, the Data Object Wizard has created two new files in your project to hold the new classes.

Phase Three—Creating a Custom User Control

When the DataSource class is completed, it's time to run the Data Object Wizard again. This time you describe how you want your data class to be presented to the user. You can choose among a grid, textboxes, or combinations thereof. When this phase is done, your project is nearly ready to run. At this time, you can add code to provide the initial parameter for the fetch query, or simply provide it in the properties dialog boxes.

If you don't like the code the Data Object Wizard generates, you can simply change it. Ripping out the DataEnvironment might be more work than you're comfortable with, but it's worth considering if you think you need the extra degree of control this change might provide.

CHAPTER 13

SQL Server 2000 and ADO 2.6

MICROSOFT HAS BEEN BUSY AGAIN. AS I was finishing Chapter 12, which was to be the last chapter of this book, the SQL Server team at Microsoft released the second beta of new versions of SQL Server and ADO. While I won't be able to offer many concrete examples that are guaranteed to work on the new version, I think it's important to discuss where Microsoft is taking its database technology. Although this book is supposed to be about ADO, we really can't ignore the innovations brought about by the folks in Microsoft's data-access development shops. One of the most significant changes we're witnessing is the apparent devolution of ADO and data-access interfaces like ADO. Yes, this means that once the tools arrive to support the new paradigms, you might find it makes sense to use newer data-access interfaces instead of ADO, especially when connecting via the Web. In this light, I suspect that you're interested in how you, as a developer, will be impacted by these changes. That's what this chapter is all about.

SQL Server 2000 is different. It has changed almost as much as SQL Server 7.0 changed from SQL Server 6.5. SQL Server 2000 (SS2K) reflects a tremendous amount of work that has been done to improve scalability. The briefings I attended made it clear that Microsoft is serious about taking the lead in NT and SQL Server markets, where millions of operations per second is a business requirement, not just a marketing check-off feature. SQL Server 2000 Enterprise Edition offers scalability and availability up to the highest levels of the enterprise by taking full advantage of up to 64GB of RAM and up to 32 processors, supporting four-node failover clustering out of the box with Windows 2000 Data Center. The new TPC-C[1] and SAP benchmarks clearly show that SQL Server has taken the lead on two fronts—raw performance and cost/TPC. This means SQL Server is faster, far faster, than its next closest competitor (over 250,000 TPS) and far, far cheaper to implement (about $19/TPS).

A primary focus of the SS2K enhancements seems to be e-commerce and the Web, but more traditional client/server implementations also benefit from these improvements. This means far more ways to implement client/server, Web-based,

---

1. TPC-C is an independently created and certified set of (rigorous) benchmarks that help in comparing various competing database engines on an apples-to-apples basis. These tests measure performance in "transactions per second" or TPS.

and middle-tier applications. In addition, TSQL has added a number of new XML and programmatic features that radically change how you can approach data access solutions. I'll give you a brief look at these paradigms, but until they are cast in stone, we can't really depend on any examples we might create with the beta. This chapter will help you prepare your SQL Server 7.0 designs, keeping these features in mind.

SQL Server 2000 and the Application Developer

While it's too early to build the list of things that'll change, work better, or simply break when you install SS2K (and thus ADO 2.6), it's not too early to build a list of cool things to fold into existing designs. You might be in the process of inventing the same technology implemented in the newest versions of ADO or in SQL Server itself. The following list by no means includes all of the new features. It does, however, list features that'll directly impact your existing and future development work.

Scalability and Performance

When the SQL Server group announces to the world that their latest offspring runs faster and does more cool stuff, I'm perhaps not as excited as they are. It's kinda like when Ford announces that their new Explorer can carry more gravel or gators and burn less gas. While I've been known to buy a new truck now and again, I'm partial to the one I have. But when I get the new model, these features will be there whether I need to carry gravel (or gators) or not. What I'll be looking for is how the features I use every day work. I'll appreciate better gas mileage, but will I have to give up my tape collection because they dropped support for cassette tapes in favor of CDs? Will I have to relearn how to program the seats, the radio, or the door locks? In other words, while those new features are cool and will help me do what I do with the truck, unless the interfaces are about the same, I'm in for a number of hours of wasted time trying to figure out how to get the headlights to turn off.

Yes, SS2K is faster and there's nothing wrong with that. Anything that lets your clients and me spend less time staring at an hourglass cursor is good. However, a faster engine won't improve my development time as much as fast, and *functional* (bug free) data access interfaces. If ADO is designed to take advantage of these features, well, okay. But unless the Visual Studio tools get a lot smarter (and a lot faster) we won't be able to leverage or even access these new features with the existing tools for quite some time—perhaps not until after my birthday in the year 2001 when Visual Studio 7.0 arrives.

MSDE Changes

SS2K also includes (in all SKUs) a version of MSDE designed to run on workstation (or Professional) NT boxes, as well as on selected Windows 9*x* systems. Remember that the Microsoft "Desktop" Database Engine (MSDE) *is* SQL Server. However, I was somewhat startled to learn that SS2K no longer supports MSDE on Windows 95 as did its SQL Server 7.0 predecessor. While this is somewhat understandable, I suspect that this will force many of you to take another look at MSDE and perhaps hesitate to move to it. On the other hand, the alternatives (Jet and who knows what else) are not nearly as attractive as moving your clients to Windows 98.

MSDE inherits most of the performance enhancements you get with SS2K. However, it's still governed at five simultaneous operations. No matter how many connections you open, once MSDE has five operations running, SQL Server slows down *all* connections to discourage you from using MSDE as a full-blown server.

MSDE can also be installed multiple times—just as Jet can. For a better understanding of what that means, keep reading. However, the database format has changed. This means if you use sp_detach_db and sp_attach_db to install your customer database, you'll find SQL Server 2000 reformats the database (automatically) when attached to the most current version. Once you detach from SS2K, the database files cannot be reattached to a SQL Server 7.0 database engine.

> **NOTE**   *While the marketing materials don't say so, the database structures have changed again. Not a single session I attended at the latest SQL Server 2000 conference discussed this issue, but it can be very important for those using sp_detach_db to deploy their databases.*

Multiple Instancing

One of the more serious SQL Server limitations has been its inability to run multiple versions at the same time. There are a number of viable scenarios in which this is a fact of life. For example, if you use MSDE as your client database (as suggested) and you install the application on a system that already has another MSDE application, or simply on a system running SQL Server, the application cannot install. In addition, because the application often sets the MSDE SA password, it won't be able to access the existing MSDE (or other version of SQL Server).

This all changes with SS2K, because it permits you to install as many copies of SQL Server as you need. Each is loaded in a separate process and can be individually named so they can run independently. This means you can run multiple copies of MSDE, or you can run MSDE alongside SQL Server 7.0 or SQL Server 2000.

Enhanced TSQL

Again, this is not a book about SQL Server, but when working with ADO and SQL Server there are a number of techniques that you may use ADO to solve that are now best solved by the backend server—at least if you're using SQL Server. SS2K now supports a number of new TSQL primitives and other enhancements:

- Table variables: These permit you to create in-memory variables that can be treated as you would any table. It also permits you to pass in-memory tables to and from user-defined functions or to and from other stored procedures. Typically, these are used in lieu of TEMPDB-based #Temp tables.

- User-defined functions: To catch up with the Access SQL extensions, and make the transition from Access easier, SQL Server 2000 now supports user-defined functions.

- Partitioned view enhancements: View functionality has been expanded to support view partitioning. This can be used to implement partitioned data across multiple tables in the same or different servers. The SQL Server 2000 query processor eliminates member tables not necessary for a given query or update.

- INSTEAD OF Triggers: These triggers can be set up to fire *before* the ordinary Update, Insert, and Delete triggers, and the new AFTER triggers implemented in SQL Server 7.0. Triggers can also be created on a view or a table. You can also order the execution of triggers so you can determine which fires first and which fires next.

- New data types:
  - sql_variant can store any of the base SQL Server types (except BLOB types). These are useful for sparse-table or object annotations.
  - bigint is an 8-byte integer used to store much larger integer values. This is supported by a COUNT_BIG( ) function, which is used to return bigint row counts. When used in an Identity column, it means you can have even larger tables.

- Database/column level collations: In SQL Server 7.0, the entire server had a single collation sequence: code page and sort order. In SQL Server 2000, each database can have a separate, default collation. In addition, each column in a table can have a separate collation. SQL Server 2000 collation encompasses code-page plus sort order. This means SQL Server 2000 can have a default collation sequence as well as different operational sequences based on how you code the query.

- Miscellaneous enhancements: SQL Server 2000 includes a number of new functions to support many oft-needed operations, including the following:

  - GetUTCDate(): Current UTC time. This lets you program against "Zulu" or Greenwich Mean Time instead of local time.

  - SCOPE_IDENTITY(): Last identity value in current scope (no triggers). This is a very cool new function that lets you trap the new identity value generated by the server, based on the last insert—the identity value returned does not get altered by triggers that fire after the local insert.

  - IDENT_CURRENT('tblname'): Last identity value generated for table. This is yet another way to trap the identity generated—also very cool.

  - CONTEXT_INFO(): A per-session value that can be set with SET CONTEXT_INFO. This is interesting for Web-based designs trying to track session-based context information.

XML Integration

We've touched on XML over and over as we marched through the chapters in this book. Based on the number of articles, books, and conference sessions alone (not to mention the internal Microsoft hype), XML is the new golden boy at Microsoft. When coupled with HTML, it's being reborn (while it's still in its infancy) as Simple Object Access Protocol (SOAP). Simply put, SOAP is becoming a replacement for DCOM and CORBA as a new standard way to communicate between systems. This by itself is the topic for another book. But consider that Microsoft is tightly integrating XML directly into SQL Server 2000 in an effort to help developers build the next generation of Web and Enterprise applications. Their Web site (http://msdn.microsoft.com/workshop/xml/articles/xmlsql/sqlxml_prev.asp)[2] sports a way to try out this innovation on SQL Server 7.0. This new technology provides a more-or-less direct URL access to SQL Server. This means you can author queries to be sent *directly* to SQL Server 7.0 via a URL, with the results being returned as XML-formatted documents. SQL Server 2000 is fully XML-enabled and includes a superset of the features available in the technology preview for SQL Server 7.0.

This technology is implemented as an IIS ISAPI extension that provides HTTP access to SQL Server and XML data formatting and updating capabilities. With the appropriate configuration, SS2K (and the technology preview) allows URL queries similar to this:

```
http://IISServer/biblio?sql=SELECT+Author,Au_Lname+FROM+Authors+FOR+XML+AUTO
```

2. The March 2000 issue of MSDN magazine has an in-depth discussion of SQL Server 2000, SOAP, and how these emerging technologies play together.

In this case, we're simply pointing the browser (not ADO) at a database (Biblio) on our SQL Server/IIS Server and asking SQL Server to execute the query and return XML. The layout of the XML returned could be specified in a variety of ways (including a useful Auto mode) and there is the option to include schema information either in document type definition (DTD) or XML-Data formats. This means you can specify an XSL style sheet along with the SQL query to make sure the XML returned is formatted correctly for the client. One special point to note: the virtual root name you choose (for example, Biblio) can be used only for accessing your SQL data. Any other Web files (such as .htm or .asp files) are not accessible from this virtual root. This space is reserved for so-called template files that contain "canned" queries.

All of this means that it's not necessary to write a single line of ADO, ODBC, or OLE DB code in your application. Now *that's* an important change.

ADO Version 2.6

ADO 2.6 has expanded its functionality to deepen its support of XML. Most of these changes have been made to the Command object to better support SQL Server's capability to pass back XML-formatted result sets. A summary of how these changes are expected to work is outlined here:

- **Command Stream**. With ADO 2.6 and the SQL Server 2000 version of the SQL Server OLE DB Provider, the user can retrieve the results of a command as an XML stream or execute an XML or Xpath command. This is to provide better integration with queries that return XML instead of "ordinary" Recordsets.

- **Support for Singleton Selects**. The Record object can now be used to retrieve the results of a singleton SELECT (a SELECT that returns a single row). This technique should result in up to a 15 percent performance improvement when executing singleton SELECTs passed to a Recordset object.

- **Named Parameter Support**. This means that when you write procedure calls, you'll have to specify parameters by name in many cases. This also means that when executing stored procedures, you no longer have to specify parameters positionally because these parameters can also be specified by name.

- **Error Status**. You can use the ADO 2.6 Field.Status property to retrieve more information about an error. In addition, ADO 2.6's overall error handling has been improved, adding far more information about errors than ever before provided.

- **User/Group Properties.** Using ADOX 2.6, the user can access properties of the User and Group objects. When using the Jet OLE DB Provider, the user will now be able to set the PIN for a user or group via the Jet OLEDB:Trustee PIN property.

- **Expose New Server Features**. ADO 2.6 adds support for SQL Server multi-instances, big-Int and sql_variant datatypes, User-Defined Functions (UDF), encryption, and column-level collation.

- **Performance Improvements**. ADO 2.6 supports new escape sequences for remote procedure calls using the new ODBC escape sequence, which is a faster alternative to the CALL escape sequence. ADO 2.6 also makes use of the internal stored procedure *sp_prepexec* for ODBC and OLE DB. This system-stored procedure reduces the metadata sent by server to client, resulting in a reduction of round trips to server (for prepare and unprepare).

SQL XML

A number of ADO 2.6 changes are planned to support SQL Server 2000's capability to return XML. These changes include:

- **Support for the new FOR XML.TSQL clause**. FOR XML is an extension to SQL Server's TSQL SELECT statement. It tells SQL Server to return the query results as an XML document fragment using one of three modes—Raw, Auto, or Explicit—to format the XML.

- **URL Access to SQL Server.** Using an ISAPI filter hosted by IIS, ADO 2.6 provides access to SQL Server 2000 data by simply pointing to a virtual root. We discussed this earlier in the XML integration section of this chapter. This new ISAPI filter supports direct execution of an SQL statement passed in the URL, through an XML template or what's called an Xpath template.

- **Annotated Schemas.** If you need a look at your database schema, ADO 2.6 supports an XML view of your relational database. A schema authored to the XML-DATA Reduced specification is annotated (additional elements and attributes are added to it) with the mappings between the elements and attributes declared within the schema and the columns of tables or views in the database.

- **OpenXML.** This is a new extension to the SQL language syntax providing a rowset interface to XML data. It can be used within TSQL stored procedures to build XML documents from data queried from the database.

ODBC Development

All ODBC work has come to a halt—the ODBC and Jet providers have been placed in "QFE" mode. This means no further changes will be made to this technology, and only serious bugs will be fixed.

Appendix

CursorLocation: Server-side Cursors

Cursor	LockType Requested	CursorLocation	LockType Opened	CursorType	Updatable	AddNew	AbsPosition	BookMark	Delete	Holdrecords	MovePrevious	Resync	BatchUpdate	Seek
FwdOnly MSDASQL														
ReadOnly	Server	ReadOnly	FwdOnly	No	No	No	No	No	No	No	No	No	No
Pessimistic	Server	Pessimistic	FwdOnly	Yes	Yes	No	No	Yes	No	No	No	Yes	No
Optimistic	Server	Optimistic	FwdOnly	Yes	Yes	No	No	Yes	No	No	No	Yes	No
Batch	Server	Batch	FwdOnly	Yes	Yes	No	No	Yes	No	No	No	Yes	No
Keyset MSDASQL														
ReadOnly	Server	ReadOnly	Keyset	No	No	No	Yes	No	Yes	Yes	Yes	No	No
Pessimistic	Server	Pessimistic	Keyset	Yes	Yes	No	Yes	Yes	Yes	Yes	Yes	Yes	No
Optimistic	Server	Optimistic	Keyset	Yes	Yes	No	Yes	Yes	Yes	Yes	Yes	Yes	No
Batch	Server	Batch	Keyset	Yes	Yes	No	Yes	Yes	Yes	Yes	Yes	Yes	No
Dynamic MSDASQL														
ReadOnly	Server	ReadOnly	Keyset	No	No	No	Yes	No	Yes	Yes	Yes	No	No
Pessimistic	Server	Pessimistic	Keyset	Yes	Yes	No	Yes	Yes	Yes	Yes	Yes	Yes	No
Optimistic	Server	Optimistic	Keyset	Yes	Yes	No	Yes	Yes	Yes	Yes	Yes	Yes	No
Batch0	Server	Batch	Keyset	Yes	Yes	No	Yes	Yes	Yes	Yes	Yes	Yes	No
Static MSDASQL														
ReadOnly	Server	ReadOnly	Keyset	No	No	No	Yes	No	Yes	Yes	Yes	No	No
Pessimistic	Server	Pessimistic	Keyset	Yes	Yes	No	Yes	Yes	Yes	Yes	Yes	Yes	No
Optimistic	Server	Optimistic	Keyset	Yes	Yes	No	Yes	Yes	Yes	Yes	Yes	Yes	No
Batch	Server	Batch	Keyset	Yes	Yes	No	Yes	Yes	Yes	Yes	Yes	Yes	No
FwdOnly SQLOLEDB														
ReadOnly	Server	ReadOnly	FwdOnly	No	No	No	No	No	No	No	No	No	No
Pessimistic	Server	Pessimistic	FwdOnly	Yes	Yes	No	No	Yes	No	No	No	Yes	No
Optimistic	Server	Optimistic	FwdOnly	Yes	Yes	No	No	Yes	No	No	No	Yes	No
Batch	Server	Batch	FwdOnly	Yes	Yes	No	No	Yes	No	No	No	Yes	No
Keyset SQLOLEDB														
ReadOnly	Server	ReadOnly	Keyset	No	No	Yes	Yes	No	Yes	Yes	Yes	No	No
Pessimistic	Server	Pessimistic	Keyset	Yes	Yes	Yes	Yes	Yes	Yes	Yes	Yes	Yes	No
Optimistic	Server	Optimistic	Keyset	Yes	Yes	Yes	Yes	Yes	Yes	Yes	Yes	Yes	No
Batch	Server	Batch	Keyset	Yes	Yes	Yes	Yes	Yes	Yes	Yes	Yes	Yes	No

Cursor	LockType Requested	CursorLocation	LockType Opened	CursorType	Updatable	AddNew	AbsPosition	BookMark	Delete	Holdrecords	MovePrevious	Resync	BatchUpdate	Seek
Dynamic SQLOLEDB														
	ReadOnly	Server	ReadOnly	Keyset	No	No	Yes	Yes	No	Yes	Yes	Yes	No	No
	Pessimistic	Server	Pessimistic	Keyset	Yes	Yes	Yes	Yes	Yes	Yes	Yes	Yes	Yes	No
	Optimistic	Server	Optimistic	Keyset	Yes	Yes	Yes	Yes	Yes	Yes	Yes	Yes	Yes	No
	Batch	Server	Batch	Keyset	Yes	Yes	Yes	Yes	Yes	Yes	Yes	Yes	Yes	No
Static SQLOLEDB														
	ReadOnly	Server	ReadOnly	Keyset	No	No	Yes	Yes	No	Yes	Yes	Yes	No	No
	Pessimistic	Server	Pessimistic	Keyset	Yes	Yes	Yes	Yes	Yes	Yes	Yes	Yes	Yes	No
	Optimistic	Server	Optimistic	Keyset	Yes	Yes	Yes	Yes	Yes	Yes	Yes	Yes	Yes	No
	Batch	Server	Batch	Keyset	Yes	Yes	Yes	Yes	Yes	Yes	Yes	Yes	Yes	No
FwdOnly Jet 4.0														
	ReadOnly	Server	ReadOnly	FwdOnly	No	No	No	No	No	No	No	No	No	No
	Pessimistic	Server	Pessimistic	Keyset	Yes	Yes	No	No	Yes	Yes	Yes	No	Yes	No
	Optimistic	Server	Optimistic	Keyset	Yes	Yes	No	No	Yes	Yes	Yes	No	Yes	No
	Batch	Server	Batch	Keyset	Yes	Yes	No	No	Yes	Yes	Yes	No	Yes	No
Keyset Jet 4.0														
	ReadOnly	Server	ReadOnly	Keyset	No	No	No	Yes	No	Yes	Yes	No	No	No
	Pessimistic	Server	Pessimistic	Keyset	Yes	Yes	No	Yes	Yes	Yes	Yes	No	Yes	No
	Optimistic	Server	Optimistic	Keyset	Yes	Yes	No	Yes	Yes	Yes	Yes	No	Yes	No
	Batch	Server	Batch	Keyset	Yes	Yes	No	Yes	Yes	Yes	Yes	No	Yes	No
Dynamic Jet 4.0														
	ReadOnly	Server	ReadOnly	Keyset	No	No	No	Yes	No	Yes	Yes	No	No	No
	Pessimistic	Server	Pessimistic	Keyset	Yes	Yes	No	Yes	Yes	Yes	Yes	No	Yes	No
	Optimistic	Server	Optimistic	Keyset	Yes	Yes	No	Yes	Yes	Yes	Yes	No	Yes	No
	Batch	Server	Batch	Keyset	Yes	Yes	No	Yes	Yes	Yes	Yes	No	Yes	No
Static Jet 4.0														
	ReadOnly	Server	ReadOnly	Keyset	No	No	No	Yes	No	Yes	Yes	No	No	No
	Pessimistic	Server	Pessimistic	Keyset	Yes	Yes	No	Yes	Yes	Yes	Yes	No	Yes	No
	Optimistic	Server	Optimistic	Keyset	Yes	Yes	No	Yes	Yes	Yes	Yes	No	Yes	No
	Batch	Server	Batch	Keyset	Yes	Yes	No	Yes	Yes	Yes	Yes	No	Yes	No

Cursor		LockType Requested	CursorLocation	LockType Opened	CursorType	Updatable	AddNew	AbsPosition	BookMark	Delete	Holdrecords	MovePrevious	Resync	BatchUpdate	Seek
FwdOnly	MSDASQL														
		ReadOnly	Client	ReadOnly	Static	No	No	Yes	Yes	No	Yes	Yes	Yes	No	No
		Pessimistic	Client	Batch	Static	Yes	Yes	Yes	Yes	Yes	Yes	Yes	Yes	Yes	No
		Optimistic	Client	Optimistic	Static	Yes	Yes	Yes	Yes	Yes	Yes	Yes	Yes	Yes	No
		Batch	Client	Batch	Static	Yes	Yes	Yes	Yes	Yes	Yes	Yes	Yes	Yes	No
Keyset	MSDASQL														
		ReadOnly	Client	ReadOnly	Static	No	No	Yes	Yes	No	Yes	Yes	Yes	No	No
		Pessimistic	Client	Batch	Static	Yes	Yes	Yes	Yes	Yes	Yes	Yes	Yes	Yes	No
		Optimistic	Client	Optimistic	Static	Yes	Yes	Yes	Yes	Yes	Yes	Yes	Yes	Yes	No
		Batch	Client	Batch	Static	Yes	Yes	Yes	Yes	Yes	Yes	Yes	Yes	Yes	No
Dynamic	MSDASQL														
		ReadOnly	Client	ReadOnly	Static	No	No	Yes	Yes	No	Yes	Yes	Yes	No	No
		Pessimistic	Client	Batch	Static	Yes	Yes	Yes	Yes	Yes	Yes	Yes	Yes	Yes	No
		Optimistic	Client	Optimistic	Static	Yes	Yes	Yes	Yes	Yes	Yes	Yes	Yes	Yes	No
		Batch	Client	Batch	Static	Yes	Yes	Yes	Yes	Yes	Yes	Yes	Yes	Yes	No
Static	MSDASQL														
		ReadOnly	Client	ReadOnly	Static	No	No	Yes	Yes	No	Yes	Yes	Yes	No	No
		Pessimistic	Client	Batch	Static	Yes	Yes	Yes	Yes	Yes	Yes	Yes	Yes	Yes	No
		Optimistic	Client	Optimistic	Static	Yes	Yes	Yes	Yes	Yes	Yes	Yes	Yes	Yes	No
		Batch	Client	Batch	Static	Yes	Yes	Yes	Yes	Yes	Yes	Yes	Yes	Yes	No
FwdOnly	SQLOLEDB														
		ReadOnly	Client	ReadOnly	Static	No	No	Yes	Yes	No	Yes	Yes	Yes	No	No
		Pessimistic	Client	Batch	Static	Yes	Yes	Yes	Yes	Yes	Yes	Yes	Yes	Yes	No
		Optimistic	Client	Optimistic	Static	Yes	Yes	Yes	Yes	Yes	Yes	Yes	Yes	Yes	No
		Batch	Client	Batch	Static	Yes	Yes	Yes	Yes	Yes	Yes	Yes	Yes	Yes	No
Keyset	SQLOLEDB														
		ReadOnly	Client	ReadOnly	Static	No	No	Yes	Yes	No	Yes	Yes	Yes	No	No
		Pessimistic	Client	Batch	Static	Yes	Yes	Yes	Yes	Yes	Yes	Yes	Yes	Yes	No
		Optimistic	Client	Optimistic	Static	Yes	Yes	Yes	Yes	Yes	Yes	Yes	Yes	Yes	No
		Batch	Client	Batch	Static	Yes	Yes	Yes	Yes	Yes	Yes	Yes	Yes	Yes	No

Cursor		LockType Requested	CursorLocation	LockType Opened	CursorType	Updatable	AddNew	AbsPosition	BookMark	Delete	Holdrecords	MovePrevious	Resync	BatchUpdate	Seek
Dynamic	**SQLOLEDB**														
		ReadOnly	Client	ReadOnly	Static	No	No	Yes	Yes	No	Yes	Yes	Yes	No	No
		Pessimistic	Client	Batch	Static	Yes	Yes	Yes	Yes	Yes	Yes	Yes	Yes	Yes	No
		Optimistic	Client	Optimistic	Static	Yes	Yes	Yes	Yes	Yes	Yes	Yes	Yes	Yes	No
		Batch	Client	Batch	Static	Yes	Yes	Yes	Yes	Yes	Yes	Yes	Yes	Yes	No
Static	**SQLOLEDB**														
		ReadOnly	Client	ReadOnly	Static	No	No	Yes	Yes	No	Yes	Yes	Yes	No	No
		Pessimistic	Client	Batch	Static	Yes	Yes	Yes	Yes	Yes	Yes	Yes	Yes	Yes	No
		Optimistic	Client	Optimistic	Static	Yes	Yes	Yes	Yes	Yes	Yes	Yes	Yes	Yes	No
		Batch	Client	Batch	Static	Yes	Yes	Yes	Yes	Yes	Yes	Yes	Yes	Yes	No
FwdOnly	**Jet 4.0**														
		ReadOnly	Client	ReadOnly	Static	No	No	Yes	Yes	No	Yes	Yes	Yes	No	No
		Pessimistic	Client	Batch	Static	Yes	Yes	Yes	Yes	Yes	Yes	Yes	Yes	Yes	No
		Optimistic	Client	Optimistic	Static	Yes	Yes	Yes	Yes	Yes	Yes	Yes	Yes	Yes	No
		Batch	Client	Batch	Static	Yes	Yes	Yes	Yes	Yes	Yes	Yes	Yes	Yes	No
Keyset	**Jet 4.0**														
		ReadOnly	Client	ReadOnly	Static	No	No	Yes	Yes	No	Yes	Yes	Yes	No	No
		Pessimistic	Client	Batch	Static	Yes	Yes	Yes	Yes	Yes	Yes	Yes	Yes	Yes	No
		Optimistic	Client	Optimistic	Static	Yes	Yes	Yes	Yes	Yes	Yes	Yes	Yes	Yes	No
		Batch	Client	Batch	Static	Yes	Yes	Yes	Yes	Yes	Yes	Yes	Yes	Yes	No
Dynamic	**Jet 4.0**														
		ReadOnly	Client	ReadOnly	Static	No	No	Yes	Yes	No	Yes	Yes	Yes	No	No
		Pessimistic	Client	Batch	Static	Yes	Yes	Yes	Yes	Yes	Yes	Yes	Yes	Yes	No
		Optimistic	Client	Optimistic	Static	Yes	Yes	Yes	Yes	Yes	Yes	Yes	Yes	Yes	No
		Batch	Client	Batch	Static	Yes	Yes	Yes	Yes	Yes	Yes	Yes	Yes	Yes	No
Static	**Jet 4.0**														
		ReadOnly	Client	ReadOnly	Static	No	No	Yes	Yes	No	Yes	Yes	Yes	No	No
		Pessimistic	Client	Batch	Static	Yes	Yes	Yes	Yes	Yes	Yes	Yes	Yes	Yes	No
		Optimistic	Client	Optimistic	Static	Yes	Yes	Yes	Yes	Yes	Yes	Yes	Yes	Yes	No
		Batch	Client	Batch	Static	Yes	Yes	Yes	Yes	Yes	Yes	Yes	Yes	Yes	No

Index

apress™

License Agreement (Single-User Products)